The Godfather Never Sleeps

The Godfather Never Sleeps

J. K. Randle

An Atoka Book

WEST AFRICAN BOOK PUBLISHERS LTD.
P.O. Box 34555 Ilupeju Industrial Estate
Lagos Nigeria
ISBN 978 153 040 5
Phototypeset by Trident Graphics Ltd.
Printed by Billing & Sons Ltd.

The Godfather
Never Sleeps

dedicated to Sade, Koshoni and the rest of my family

WHO IS FOOLING WHO?

Note from the Publisher

When we first considered the publication of various newspaper articles written by J. K. Randle in book form it was initially felt that considerable rewriting would be necessary to achieve continuity of style; the various satirical observations did not happily blend with the serious passages. We soon realised that to do so, would spoil the very important moods and feelings of the author at the particular moments they were recorded.

The author expresses what many people were thinking at a particular time in the events of our country. If serious subjects have been treated in a humourous way, it is because to laugh at some problems is the only way to build the necessary will to overcome them. Humourous commentators are also able to say far more in a few words what politicians and historians need volumes to explain. Future historians will rewrite history but J. K. Randle's book records the way ordinary people felt at the time.

IS THIS THE CITY PERHAPS?

THE traffic situation in Lagos is getting more chaotic and we are confronted with the apparent inability of the authorities to adopt and implement meaningful solutions. The short-lived exercise based on helicopter surveillance was a glaring irrelevance that demonstrated to even the most faithful minds how little homework had been done by the authorities to grapple with the problems.

In fairness to the police, we must admit that they did manage to get some lovely aerial photographs of the 'traffic jam' if only to prove that the chaos looks twice as bad from the air.

The lost man-hours, the erosion of manpower and the wear and tear on vehicles must be so staggering that it is about time the business community woke up to the fact that it has a vested interest in finding a sensible, practical solution to the problem of congestion on the roads. A realistic approach to the problem would have to recognise that congestion on the roads is tied up with a larger problem – that of a steadily *declining quality of life* in Lagos.

More and more people are being cut off from the mainstream – their lives reduced to the sheer physical routine of getting to work and getting back home. There cannot be many of us who do not personally know of workers who have to leave home at 5.00 a.m. in order to get to work for 8 o'clock and close at 5.00 p.m. but do not reach home till 10.00 p.m. The mental exhaustion, the fraying of tempers, poor productivity, the disruption of family life are all obvious consequences.

It would be a mistake to think that bus-users are the

only sufferers. Perhaps the only difference between bus-users and the car-owners is that the car owners wait and suffer in their cars. Even in your air-conditioned car, you could not miss the glum resigned faces of people queuing at bus stops. It must occasionally occur to you that some of them have been waiting for three or four hours – but how long will they remain passive? Anyway, we are all bound by a common bond – we are all eminent citizens of CITY PERHAPS.

Perhaps we'll get to work; perhaps we'll get home before dark; perhaps we'll find a doctor at the hospital; perhaps our rubbish will be cleared; perhaps your children will find schools; perhaps the telephones will work; perhaps there'll be electricity; perhaps we'll find petrol to buy; perhaps the cost of food will triple, perhaps, perhaps, perhaps we'll survive.

Our claims to self-respect, decency and civilisation crumble in the overwhelming shame of our slum dwellers who live a 15th century existence, while, we are determined to build 21st century stadia, theatres, television studios,' . . . the show must go on, gringo . . .'.

It is up to the business community to realise that the problems have been identified and solutions have been offered and yet nothing has been done or at least not quickly enough. The business community is then confronted with the stark naked fact that if it waits for the Government, it may just as well wait for ever. This is the time to grab the initiative.

It never ceases to amaze me the number of times traffic to the Apapa Docks grinds to a halt while cows amble along the main road. Then, there are the famous Lagos traffic lights. If you know any that actually works – let me know. Dahomey and Ghana are nowhere near as rich as we are, yet both Cotonou and Accra have streets that are clean and traffic lights that actually work.

If the business community is really concerned with the welfare and consequent productivity of available manpower this is the time to start doing something about it. The problem of congestion on the roads is well outside the terms of the Udoji report as well as any imminent serious Government effort. In dealing with the problem we have to recognise that the basic flaw is the 'troublesome square-mile' or 'danger zone' embracing Tinubu Square, Yakubu Gowon Street, Marina and Martin Street. This is where everything seems to come to a standstill and anything that can be done to reduce the number of cars entering the 'danger zone' must result in a measure of relief.

The business community in that area – banks, insurance companies, retailers etc. can voluntarily reduce the number of company cars brought into the area. For example, instead of six executives who live in the same area e.g. Ikoyi or Victoria Island bringing in a car each, a small bus or two cars could pick them up in the mornings and return them to their homes in the evenings. A similar arrangement could be worked out whereby company buses would pick up employees living in Apapa, or a section of Surulere or Somolu.

The problems of congestion in Lagos will not necessarily be solved by moving the capital. If we did, the new capital will sooner or later be faced with the same problems and we shall end up with two congested cities instead of one. Rather we have to realise that the problems of Lagos are beyond the resources of a state and can only be tackled by complimenting the efforts of the State Government with the might and resources of the Federal Government in its determination to create a worthy capital.

Unless, these problems are tackled urgently, the impossible will soon become the inevitable as everything grinds to a standstill.

Perhaps we'll have a city, perhaps we won't.

'I AM FRANCIS, COME FLY WITH ME'

IN 1973, American Airlines came up with an advertising campaign which turned out to be a winner with passengers. The adverts showed a very attractive barely clad hostess relaying an invitation: 'I'm Linda, fly with me . . .' It was an offer that prospective travellers couldn't refuse. The suggestion of a personalised service and the hint of sexual adventure in exotic lands sent passengers queuing for tickets. There were several variations of the same theme with the substitution of 'Cynthia', 'Tina', 'Vicky', or 'Jill' for 'Linda'.

However, it would be unkind to interpret newspaper reports of Mr Francis Obi's (General Manager of Nigeria Airways) personal supervision of the airlift of pilgrims to Jeddah, Saudi Arabia as a development of the same theme. Mr Obi was sighted at Lagos, Kano, Jeddah and various locations en route. His personal service may well justify the slogan: 'I'm Francis, come fly with me'.

Rather than condemn Mr Obi for carrying the 'do-it-yourself' principle too far, I'm inclined to believe that he has simply recognised the Nigerian malaise i.e. if you want anything done by your subordinates, you have to be there yourself and if you want it done *efficiently*, you'd better do it yourself.

The chap who got the roughest deal was a certain Nigeria Airways official, Malam Musa Uba who ended up in a Jeddah clinic after a religious war with pilgrims newly-emerged from the purification rites and sublimity of the blessing of the holy pilgrimage. They charged him with blasphemy – instead of quoting excess baggage rates from the Nigeria Airways blue book, he should have been chanting quotes from the Holy Book.

4

The Americans may well groan about Saudi Arabians buying up everything within sight but the Nigerian pilgrims taught the Saudis a thing or two. Nigerian pilgrims bought just about everything that could possibly move much to the delight of Saudi merchants. The pilgrims bought first and worried about the transportation and baggage limit afterwards – and that was the beginning of Mallam Uba's troubles.

Even at the best of times, Nigerian airlines' passengers must rank as one of the most aggressive in the world. I once heard a report of a Nigerian woman who was returning to Nigeria – she carried a sewing machine on board and insisted it was hand luggage! A more enterprising soul strapped her six-year-old daughter to her back and refused to pay on the pretext that her little girl was her only luggage. Embarkation time at Heathrow is really something out of this world. Ha! The fights that go on!

As for the airline itself, it once enjoyed a wide reputation for the excellent absence of service on board. I cannot vouch for stories of stewardesses fighting on board – but I do know that Nigeria Airways, (particularly on its DOMESTIC flights) has earned itself the name 'Air Perhaps' – perhaps the plane will arrive on time, perhaps it will be five hours late taking-off, perhaps the flight has been cancelled, perhaps your name isn't on the manifest even though you booked your seat five years ago.

NO VACANCIES?

THE announcement by the Federal Public Service Commission that it has no vacancies for university graduates with qualifications in 'agriculture, mechanical engineering, electrical engineering, civil engineering, petroleum engineering, vetinary science, zoology, food technology and science subjects, must rank as one of the most astonishing pronouncements of all time. We have to go a hell of a long way back into our history to find anything more ridiculous.

If the Public Service Commision has no vacancies for science graduates, we must perforce ask – for whom do they have vacancies – messengers, cleaners, money-doublers or acrobats?

We are supposed to have a gigantic 4-year development programme that's going to completely change our lives for the better. How can we possibly implement it without a steady infusion of science graduates. How can we execute projects involving millions of naira unless we are able to involve scientists at all levels? No way. This is the time to start the technological revolution. We have the money and we have the men – all that is missing is the sense of direction as well as commitment.

In Europe and America, one finds Nigerians with the highest qualifications living in permanent exile because their own country doesn't appreciate them. Some of them are right in the front rank in medicine, engineering, metallurgy, aeronautics, mathematics and it has even been reported that there are Nigerians working on the American space programme.

Every hoe-carrying, skinny-legged, emaciated, illiterate farmer is a resounding indictment of government policy. Instead of carrying a hoe and a matchet, that farmer ought to be driving a tractor; attending farm shows organised by the government, experimenting with seeds and readily available subsidised fertilisers, living in his own home spending his evenings baking his own bread, watching new farming techniques on television or attending adult educational classes.

I have little faith in gigantic programmes. Think of all the time, effort and brain-work invested in producing beautiful volumes that will only be left to rot away in somebody's cabinet. We are more likely to be impressed by a government that announces on January 1, that within a year the whole country will have water, electricity, x number of hospitals and x number of low-cost housing units. If by December 31, we haven't got them, then we want to know why.

How can we be anything but dumb-struck when the Governor of the Central Bank publicly announces that we have foreign reserves piling up abroad and we don't know what to do with the money. This is money that is badly needed here. One shudders to think how much we must be losing daily by leaving such vast sums idle. It sounds too much like a bad joke when our own government announces that we are lending money to the World Bank!

Fifteen months after the low-cost housing was supposed to take-off, the Western State says it can't find suitable land. By the time the Western State finds land, there probably won't be cement – and by the time it finds both land and cement, there won't be any money!

In terms of foreign reserves, Nigeria ranks seventh in the world but the only way oil money can mean anything to the ordinary Nigerian is for the government to realise that more money means greater responsibilities and a larger vision. The slipshod manner in which half-baked ideas are pursued frantically for a few months and then suddenly abandoned, to be replaced by something even more baffling points in only one direction – we are in danger of remaining THE RICHEST UNDER-DEVELOPED

COUNTRY.

Our march on the road to development and self-fulfilment must be underpinned by a healthy respect for science and technology even if it means deliberately encouraging the universities, to be more science-orientated and making scholarships more easily available for students who wish to study science or agriculture. The last thing this country can afford is to produce a pool of science graduates without meaningful and satisfying employment.

I suspect that when the Chief Justice complains about 'suffering in silence' he is not talking about just the Udoji report and the White Paper. Such comments should be seen more in the light of a man who has had a ringside seat at some of the most traumatic events in the history of this country and is forced to remonstrate at how we live from one crisis to another.

The message is clear – nothing good can come out of all this. We live in a multi-plural society with cultural, ethnic and linguistic differences. Our relationships are so finely balanced that it is impossible to do one thing without throwing a lot of things out of rhythm. Anyone who doesn't understand this, doesn't understand this country at all.

THE SPIRIT OF ITOIKIN

LAST week the Head of State addressed the conference of Commonwealth Law Ministers at Victoria Island and without mincing words, told them that the detention of persons considered to be security risks did not in any way derogate the rule of law. A few days later, while declaring the new Itoikin road open, the Head of State 'dispelled rumours that his salary is ₦32,000 a year' in three minutes flat. He did it by responding briskly to the entreaties of two drummers who were demanding their own 'Udoji'. It is reported that General Gowon dipped his hand into his right-hand trousers pocket and turned it inside out for everyone to see – 'Let it all hang out.' The Head of State declared 'Look! I have no ₦32,000 in my pocket. In fact, I don't earn ₦32,000 being currently peddled about.'

These two events are both remarkable and are not unconnected. The learned gentry of the Commonwealth made a good job of concealing their surprise even if they felt that arbitrary detention and the rule of law are a contradiction in terms. In analysing the Head of State's speech, one can conclude that he was merely reminding the august gathering that the Nigerian judiciary is free to interpret the law as it thinks fit but the ENFORCEMENT of the law is the exclusive prerogative of the government.

The rate at which decrees are being churned out can only leave the citizen reeling with confusion. When we had parliamentary democracy, it was obvious that it had serious imperfections. However, as a bill went through its first, second and third readings it at least gave the people a chance to familiarise themselves with what was going on, think about them, debate the issues involved and finally make up their minds. With decrees, we are dealing with a *fait accompli*. This should not necessarily be so.

The great lesson to be learnt from the chaos of the 'Udoji' awards is that where great issues are involved, the Government should not only listen to advice but invite comments and criticism from the widest possible sections of the community. We could easily have saved ourselves a lot of agony simply by publishing the Udoji report in full, inviting public commentary BEFORE publishing the government white paper. Even the debacle over the census figures could have been avoided by releasing the overall figure of 80 million but withholding the figures for each state until the anomalies and discrepancies had been ironed out.

The wave of industrial unrest that followed the 'Udoji' award demonstrated once more that everyone is important. The strikes denied the generality of the public water and electricity, as well as medical and transport facilities, thus making life close to impossible. Everyone felt the impact. I report a conversation between a senior army officer and the telephonist at one of the banks during the strike.

Army Officer: 'Could I speak to the manager?'
Telephonist: 'I'm hungry, sir.'
Army Officer: 'What? Have I got a wrong number?'
Telephonist: 'No, you have the right number – but I'm hungry.
Army Officer: 'I didn't ask whether you were hungry, I asked to speak to the manager.'
Telephonist: 'How can you speak to the manager when I'm hungry?'
Army Officer: 'This business of your hunger is something between you and your manager.'
Telephonist: 'But I'm still hungry . . .'.

In theory, the government could break any strike simply by moving soldiers in to take over. However, this is an exercise with limited effectiveness. Soldiers may be able to take over from bank workers, NEPA, or the Water Works, but can they also take over from doctors or nightsoil men?

This is not a country of two nations – one for soldiers and one for civilians. Rather, this country is made up of soldiers who have brothers and sons at University, sisters who are doctors; and teachers whose children are in the Navy or Air Force; farmers who have nephews and cousins in the Army. Therefore in dealing with explosive situations, the government should be guided not by the expediency of meeting force with greater force – this only leads to escalation. Rather, the message is that the enforcement of law and order calls for the highest demonstration of restraint.

Even the most explosive situation can be diffused by explaining government programmes and winning maximum public support for their implementation and if the public has been misled by unfounded rumours, then it is the job of the government to disabuse their minds and set the records straight simply by putting the facts before the public. This is the lesson of the Spirit of Itoikin – the public now knows that the rumour that the Head of State's salary is ₦32,000 is untrue.

It is very much to the credit of the military regime that it has so far avoided the use of mass torture, jailings and blackmail which are prevalent in other military regimes scattered all over the world. In our own case, the military can demonstrate its superiority to a civilian administration by proving that it can get things done and is more protective of the rights and freedom of its subjects. The military can win more friends by its readiness to act with strict legality rather than force. The government has less to fear from the Aper Aku's of this world than from the manner government policies are implemented and executive response to the matters of the day.

It is reported that at Itoikin the Head of State 'danced openly to the Yoruba "gangan" tune for about three minutes amidst laughter'. This country has a lot to be thankful for – it has a lot to dance about and it has more than enough to laugh about. – Why then are we wasting time locking each other up? Give me the spirit of Itoikin anytime.

KEEP ON DANCING.

DON'T SHOOT ME, I'M ONLY THE BISHOP

THE Bishop of Gogobiri once opened his address to a congregation consisting mainly of starving unemployed, malnutrited children, diseased snake-bitten farmers, out-of-work thugs, and delirious coffin-makers with the immortal words 'blessed are the poor'.

The congregation insisted on an immediate and accurate census – 'the most thorough head count of human beings by human beings anywhere in the world' to determine whether anyone had seen any blessing in the midst of their poverty.

Since the answer was a unanimous 'No', the congregation immediately fled into the bush and have remained there, stubbornly refusing to recognise right-hand driving, Universal Primary Education, colour television, Black Arts Festival, the Third Development Programme, 'Udoji', the 2nd All African Games, the new currency and the appointment of Professor Adedeji (Federal Commissioner for Economic Development) to head the United Nations Economic Commission for Africa – 'if he can't help us while he is HERE, how can he help us when he is OVER THERE?'

On another occasion, the Bishop started his address to a congregation of tax-collectors with the words . . . 'It is more difficult for a rich man . . .' Even before he could finish, he was interrupted by a voice from the audience 'Your Worship, these days the rich are not just entering all sorts of kingdoms – they are buying them up.' At which point the congregation broke up in uproar, took to the streets and marched to the office of the local army commander to demand the immediate removal or liquidation of the Bishop.

Brigadier Akpanah being a very sensible man placated the angry crowd with the immortal words. 'These are trying times, I'm only interested in saboteurs, arms dealers, profiteers, milk-hoarders and girls. Don't shoot him – he is only the bishop.'

The Bishop having narrowly escaped death, found himself in Afemaeze, deep in the Midwest.

When income tax was first introduced in England, the Bishops condemned it as the work of the devil – and insisted that the church would have absolutely nothing whatever to do with it, in spite of the King's assurances that the tax was for only one year and was only a penny anyway. The Bishops were adamant and pointed out that once you let the devil in, he stayed for good. Consequently, they insisted on and got exemption for all bishops, clerks, and church property.

At various times since then, kings desperate for money have been tempted to shoot bishops in order to get hold of the vast property and artworks in the custody of the bishops. The bishops always coolly explained to the kings that since the property were not personal to them but were in fact vested in the church, no useful purpose would be served by shooting bishops. In order to get the message across to the king, the bishops came up with the slogan 'Don't shoot us – We Are Only Bishops'.

It is not often that I find myself agreeing with bishops, but on this occasion I must make an exemption. The Anglican bishops of the province of West Africa met last week. Just as the bishops were right about income tax, it is just possible that they may be equally right in their criticism of the proposed introduction of colour television. They declared that there was no justification for the Black Arts Festival which they condemned as the work of the devil. The bishops rightly implored the Government to 'first provide its citizens with good sanitation, water and roads before it embarks on such expensive projects'.

No doubt, many will endorse the bishops' views as regards the Black Arts Festival. However, it looks as if the lords bishops have left their protests too late! Far too many 'agba contracts' have already been awarded; and far too many globe-trotters have jetted round the world in search of vestiges of black culture in such unlikely places as Alaska, Hong Kong, Iceland, Outer Mongolia and Siberia for the festival to be cancelled at this stage.

As for colour television, that is a different kettle of fish altogether. It must take at least six double-gin and tonics followed by four treble brandies and quadruple vodka and limes plus a repeat order for anyone to even think up the idea that with all the problems before us, the abject poverty amidst us and rank illiteracy, colour television has any place in our scale of priorities.

Anyway, perhaps we should be thankful to God in His mercies that the people who dreamt up the colour-TV idea stopped there. Why, with a few more gin and tonics they could easily have added on a change back to left-hand drive, replacement of naira with cowrie shells, atomic missiles, a defence pact with Israel, and the introduction of Chinese as our lingua franca.

Following closely on the Bishops' protest, the ex-Governor of the former Eastern Nigeria, ex-'Sir' and now Dr Akanu Ibiam, a very devout Christian, put forward the following suggestions as the 'panacea' that can cure Nigeria's ills and usher in perfect peace in the country:

1   The institution of a constitutional assembly
2   The demobilisation of the army soonest
3   A stop to the building of army barracks everywhere and anywhere
4   The creation of a reconciliation committee
5   The release of all detainees
6   The sending away from the country of all the false friends of Nigeria
7   Allowing the court to try the supposed offenders before punishment
8   Don't shoot me – I'm ONLY AN EX-GOVERNOR

A few days after Dr Ibiam's address to the Peace Research Institute of Nigeria, at which the Bishop of Gogobiri surprisingly resurfaced and in fact said the closing prayers, the Bishop fired off the following telegram to Mr Edwin Clark, the new Federal Commissioner for Information who had just emerged from a stormy press conference.

'Dear Ed,

'I congratulate you on your first press conference as Commissioner for Information. It is a pity you took it for granted that the press would give you a warm reception, blow kisses all round, consider your points soberly and comment with mature judgement.

'I feel I ought to congratulate you because your press conference marks the first occasion since 1967 that the Government has volunteered not only the number of people in detention but also their names, age, sex, height, weight, religion, skin-colour, tribe, last known address as well as food preferences. Now, simply by telling all, you have put the lie to all those wild stories about the number of people in detention.

'Dear Ed, however, I do wonder whether you may not be taking this job too seriously. You see, the change from being Commissioner in the Midwest to being a Federal Commissioner calls for a "new game plan" as my good friend Richard Expletive Nixon (another work of the devil) would say, I feel that the very qualities that made you such a resounding success in the Midwest are the very ones guaranteed to get you into trouble in Lagos. Please take my word for it, there is nothing the Lagos Press dislikes more than a Commissioner for Information who is determined to release information.

'Why not borrow a leaf from your predecessor in office – Chief Anthony Enahoro, a fellow Midwesterner who really knew how to handle the press. This is not surprising since he is an ex-journalist himself. Between you and me let me tell you a secret – anything Chief Enahoro does not know about the press is NOT WORTH KNOWING AT ALL. At the beginning of each press conference, the "Chief" or the "Old Maestro" as his friends call him, would announce to the journalists present:

'"I do not intend to answer any questions about census, creation of new states, Udoji, National Supply Corporation, inflation, lingua franca, strikes, students, protests, poverty, disease, sex, illiteracy, unemployment, water shortage, power failure, iron and steel, state governors. . . .'' At which point he would invite questions from the floor and seeing no impetuous hands shooting up, he would declare the press conference over and invite the journalists to feel free with the ample supply of free drinks. The following day's headlines bore witness to his excellent performance as every reporter felt free to invent his own version of the questions and answers.

'Those of us who have been privileged to know Chief Enahoro can confirm not only his versatility (combining, labour, sports, culture, antiquities, and weather forecast with the Ministry of Information) but also his wonderful sense of humour. For many years, journalists were baffled by his constant reference to the Nigerian press as the FREEST in the world. Revelation came when a passing journalist overheard the Chief explaining tongue-in-cheek to a foreign journalist that the Nigerian Press, more than any other journalists anywhere else in the world liked FREE drinks, were fond of FREE food, solicited FREE trips abroad and were crazy about FREE information.

'Just to illustrate the point I was making about the consequences of taking your job too much to heart, let me remind you that a few weeks ago the workers at Lagos City Transport Services named a bus after their ex-Chairman, Lt Commander M. A. B. Elegbede. However, the bus they chose was a rickety, wheezing, dilapidated bus. I leave you to draw your inference of this opinion of their boss, who against formidable opposition tried to give the place a clean sweep.

'Let me assure you that I fully share your enthusiasm for plain and accurate information. I remind you of the misfortune of my fellow bishop, the Bishop of Isale-Eko who was in the middle of his Sunday sermon when he heard of Brigadier Mobolaji Johnson's call to church leaders to pray for the soul of the nation, to pray for rain in

17

drought-affected areas and to pray for the success of the Black Arts Festival.

'The Bishop of Isale-Eko read the message in such a hurry that he got it all wrong and instead led the congregation in prayer for RAIN DURING THE BLACK ARTS FESTIVAL. Needless to say, the Bishop of Isale-Eko has been declared a SECURITY RISK.

'I must stop here, the electricity is gone, the water is gone and I don't even know whether this telegram will ever reach you, but trust in the lord and be rest assured that I remain.

'Your brother in Christ.

'The Bishop,

'Gogobiri Lodge.'

'REMEMBER THE GODFATHER NEVER SLEEPS'

A FEW years ago, the Prime Minister addressed his newly appointed cabinet as follows:

'Gentlemen, you will no doubt wonder why I have not issued a press statement as regards the newly appointed ministers. The answer is simple. Over the years I have found that the Nigerian Press is only interested in printing erotic photographs, obituaries, petitions for the creation of more but obviously unviable states, gossip about my ministers, allegations of bribery and corruption in high places and innuendoes about dubious deals and shady characters both within and outside the government. I warn you – don't listen to the press and don't even talk to them.

'I don't want to hear about ministerial wrong-doings or press leaks of cabinet discussions. Be on your guard. I shall myself be watching you not because I do not trust you but because I wish to avoid any embarrassing stories in the press. I shall be watching your movements; your contacts; the company you keep; your bank accounts both here and in Zurich; and of course all your telephone conversations must be pre-recorded and sent to the Cabinet Office for vetting. Remember the slogan "The Godfather never sleeps"!

'You may think the measures I have adopted are stringent but I assure you they are absolutely necessary. I am sick and tired of hearing stories of personal aggrandisement and official corruption especially when I know them to be true! Can you imagine my embarrassment when the American Ambassador whispered into my ear the other day, that one of my ministers had addressed the American Chamber of Commerce and was asked –

"Mr Minister, is it true we have to pay 10 per cent of any deals we fix to you as commission?" His reply was "Nonsense. All these stories you people hear about TEN PER CENT are not true. Me, I always charge FIFTEEN PER CENT."

'I was even more embarrassed when the British Ambassador told me that one of my ministers had confided in him that he liked dealing with Lebanese because:

"They know the score. You don't have to ask them for a bribe. Their gifts are never too small to insult you and never too big to compromise you."

'Gentlemen, as ministers you will be open to all sorts of offers and temptation but I warn you, be careful because nothing you do will remain a secret for ever. Why, only a few months ago, I heard that another of my ministers was being pestered by a contractor who desperately wanted a favour. The contractor offered my minister a very attractive deal but the minister was very worried in case it leaked. To reassure him, the contractor declared: "Don't worry, Mr Minister. After all, only last week, I paid off the Honourable Minister of . . . AND NOBODY KNOWS ABOUT IT."

'Gentlemen, you will no doubt recall that my last Minister of . . . was a rabid socialist. He was always telling me things about a German with a funny name – Herr Karl Marx or something like that. I have the name written somewhere – I'll look for it later. Anyway, at the last cabinet meeting, I called him aside and let him know that I knew about his deals. Herr Minister, I see you have enough money to keep you in champagne for a long time to come. I also see you have five houses in Victoria Island, eleven cars and money in WAKIKI. What has happened to all that stuff about socialism with which you were always bugging me?'

'He coolly replied: "Your Excellency, Mr Prime Minister, Lion of Lagos – socialism is the sharing of wealth NOT poverty."

'As Ministers, you will often have to travel abroad. I

warn you to be careful in choosing your words. Last year, one of my ministers who was visiting London during the Easter holidays was asked by Robin Day, "Mr Minister, will you be going away?" (Meaning will you be travelling during the holiday?) My Minister retorted angrily: "Go away you." (Meaning shut up and get out of my sight).

'Only a few weeks ago, the Swedish Ambassador reported to me that my Minister of . . . was addressing a group of businessmen in Stockholm. The question asked was "Is there stability in Nigeria?" His answer was: "Of course, there is stability. Today, I Francis Gogo, am Minister of . . . if my party wins the next elections, I Francis Gogo will still be Minister of . . . if on the other hand my party should loose the election, I shall cross-carpet and I, Francis Gogo will still be Minister of . . . Gentlemen how can you say there's no stability?"

'I think it is only right that I should tell you that hence-forth no minister will be paid "Overseas allowance". I made a mistake last time when I approved an allowance of £100 per night plus expenses for the last cabinet but to my horror, I found that some of my ministers were living permanently outside the country in order to collect over-seas allowance: NOT ONLY THAT, I discovered that the bills from Hilton, Dorchester, Plaza, Americana, and of course Playboy included such items as Elliot skin-coloured boots for Rita, Agnes, Comfort, mink coat for Zsa Zsa; 17-hour trans-Atlantic phone call to Racquel Welch and a country mansion for my minister for . . .

'Gentlemen, hotel expenses in that year cost my Government 56 per cent of the budget. I'm sure you all know that there is something seriously wrong with a government that spends more on entertainment than on its defence.

'Finally, my advice to you all is simple: Be wise, be careful and above all remember I shall be watching you. Think clean thoughts, do good deeds and collect your reward not here in Swiss francs but in heaven. Remember – THE GODFATHER NEVER SLEEPS.'

UDOJI: A CASE OF
RIGHT MEDICINE TO WRONG PATIENT?

THE more closely one looks at the inconsistencies and platitudes in the Udoji report, the more clearly one realises that the whole exercise is a case of giving the wrong medicine to the wrong patient or a case of claiming that the 'operation was successful, but sorry the patient died'.

The Udoji award has certainly done very little to bridge the gap between the lowest paid workers and the 'super-permsecs', otherwise known as the 'miracle workers'. It looks more and more as if the award is based, more on political considerations rather than economic reality.

The reality of the situation is that faced with our lopsided economy, steadily rising prices and extremes of poverty and affluence, our rightful course of action is not simply to pump more money into the economy but rather to aim at an increase in REAL INCOMES i.e. an increase in the purchasing power of the naira.

There is no real increase in income if the award is eaten up by increases in rent, food, drugs and transport. This is the pattern that is rapidly evolving, and that is why it would not be surprising if six months from now workers start pressing for another round of increments.

A far more fruitful strategy would be to increase the amount of goods available, expedite the low cost housing programme, subsidise public transport, accelerate the rural electrification programme, expand the health services and above all bring our agriculture into the 20th century. It's rather odd that at a time when every other nation is battling to contain inflation, we are determined to manufacture our own.

The Udoji award has awarded Permanent Secretaries pay increases to bring their salaries in line with those obtainable in the private sector. This is rather strange because the functions, security and responsibilities of a permanent secretary are vastly different from those of a general manager in the private sector. Besides, the Permanent Secretary invariably enjoys far more POWER AND INFLUENCE.

A Permanent Secretary is no more comparable to a General Manager than a horse is comparable to a camel, even though both have four legs and are used for transportation. The irony of the Udoji award is that the Permanent Secretaries it seeks to reward the most are the very ones whose ministries are crying out for massive re-organisation and dismantling.

I am entirely in favour of paying attractive salaries to Permanent Secretaries PROVIDED they are delivering the goods. As for the suggestion that such salaries will attract top management from the private sector, this is wishful thinking. The private sector will simply pay its efficient managers more in order to retain them.

The really strange thing is that the report could easily become an instrument of sectionalism – private sector versus public sector; administrators versus professionals; technicians versus non-technicians, etc. For example, while the Permanent Secretaries are on 'Cloud Nine', the Accountant-General, the Chief Medical Adviser, the Chairman of the Inland Revenue, are way down below.

The doctors and nurses have obviously got a pretty poor deal. So also have the engineers, accountants, and other professionals in the civil service who are supposed to form the hard core of middle management.

As for the private sector, the Udoji award could easily trigger off industrial unrest. Many of the indigenous companies are going to have a hard time paying the award particularly as some of them have still not paid the Adebo award.

The Udoji report looks like a bad mess, maybe we should just treat the awards as PROVISIONAL.

MR & MRS UAC CORDIALLY REQUEST . . .

THE United Africa Company has sent 85,000 invitation cards to its multitude of shareholders scattered all over Nigeria to attend the 'Annual General Meeting of the members of UAC of Nigeria Limited at the Indoor Sports Hall of the National Stadium Western Avenue, Surulere Lagos, next Thursday at 11.00 in the forenoon.'

Even though the invitations were posted eighteen months ago, there will be many shareholders who won't receive theirs until the party is over. For those who manage to make the trip from Gboko, Nasarawa, Obubra, Uzuakoli, Ake, Molete or wherever and survive the Surulere traffic here are a few hints as to what to expect.

First of all you are expected to turn up in full and colourful regalia: medals and braids are in order but please do not come in evening dress – your hosts do not expect the party to go on for that long, after all they have a business to look after. Secondly, it may come as a shock to find that you won't be getting a personal introduction to an handshake from the Board of Directors – 85,000 are far too many to expect Messrs F. A. Pardoe, C. E. Abebe, G. U. II. Gardner, Chief S. O. Adebo, Messrs J. R. Bell, D. H. Boyles, J. F. Brown, J. G. Clark, S. B. Daniyan, Chief E. A. Silva, Mr W. B. Smart and Chief L. O. Edet to stand in line.

When you do get in, don't be too disappointed if you find that there are far fewer than 85,000 other guests – some people have to be at work you know. Also, don't be too put off when you discover that all the proceedings will be in English. If Swahili is the only language you speak, just take out your hearing aid, relax and enjoy the scenery, but remember to clap whenever everybody else is clapping – it'll probably be the dividend being announced.

At some point, the Chairman and Managing Director Mr F. S. Pardoe will offer to answer questions. Here is a sample of what NOT to ask:

1 'Your Excellency, Mr Chairman when is the price of the shares going to drop so I can buy some more?'
2 'I have travelled here from Gboko – will the Chairman accept the humble offer of the people of Gboko to hold the next Annual General Meeting in Gboko?'
3 'Your Highness, I have been unemployed for the past six years. I hold four shares bought in my name by my greedy cousin, can you give me a job?'
4 'On hearing that Dr Arikpo had resigned from the Board of Directors in order to concentrate on our border dispute with Australia I applied under sixteen different names to replace him on the board. Why have I not received a reply?'

Before question time is over you can be sure to see Mr Akintunde Asalu leaping to his feet. If you have been reading your newspaper regularly, you would have noticed his photograph on the front page of Daily Times.

When Mr Asalu is not venting his spleen as 'President-Director Proprietor-General' of the Lagos University Alumni, on the Military Government for daring to close the universities, he is likely to be attending company annual general meetings where he is constantly baiting Chairmen. He can be relied on to ask a few awkward questions.

Incidentally, rumour has it that one or two chairmen have been so embarrassed by Mr Asalu's tactics that they contacted him in advance with a view to anticipating any awkward questions he may have up his sleeve. You should have seen the relief at the AGM of Alfamanshudanwikolit Group of companies when Mr Asalu's only question was to ask what the time was.

The Chairman will personally deliver your invitation to next year's party and have you and your wife collected in a chauffeur-driven Mercedez-Benz, if you get up to make any of the following statements.

1 'On behalf of ALL SHAREHOLDERS, MY WIFE AND I congratulate the Directors on the wonderful job they have done, are doing and will no doubt continue to do'.
2 'Three hearty cheers to the Directors.'
3 'My fellow shareholders and I INSIST that the Directors IMMEDIATELY collect their own Udoji award with arrears back-dated to the end of the civil war.'
4 We insist on carrying the directors shoulder-high for declaring such a generous dividend in excess of what was promised in the prospectus'.

Towards the end of the proceedings, you are likely to hear the Chairman announce:

'After the next question, I shall declare the meeting closed and invite all shareholders to partake of refreshments laid on at the back of the hall.' Please do not be unduly upset at the mad rush that is sure to ensue as your fellow shareholders stampede towards the chicken and jollof rice.

'Last year, at the AGM of a company whose main product is soap powder, free samples were issued to the shareholders and I'm sure you would have been most upset at the pandemonium that ensued as each shareholder tried to grab as many packets of detergents as possible. Much to the distress of the hotel at which the meeting was held, soap powder was strewn all over the Conference Hall.

'On your way home, just in case you start wondering whether it would not have been better to stay home in bed, I urge you to consider that there have been occasions in the past when the company and the shareholders have benefited from the goings on at AGM's. I admit that they are rare occasions but they are worth recording anyway.

In 1970, when Rolls-Royce Limited was on the brink of financial disaster, Michael Wynford, a shareholder, got the other shareholders to vote unanimously in support of a resolution which called on the Directors to pass the following instructions to all Rolls-Royce employees:

'Due to the excessive number of absences during the past year and the imminent collapse of the company, it has become necessary to put the following rules and procedures into operation immediately.

1 SICKNESS: No excuse. The company will no longer accept your doctor's certificate as proof. We believe that if you are able to go to your doctor you are able to attend work.

2 DEATH (Your own): This will be accepted as an excuse. We should like two weeks notice however since we feel it is your duty to train someone else to do your job.

3 DEATH (Other than your own): This is no excuse. There is nothing you can do for them and henceforth no time off will be allowed for funerals. However, in case this should cause some hardship to some of our employees, please note that on your behalf the company has a special arrangement for lunchtime burials thus ensuring that no time is lost off the job.

4 LEAVE OF ABSENCE FOR ANY OPERATION: We wish to discourage any thoughts you may have of needing an operation and henceforth no leave of absence will be granted for hospital visits. THE COMPANY BELIEVES THAT AS LONG AS YOU ARE AN EMPLOYEE HERE, YOU WILL NEED ALL WHAT YOU ALREADY HAVE AND SHOULD NOT CONSIDER ANY OF IT BEING REMOVED. After all, we engaged you with all your parts and having anything removed would mean that we are getting less than we bargained for.

5 VISITS TO THE TOILET: Far too much time is spent in this practice. In future, the procedure will be that all personnel shall go in alphabetical order. For example,

those with surnames beginning with letter 'A' will go from 9.45 to 10.00; 'B' will go from 10.00 to 10.15 etc. Those of you unable to attend at your appropriate time will have to wait until the next day when your time comes again.

With all good wishes for a memorable Annual General Meeting.

FIRST THE BAD NEWS

It's really terrible that with the introduction of the first ever assembled Peugeot car in Nigeria, people have already taken it for granted that the car may not have an engine; would be incapable of going into reverse or travelling faster than 30 M.P.H. Admittedly, the public have had very poor experience with made-in-Nigeria textiles, matches, cigarettes, alcoholic drinks, drugs etc., hence a formidable amount of market resistance has built up over the years.

NOW THE GOOD NEWS

All the indications are that the 'made-in-Nigeria' Peugeot cars will meet the challenge. Owing to the relatively small number (20,000 a year) to be produced. They may well prove to be a better product than the imported mass-produced version.

The following story augurs well for the future of Peugeot cars:

Mathias Ebionseriah took his brand new Volvo 144 home to the Midwest last week. He was severely reprimanded by his uncle who said 'that's the trouble with you educated young men, you think you know everything. If only you had added a little more money, you could have got yourself a nice Peugeot 404.'

POSTSCRIPT

There is no truth whatever in the story that a state government is negotiating with a foreign partner to ASSEMBLE safety pins and paper-clips in Nigeria.

28

THE IMPOSSIBLE DREAM

I HAVE very strong reservations about whether the salary structure for doctors can be dealt with along with the anomalies and petitions being examined by Williams & Williams (otherwise known as the Review Panel).

This is no reflection on the competence of the panel – rather it looks more and more as if the salary structure for doctors calls for a sober, thorough and comprehensive review of the practice of medicine itself and the availability of medical facilities not just in the urban areas of the country but also in the far flung nooks and corners. This would take at least a year.

For doctors the problems are personalised and to understand them, we have to bear in mind that most of the people who are today doctors were very bright students, perhaps the 'creme de la creme' of their class. College was followed by impressive academic performance at university, long hours of study and years of self-denial.

Ten years after graduation some of them find they are tenants renting flats and surgeries from people with whom they went to school – the dull ones who barely passed the School Certificate or the not terribly clever ones who drifted into law, accountancy, civil service, surveying, architecture, import and export and of course smuggling, counterfeiting and highway robbery.

A lot of doctors caught in this situation in which they find themselves in spite of the length of their training, their specialised skill and scarcity value, poor relations of their counterparts in other fields are asking themselves WHERE DID WE GO WRONG?

This is further illustrated by the case of a doctor friend

29

of mine who is a consultant at Lagos University Teaching Hospital. His wife holds a Bachelor of Arts degree and is in the civil service. She hadn't even entered university at the time when her husband qualified as a fully-fledged doctor. Now, thanks to Udoji. She's earning a clear ₦1000 per annum more than her doctor husband.

It would of course be silly to portray doctors as a poverty-stricken brotherhood. However, the fact remains that the affluent doctors with swanky surgeries or multiple nursing homes constitute only a small minority. Neither are doctors saints. We are all too familar with stories of doctors thriving on sick-leave permits, unnecessary injections and drugs as well as illegal, abortions.

It is equally true that such doctors are in the minority and some of them will frankly tell you that they are driven by desperation to such exploitative pursuits. For the most part doctors would be happy to work 8 a.m. to 5 p.m. for a decent salary and spend their evenings with family and friends rather than running moonlight surgeries or chasing cement deals.

This country needs doctors and needs them badly and fortunately it can afford to pay them generously. Unless we recognise this, all talk about producing more doctors or spreading medical facilities to the rural areas will forever remain an impossible dream.

The public are rightly critical of doctors but the doctors in turn blame it all on the medical service itself; strangely enough there is quite a lot of truth in this. Only the other day, a doctor made the point that even doctors are alarmed at the wastefulness of the medical service.

For example, at LUTH there is a brand new ₦1,000.000 electron microscope purchased from Japan which is now rendered completely useless because nobody knows how to repair it. Also there are some highly sensitive and expensive equipment in the Chest department and in the Cardiac department. In order to function properly, these equipment depend on a steady and UNINTERRUPTED SUPPLY OF ELECTRICITY. Thanks to the inefficiency of

NEPA, the vulnerability of these equipment is guaranteed.

As regards charges that doctors who are supposed to be on call duty will often disappear for hours on end, the doctors say that this is the fault of the hospital. I find a lot of sense in the suggestion that a hostel should be built within the hospital itself so that doctors who live far away from the hospital or cannot be contacted by phone can spend the night in reasonable comfort with meals readily available so that there is no need for them to go outside the hospital premises.

Perhaps the most distressing aspect of the whole set up is the co-ordination between doctors and anaesthetists. Most of the anaesthetists live outside the hospital in such 'classy' areas as Bariga, Somolu, Aladire, Agboyin, and Idi-Oro.

What seems to be happening is that a doctor who finds himself with a case requiring immediate surgery is confronted with the problem of how to get hold of an anaesthetist who will almost certainly not have a phone in his house. So the doctor writes a nice little note [which he hands in to the matron] for delivery to the anaesthetist and pleads that his services are urgently required.

Because of the urgency of the situation the matron gets hold of a hospital driver, gives him the note and the search is on. Anyone who has ever tried to locate a street in Bariga or Somolu must be familiar with the fact that a street that was 'Awoyinfa Street' until last week may well now be called 'Adeyinka Close' only to be changed to 'Olabunmi Plaza' next week.

Even if by some stroke of fortune the driver was able to locate the house, the anaesthetist may be out at a party or be receiving spiritual guidance at the local 'aladura' church.

The deficiencies in the service at LUTH apply to a lesser or greater extent to the General Hospital, Massey Street Children's Hospital and Island Maternity.

At Island Maternity, the slogan is "if your wife is

31

having a baby better bring your own water." The water shortage is so bad that doctors complain that they have to spend their own money to buy bottles of water to wash their hands after surgery. Can you believe that? This is happening right in the middle of Lagos.

It is difficult to believe that the problems of the medical profession could be dealt with in isolation without looking into the medical facilities available to the nation as a whole. This involves recognising that the expense and complexity of an efficient medical service are too much for the resources of the State Governments.

The running of the hospitals whether in Lagos, Ibadan, Benin or Kaduna should be handed over to the Federal Government and the programme should be such that the facilities are of a uniform minimum standard. There is no reason why the Ilorin General Hospital should be the poor relation of the Lagos General Hospital. Once the Government accepts this, purchase of equipment can be tied in with adequate training programmes to ensure proper maintenance and repair facilities which are freely available to all the States.

For example, if Kano State should purchase an electron-microscope identical to the one in say Benin and both of them break down, as of now, both Kano and Benin would each have to send for an engineer from Japan. It seems only reasonable to train enough engineers who regard their services as readily available to all the hospitals irrespective of the State Government involved.

It is only within the context of a truly national scheme that the differentials between doctors in the teaching hospitals as opposed to doctors in the General hospitals, or doctors in the rural areas; the advantages of bulk buying of drugs and exchange of stocks of a particular drug in excess of the hospitals' immediate requirement; and the grading of nurses and para-medical staff can be ironed out.

It is possible that in a place like Canada where clean water, good food, basic hygiene and sanitation are taken for granted and most of the population have a basic knowledge of antibiotics, a doctor on the scale of relativities may come no higher than the hair-dresser but here in Nigeria, at least in the rural areas, the doctor is God or a pretty close second.

If anyone is in any doubt about the despair caused by the lack of medical facilities, take a trip to Aba or Onitsha where right in the market place, quack doctors do a thriving trade in giving phoney injections. Believe it or not, people are so anxious to receive injections they don't even bother to take their trousers off!

'THIS IS YOUR GOVERNOR SPEAKING'

A FEW days ago, Brigadier Oluwole Rotimi,. Military Governor of the 'ungovernable' Western State delivered his Budget speech. It was very much in character that the governor chose to do away with pre-recording and editing his speech. Instead, the budget was broadcast 'live simultaneously over radio, television, telegraph, talking drum, 'ganggan', and of course, word of mouth.

A very loyal citizen, Mr Moyo Salami had only six weeks before bought a television set with his 'Udoji Award.' He gave a big 'Khaki', palm wine cum 'Odeku' (Guiness Stout) party to mark the occasion and announced to his guests that as a gesture of appreciation of the generosity of the Military Government, the first picture he wanted to see on the screen of his new TV set was that of his Governor. He apologised for not demonstrating the new equipment right away.

He however, implored his guests that they should keep their eyes and ears wide open for any announcement of the Governor's appearance on TV so that they could re-assemble and listen to the Governor's words of wisdom. It was six weeks of torture for Mr Salami and the rest of the village. They listened to the radio all day and all night; forced their literate children to go through all available newspapers; and even sent a scout to the next village for news.

In desparation they turned to the oracle, 'Ifa' and demanded to know when the Governor would next appear on television. The 'Ifa' priest apologised to Mr Salami that owing to the black-out by NEPA (National Electric Power Authority) there were considerable difficulties in communicating with the spirits of their ancestors. Mr Salami got more and more desperate and finally decided to go to the Secretariat at Ibadan to make enquiries.

He checked at the Governor's office but was directed to the Ministry of Information. At the Ministry of Information, the Principal Information Officer didn't know but suggested maybe the Deputy-Permanent Secretary might know. The DPS didn't know but being anxious to help, he telephoned the Permanent Secretary to enquire: . . . 'Sir, I have a Mr Salami here. He wants to know when the Governor will next appear on television?'

The Perm-Sec. asked, 'Which Mr Salami is that? Is it Salami the Contractor, or the medicine-man, or rain-maker, or Salami 'tycoon'? The Deputy-Perm. Sec. replied, 'This one is Salami nothing.' The Perm-Sec. getting irritated ordered his deputy, 'In that case tell him to mind his own business.'

Since Mr Salami was able to overhear the conversation between the DPS and the PS, he realised he had come to the wrong place. Apart from smarting from the insult of being described as Salami 'nothing'. He was so outraged, he burst into tears outside the Ministry of Information. A passer-by Mr Somorin consoled him and on learning of his problem, directed him to the studios of Western Nigeria Television.

At WNTV, Mr Salami asked everyone and anyone he could get hold of – gatemen, messengers, programme executives, actors, actresses but drew a blank everywhere. Nobody knew when the Governor was due to appear. Finally, he confronted the Managing Director with the question. 'I am a loyal citizen of the State. Can you tell me when the Governor is due to appear on TV?

The Managing Director replied 'I am sorry, I don't know. I mean, I do know but for security reasons, I am not allowed to tell you! The only person who can tell you is the Governor himself.'

'Mr Salami':   Are you suggesting I have to
                           ask the Governor himself?'

MD: 'Yes'

Mr Salami:	'Where does he live?'
MD:	'Government House, of course.'
Mr Salami:	'Where is that?'
MD:	'I'm very busy at the moment but if you wait five hours I can give you a lift there.'

Five hours later, Mr Salami duly got a lift to Government House. He went up to the soldiers guarding the entrance only to be confronted with a harsh enquiry:

'Who goes there?'

His reply:	'ME'.
Questioner:	'Me who?'
Reply:	'Emi Salami ni o!'
Questioner:	'Do you know the password?'
Reply:	'What password?'
Questioner:	'Scram! You have no business here. YOU HEAR.'
Salami:	'I'm not a business-man. How can I have a business here? All I want to know is when the Governor is due to appear on TV.'

At this point, the soldier cocked his rifle and ordered Salami to leave immediately. Salami was so frightened, he collapsed in a faint. The soldiers gave him first-aid, but to no avail. They therefore rushed him to the nearest hospital. The doctor on duty tried everything he could to revive Salami but as the patient was not responding to treatment, he concluded that Salami was suffering from an advanced state of shock.

The doctor therefore recommended the best thing to do was to rush him to Aro Mental Home where psychiatric treatment would be available. At Aro, Salami was quickly attended to by the psychiatrist on duty. He was given all sorts of injections and tablets but still no response.

It was at this point that one of the young radical doctors suggested trying 'Khaki.' It worked! However, the psychiatrists were most puzzled by the fact that Salami kept mumbling only two words 'Governor' and 'Television' and decided he needed special treatment. He was promptly given a mattress and locked up.

The following morning he was hauled before the Superintendent who told him that the psychiatrist's tests showed conclusively that he was schizophrenic paranoid. At this point Salami burst into tears and demanded to be set free as there was a madman in the ward who had been winking at him. Furthermore, every ten minutes, the said madman would confront Salami with the now famous words: 'Where is my Udoji?' At this point, the Superintendent assured Salami that the best treatment available would be given to him and he should consider himself surrounded by friends.

Salami exploded: 'What friends? I DON'T WANT MADMEN AS FRIENDS.'

That same night, Salami escaped from the mental home and after two days of riding a bicycle which he had stolen from a farmer he finally covered the 400 miles to his village. He was greeted with wild jubilation and the village Chief declared a public holiday or 'LAZY DAY' to mark the occasion. The drinks ('Khaki' of course) flowed freely until the early hours of the morning and the 'long-distance runners' whose capacity for 'Khaki' knew no limits were determined that the celebration should go on all of the next day and night as well.

Over and over again, Salami was prodded into retelling the story of his adventure accompanied by sympathetic 'ha' and 'ho' from his enthralled audience.

The following night when even the sturdiest drinkers were beginning to wane in spirit and the supply of 'khaki' had been exhausted, word suddenly came from the next village that they had foolproof and absolutely irrefutable information that the Governor would indeed appear on TV at 9 o'clock that night; wild jubilation followed. The village Chief ordered a fresh supply of 'Khaki' and ordered all villagers to assemble before Salami's television set at 8.30 p.m.

At the appointed time, the village Chief poured libation, prayed for the souls of their ancestors and led the congregation in special prayers for long life and prosperity for the Governor. A few minutes before 9 p.m. Salami nervously turned the knobs of the TV. As the National Anthem came on, the audience burst into wild applause and this was followed by the picture of the smiling Governor in full Military dress. As the Governor commenced his speech with the now famous words: 'This is your Governor speaking . . .' the audience burst into even wilder applause.

As the Governor's speech went on, the audience got more and more excited. Every time he mentioned 'Million' or 'billion', Salami translated it as 'Uncountable' or 'Double Uncountable' and the response from the audience was rapturous – millions for health; millions for education; billions for agriculture; and more billions for infrastructure.

Finally, the Governor got to the last paragraph. 'As from next year we shall have COLOUR TELEVISION and even though I won't be able to see you, you at least will be able to see me in colour. Every effort will be made to assist you to purchase colour TV sets and . . .' At this point, there was total blackout, (NEPA) again! Pandemonium immediately broke out among the audience as everybody scrambled for the exit.

Salami started rolling on the floor, wailing and weeping, and loudly bemoaning that by next year his new TV set would be useless, and where was he to find the money for the colour version? He pulled himself together, got on the stolen bicycle and rode straight back to Aro Mental Home where he found the Superintendent coolly waiting for him. All that the Superintendent could understand from Salami's repetitive mumblings was the question: 'Your Excellency, the Most Reverend Superintendent, will you be getting colour television?

Superintendent: 'Oh no. Not television again. We have enough trouble with the one we have now. I told you before – you are a schizophrenic paranoid.

Salami: 'What does that mean?'

Superintendent: 'It means you IMAGINE things – You

even imagine you have enemies.'

Salami: 'I KNOW I have enemies but I don't want to see them in colour.'

At this point, the Superintendent directed Salami's attention to the sign outside the hospital – 'THEY ALWAYS COME BACK.'

A NATION OF 80 MILLION CONTRACTORS

Last Saturday, the Head of State launched the Third National Development Plan and within a few minutes some of the dignitaries who had attended the ceremony had retired to the Island Club to ponder on the more profound implications of the Plan. They were soon joined by others who only heard it on the radio.

The general concensus of opinion was that this was the 'operation fantastic' to beat them all – unlike any of its predecessors, the Third Plan is for EVERYBODY and 'anyone who doesn't make it during the Third Plan is never going to make it'. Everybody from doctor, engineer, dentist, lawyer, right down to messenger, taxi driver and steward is going into the contracting business. This is a nation of eighty million contractors!

The discussions got so animated that some of the older members of the club couldn't help recalling the great days of Sir Adeyemo Alakija, Mr Ernest Ikoli, Dr Omololu and Chief Oladipo Moore and how the Governor used to come down to the club straight after delivering the budget and declare 'now what do you think of it gentlemen? – all the jokes are on me.'

He didn't always hear what he wanted to hear and neither did he always like what he heard but at least he listened.

A few days earlier, Mr Simon Shodipo, the co-ordinator for the multi-million naire Black Arts Festival disclosed to the Head of State that more than 20 per cent of the houses will not be completed on schedule for the 2nd Black Arts Festival to be held in November this year.

Considering what is at stake, this is an event for which it is not enough to be only 60 per cent; 70 per cent; 80 per cent; or 90 per cent prepared. In fact we need to be 200 per cent ready. If Mr Shodipo is to be believed, the best we can hope for is to be 80 per cent ready.

In order to illustrate just what this means I asked various people what 80 per cent success means. Here are some of the answers:

Banker: 'When you lend ₦100 and recover only ₦80.'

Builder: 'When the money runs out before you've built the roof.'

Lawyer: 'When eight out of your ten clients end up in jail and the remaining two refuse to pay your fees.'

Accountant: 'When twenty per cent of your clients end up in detention for tax evasion.'

Housewife: 'When your husband spends 80 per cent of his time in the office and the remaining 20 per cent with the other woman.'

Central Bank Official: 'When 20 per cent of all the money in circulation is counterfeit.'

Right now the reputable contractors are having to turn down jobs either because they feel that the time allowed for completion of the work is unrealistic or because they feel that their managerial resources are so strained already that they cannot adequately supervise new jobs. Incidently that is why apart from the 'maza maza' people hardly any of the big contracting firms are involved in constructing houses in the Black Arts village.

I haven't seen the list of the Black Arts contractors and sub-contractors but if some of the names being mentioned have in fact been given work, then there's something wrong somewhere. I wouldn't trust some of them to build me a chicken shack for fear of being landed with a piggery!

The whole country is littered with contracts that were either never started at all or were done in a mad hurry with very poor results. After one or two bouts of rainfall new tenders have had to be invited for the same jobs to be done all over again.

Some contractors seem to have mastered the art of how to take the government for a ride. The classic scenario is as follows: Before the contract is approved – collect 20 per cent 'mobilisation fee': then drive your brand-new Mercedes-Benz round the ministry three times, so that even the Permanent Secretary can see that the money has gone towards a good cause.

Next, get all your creditors to pay for a newspaper supplement extolling your virtues; then proceed on a world tour lasting two years in order to recruit experts; next obtain a letter from your bank manager to the effect that your funds are totally exhausted and no further credit will be allowed and attach same to your letter addressed to the appropriate ministry and let them know that unless you receive more money you will not be able to (i) commence the contract; (ii) bring in your experts and (iii) pay the 'Udoji' award.

The Permanent Secretary would then reply:

> 'Unless you (i) commence the contract immediately (ii) bring in your experts and (iii) pay the 'Udoji' award, no further funds would be released to you.

Result – STALEMATE or if you are a chess-player, CHECKMATE. Two years afterwards the same contract is re-advertised, and of course since your face is already well-known at the ministry, your tender gets priority treatment and you can start all over again!

'ASK MY ADVISERS'

A few days ago, it was reported by 'Daily Express' that 'At a rousing send-off party held in honour of the retiring head of the Federal Civil Service, General Gowon declared: 'Advisers of the Federal Military Government should be blamed for any of my shortcomings'. The report continued 'General Gowon in a very light-hearted mood added: 'There is no bad ruler BUT BAD ADVISERS. If I had done anything wrong it was not my fault but the fault of some others'.

Therefore it seems quite clear that in addition to the six new ministries to be created – Co-operatives and Supply; Civil Aviation, Social Development; Youth and Sports; Petroleum and Energy; Urban Development, Housing and Environment and Water Resources we URGENTLY need two more ministries:

1   THE MINISTRY OF UNCOMPLETED CONTRACTS
2   THE MINISTRY OF BAD ADVICE

Of course each ministry qualifies for the services of a super-permsec. These are vital ministries and the success or failure of the Third plan depends entirely on the efficient running of these two ministries. The Third Plan envisages the spending of a staggering 33 billion naira. This is no small money. Incidentally, out of the 400 or so languages in this country, not a single one has a word for 'million' or 'billion'.

On paper we seem to have everything we need to implement the plan except two vital factors: MOTIVATION AND COHESION. There is an urgent need for EVERYONE to get involved. This can happen if everyone gets motivated once it is realised that the goal is not only desirable but also identifiable and all our efforts are cohesive. On several issues state governments proceed in directions that are completely opposite to the policy declared by the Federal Government.

We have to realise that the countries that have succeeded in revolutionising their rate of advancement have done so by proceeding from the BOTTOM TO THE TOP – we seem to be attempting to secure advancement from THE TOP DOWNWARDS. This is no easy task. Our development programme has leapt elevenfold from the previous 3 billion to 33 billion naira. In athletic terms this is equivalent to programming a baby that's just learning to walk to suddenly do a four-minute mile.

Much as I believe that no one should be made to feel indispensable, it is a matter for regret that Professor Adedeji, the Commissioner for Economic Development won't be around to oversee the implementation of the plan – after all it's his baby.

His new job at Economic Commision for Africa carries a salary of $60,000 TAX FREE plus a budget of $200,000 to cover travelling and entertaining expenses etc.

(These figures are available in 87 different currencies from the UN Secretariat).

CORRECTION

A few weeks ago, we misquoted an ex-governor. What he actually suggested as the panacea to cure Nigeria's ills were:

1 The institution of a constitutional assembly everywhere and anywhere.
2 The demobilisation of the army soonest everywhere and anywhere.
3 A stop to the building of motor assembly plants and oil pipelines everywhere and anywhere.
4 The creation of reconciliation committees everywhere and anywhere.
5 The release of all detainees everywhere and anywhere.
6 The sending away from the country of all the false friends of Nigeria everywhere and anywhere.
7 Allowing the courts to try offenders everywhere and anywhere.

FIRST THE BAD NEWS

The Chief Executive of a newly-opened partly-government owned motor-assembly plant put up a virtuoso performance before the press last week.

Question: How many cars do you expect to produce this year?
Answer: I don't know.
Question: How much will each car sell for?
Answer: I don't know.
Question: Will you be flying in spare parts from Outer Mongolia?
Answer: I don't know.
Question: Have you done any market research?
Answer: I don't know.
Question: Would you like to ask the questions?
Answer: I don't know.

AND WORSE NEWS

Competent sources revealed that the Posts and Telecommunications authorities in Umuahia have since March 12 sent an urgent telegram to P & T headquarters in Lagos requesting that ₦50,000 be transferred to Umuahia urgently. According to the sources it is possible that the P & T has been caught up in its own 'go-slow' or 'DEAD-SLOW' web because 'we are suspecting that the telegram may not have reached Lagos almost two weeks after it was despatched'.

NOW THE GOOD NEWS

The people of Ajegunle have voted unanimously in favour of a new pipe-line but only on the condition it is connected directly with the brewery at Iganmu. Beer instead of oil is better than no oil at all, and far better than no beer at all.

FALSE NEWS

Memo from the Hon. Minister of Information
To: (i) President Nigerian Union of Journalists
    (ii) President Nigerian Guild of Editors

Gentlemen,
          In view of the current rumpus over false
news reporting, you have requested me to furnish you
with specific instances when the press carried false news
items. Before granting your request, I must first of all
enquire whether either of you gentlemen ever read our
papers. If the answer is 'No', then it is my duty as
Minister of Information to assure you that you are not
missing anything! Here are a few examples:

OBVIOUSLY FALSE NEWS

'On 6 April, the 'Aguda Village Echo' carried a report
that the delay in announcing the successor to Chief Dr
C. O. Lawson as Secretary to the Military Government
was because the Government had decided to implement
Chief Jerome Udoji's recommendation that the post
should be declared vacant and applications invited from
the public. Furthermore, neither age nor sex, physical
disability, tribe, rank nor sector (private, public or
neutral) would be considered a barrier.
    'As a matter of fact an application has already been
received from a one-eyed, 102 year old ex-farmer who is
determined not to die until he has attained his life's
ambition to become the SMG. When tackled about his
qualification, the gentleman replied – 'anyone who can
dig a hole; put a seed in it, water it every day, come rain
or shine and wait nine months to harvest it is clearly of a

sane mind and certainly deserves to attain the highest station in life'.

Furthermore, the appointment will be done by acclamation and since it's such a long time since we last voted for anything, this time every Nigerian over the age of 16 will be allowed to vote for any candidate of his own choice.'

DEFINITELY FALSE NEWS

'The 8 April issue of the 'Nassarawa Times' carried the headline – '547 MILLION NAIRA TO BE SHARED OUT'. The main story reported that the government had agreed that the ₦547,000,000 ment for Defence in the budget should be shared out among all Nigerian citizens. At the same time, a special fund to be known as the 'Defence Fund' would be set up, so that all those who wish to be defended can voluntarily contribute to the fund.

'Needless to say, in an emergency only those who can produce the green card as evidence that they have paid their dues will be defended. Similarly, the ₦30 billion for the Third Development Plan is to be shared out so that those who do not desire any further development can opt out'.

'This I consider to be lamentable and irresponsible news reporting. It was predictable that a few hours after the publication of this stupid and definitely false report, all those who have no intention of travelling by Nigeria Airways or Nigerian Railways, demanded that the amount of ₦800,000,000 budgeted for the expansion of the railways and airways should be shared out and special donation boxes put at Iddo Railway Terminus and Ikeja Airport for those who are genuinely interested in the expansion and improvement of these two services.

INCREDIBLY FALSE NEWS

Even more disturbing is the fact that the press cannot even accurately report incidents involving its own members. For example, the 'Auchi Express' of 9 April reported as follows:

(i) 'Haroun Adamu of "Daily Times" had been appointed special consultant to the Ministry of Lands and Survey for being the first man to discover that Sokoto is at the back of Dodan Barracks.

(ii) 'The same man narrowly escaped the services of the firing squad for advocating the postponement of the 2nd Black Arts Festival.

(iii) 'A plane-load of United Nations observers have arrived in the country to observe whatever happens first – the liquidation of the said Haroun Adamu or the postponement of the festival.

RIDICULOUSLY FALSE NEWS

'The Imodi Observer' of 10 April quoted Gbolabo Ogunsanwo of 'Sunday Times' as saying that corruption exists everywhere. In Nigeria what we call corruption are regarded as tips everywhere else.

'In America, bribery is a science; in Europe it is a fine art, but in Nigeria it is crude'.

BLANTANTLY FALSE NEWS

'According to the "Isale-Eko News", on collecting his "Udoji Award" Alhaji Jemiola decided to buy the one thing he wanted more than anything else – a large fridgedaire. He had to knock down a wall to get the fridgedaire into his room. Unfortunately Alhaji Jemiola lives in a room 10 feet by 6 feet with two wives and eight children. Now they have a fridgedaire but nowhere to sleep.'

FALSE CONCLUSION

'My market research suggests that the public prefer false news to genuine facts and irrespective of what I say, the press will go on publishing false news anyway. Personally, this does not bother me at all because by publishing false news. the press are ironically JUSTIFYING THE NEED FOR A MINISTER FOR INFORMATION! Furthermore, the press is the least of the government's problems. I need only remind you of the words of Mr George Gthii – "We have known many instances where governments have taken over newspapers but we have not known of a single incident in which a newspaper has taken over a government".

FUTURE NEWS

'The Nigerian Press has acquired so much expertise in falsifying news that they are even printing newspapers in advance. For example I have been informed that the Christmas Day edition of the "National Times" coming up at the end of the year carries a report that at the annual general meeting of the Union of Journalists I was voted the "Man of the Year" and the President of the Nigerian Union of Journalists and the President of the Guild of Editors led a six-mile long procession carrying placards that urged the government to make me the Minister of Information FOR LIFE. I can't wait!

THE NON-NEWS

'The "Daily Times" of 11 April reported (correctly, I hope) Alhaji Babatunde Jose as saying: "No press enjoys the kind of freedom being currently enjoyed in Nigeria under a military regime."'

FALSE NEWS (Vol. 2)

FROM: The President Nigeria Guild of Editors
              and
          The President Nigeria Union of Journalists
TO: Hon Minister for Information.

THANK you for yours of the 20th ultimo. We find your views on false news most forthright and we were most surprised and of course delighted that your views are entirely in accord with ours – or does that ring false?

If you had asked us, we would have saved you the vast expense of extensive market research carried out by your Ministry to discover what we already know – namely that the public prefers false news to strange facts. The public's appetite for false news is fantastic and insatiable. The more you give, the more they want. They even write to ask for the extras and embellishments.

You see, both the Press and Government are victims of public demand. When the people want water, Government gives it to them; when they want electricity – the Government gives it to them; when they want the port decongested the Government rolls up its sleeves and does just that. The same goes for roads; planes that arrive on time; hospitals; milk, food, cement, and of course schools and telephones.

Incidentally, we have great difficulty in passing false news to State capitals, because from Lagos you can only call three of them direct. As for the others, a voice at the exchange always answers:'Calabar lines are out of order, please try after June'. No point in arguing with her that you didn't want Calabar in the first place but rather Benin. She just repeats 'Calabar lines are out of order

. . .' and goes back to sleep.

Also we feel sure you would have noticed that the people at the exchange seem to be under strict orders not to pick up the phone until it has rung at least fifty times. It's gone up to SEVENTY-FIVE since Udoji so that everyone can have an extra one hour sleep at work.

The Press finds itself committed to meet public demand for false news. In fact, at our last convention, our members unanimously voted that when the Consititution is re-written there must be a clause guaranteeing each citizen's right to false news.

Since we are mature men of the world, we are open to persuasion on this issue. Perhaps we can work out a quota system – 70 per cent false news; 10 per cent facts; and 20 per cent no news.

We have personally checked every single publication of false news listed in your complaint and are able to confirm that your points are entirely legitimate. In order to enable you update your files, we list hereunder those other false news items which you appear to have overlooked. Not to worry – nobody is perfect.

ALARMING FALSE NEWS

The 'Arondizuogulu Town Crier, on April 14 reported that a new fire engine had been purchased by the Local Council at the alarming price of ₦150,000. The only trouble was that the damn engine had stayed three years in the ship [specially chatered to bring it from South Africa] owing to congestion at the Apapa port and had therefore suffered extensive rust.

In any case, the fire engine was far too big to enter any of the ridiculously narrow streets of Arondizuogulu. The problem was how to raise 10 million naira to finance the widening of the streets so that the new fire engine could pass freely.

After 37 hours of intensive deliberation, the Council voted unanimously in favour of keeping the old engine for genuine fires and using the new engine for false fire alarms!

SENSIBLE FALSE NEWS

According to the 'Ikoyi Guardian' of April 15, hundreds of residents of Ikoyi have had to complain to Bhojsons Stores as they were getting SEVEN different bills for each credit purchase. A spokesman for Bhojsons Stores explained; 'The postal service is so bad in Ikoyi that we have to post seven different bills and hope that ONE of them at least would reach the customer.

'We are sorry for the inconvenience to our customers, but we assure all customers that it is even more inconvenient to us when they tell us that the reason they haven't paid is because they didn't get our bills. After all, even a registered charitable organisation like ours needs money these days to pay Udoji wages.'

FALSE NEWS IN BLACK AND WHITE

On the 16 of April, the 'Kakawa International Observer' reported that Mackintosh Chocolates Ltd have stopped making 'Mackintosh's Assorted' chocolates on the orders of the South African Government who now own a controlling interest in the Company. The South African Government insists that henceforth, black chocolates and white chocolates must not be sold in the same box.

FALSE TRAVEL NEWS

On the 17th of April, 'The Kainji Damn News reported that Interpol had apprehended thousands of businessmen who had travelled to Johnnesburg to sell Nigerian oil for gold. They were found to be carrying Nigerian passports even though they were not and had no intention whatever of becoming Nigerian citizens. Such a pity – since we import everything, we may as well import 'Nigerians' since we are incapable of producing them ourselves. Anyway, now we know why it's so difficult for genuine Nigerians to obtain passports. All passports will until further notice be stamped 'For Export Only'.

FALSE COMMERCIAL NEWS

On learning that his company would have to pay three years 'Udoji' arrears to all its workers, the General Manager of Swingway Stores Limited wrote according to the 'Kirikiri Express' of 18 April, to the Union as follows:

'The company is quite agreeable to paying the Udoji arrears, even though it is going to cost us ₦50 million naira. We have therefore reluctantly had to increase all prices by 250 per cent. In addition we have written to all five million customers who bought goods from our 87 different branches during the past three years to send us cheques to cover the difference between the price at which we sold to them and the new prices. As soon as the money is received, we shall pay the arrears. We feel sure your members will be patient'.

WISHFUL FALSE NEWS

It's quite interesting that the appetite for false news is not restricted to civilians. You could not have failed to read the 'Army Chronicle' of 18th April. The lead story stated that Brigadier Godwin Ally DSO (President General of the Lagos Garrison Organisation and Commander-in-chief of the Lagos Chamber of Commerce) who was acting Governor of Lagos for SIX WEEKS, had during his short tenure in office built six new oil refineries for Lagos, as well as fourteen hospitals, six medical post-graduate colleges, eight new dockyards, and commissioned 700 miles of new roads, as well as 25,000 low-cost houses not to mention a giant bridge to link Victoria Island with Victoria Island.

THE NON-FALSE NEWS

Our members are already complaining that you are the best Minister for Information we have ever had.
    Signed
    President, NGE
    Signed
    President, NUJ

NOW THE GOOD NEWS

When word leaked out that a new Commissioner for Transport would soon be appointed, the Head of the Railways, the Airways, the Ports Authority etc. got together and decided that the sort of person they needed was someone with a beard, preferably looking forward to imminent retirement and just literate enough to sign fat Government cheques.

They got a bearded man alright – in the person of Navy Captain Olumide, but much to their annoyance, rather than sit behind a huge desk and play with his beard, the youngish Commissioner has been clocking a lot of mileage, using the big stick and telling everyone to get off their – you know what. There has been much specualtion as to whether he represents Egbaland or Lagos in the Federal Cabinet.

The truth is that though of Egba ancestry, he was born and schooled in Lagos and went to University in the north. He represents not any one state but rather a generation of young Nigerians who would do ANYTHING for their country except lose their self-respect.

One of his ex-tutors says of him: 'He was a bright lad – all he now has to do is remember there are things an "Igbobian" will not do. If some of the encomiums being showered on him at the moment can still be repeated in three years time, this country will have come a long way.'

YOUR EXCELLENCY, IT'S TIME TO SAY GOOD-BYE

THERE are far too many people who don't know how to say goodbye or when, for that matter. Which reminds me of a character who said 'I'd like to say goodbye to your wife'. The harassed husband's reply was 'who wouldn't?'

The elegance of how and when to say goodbye suffered another major set back with the goings on in Calabar where Professor Essien-Udom, the Secretary to the Military Governor, was honoured with a lavish farewell party by his boss. The Govenor had finished his speech and just as the Professor was clearing his throat and rearranging his outfit, he was astonished to hear the familiar strains of the National Anthem – The party was over!

As a political scientist, the Professor is not necessarily bound to the theory that for everything a character does, we should be given a nice neat reason why he did it. For the benefit of all those who were deprived by official high-handedness from hearing it, here's the Secretary's goodbye speech –.

"Your Excellency, super-contractors, sub-contractors, ladies and gentlemen, I am deeply honoured to be called upon to respond to my toast. Needless to say, amongst such an august gathering there are many more qualified for the task than my humble self. Let me say right away that there is no rift whatever between H.E. and myself (standing ovation from His Excellency).

'In fairness to H.E. I must admit that he has always been nicer to me than I have been to him. I recall my first night in office, when H.E. invited me to his private quarters at Government Lodge – a rare honour. It was a glorious night – he sat on the bed and I stood at attention until the early hours of the morning talking politics.

'Incidentally H.E. has the finest collection of classical music in the land. It was a night of revelation, a union of two minds enjoined in a great enterprise – OUR STATE WAS DUE FOR A CHANGE.'

As I walked home, I was overcome by elation. I knew that I as a Professor of political science had in my hands the best student that I would ever have. I got home only to find that my wife feared the worst, maybe I had been detained on my first night in office. The police had been alerted, a search party had combed every corner of Calabar looking for me and an appeal was about to be broadcast on the six o'clock news.

'Without bothering with sleep, drink or food, I sat down and meticulously recorded all the reforms which would usher in a new dawn. First thing in the morning, I took it round to H.E. for his formal approval. You can imagine my surprise when he took one look at it and very politely asked "Very interesting, but what country is it meant for?" Ladies and gentlemen that is the origin of my "theoretical approach to the practical issues of government". (Outburst of laughter from H.E.)

'I must confess that I did have reservations about accepting the job in the first place, even though it carried an attractive salary (pre-Udoji) – I already had a handsome salary from the University plus royalties from my books. Neither was I unduly impressed by all that talk about "service" as I felt I was already serving the nation enough at the University. As for the prestige, that was one thing I didn't need at all. (Prolonged laughter from H.E.)

'I want to declare with all the emphasis at my command that my departure has no connection whatever with the "Charles Abia affair". This incident amusing as it was served as a useful illustration of the mischief of the Nigerian Press and the glaring differences between what you read in your newspaper and the reality of the situation. (Mild applause from H.E.)

'According to the press, Mr Charles Daniel Abia, Permanent Secretary, Ministry of Finance had released government funds to a certain motor company without proper authorisation while His Excellency was away on a business tour of Europe. The motor company was so anxious to collect the money that it hired a private plane and had the raw cash put on board for delivery in Lagos. The Acting Military Governor, Col. Bajowa immediately ordered an investigation which I effected with what some people considered undue haste. As a result of "other irregularities" discovered, the Acting Military Governor ordered the immediate suspension of the said Mr Charles Daniel Abia. The Public Service Commission reviewed the situation and ordered the sacking of the aforesaid Mr Charles Daniel Abia. The press further purported that on his return from abroad, the substantive Military Governor was furious with me for having got rid of his life-long friend and it was only a matter of time before I got the sack myself. NOTHING COULD BE FURTHER FROM THE TRUTH.'

I leave it to you to compare the press version with the actual sequence of events: When the substansive Governor heard of the suspension of Mr Abia, he cut short his trip and immediately proceeded home. Any misgiving I may have had were immediately removed by the fact that on getting down from the plane, His Excellency embraced me warmly, kissed me on both cheeks, French style and put a garland round my neck; and assured me that my diligence would be rewarded by making the post of SMG personal to me for life together with a nomination for a Knighthood. His Excellency next shook hands with the acting governor and thanked him for his excellent work; and also assured him that the fight against wrong-doings by officials no matter how highly placed transcended personal friendships.

The really funny aspect of the incident was its origin and how it was entirely forced on me. I was quietly smoking my pipe and telling my wife how badly I missed H.E. when suddenly a soldier came up running and asked me to proceed immediately to Government Lodge. There Col. Bajowa informed me that there was pandemonium all over Calabar and he wanted an immediate investigation. Apparently, currency notes were falling from the skies. Bundles of them in all sorts of denominations but mostly ₦10 notes. The 'Jehovah Witness' people said it foretold the second coming of Christ while the native doctors equally demanded six goats or seven maidens for the appeasement of the Gods. You see, you can fool Nigerians about a lot of things – BUT YOU CAN'T FOOL THEM INTO BELIEVING THAT MONEY FALLS OUT OF THE SKY.

The people of Calabar are no different. Anyway, our investigation soon revealed that the plane sent over by the motor company had run into fuel and engine trouble on leaving Calabar on its way to Lagos. Consequently it had to jettison the currency on board. The pilot realised that it would be too risky for the plane to lose weight too quickly. Being a very sensible chap, he threw out only a few naira notes at a time. Some landed on people's heads, some landed in cooking pots, some landed in beer glasses and some landed straight in one soldier's left hand pocket. Ladies and gentlemen, so now you have the inside story on how the investigation started. (Laughter and applause from H.E.)

'Finally, I want to thank His Excellency [for appointing me in the first place and] without whose co-operation and encouragement this speech would not have been possible. The only reason why I have not been allowed to make this speech is because H.E. does not suffer fools gladly and he would be embarrassed by such a flattering speech.

'Ladies and gentlemen, now is the time to say goodbye.' (H.E. ordered band to play National Anthem.)

GOODBYE PHASE TWO

Aristotle Onassis last week told Jackie Kennedy 'Now is the time to say goodbye'. Her reply: 'What about the ₦200,000,000?'

FIRST THE BAD NEWS

On receiving a cable from home that his mother-in-law had died in Port Harcourt, Bernard Koko who has been a law student in London for the past 23 years had wondered why his wife bothered to ask him whether her mother should be cremated, buried at sea or embalmed. Since he never got on well with her and was covinced that she had cast a permanent juju spell on him to prevent him from qualifying as a lawyer and returning home to 'playbig', his reply was 'TO MAKE SURE – DO ALL THREE'.

AND NOW THE GOOD NEWS

The Government is to be congratulated for resisting the temptation to 'teach the students a lesson' by keeping the universities closed. Had the universities remained closed much longer, it is conceivable that they may have turned out a generation of doctors who won't be able to cure anyone; lawyers who can't draft deeds of conveyance; accountants who can't balance books; language graduates who can't translate letters and of course journalists who won't mind their own business.

THE WALDORF-ASTORIA (NEW YORK)

IT'S rather unfortunate for Mallam Dijani Dagavau that on the very day that the 'New York Times' gave front page headline to the Mallam's story of how he was relieved of $140,000 at the Waldorf-Astoria Hotel by one of the 'happy hookers' of New York, the film 'Midnight Cowboy' was being shown just round the corner on Lexington Avenue.

The film is about an up-country boy who comes to New York in the mistaken belief that anything and everything is for free in New York. Even more unfortunate was that on the same day the 'Herald Tribune' published a story declaring Nigerians the biggest 'tippers' in the world and how 'what we call bribes in America are called tips in Nigeria'.

The result was that when Mallam Dijani alerted the hotel manger Mr Tim Rawlings, his response to the Malam's complaint was 'Sheik, you mustn't believe everything you see in films – nothing is for free in New York and secondly Sir, I've been reading about you people in the "Herald Tribune" and surely with all that oil money, you can afford a decent tip.'

Nevertheless, Mallam Dijani insisted on repeating his story of how he met a young woman and took her back to his room. They talked (and that's all, he says). He put his $1000 watch, his ring and his cuff links into a briefcase with more than $140,000 in cash and cashiers' cheques. Being a cautious type, he locked the briefcase and then still talking, he dozed off.

When he woke up his briefcase containing his money and valuables was gone! Dijani claimed the woman had walked up to him on Lexington Avenue at about 1 a.m.

and had said: 'Hi there'. She was very pretty, so I stopped to talk with her. . . . It seemed as if we had known each other for years. I started to walk back to the hotel and she just sort of followed me.

When we got up there to the room, we talked of many pleasant things – but nothing immoral. She did not even ask me if I would like to kiss her. I must really have been tired because I dozed off. The reason I went for that walk was to get some cold pills and aspirin.

Mallam Dijani added that he was in New York on business – 'construction and railroads and dabble in oil'.

The Hotel Manager gave Mallam a knowing look and reminded him (a) that there is a safe deposit box in the hotel and it's available 24 hours day and night for the benefit of customers and (b) considering the cheapest room in the hotel is $130 (i.e. ₦100) per night, aspirins are available 24 hours on every floor.

The manager consoled the distraught guest with the following words:

'Sheik, I assure you, the only man within living memory who has taken a midnight walk in New York and not lived to regret it is Arab guerilla leader, Yassir Arafat who was here last December. He was surrounded by 1000 CIA men as well as 750 Fedeyeen and he himself was carrying 25 hand grenades. Somehow even he didn't go entirely scot free – he lost his wallet containing a photo of stunning Jewish actress Dahlia Lavi.'

THE WALDORF-ASTORIA (LONDON)

Last Easter, Mr Emeka Ehimasi of Issele-Uku was staying at the Waldorf-Astoria Hotel, London which is only a mile away from Soho, the number one 'sin centre'. It was Mr Ehimasi's first visit to London and needless to say he had heard all the wild stories about Soho and the incredible varieties of sin on offer to make your visit to London unforgetable. Being a Catholic and the headmaster of a government secondary school, Mr Ehimasi knew that it was his Easter duty to find somewhere to pray.

He kept reminding himself that on no account whatever would he give way to curiosity and temptation. He was determined not to set foot in Soho. At midnight, he found himself unable to sleep and like Mallam Dijani he decided to go for a walk in search of aspirin and thereafter to attend the midnight mass.

He went up to the first policeman he came across and asked where the nearest Church was. The policeman took one look at him and asked: 'What's wrong with you people? A few minutes ago, a Mallam from your country stopped me to ask where to find aspirins – now you tell me you want to pray! Anyway, the nearest church is St Mary's Sacred Heart Church and it's in Soho.'

On getting to the church, Mr Ehimasi found the doors securely locked. Pasted on the door was a notice that said 'If you are fed up with sin, come in and pray.' However, just below the poster, an enterprising young lady had scrawled: 'If you are NOT fed up with sin, ring SOHO 9988 and ask for SUZY.'

THE WALDORF-ASTORIA (TEL AVIV)

Last February, Chief Morakinyo from Ikenne, Ijebu was staying at the Waldforf-Astoria, Tel Aviv. He was quite unable to sleep because every time he dozed off, he was startled back into wakefulness because he kept imagining there was an Arab guerilla hidden somewhere in the suite and ready to hold him hostage as soon as he fell asleep.

At midnight, just like Mallam Dijani, he decided to go for a walk. As he went past the hotel bar, he was accosted by a waiter who informed him that the gentlemen seated at table eight would like him to join them for a drink. Chief Morakinyo being a man who had never refused a good offer accepted gladly.

The five gentlemen were of different nationalities and when a few minutes later, a fly landed in the Frenchman's glass of beer, the Chief watched the Frenchman's reaction closely. Coolly, the Frenchman picked up a spoon, got rid of the fly and carried on drinking.

Next, the fly landed in the Englishman's beer. He exclaimed 'Oh dear' and asked the waiter to pour the beer away and bring a fresh glass.

Next, the fly landed in the German's beer. There is nothing Herr Otto hates more than wasting beer. He ignored the fly and went right on drinking his beer.

Next, the fly landed in the Japanese's beer. Mr Takada spooned it out and munched it with obvious relish. He declared: 'In Tokyo, I'll have to pay ten dollars for such a delicious fly.'

A few minutes later, a fly landed in Chief Morakinyo's beer. He spooned it out and offered it to Mr Takada – 'ten dollars please', he demanded.

THE WALDORF-ASTORIA (PARIS)

Last Christmas, Mr Edwin Karikari, a very senior government official from Warri checked into the Waldorf-Astoria, Paris. It was his first visit to Paris, and he was determined to fully exploit the delights of the famous city. He had two problems – first he was accompanied by his incredibly plain wife and two, everything was so expensive. Throughout their five-day visit Mrs Karikari kept a rigorously watchful eye on her errant husband.

On the eve of their departure for home, Mr Karikari realising he was no nearer to fulfilling his fantasy about Paris made sure that his wife drank a generous dose of strong wine. In no time at all, she was asleep much to the delight of Mr Karikari.

He dressed quietly and crept stealthily downstairs and seeing that it was nearly midnight, he, like Mallam Dijani, decided to go for a midnight walk. He was soon accosted by a stunning young lady who promptly offered to show him the delights of Paris.

'How much?' Mr Karikari '140,000 francs.' declared the Parisienne.

'Lord have mercy! That's ten times my salary. I don't dabble in oil you know. Let's make it 5000 francs and you can show me the art galleries, the Champs Elysee;

the Louvre; the Seine, the Eiffel Tower and all the other delights of Paris.'

'Monsieur, no way. Everything in Paris is expensive.' declared the young lady as she walked off in huff.

The following morning, as the frustrated and gloomy Mr Karikari accompanied by his wife came out of the hotel lift he walked straight into the young French lady of the previous night. She was covered in mink and looked even more gorgeous than she did the night before. After giving plain Mrs Karikari a look over, with a triumphant sneer she whispered into Mr Karikari's ear.

'Viola! Monsieur, that's what you get for your 5000 francs!'

THE MAN WITHOUT WHOM THE NEWS WOULDN'T BE THE NEWS

Chief Henry Fajemiorkun while briefing newsmen of the aims of a 62 man trade mission to Europe declared:

'Before you can distribute wealth, you must create wealth, otherwise you will be distributing poverty.'

Asked by a reporter whether he planned to take any midnight walk while on tour, the eminent Chief refused to answer.

AND NOW THE GOOD NEWS

We are still waiting.

NO LAUGHING MATTER [the man died]

ON Wednesday, 7th May, a Lagos newspaper carried a photograph of Mr Clarkson Onogboete Odolomerun aged 38 in its Obituary columns. Apart from the shock at the death of the youngman, I was astonished at the reference to a fatal aircrash at the Benin Airport in the early hours of Saturday, 3 May.

Besides the fact that the obituary column is hardly the place to announce an aircrash, it was unbelievable that the crash had occurred four days before and there had been no public announcement on radio, television or in the newspapers. Worse news was on the way.

On Thursday, May 8, the same newspaper carried an announcement from the Ministry of Transport which not only confirmed the previous day's story of the Benin aircrash but went on to confirm that on March 3 (SIXTY SIX DAYS EARLIER) another aircraft had crashed at Oturkpo in Benue Plateau State, killing the two occupants; and that on Friday April 25 (THIRTEEN DAYS EARLIER) after an air and land search, an aircraft and its student pilot were still missing.

The Ministry then WARNED all operators of light aircraft of flight hazards and enjoined them to 'avail themselves of the flight information service provided at government aerodrome'. The incredible delay in announcing the crashes, carrying out investigation and alerting the public to the danger left people wondering whether MR ODOLOMERUN's LIFE WOULD NOT HAVE BEEN SAVED if the warning from the ministry had been made earlier.

Those who knew Mr Odolomerun from his student days at International Students House London can testify that he was a fine young man. At ISH he made friends easily – Indians, Swedes, Americans, Greeks and English. He qualified as a surveyor and whatever success he achieved on coming back, he did it the hard way – through hardwork. To the question – How's business? Clarkson's reply would always be an honest admission: 'I'm ABOUT TO MAKE IT'. Well, very sadly, he was still about to make it when he lost his life under tragic circumstances.

It is amazing how many young people lose their lives under tragic circumstances that could have been avoided. The question is whether as a country, we can afford to lose such fine people. Professor Olakanpo lost his life through someone else's bungling ineptitude. The same fate befell Oyewole Brown who at 22 years old already held a law degree from Cambridge University. Two years later he was dead. He was the victim of a motor accident less than half a mile from a hospital. When he was eventually rushed to the hospital he was left unattended until someone told them who he was. It was too late. He had lost too much blood already. AND THESE ARE ONLY THE ONES WE KNOW ABOUT.

THE PILGRIMS WHO DIED

A few weeks ago a newspaper announced with bold headlines that 985 people had lost their lives while performing the holy pilgrimage to Mecca. 985 is an awful lot of people. These were people who carried medical certificates testifying that they were fit to travel. Many of them died of STARVATION. They carried forged traveller's cheques and counterfeit foreign currencies which sent the Saudis yelling: 'Allah may be merciful but there is no record anywhere that he ever sold food in exchange for counterfeit money'.

Many of the pilgrims who were travelling out of the country for the first time fell easy prey to the black-market operators who duped them of their genuine travel allowance. They suffered the humiliation of quarantine both here and in Saudi Arabia. I don't know what the Saudi Connection was like but the toileting and feeding arrangement provided for pilgrims at this end would put even infidel dogs to shame.

GUESS WHO'S STARVING

The UN expert seconded to Nigeria to advise on the problem of nude madmen who appear to have taken over all our major streets astonished an august gathering at a lavish party by declaring that from exhaustive interviews with the so-called madmen, he had come to the irresistable conclusion, that they were not mad at all but simply STARVING.

He challenged the incredulous audience to go without food for three days and report the result to him. This prompted one of the distinguished guests to speculate: 'I think our Mr Expert must be either drunk, mad or inspired.'

The expert promptly and soberly replied: 'Our studies indicate that every time the price of food goes up, the number of people who take to the streets goes up correspondingly. In fact we were 100 per cent accurate in our forecast that the number of the 'lords of the streets' would climb sharply following the Udoji award.'

GUESS WHO'S NOT STARVING

(i) At a mammoth Lagos party the other day, the guests started 'spraying' the musician with 'fivers' and 'tens'.

Every time someone pasted 100 naira on the forehead of the band-leader, someone else went a little further by 'spraying' 200 naira and on and on it went. The escalation got completely out of hand when Alhaji Toyota came on the scene. After 'spraying' ten naira notes, Alhaji Toyota caused consternation by doing the ultimate in spraying – HE SPRAYED WITH A TOYOTA CAR!

(ii) An ambassador from one of our tiny landlocked neighbours looked out of the brand new swanky Eko Hotel at the splendid array of ships with their lights glittering but unable to find berths at the congested Lagos port. His comment: 'What a breathtaking sight – but what a waste. Those ships are loaded with goods slowly rotting away. If my country could get hold of those goods – We WON'T HAVE ANY SHORTAGES FOR THE NEXT FIVE YEARS.'

SLOWLY AS I LEAVE YOU

Former South Vietnamese premier and Vice-President Nguyen Cao Ky told a Saigon rally that all talk of the imminent collapse of the country was foolish and those who left the country were cowards. The next day, the same man coolly commandeered a helicopter and personally piloted to safety to join his wife and children who were already out of the country.

SWEET COMFORT

Lagosians who were distressed at government plans to dig up Ajele cemetary in order to re-develop the site got terse comforting news from the Ministry of Information. 'THE DEAD MUST MAKE ROOM FOR THE LIVING'.

THAT'S A LOT OF MONEY

When the last Governor-General of Ghana handed over to Kwame Kkrumah, his last official duty was to hand over the keys to the treasury and personally hand over the 400 million pounds held in the vault.

The G-G's last words were: 'Kwame, that's a lot of money for a small country'.

A few years later, when Kkrumah was topled, the BBC rang up the ex-Governor-General and informed him that the treasury at Accra was empty and in fact foreign debts were a massive 1200 million pounds. On being asked to comment, the ex-G-G's words were: 'That's still a lot of money for a small country'.

NO WAY TO TREAT A KING

A newly-appointed 80 year old 'natural ruler' reluctantly accepted an invitation to attend his first party at Government House. Everything was fine until it was champagne time. To the great embarrassment of the host, everytime a bottle went 'pop' the natural ruler thinking it was gun fire quickly hid under the table only to emerge a few minutes afterwards pleading to be allowed to surrender the crown. This caused much laughter among the distinguished assembly of diplomats, judges, doctors etc.

NOW THE BAD NEWS

Faced with acute shortage of fuel, sharp increase in food prices, closure of schools, and hospitals, no water and electricity, cinema houses in the Western have started playing the famous Shirley Bassey hit record, 'I WHO HAVE NOTHING . . .' at the beginning and end of each performance.

THE FIRST LADY, 'AMADI', AND 'SUPERSTAR' ASIKA

MRS Victoria Gowon took Enugu by storm last weekend and she did it by going about her official duties with cool dignity and it was not lost on the welcoming crowd that her attire was refreshingly simple and subdued.

On her last night, she climaxed her round of official engagements with her attendance as guest of honour at the premiere of Dr Ola Balogun's film 'AMADI'. The film is in Igbo language, a remarkable 'first' and was partly financed by the East Central Government.

Any fears that such a bold joint venture between an imaginative and articulate artist on the one hand and government on the other hand was sure to land the artist in a straight-jacket and consequent artistic cramp have proved unfounded.

Truly, Dr Balogun has made a great film. With 'Amadi' he has made his peace with his maker – the promise and genius that were only faintly hinted at in 'Alpha' have been fulfilled.

There has never been any doubt that Dr Balogun is gifted – aged only 30 years he has been a successful academic, diplomat, author, film-maker, linguist etc., but what has worried many is that for one so versatile, his genius many be thinly-spread. That this is not so is amply demonstrated by the vigorous wit and the excellent camera work with which he handles his delicate theme.

'Amadi, a young Nigerian from the East Central State decides to abandon the absurdities of city life in Lagos and return to his home village to begin a new life. He is brought into contact with old traditions and customs and in turn helps to stimulate the villagers into new awareness. Aided by his friend Obi, he is instrumental in encouraging his fellow villagers to rebuild the local "Mbari" shrine dedicated to the earth-goddess "Ala", while at the same time helping to introduce modern agricultural techniques in the village.

'He meets a young girl named Ngozi while watching a traditional dance display in a neighbouring village and after a brief courtship enlivened by some confusion with Ngozi's sister, they are married in the traditional manner. At the end of the film, the birth of his first child coupled with a vision of the earth-goddess "Ala", and the death of his uncle inspire in Amadi a deeper awareness of his past and the promise of the future – all the best things are still to come.'

What 'Alpha' lacked in passion and depth, 'Amadi' evens up with rage, incisiveness, dimension and disciplined pace. John Chukwu is a winner as Amadi and in spite of having lost a leg during the civil war, George Okoye gives a very credible performance as Obi. In the film he drives a tractor using only one foot on the pedals and in real life he enjoys a wild reputation as a hairy driver rasing a lot of dust with his Peugeot 404.

The film has a generous dash of pulsating jungle rhythms and the uninhibited music and esoteric dancing are entirely relevant. There is a scene – the death scene, that is so incredibly riveting, that I have no doubt that for me that was the highpoint of the film. The audience was very visibly moved by it.

Ironically, I fear that such a scene would probably be lost on a European or American audience. I understand that there are plans to dub English and French subtitles, but I rather think that would be superfluous. Amadi as a film is so vividly constructed that even non-Igbo speakers should have no difficulty in following the narrative.

The Administrator of East Central State, Ukpabi Asika acquired 'Superstar' status with his brief appearance in the film. I imagine this must be a record.

THE OTHER VIEW

Since we have decried the 'Udoji' award so vehemently, it is only right that we should give the other view. Mr Etim Abaoka has declared the 'Udoji' award as the BEST THING THAT HAS EVER HAPPENED TO HIM.

'Them declare "Adebo", I no get.

'Them declare "Ani", I no get.

'But this one, I get am FINE FINE.

'After 27 years of working,

I have bulk money.

'I buy one fridge, one Suzuki, one fan, and for my home town.

'I buy land,

'And still have money for hand!'

THE OTHER VIEW

Mr Aroti Idoko says all this talk about traffic congestion in Lagos are lies. He refuses to believe that there are too many cars on the roads until he has bought his own.

STILL ON THE SUBJECT OF 80 PER CENT

Dr Perez Francise of the institute of Lifeguards says you are 80 per cent successful, if you see a man drowning 100 feet away and send him a rope 80 feet long.

LIFE BEGINS AT 45

WITH the announcement of 45 year old Allison Akene Ayida as the new Secretary to the Federal Government and Head of State, all the wild speculation surrounding the appointment of Mr C. O. Lawson's successor hit the dust. All sorts of names were being bandied about and strangely enough Mr Aydia's name was hardly mentioned.

On learning of his appointment, the obviously delighted new Head of Service declined to make any comment other than to say 'LIFE BEGINS AT FORTY-FIVE' and carried on trimming roses in his garden . . . He did however add that he would remain in his former office, the Ministry of Finance, 'for at least one week before going to assume duties at the Cabinet Office'.

We understand that this is to enable the Post and Telegraphs Department to return the applications of Mr Aminu Kano, Dr Tai Solarin, Professor Samuel Aluko and Mr Godwin Daboh and Mr Haroun Adamu marked 'return to sender'.

Unknown to the public, it is established practice in the Civil Service that on the appointment of a new Head of Service, all permanent secretaries submit their formal hand-written letters of resignation and await his decision as to whether they would be re-appointed 'without loss of seniority' dismissed or reassigned.

Furthermore, it is also traditional that the new head will not be allowed to take his old desk and files with him to his new office. Incredible as it may sound, it is also traditional that for some strange reason, the desk of the head of Service must be no more than six inches longer than the desk of the Permanent Secretary, Ministry of

Finance.

Mr Ayida comes from a solidly impressive background. He was educated at King's College, Lagos, followed by Queen's College, Oxford; and the London School of Economics. His civil service career straddles the Ministry of Education;, the Ministry of Finance;, Ministry of Economic Development and Reconstruction, and the National Economic Council.

It is obvious that his appointment is not based on narrow considerations of seniority, or ethnic balancing. His elevation to the most powerful office within the civil service provides refreshing confirmation that it is still possible for a talented man of modest origin to reach the pinnacle, provided he is prepared to work hard and successfully utilise the opportunities that come his way. Whatever one may think of the new head of Service, there is no denying the fact that he has for close to a decade been within firing range of many of the most traumatic events in the history of this country.

It has been suggested that in the context of a Military Regime, the public's conception of the importance of and the influence of the Head of Service is exaggerated, and also that his control of permanent secretaries is limited. On the first point, it would appear that the truth is that the power and influence of the Head of Service depend on the personality and background of the incumbent.

As regards the control he exercises over permanent secretaries, it would appear that it is only in the states that the control state SMG's have over their lieutenants is absolute. The Federal SMG operates on a different plane. it is conceivable that because certain permanent secretaries themselves control such vast power-centres, control is on the basis of give and take or live and let live.

On at least two occasions, Mr Ayida has won great respect for himself by his public candour. I refer first of all to the lecture he gave last year at the Institute of International Affairs in which he set out in lucid details the power-axis on which the relationship between policy-makers (whether civilian or military) and civil servants revolves.

According to him, the relationship is not based on coincidence of self-interest, or self-preservation or fixed delineation of roles. Rather it is based on a fluid inter-changeability of roles between the policy-makers and the civil service as regards the initiation of policy and the execution of policy.

At the same lecture, Mr Ayida gave a ringside account of the history behind the 12 state structure which is the foundation of the present administrative network.

Even more endearing was Mr Ayida's candid and public admission that he agreed to the setting up of the Price Control Board even though he knew it was doomed to fail. Any public figure that can openly admit human frailties or accept his short-comings should command respect – these days, they are a rare breed.

In one of his farewell speeches, Mr C. O. Lawson, the last head of service, admitted that in restraining over-zealous policy makers, the permanent secretaries may have to resort to 'gentle blackmail'. This opinion as well as many others which Mr Lawson has expressed recently are futher reinforced by the fascinating revelations of the 'Crossman Diaries' which have caused such a storm in British politics by their detailed account of a former minister's relationship with formidable civil servants.

Mr Ayida is clearly a formidable civil servant, well seasoned in the departmental in-fighting. However, the forecast is that under the new Head of Service, the civil service had better be ready for a lot of changes once the dust of the Ujoji exercise settles. It is confidently expected, that the professionals and the administrators will close ranks behind the new Head of Service and a serious effort will be made to give the professionals a responsible say in the running of the affairs of their various ministries.

After that we may well see Mr Ayida, spearheading and even grabbing the initiative in dealing with our chronic 'POV-FLUENCE' a disease roughly defined as the inability to deal with either poverty or affluence. In dynamysing our efforts in this respect, we may well find Mr Ayida broadening the base of advisers. In his words, "rather than confine itself to civil servants, government will draw on the ready pool of knowledgeable engineers, city-planners, bankers, teachers, doctors, and even students."

We may even find the introduction of 'inner-outers' i.e. a system developed by the Americans whereby deserving people from various fields are invited into the civil service for a year or two for special assignments related to their professions. It is even conceivable that Mr Ayida may be persuasive in counselling that a realistic pruning of the Defence budget is not only in the national interest but also that of the army itself.

As regards the relationship between the Federal Government and the states, it is likely that, more than ever before, the states will find their views not only being listened to but also incorporated in the formulation of policy. Since the Government has confirmed that Lagos will continue to be the Federal capital, it goes without saying that the Secretary to the Military Government has to live in Lagos.

Well, the problems of Lagos as a capital are enough to keep the SMG busy all year round. For a start, there are few capitals that match Lagos for squalor and filth. The slums of Okepopo, Ita Faji, Idumota and Agege are clearly not meant for human habitation. I don't know anywhere where there is so much human despair as well as frustration.

In 1973, Dr Gabby Williams, the Chief Medical Officer for Lagos reported that Lagos was fast becoming another Calcutta, a city crumbling under its own dirt. Today, his observation still holds true.

It goes without saying that sooner or later, the SMG will travel abroad and will no doubt call at our embassies. Our embassies are located in the choicest areas of New York, London, Paris, Rome etc. but nevertheless they seem determined to create a negative home away from home – an export model of ITA FAJI or Dugbe market. No visitor is unlikely to be astonished at first the noise and then the dirt as well as the slovenly manner in which enquiries are attended to. This for sure won't go down well with the new SMG.

AND NOW THE CIVIL SERVICE NEWS

The astonishing discovery by Chief Udoji of the power struggle between the administrative class and the professionals within the civil service has been totally eclipsed by an even more fantastic discovery by the Williams and Williams Committee. It appears that the first decision to be made by the new SMG is the number of typewriters each Ministry is allowed to buy.

One would have thought that with all our oil money, this should be no problem at all. Not so. It is common knowledge within the civil service that the importance and respect accorded to each ministry depends on the number of typewriters under its control. Typewriters enjoy a celebrity value because every government decision at some stage or the other goes through the typewriters and it follows that the typewriters know all government secrets.

The situation is so delicate that given the choice of two ministries, certain Permanent Secretaries have been known to insist on a secret midnight count of the typewriters in the respective ministries before making up their minds.

The Williams and Williams Committee were surprised at the depth of resentment at the Ministry of Finance, when the Ministry of Mines and Power acquired 55 per cent of all the shares in the oil companies. This meant that in addition to controlling all the typewriters at NEPA and the National Oil Corporation, the Ministry of Mines and Power automatically controlled 55 per cent of all the typewriters at Mobil, Gulf, Elf, Philips and Shell Oil Companies thus beating the Ministry of Finance.

The Ministry of Finance's pre-eminence had to be

promptly restored by government acquisition of shares in Barclays Bank, United Bank for Africa etc. so that their typewriters as well as those of the Central Bank, and National Insurance Corporation could come under its control. In order to guarantee the respect properly due to it, the Ministry of Finance has signed an agreement with the World Bank to borrow an unlimited number of typewriters.

OLD BOYS NEWS

Next Thursday at 7.30 p.m. the new SMG will respond to his toast before a gathering of King's College, Lagos Old Boys. His opening words will be the now famous . . . 'I didn't know I had so many friends . . .'

FALSE NEWS

The Ministry of Information has categorically denied that the only copy of the Williams and Williams Committee report which was specially flown out to General Gowon in Jamaica last week was lost-in-transit by AIR PERHAPS.

Neither was it confiscated by the Jamaican authorities who insisted on exhaustive forensic tests to reassure themselves that the parcel did not contain a certain brand of "vegetable" (hemp) which has proved to be an irresistible naira earner for Nigerians.

THE NO-NONSENSE GOVERNOR

IT IS quite interesting to observe that the characteristics displayed by Brigadier Oluwole Rotimi during his tenure of office as Governor of Western State were firmly established twenty odd years ago when he was a student at King's College Lagos. Way back then he enjoyed a solid reputation as a 'no-nonsense man'. He played football in the first eleven as a halfback and anyone who was foolish enough to bring him down with a foul tackle pretty quickly got a full measure of the same treatment back.

In fact, it was widely known that if the young Rotimi didn't even strike back on that particular occasion, it was a dead certainty that redress would be inflicted at the next match. One sure thing – he never forgot a foul tackle. Very soon word got around, he was one fellow you didn't mess around with. ('Papa don't take no mess'.) As for stamina, he had it in abundance. In the closing minutes of even the most hectic matches, he would still be bounding with energy, ready to take anyone on. The rougher the going, the more he relished it.

It is therefore not surprising that from his first day in office, his administration has been dominated by the 'no-nonsense' approach. He took one look at the Treasury Coffers and finding only a few coins, he promptly told the world at large that the Treasury was empty, and would contractors please, stop bothering him!

Over the years, the Governor's no-nonsense'' reputation has been reinforced by several incidents. On a famous occasion, he was confronted by a high-powered delegation of Egba Chiefs from the Governor's home land, Egbaland. The Chiefs drew the Governor's attention to the fact that he appeared to be deviating from establshed practice by not favouring his own homeland in the location of industries and creating jobs for the boys back home.

Without wasting time on niceties, the Governor astonished the distinguished delegation by declaring – 'I'm Governor of the WHOLE of the West', and that he had no intention whatever of favouring any particular area.

This did not go down well at all with the delegation. So much so, one of the Chiefs remarked that, had a politician made such a blunt, and candid negative response to the wishes of his 'countrymen', he would be able to count on only THREE votes at the next election – his wife, his ' assistant' wife and his bank manager!

On another occasion, a senior official who was outraged at comments made about him in the Western State's press confronted Governor Rotimi. After listening to all his complaints, the Governor pulled out his pocket book of press cuttings and handed it over with the comment:

'You should see the things they write about ME!'

Whatever measure of freedom, the Nigerian Press enjoys today some of the credit no doubt belongs to the West, as well as the restraint and tolerance with which the Governor handles the press. It is very much to his credit that in spite of the massive criticism of some of his policies, the Governor has nevertheless refrained from sending journalists to detention.

It's quite interesting to note that Administrator Asika and Governor Rotimi are the two heads of Government who have never once complained about being misquoted by the Press. It may well be that since both of them come from such sound educational background and are so articulate there is no chance whatever of their having words put into their mouths or saying 'green' when they in fact mean 'red'. If one were to categorise heads of state governments, the 'thinkers' would be led by Governor Rotimi and Administrator Asika while the 'doers' would be headed by Governor Ogbemudia of the Mid-

West.

Last year, the 'Daily Times' published the full text of Governor Rotimi's lecture on the role of the Military in Politics. By any standard, the dissertation was clearly the product of a scholarly intellect. It covered the historical processes that make military intervention inevitable; the prevention of counter coups; and how the military should handle power having secured it.

The West has been a chain of 'firsts' and Governor Rotimi added another first when he said a public 'Thank you' to his departing Commissioners by giving a farewell dinner in their honour.

On students' protests, quite a few people were surprised that in spite of being a graduate of University of Ibadan, the Governor took such a tough line, but this was predictable. Once the students had resorted to the damaging of government property, the Governor's 'no-nonsense' approach was inevitable.

It is quite ironical that while most other states have too few graduates, the Western State probably has too many and unfortunately they are concentrated into a limited field. An ex-Premier of the West once made the poignant observation that the West is saturated with graduates who are saturated with 'book knowledge!' The result of this is that quite a few Ph.D's of Western origin find themselves queuing for jobs while their counterparts in other states with lower qualifications are being propelled into top jobs in their own states.

A lot of criticism has been generated by the state's take over of private schools instead of 'flooding the market' with government-built schools. The government may well have chosen the worst of all the alternatives open to it. However, what is indisputable is that something needed to be done about the schools. The disparity between the best schools and the worst ones is staggering.

Some owners of private schools were clearly exploiting the insatiable demand for education and the situation had degenerated to the extent that some of the worst schools were entering students for science exams even though they had neither science teachers nor science laboratories.

Even more criticism has been generated by the decline in the economy of the West. Prior to the Civil War, the West probably had the most flourishing economy in the Federation. Its bold innovations paid handsome dividends and the slogan 'life more abundant' was realistic enough, at least for some. The stagnation that set in must in part be due to the numerous public corporations that had grown too large, too amorphous and too unmanageable.

Originally, the thinking behind the setting up of the corporations was that they would generate profits which could be invested in more industries which would in turn create more jobs and repeat the process. This was fine in the early years but in recent years, the corporations have gone into reverse gear. They were gobbling up public funds so fast that rather than create more jobs they were biting hard into limited funds. Their expenses and losses ran into millions but nobody knew about them until two or three years after the damage had been done and revelation came with the auditors' report.

Furthermore, the corporations became private kingdoms for tribal gods and ethnic rivalry. The situation had degenerated to such an extent that the newly-appointed secretary to the State Military Government, Mr Adebayo publicly declared a little while ago, that henceforth promotion in the entire public service would be by merit, implicitly admitting that, that had not been the case hitherto.

Governor Rotimi's style in office is entirely without ostentation, and if you discount his polo-playing, it borders on the austere. He obviously prefers the company of old friends, mostly ex-classmates, even those going back to primary school days.

His administration has been characterised by a refusal to prefer the parochial interest of any one area against another; or encourage statism at the expense of the nation as a whole; and when the Federal chaps get their sums wrong, he has refused to defend the indefensible.

Much to his credit, there is a marked tolerance for all shades of opinion in the West. A case in point is that of a gentleman who declined to serve as a Commissioner. He is still a free man, unharrassed and unmolested.

AND NOW FOR SOMETHING COMPLETELY DIFFERENT

One of the state Governors who had just been awarded an honorary LL.D. by Nsukka University could not resist warning members of his Executive Council, several of whom held University degrees – 'All you people who have been trying to confuse me by using big grammar had better watch out!'

UNIVERSITY NEWS

Following Professor Aluko's one-man protest at the newly enacted University of Ife (Amendment) Edict giving vast powers to the VISITOR of the University of Ife (at present the Military Governor of the West) all public notices at the University which previously read: 'No Visitors allowed after 8 p.m.' have been changed to read: 'NO VISITORS ALLOWED AT ANY TIME!'

THE MAN WITHOUT WHOM THE NEWS WOULDN'T BE THE NEWS

While visiting UK at the head of a 62-man delegation, Chief Henry Fajemirokun, President of the Nigerian Chamber of Commerce complained to British Government officials that he could not SEE why the British Government's Export Credit Guarantee Department would not GUARANTEE goods valued at ₦500,000 to a Nigerian company with a paid-up capital of only ₦1000.

FIRST THE DOCTORED NEWS

At an impressive ceremony conducted in Latin, General Yakubu Gowon received an honorary doctorate in Law (LL.D) from Cambridge University. It was in recognition of his contribution to peace by his humane conduct of the Civil War.

It is worth remembering that had the Civil War been fought differently, we would now have a generation totally ignorant of peace time life or what it is to go to bed without the rat-tat-tat of machine-gun fire or wake up without the howls of bazookas. What is not generally known is how close General Gowon got to winning the Nobel Peace Prize that eventually went to Sheik Henry Kissinger.

THE 'MADE-IN-NIGERIA' CAPITAL

A FEW days ago, Dr Nnamdi Azikiwe (LL.D) was in top form when he launched, his new book 'Dialogue on a new Capital', before an enraptured audience at Hamdala Hotel, Kaduna amidst incessant shouts of 'the old man is still great'.

Dr Azikiwe suggested that the Federal capital should be moved out of Lagos to Kafanchan, and enjoined the audience to consider the suggestion as a matter for mature public debate and objective criticism. We are sorry to report disappointing public response.

The first salvo was a dignified 'no comment' from the Commissioner for Justice Dr Graham Douglas (LL.D) who declared at Kano Airport. 'I am not one of those senior government officials who go around parroting their views in public. If you want to know my comments, come to my chambers.'

Dr Douglas was on his way to Russia and no doubt when he comes back he will have something to say about what the Russian Government does to people who agitate for the shifting of the capital from Moscow.

The second salvo came from Col. (Dr) A. A. Ali, LL.D, Federal Commissioner for Education who flatly refused to comment when asked whether he thought Dr Azikiwe should have built the new capital while he was President of the country.

Col. Ali also reminded the journalists that when he used the word 'Windbag' he was referring to another ex-politician in a completely different context.

The third salvo came from the Sheik of Kafanchan who had to be restrained from exploding with wrath. He declared. 'Dr Azikiwe can build his capital wherever he likes, but the presumptiousness of Southerners never ceases to amaze me. How can he come and build the capital here without so much as a by-your-leave? I would have thought the least he could do would be to come here and ask the people of Kafancham – do you want the new capital built here?'

The fourth salvo was fired by Chief (Dr) Mrs Irene Ikerechuwa (LL.D inherited) who declared 'I think when a man of Dr Zik's stature speaks, we ought to listen. If only we had listened to him, we would not be in such a mess now.

She was immediately contradicted by Mrs Adeola Figbati (LL.D 'Attempted') who vehemently declared: 'We have been listening to Dr Zik for 30 years – see where it got us.'

The strongest comment of all came from Sir Sanyo Egbuaki (LL.D. Japan) who declared: 'Dr Zik is a great man. He is a man before his time. I agree with everything he says. In fact I think there ought to be a Federal Capital in every state.' For the benefit of those who don't already know, Sir Sanyo's doctorate thesis was on CONFUSION.

Even more irresponsible was the contribution of Chief J. J. J. J. Akpanudo (LL.D. 'Failed') who declared that what Dr Zik is really saying is that it's about time we built our own capital – a sort of 'MADE IN NIGERIA' Capital!

The Chief however, went on to add that he had great difficulty in believing that on our present from we could handle such a gigantic project. Take the smallest things such as made in Nigeria matches – there's a real danger that every time you light one, the flame just leaps at you and you have to take cover so as not to get a serious burn.

Now completely beyond control, the Chief went on to add that he could not even see anything 'BLACK' about the Black Arts Festival, (even though the theatre was 'designed and built by Nigerian Architects and all the furniture as well as the lighting equipment will be entirely made in Nigeria!)

Dr Sam Okuloma (LL.D 'dashed') commented that Dr Zik had made a brilliant analysis of the inadequacies of Lagos as a Federal Capital and his solution is a logical progress of the 'Diarchy Theory' – one capital for the Military in Kafachan and one for civilians in Lagos.

Dr Okuloma's wife (LL.D 'by association') added that Dr Zik was right in his 'flexible' approach and that she is certain that at his next press conference to be held in Lokoja, he will suggest Ikenne as the Capital; and at the following press conference to be held at Warri, he will suggest Gboko as the capital; and of course when he gives his Lagos press conference, he will suggest Nsukka as the Federal Capital.

Needless to say, when he gives his press conference at Kafanchan, he will give a sixteen-hour non-stop 'syllogistic discourse' on WHY WE DON'T NEED A FEDERAL CAPITAL AT ALL!

Some sanity was restored by Dr Franfurter Jackopoto 'the first' (LL.D 'borrowed') who reminded a television panel that it is all very well giving examples of other countries which have succeeded in building alternative brand new capitals but that what is often forgotten is that in every single case, those countries had tried their hands and made a success of running things such as electric and water supply, iron and steel, oil supplies and last but not the least – accurate census to determine in advance likely population redistribution as a consequence of shifting the capital.

A fellow member of the panel, Architect Dr Hubert Lanre Towry (LL.D 'planned') suggested that the idea of a permanent capital is completely foreign to the African personality which is essentially nomadic – 'WHEREVER MY COW GOES, I GO!'

Therefore, what we must think of is the 'Disposable Capital' – based on INFLATABLE OFFICE BLOCKS AND PREFABRICATED INFRASTRUCTURE which can easily be dismantled and shifted to wherever the new capital is required.

Chief Ukpabia Senako who paid ₦100,000 for his LL.D caused great confusion by declaring that he had already put in his tender for the building of the new capital and reckoned that with the 20 per cent 'mobilisation fee' of at least three million billion naira he should be comfortable for his next three lifetimes.

Dr Jolalo Okure caused raised eyebrows by declaring that he didn't want to talk about the new capital at all. He would rather talk about Dr Tony Enahoro's attempt to justify the Black Arts Festival by claiming that 'it did NOT in any way hamper other Federal projects.'

Dr Okuru insisted on arranging an immediate meeting between Dr Enahoro and the Engineers and Architects of the Federal Ministry of Works to confront Dr Enahoro with complaints from government engineers and architects who find themselves supervising five different major projects as well as running to and fro between their offices and the festival site.

More digression was caused by Dr Kole Olayomi (LL.D 'genuine') who informed the audience that he didn't want to talk about the new capital or Black Arts Festival. He would rather talk about DISCLAIMERS.

The eminent professor of Law warned that the country is full of extremists and it is conceivable that some crazy fellows may publish a photograph of the Minister of Information with the warning that 'this man no longer represents us and anyone dealing with him does so at his own risk'.

Also, in view of the feud between the Bishop of Lagos and his Provost over mode of worship, it is conceivable that someone might forge the Bishop of Lagos's signature and advertise the photograph of the Provost with the caption: 'Anyone praying with or through this gentleman does so at his own risk.' These would be clearly unlawful acts and the government must do something urgently before things gets out of hand.

The panel discussion ended with Asege Balogun-Okimade's (LL.D 'imported') summation that it is fortunate for this country that we have been blessed with such an illustrious personality as Dr Azikiwe – a man of prodigious intellect, undoubted foresight, and immense political astuteness.

He therefore called on the Federal Government to award the contract for the building of the new Capital immediately SO THAT IT COULD BE COMPLETED IN TIME FOR THE BLACK ARTS FESTIVAL!

DIG-HOLE; FILL-HOLE

LAST week at the Institute of Contemporary Affairs, Victoria Island, Professor R. O. K. Oki-Balogun delivered his annual 'State of The Nation' speech. This year his theme was 'The DIG-hole; FILL-hole' syndrome in contemporary public affairs. I had interpreted this rather baffling title to be a reference to the rumoured existence of a phantom man specially employed by State Governments to patrol their main roads looking for pot-holes which he would ferociously attack to make them bigger before the rains! If Areoye Oyebola, Editor of 'Daily Times' is to be believed, this phantom gentleman, the curse of all road users has been particularly active in Ibadan and has according to the Nigerian Union of Students, been devastatingly efficient in the East Central State, particularly in Aba and Onitsha.

As it turned out, the Dig-hole; Fill-hole syndrome refers, to something even more serious. According to the learned Professor, contrary to popular misconceptions, Nigerians do not give or receive bribes. What is at work is something else entirely. It is the exchange of coded messages between those awarding contracts or favours and those accepting them. To illustrate his point. The Professor showed a film slide of a contractor chasing a deal. The rules of the game forbid him to offer a bribe or BEG. What he must do is walk up with 'bold face' to whoever is awarding the contract and spend the next two hours chatting with him about the price of food, power failure, infant delinquency, traffic, water shortage, indiscipline in schools, etc. – anything except the contract. Having proclaimed how terrible things are in the country, the contractor would then climax by thanking God that there are 'still people like you around' – a reference to the wisdom of the Mr Big – the man who is going to award the contract. The contractor would then get ready to go and almost as an afterthought, he would set in his punch line: 'Before I forget, I hear you are about to award a contract for ₦100,000. You know I'm a man of few words but you of course know that ₦10,000 is yours plus extras from "variations".' As the contractor has at this stage completed the 'Dig-hole', The Big Man responds by declaring: 'Chief, Thank God, there are still people like you around – of course you'll get the contract.'

To 'Dig-hole' even further, the contractor would then subtly hint: 'Oga, it's too bad that you have to work so hard. You seem to spend all your time in the office. There are several attractive young ladies I know who are just dying to meet you. In fact I have one waiting in my car.' Of course Mr Big has got the message and declares 'Send her right over and bring a pen along as well – I think we ought to sign the contract right away ("Fill-hole").'

According to Professor Oki – Bally, one interesting variation of the 'Dig-hole; Fill-hole' syndrome is the 'Hire Purchase' whereby the recipient of a favour doesn't have to 'compensate' the giver of the favour in one lump sum – instead payment in cash or kind is spread over several months and even years either in genuine appreciation of past favours or in expectation of more favours. The Professor even dug up the case history of a certain Pius Uwalaka – Obembe who had been paying 'HP' to Chief Akpuese Oookah for so long he couldn't even remember what the favour was in the first place!

The eminent Professor added, that the system of 'Dig-hole; Fill-hole' is so extensive that people will even pay for things that they are entitled to have for free. Such things include passport forms, road tax renewal forms, electricity connection, etc., and strangely enough there have been reported cases of people 'tipping' before being issued with tax receipts. However, it seems to be common knowledge that everyone who is seriously interested in getting a telephone, a driving licence, government quarters, overdraft, scholarship, employment, foreign-exchange, promotion, hospital bed, plane ticket on domestic flights or clearing goods from the ports would have to pass the 'Dig-hole; Fill-hole' test.

The system seems to work smoothly as long as both the 'diggers' and the 'fillers' are happy. The snags develop when the 'diggers' find they are doing a lot of 'digging' but nobody is doing any 'filling' or the benefits of the 'filling' are going to others who were not in any way connected with the original 'digging'. A classic example occurred when a certain American gentleman discovered that after putting a considerable amount of dollars down the 'hole', when it came to raking in the 'filling', there were so many people demanding cuts that he began to wonder what the hell would be left for him and his lieutenants who set up the cement deal in the first place. The last straw came when someone demanded a cut for a certain 'His Royal Highness'. The outraged American totally unfamiliar with the 'tradition' and 'culture' fumed – 'I ain't working for any Godamn Royal Highness!'

At this point, an impressively-clad Chief interrupted the Professor and declared himself a rabbid supporter of the system and that already he had formed his own political party to contest the next election (to be held next year even though the government hasn't announced it) with the slogan 'DIG-HOLE; FILL-HOLE'. The Chief lighted a very large cigar and reminded the audience that he at least was perfectly happy with the system and that from time immemorial every Society has flourished by 'robbing Peter to pay Paul' to a greater or lesser degree. He was immediately contradicted by a bearded fire-eating Dr Sam Walukolo who warned that unless something was done urgently, the country would degenerate into an organised system of 'Robbing everyone and Paying nobody'.

The lecturer had to ask for Police protection when

fighting broke out between those who wanted to be 'robbed' and those who wanted to be 'paid'. Peace and tranquility were restored when six nude girls came on stage carrying postcards inscribed 'I'm Linda – I want to be robbed'. They were followed by six 'agba' tycoons carrying placards with the message: I'm Henry, I want to be PAID'.

VIGNETTES OF THE NIGERIAN

YESTERDAY at the United People's Convention, all the major and minority tribes were fully represented. After serious and prolonged deliberation, they passed a resolution calling on The Federal Government to abolish all states and start afresh or failing that, the Government should create (in addition to any number of states which the Irikefe Commission might recommend) an extra state to be called THE FREE STATE for all those thousands or hopefully millions of Nigerians who irrespective of their state of origin are willing and even anxious to live together without caring two hoots whether their neighbour or co-worker is a Hausa man, Yoruba man or Ibo man. The Chairman of the Convention, Alhaji Mustapha Alagbara declared that true unity will not come until one can go into a household and find Hausas, Ibos and Yorubas all living together. Of course they will quarrel, argue and fight but that's what living together is all about. The Alhaji went on to point out that it was because General Gowon did not understand this basic complexity that he chose insipid irrelevancies such as lighting the 'Torch of Unity', and believing that the problem was thereby solved. He went on to ask – 'What significance has the lighting of the Torch of Unity on the Lagos Racecourse got for the "Mallam" living in Yola, the "Ete" living in Calabar, or the "Alagba" living at Abeokuta? The answer is zero.'

Finally, the Chairman reminded the Convention that a nation's degree of civilisation corresponds very closely to its ability to laugh at itself. He therefore called on each delegate to tell a story about his own area of origin. Here are some extracts:

KANO STATE

Mallam Umaru Pateshi spoke of how a few weeks ago the American Ambassador got an urgent message from Dr Kissinger, the American Secretary of State, asking him to find three Nigerians to participate in the last joint American/Soviet Mission to the Moon. The first man the Ambassador got hold of was a Hausa man who agreed to risk his life for ₦100. The second man was an Ibo who demanded ₦200. Asked why he was asking for ₦200 even though a Hausa man was willing to go for only ₦100, the Ibo man coolly explained that he needed ₦100 to leave behind for the welfare of his family and with the remainder he would hire a smart Ibo lawyer to draw up the contract. The third man was a Yoruba man who demanded ₦300. This puzzled the American Ambassador even more. However, the Yoruba man went to explain that with the first ₦100 he would throw a lavish farewell party; with the second ₦100, he would hire a smart Ibo lawyer to draw-up the agreement and with the remaining ₦100 he would hire the Hausa man who was so willing and ready to risk his life.

EAST CENTRAL STATE

Prince Ike Nwalagu-Ositame spoke of how God once gave St Peter a lamp with which to go round the world in search of an honest man. When St Peter got to Aba, the lamp was stolen.

KWARA STATE

Alfa Ahmed Bamgbola told of how the German Managing Director of a newly established shoe factory at Ilorin was most surprised when the local distributors kept insisting that all shoes sold to the public should be clearly marked 'Left' and 'Right' in order to stop the hundreds of shoes returned by customers with the complaint 'wrong size'.

SOUTH EASTERN STATE

Chief Esopi Ita told of how during the last Civil War a Chief on hearing that soldiers were approaching his village, immediately locked up his young brand new wife and gave the key to his best friend.

Before fleeing, he told his friend that if he did not return within a year he should be presumed dead and his friend should feel free to open the room and inherit the young wife. He had hardly got to the next village when his best friend came running and shouting 'My friend – you gave me the wrong key'.

LAGOS STATE

Dr Wole Saifudeen spoke of how when he was a student in London, his friend Bayo Oyinbogo managed to collect unemployment benefit from the British Government for eight years by insisting that his last job was that of 'Elephant Hunter' and that any attempt by the Welfare Authority to find a job for him would be unacceptable because they were bound by law to find him a job similar to his last one. The Welfare Inspectors in desperation reminded him that there were no elephants left to be hunted in London. Bayo (previously of Isale-Eko) coolly reminded them 'That's proof of how efficient I have been'.

RIVERS STATE

Chief Mariere Diette-Bekami told of how he had to complain to the Port Harcourt police about his next-door neighbour at Umekuruche, a young army officer named Mike Asabeka. 'He must think I'm in the Coast Guard. He keeps telephoning my young wife to ask if the coast is clear'.

NORTH EASTERN STATE

Alhaji Momoh Sadiku told of how a few weeks ago on getting to Iddo Railway Station, he found himself 5 kobo short of the correct fare back to Maiduguri. He turned to a man from Lagos State who was standing nearby and pleaded:

'I need 5 kobo to get back home'.

He got a very prompt reply. 'Here's 50 kobo – you can take NINE more with you'.

NORTH WESTERN STATE

Mallam Dagu Muka of Bauchi spoke of how during the Second World War he served as a sergeant-major in the West African Riffles. His Brigade Commander was a British Officer named Coombes who had split the brigade into three contingents comprising of Hausas, Ibos and Yorubas respectively. On a certain occasion, Major Coombes turned first to the Ibo contingent and announced 'Break ranks and assemble at 1515 hours'. To the Yoruba contingent, he announced 'Break ranks and reassemble at quarter past three'. To the Hausa contingent he announced 'Break ranks and reassemble when you see both hands of the clock on "3"'.

MID-WEST STATE

Prince Oruame Ihebora of Warri spoke of how his grandfather married so many times, he even married one of his former wives again and didn't even know it. The Chief was on his death bed before he found out. He recognised his mother-in-law, the formidable Madame Irekah Ajime who during her lifetime attended the funeral of seventeen husbands. (all of her own!)

BENUE PLATEAU STATE

Mrs (Dr) Dorcas Benkaga recalled of how when the first Mission Hospital was built in Gboko, she was amazed when she discovered that the first patient had spent the whole night studying for his 'urine test.'

NORTH CENTRAL STATE

Mallam Sanni Jubatu spoke of how he once discovered his young son, the first scion of the family to go to school busy with pen and paper. He enquired of his son 'what are you doing?' His reply: 'I'm trying to write a letter to myself. It's my homework'.

'What do you tell yourself?'

Answer 'How do I know? I won't get the letter until Friday'.

WESTERN STATE

Chief Abiola Iroko spoke of how he once came across four people at Government House Ibadan. They were standing one on top of the other, trying to measure the flagpole on which the Nigerian flag was hoisted.

He suggested to them that it would be more sensible to take the pole, lay it down on the ground and measure it. Their unanimous reply was 'we are not interested in the length – it's the HEIGHT we want to measure.

AND FINALLY, FEDERAL

On behalf of the Federal Capital (wherever it is), Chief Awalawanbe admitted that his story owes its origin to Cleaver. According to the Chief, after the American Civil War, the negroes were allowed to vote for the first time. However, before they could be registered on the Voters List, negroes were required to prove that (1) they could write their names and (2) they could READ English. One of Chief Awalawanbe's ancestors called McLangston was one of the first to try to register. He went up to the white polling officer who asked him to write down his name. This was no problem for McLangston and he readily wrote his name (he managed to mispell it). However, when it came to the reading test, McLangston was all at sea and completely confused because the Polling Officer deliberately gave him a CHINESE newspaper to read instead of an English one.

'Hurry up McLangston – can't you read it?' asked the Officer.

'Yes of course, Massa,' replied McLangston.

'What does it say?' demanded the Officer.

'It says, er-er-er.' stammered McLangston turning the paper upside down, 'er-er this is one blackman who's not going to get the Vote.'

BUT ALSO THE ENGLISHMAN

An English diplomat who had been attending the convention as an observer declared that he couldn't resist making his own contribution. He spoke of how on June 5, the date of the last Referendum held in UK to decide whether Britain should stay or leave the European Economic Community, in the mistaken belief that there would be postal votes, fifty Englishmen turned up at the British High Commissioner's Residence to cast their Votes. The result:

5 voted that Britain should stay

5 voted that Britain should leave

and the remaining forty voted that THEY wanted to remain in Nigeria.

ALL RISKS COVERED

FIRST THE INSURANCE NEWS

TOMORROW at 9 p.m. The President of the Insurance Institute will deliver the principal speech at a tycoon-studded annual dinner. The atmosphere will be supremely charged on account of the 'will-he-won't-he' faction amongst the gentlemen of the 'all risks covered' fraternity who are determined to censor their President's speech.

The advance text of the speech reads as follows:
'Gentlemen!

More than at any other time the moment has come for indigenous Nigerian companies to seriously consider combining to form larger units so as not only to take on bigger risks but also to reinforce the confidence of the insuring public in the ability and resources of the indigenous companies to meet their obligations arising from risks they have undertaken to cover.

Needless to say, in every country where insurance business now flourishes, there has occurred the moment of decision which has had to be faced – whether or not to remain a mixed bag of mushroom companies engaged in the legitimate business of insuring other people's risk with their attendant gains or losses; or become larger units.

To illustrate my point, I would remind you of the period immediately following World War II. The British insurance companies got together because they realised that the only way they could compete with the American companies on equal terms was to amalgamate and form a giant company that would be known as Mammoth Insurance Co.

On July 27 1946, the four Managing Directors of (I) LEGAL & GENERAL INSURANCE CO. (II) COMMERCIAL UNION INSURANCE (III) PRUDENTIAL INSURANCE and (IV) ROYAL EXCHANGE held their final meeting prior to making the official announcement of their amalgamation.

There was one little snag though – the four Managing Directors could not agree on which company's emblem should be bestowed on the new company. Each Managing Director insisted that his company's emblem and the years of tradition and public confidence that were associated with it should be preserved. As there was complete deadlock, the Directors decided to invite the public to offer suggestions.

A few days later, as the directors went through the thousands of suggestions that had turned up through the mail, they were totally mystified by an emblem suggested by an Irishman, William O'Risk. It was a circle divided into four segments and each segment contained a picture of a man and a woman in an amorous position in bed. The directors were so intrigued that they felt compelled to invite Willaim O'Risk to their next meeting so that he could explain his suggestion.

William O'Risk patiently explained as follows: Gentlemen, the circle itself represents MAMMOTH Insurance. The first segment with a picture of a man in bed with his own wife represents LEGAL & GENERAL INSURANCE CO.

The second segment showing a man in bed with a CALL-GIRL Represents COMMERCIAL UNION INSURANCE CO; the third segment showing a man in bed with a girl who is on the PILL represents PRUDENTIAL INSURANCE CO; and the fourth segment showing his Royal Majesty in bed with his BEST FRIEND'S WIFE represents ROYAL EXCHANGE INSURANCE CO.'

NOW THE POLICE NEWS

Inspector Pius Jerasako was quietly contemplating the prospects of a comfortable early retirement when his peace of mind was shattered by a radio message alerting him that a vicious cold-blooded murderer and rapist was

100

at large and Headquarters had good reason to believe that the murderer was someone with fairly good knowledge of the neighbouring area of Kamukamu thus giving rise to speculation that he was either born there or had lived there in the recent past.

Inspector Jerasako promptly assembled everyone between the age of six and eighty-five, MALE AND FEMALE. He asked each one of them a simple question. 'Are you the Kamukamu rapist and murderer?

On receiving the answer 'NO' the inspector patiently recorded the reply. At the end of the question and answer session, the inspector sent the following message to Headquarters – 'I have interviewed all 965 suspects, the Kamukamu rapist/murderer is not here.'

AND NOW THE PRISON NEWS

On Wednesday Brigadier Mobolaji Johnson, Military Governor of Lagos State visited the old 'Broad Street Prison.' On the same day, Sikiru Amona, Chief Sub-Editor of the 'Eko Times' got the sack for printing a first edition with the blazing headline – 'Governor Goes To Prison.' His editor was furious with him for making light of a serious visit.

The Governor's visit was symbolic for two reasons. First, the prison is to be demolished and a new annexe to the Island Maternity Hospital is to be built on the site. Secondly, the site is a gift from the Federal Government to the Lagos State Government – given in the true spirit of give and take. This should pacify that section of the Lagos community who are forever complaining about Lagos land being ceded to the Federal Government.

Unfortunately, the Governor's remarks about 'air-conditioned prisons' which exist in America has been completely misconstrued. The remark was only to emphasize that prisons need not necessarily be centres of harsh primitive and punitive vilification of the human spirit. Rather the emphasis should be on corrective programmes to enable convicts to prepare themselves for re-absorption into the mainstream of society.

Chief Eko Gbagbakugba who was present at the ceremony commented as follows:

'Brigadier Johnson's problem is the Herculean task of planning for an indeterminate and staggering population. For instance, by the time the extension to the hospital is completed, Lagos Island alone will need six hospitals not to talk of places like Mushin, Ikeja, Ajegunle, Ketu and Papa Ajao.

'The same goes for the 100 buses purchased from British Leyland. By the time the buses arrive at the ports, manage to land and get through Customs clearance and finally start plying the roads, Lagos will need not 100 but 500 more buses. That is why the Governor's comment on the census figures – "WE KNOW HOW MANY MOUTHS WE FEED" is so poignant.

'Last week I was at Ajegunle and got the shock of my life. I have never seen so many people out on the roads – as many as six abreast just gushing like water from a waterfall. I couldn't make out where they were heading for or where they were coming from.

'It was as if they live in the streets. They dance in the street, hawk their wares in the street, eat in the street, wash in the street. It wouldn't surprise me at all if a proper census revealed that there are THREE MILLION PEOPLE living in Ajegunle alone. These are people living beyond the law – they don't recognise any Government, they pay no taxes; even the police have given them up and they openly sell goods obviously stolen from the docks. With the rate of juvenile delinquency in that area how can their children end up anywhere other than jail?

Let me add another example – beggars. After a lot of stop-go-stop-go, the settlement for beggars was finally set up at Oshodi. For a few days, Lagos was free of beggars. No sooner were the beggars rehabilitated (albeit not entirely successfully) than Lagos was invaded by a FRESH set of beggars from across the northern borders. During the day – their children tout and at night their fathers are fleet-footed night marauders perpetuating organised burglary. Where do we go from here?

THE LORD MAYORS

JUST before the Udoji Salary review panel completed its work, details of the recommendations, particularly the salary increases leaked to the 'Lord Mayors.' The 'Lord Mayors' are the hundreds of nude mad men who openly parade their masculinity along the major roads of Lagos.

The Lord Mayors decided to send a petition immediately to Chief Udoji warning him that nothing but trouble would result from the recommendations. The President-General of the Lord Mayors, Alhadji Jimoh Ina Njo Ogiriosa called an emergency meeting of all Lord Mayors.

The meeting was to be held under the Eko Bridge which is the official residence of many of the Lord Mayors. The invitation read 'Dress strictly formal or come as you are.'

Alhaji Jimoh Ina Njo Ogiriosa addressed the meeting as follows: 'You all know that Chief Udoji is a good man. He has been given a most difficult task – which is no less than to start again from scratch and create a first class civil service, the finest in Africa for the benefit of the most populous country in Black Africa.

'I have read the draft recommendations from page to page (don't ask me how I got it, after all you know we have representatives everywhere). Some of the recommendations are brilliant but the tragedy is that while Chief Udoji no doubt knows what he is talking about, his audience don't.'

The result is predictable chaos. You are yourselves witnesses to the fact that since word leaked that hefty pay increases were on the way, prices have shot up so fast that a lot of ordinary, perfectly sane people find they can't afford to eat.

Hunger and hardship are forcing them to join our party thus causing serious congestion under the Eko Bridge. Henceforth only members who have paid their dues up to date will be allowed to sleep under the Eko Bridge. All others are being directed to the Black Arts Village.

As for employment, I can see nothing but massive retrenchment when employers find they just can't pay the new rates for labour. This means more members for us because a lot of nice people who like to get up in the morning, dress for work and head for their various offices and factories will suddenly find that they are not wanted.

Shame and degradation will drive them to us. Even the ones who manage to retain their jobs will find that their increased pay packet would purchase even less than what they were getting before.

Their frustration and anger mean more members for us. Now you all know that in the national interest there should't be too many of us. Each society can only cope with a limited number of 'Lord Mayors.' Once there are more Lord Mayors than sane people, there's going to be trouble.

Alhaji Ogiriosa then led a delegation of Lord Mayors to the Cabinet Office to petition Chief Udoji to reconsider his proposals. They were confronted by one of the Chief's attractive secretaries who told them with impeccable Oxford accent.

'For a start, you are not properly dressed; secondly, this is international Women's Year and I'm ashamed to see women amongst you; and thirdly there is nothing Chief Udoji will not do for this country – but you are much mistaken if you think he is going to listen to madmen.'

ARE ALL THESE PEOPLE LYING?

Mallam Bukar Oniro a reporter for one of the Northern newspapers has been going round Lagos, making enquiries about whether there is any truth in the following complaints about Lagos traffic:

(i) last Thursday, a nursing sister at Lagos University Teaching Hospital rang her home at 10 p.m. to tell her maid to get her food ready as she was on her way home. She did not reach home at Ilupeju (a distance of 8 miles) until 4 a.m.

(ii) the week before, a Lagos State Commissioner was on his way home from a conference at Ibadan. His LSG car reached Bata, Mushin at 2 p.m. He did not get to his home at Surulere, a distance of $6\frac{1}{2}$ miles, until 7.30 p.m.

(iii) Last Tuesday, a young lady left her office (The Mint, Victoria Island) at 5 p.m. She did not get to her home at Yaba (a distance of 10 miles) until 10.30 p.m. She was carried unconscious out of her car.

(iv) on Saturday, relatives of a prominent Ikorodu citizen set out from Lagos at 2.00 p.m. with the coffin meant for his burial. At 10.30 p.m. they had covered a distance of only 11 miles and were forced to picnic by the roadside at Anthony Village.

Burial could not take place until the following day.

ABSENT GUESTS

Last week Mallam Faji Repete threw a fantastic house-warming party at his Ikeja residence. By 2 a.m. having said goodnight to the last guest, the Mallam and his wife retired upstairs only to fall fast asleep within minutes.

At 2.45 a.m. thieves broke in and cleared Mallam Faji Repete's TV, Radio, furniture and even the carpet. Everything that could possibly be moved was bundled into a waiting van.

The thieves then started to help themselves to the drinks left over from the party and decided there was no reason why the party should not continue.

At 6 a.m. the Mallam came downstairs only to be confronted with a bare sitting room and six drunken thieves in a coma. Mallam too shocked to believe his luck called the Police to arrest the gate-crashers. Since then the police have recommended the 'Mallam Repete special' to all inhabitants of Ikeja.

As for Mallam, every night before going to bed, he makes his sitting-room look as if he's just had a party and leaves six bottles each of Brandy, Whisky, Schnapps, Champagne, Beer, Stout and of course 'Ogogoro,' in a tray. Finally, every night at the stroke of midnight, he plays the National Anthem and drinks a toast to ABSENT GUESTS!

MOTORCYCLE NEWS

Mallam Raji Gamara shook his head violently and declared that there must be something wrong somewhere because every time the government sets out to please everyone it ends up pleasing no-one. The Mallam pointed out that a good example of this was the Udoji award and the consequent easing of loans to civil servants who wish to buy motorcycles.

'My friend, I don't know what to do. As the Deputy Permanent Secretary in this Ministry, I have to approve all loans for the purchase of motor-cycles by our clerks. If I say "no," they complain and yet I know every time I say "yes" it is like signing their death warrants.

'Let me emphasize that I have nothing against motor-cycles, in fact I know that a particular brand is a very fine machine.

'However, since January, there hasn't been a single month when I have not been invited to the funeral of at least two of our clerks or messengers involved in motor-cycle accidents.

'Every month, we have at least forty reports of injuries necessitating absence from work. Wallahi Tallahi, this Udoji "wahala" is going to kill me.'

TERMINAL NEWS

At the last count, there were 230 ships waiting to berth at Apapa docks and many had been waiting for upwards of four months. It has been reported that a whole community on water has grown around the ships.

They have their own currency and radio station: they

exchange letters and records; they have excellent fishing and water skiing facilities; they have street lights and some Captains have had streets named after them.

Some bright fellows have even taken up learning Yoruba and Hausa languages. This report was violently repudiated by a captain who declared that life out there is no joking matter. He declared he had spent 'more than two months without water, food or medical care.'

A United Nations observer has just submitted a report in which he concludes that the only way we can decongest the port is to do what the Swedes once had to do – ABOLISH CUSTOMS AND EXCISE DUTY AND ASK EVERYONE TO REMOVE HIS GOODS WITHIN SEVEN DAYS.

MRS TEN PER CENT AND ALL THAT . . .

FIRST THE INTERNATIONAL NEWS

JUST to confirm, that now more than ever before, women are determined to get their own share of the goodies particularly as this is International Women's Year.

It has been reported that in Indonesia, the President's wife, Ibu Tien Suharto, is widely known as 'Ibu Ten Per Cent' for the rake-offs (bribes) she has been collecting from businesses operating there.

NEPA AGAIN!

An over-ambitious youngman on seeing a full-page advertisement by the National Electric Power Authority promptly applied for a job as a SYSTEMS ANALYST.

The over-optimistic applicant added that in the event that the vacancy had already been filled he would be quite happy to accept an alternative job as a PROGRAMME ANALYST and failing that as a STARDARD AND TECHNIQUES OFFICER.

He has since been informed that NEPA has (1) – No systems, (2) – No programme, (3) – No standards, and no techniques and (4), just in case he didn't already know, NEPA has a new slogan:
ALL THE BEST THINGS HAPPEN IN THE DARK!

SMOKING NEWS

After a long drawn out battle, the Medical Council backed very strongly by the government has finally forced cigarette manufacturers to print a health hazard warning on every packet of cigarette sold to the public.

The warning reads: 'CIGARETTES KILL SLOWLY'. However, the Cigarette Consumers Association has now written a strongly-worded petition to the Medical Council and the government. The last line of the petition reads: 'We are NOT IN A HURRY TO DIE'.

EMPLOYMENT NEWS

Alhadji Bisako Adimu who was carpeted by the Public Service Commission for giving a juicy government job to his brother instead of advertising it and going 'through the proper channels' with the attendant risk that the job might go to someone else, has strongly defended himself against charges of nepotism by asking the PSC:

'If you have to choose between giving the job to a complete stranger and SOMEONE YOU'VE BEEN FEEDING FOR THE PAST TWO YEARS, who would you rather choose?'

AIRLINE NEWS

Ayinla took another look at the newspaper heading 'HIJACKERS DEMAND ₦1,000,000'. He turned round to Dr Okon LL.D:

'You know, I'm not educated, but I'd like to ask you to explain what it means to Hijack a plane.'

Dr Okon replied – 'That's simple enough, to HIJACK a plane means to seize it.'

Ayinla, looking very confused, declared: 'You are joking. A plane is about the size of four houses – how can you seize something that is that BIG?'

Dr Okon coolly replied: 'Simple. You wait until it gets off the ground and when it's right up – miles away, it gets SMALL, that's when you seize it.'

AND NOW DODAN BARRACKS NEWS

Several national newspapers recently gave front page prominence to the photograph of the Head of State shaking hands with Professor Sam Aluko while Chief Simeon Adebo, former Nigerian Permanent Representative at the United Nations looked on.

Both gentlemen along with other members of the statutory National Universities Commission had been invited to Dodan Barracks for a chat with General Gowon. It is quite interesting to compare the style of the two gentlemen.

While Chief Adebo has maintained dignified silence about the issues of the day and some perennial crises. Professor Aluko has been a consistent critic of the conglomeration of absurdities inherent in government policy and spending programmes.

This has prompted Peter Welstaff, who represents a foreign newspaper here, to suggest that henceforth more and more eminent citizens representing the widest spectrum of opinion will be called upon to participate in 'OPERATION HELP OUR NATION' irrespective of their publicly stated reservations about policy decisions.

No one who has any serious contribution to make will be left out – even those who staunchly refuse to book newspaper adverts extrolling the virtues of any particular individuals.

SIGN HERE, HERE, HERE AND HERE

On Monday, Ralph Nickswell of Rextol Enterprises flew in from London on the midday flight. Two hours after arrival he was still at Ikeja Airport signing away like mad.

His signature was required on various documents – customs, immigration, health . . . all the forms seemed to be in sixplicates and a little man kept following him around extolling him to 'sign here, and here, and of course here . . . and four more copies . . . .'

On emerging from the Airport, Ralph got hold of a taxi only to find himself trapped by the famous Lagos traffic for the next four hours. When he finally made it to the hotel, he was barely conscious enough to make it to the reception desk.

On being confronted with more forms to sign, Ralph passed out. For the next two days, Ralph was confined to bed, a half-conscious victim of nervous exhaustion inflicted by the terrible combination of Lagos traffic and 'sign here, sign here . . . and here'.

On Thursday, Ralph set about the urgent business of contacting various government officials. He very quickly discovered what everyone in Lagos knows i.e. you can't get hold of anyone on the telephone unless you are prepared to dial the same number a dozen times and are willing to devote the whole day. Sheer frustration drove him to hire a taxi in order to call personally at various ministries.

Eight hours afterwards, after fainting twice while his taxi was stuck in the traffic hold-up and managing to get to only two ministries before closing time and being confronted at the ministries by the same little man who again kept extolling him to 'sign here, here, and here . . .' wherever he went, Ralph was back once again bedridden with exhaustion.

The hotel manager was most concerned and politely asked if there was anything he could do for Ralph. 'Yes, please telex my Head Office and relay this message.' On the piece of paper which Ralph handed to the Hotel Manager were written just two words: 'MISSION IMPOSSIBLE'.

On being asked to comment, a spokesman for the Lagos Chamber of Commerce declared: 'Mr Nickswell's case is a familiar story. All our members know that if you can do business in Lagos, you can do business anywhere, even on the moon.'

IF YOU 'AIKPE' ME, I WILL 'KEREKOU' YOU

Before President Kerekou of Dahomey set out for Lagos to attend the launching ceremony of ECOWAS, he passed a coded message to Captain Michel Aikpe, the Interior Minister.

The message was restricted to three letters 'TCB' which translates as 'Take Care of Business'. It now appears that Captain Aikpe was a little too diligent in looking after Internal Affairs, particularly the President's household and more particularly the President's wife.

A few days after the President's return, 32-year-old Captain Aikpe was a dead man. According to an official governmental statement: 'he met his death at the hands of presidential guards when he was trying to escape, having been found COMPLETELY NAKED (no way to treat the First Lady, a clear breach of protocol) with the President's wife. The President was at the scene of the murder.

A cynic declared the episode as a put up job – a classic 'Lady Macbeth' set-up to eliminate Captain Aikpe who was a thorn in the President's flesh and was clearly a rival who enjoyed immense popularity in the army.

Another commentator blamed the episode on ECOWAS, his thinking being that had the President not neglected his Internal Affairs and gone off to ECOWAS the illicit affair would not have started in the first place.

A third commentator has declared that if the President was determined to take the law into his own hands, the least he could have done would be to issue a public disclaimer before hand with a photograph of the President's wife and the Captain: 'ANYONE CAUGHT COMPLETELY NAKED WITH THE FIRST LADY DOES SO AT HIS OWN RISK.'

The Nigerian Minister of Information has declared: 'We are watching the situation closely but we are not unduly worried. Afterall, the last time I was in Ibadan I saw illicit affairs everywhere.'

ZOOM ZOOM

AYINLA was lying in the sun 'taking breeze' outside his shack in Rio de Ajegunle when his friend Okon came running up waving a newspaper excitedly. 'Ayinla, now is our chance at last. We must make quick money double quick.'

Ayinla: You know I can't read. I was already too old to benefit from Chief Awolowo's free education scheme.

Okon: Look at this photograph. It is an aeroplane and it's for sale. It is an executive jet bought by the last civilian government. It now rests at Hangar 3 at Ikeja Airport waiting for a buyer.

Ayinla: What has all that got to do with me?

Okon: Plenty, plenty. We must go the the Airport immediately and make Mr Francis Obi, the General Manager of Nigeria Airways an offer he can't refuse.

Ayinla: How are we going to pay for it?

Okon: Who mentioned payment? What we must do is to so totally confuse him, he'll let us have the plane for free.

Ayinla: That sounds interesting. In fact, only this very minute I was thinking how in this country, there are three types of power that are superior to even gun power.

Okon: What do you mean?

Ayinla: The most important power is bank power – the ability to borrow money you have no intention of paying back.

Okon: Go on.

Ayinla: The second is road power – that is the power

113

	to buy the biggest Mercedes-Benz and clog up the roads.
Okon:	Which is the third?
Ayinla:	Bottom power – I leave that to your imagination. Anyway, about the plane business – how can you possibly hope to confuse a man like Mr Obi? He is a hard-working man – really smart, and you seem to forget that he was already Deputy Permanent Secretary before he transferred to the Airways.
Okon:	You shall see!
Ayinla:	In any case how are we going to get there?
Okon:	By horse, of course, you mean you never heard of horsepower? It's the only way to travel in Lagos these days. All those Mercedes-Benz cars are stuck in the traffic; the Suzuki – people (landlords of Igbobi) are forever being run over and even pedestrians are not safe. Didn't I tell you about my friend Aremu who was riding home on his bicycle and stopped to buy cigarettes just below the Apapa flyover overhead bridge. A car above him on the flyover hit the ramp and next thing it fell right on top of Aremu.
Ayinla:	What a way to die.
Okon:	No doubt about it the only way to travel is by horse. Have you heard of any horse rider being killed in the traffic?
Ayinla:	Maybe you are right.
Okon:	Right on. I have a horse ready. I stole it from the Army barracks. A soldier asked me what I needed it for and I said it was for a cultural show. He didn't mind at all. He just laughed – 'If it's for culture it's okay.' Without much ado the two gentlemen set out for Ikeja on horseback with Ayinla waving a very majestic fly-wisk while Okon insisted on bringing along his walking stick for moral support.
Ayinla:	Why is everyone staring at us?

114

Okon: Because everyone else is stuck in the chaotic Lagos traffic but we are moving – can you see anyone else on horseback?

Ayinla: I wish they wouldn't gape at us if we invented horses.

Okon: Maybe we ought to offer that Alhaji in the Mercedes-Benz our horse in exchange for his car.

Ayinla: Did I ever tell you of two people, Sadiq and Aminu who set out from Kano with their only possession – a goat, which they intended to sell at a profit in Lagos. They walked all the way from Kano. Aminu held the rope tied round the neck of the goat while Sadiq held its tail, but by the time they got to Lagos, the goat had escaped! Aminu and Sadiq started blaming each other. Aminu accused Sadiq of being irresponsible – if he had held tightly to the rope, the goat would never have escaped. Sadiq equally furious blamed Aminu – if only he had held tightly to the tail, the goat wouldn't have escaped.

Okon: That's a very interesting story. It is exactly what is happening in this country – nobody is responsible for anything and everybody is busy blaming everybody else. When your goods disappear from the docks, the Ports Authority blame the Customs and Excise who in turn blame the Clearing and Forwarding Agents.

Ayinla: Do I sound like an arm-chair critic?

Okon: No, you sound like a horseback critic.

Ayinla: Okon. Do you know something? Ajegunle is the most beautiful part of Nigeria – lagoons, streams, waterfalls, creeks, ducks, baboons, palm trees, coconuts, mangoes, blue skies, fantastic beaches etc. That's why we call it Rio de Ajegunle.

Okon: Shut up immediately, Ayinla. Have you forgotten that we are under oath not to tell anyone how beautiful Ajegunle is? Remember Chief Agbam, 'The man they couldn't arrest, the Jesus of Ajegunle and the Black Prince of Morocco' warned us that it is the duty of every responsible inhabitant of Ajegunle to keep telling the Government and the public that Ajegunle is a rotten place unfit for human habitation; no roads, no telephones, no electricity; no water; The place is entirely in the grip of man-eating mosquitoes and giant snakes. Fifty-five murders, eighty rapes and at least 500 burglaries are committed every night.

Ayinla: I wonder why the Chief said that?

Okon: That way, the government will leave us in benign neglect, and we'll be able to go on running our own affairs.

Ayinla: You mean, if we let the Government know about all the goodies in Ajegunle, they'll just drive us out like they did at Ikoyi, Marina, Tarkwa Bay, Badagry, and Victoria Island?

Okon: That's correct. We have even found oil – but we won't tell the government.

Ayinla: Next time I see any Government official, I'm going to tell him an atomic bomb has just exploded in Ajegunle – that should keep them away.

On reaching Ikeja roundabout the two gentlemen were stopped from proceeding further by a Police siren and a long procession of Mercedes-Benz cars carrying several Heads of State to the Airport.

Okon: Ayinla, do you know what ECOWAS means?

Ayinla: Of course not.

Okon: It stands for Economic Community of West African States.

Ayinla: That's a grand title – but what does it really mean?

Okon: It means Ghanaians, Ivorians, Dahomeans,

	Sierra Leoneans and other West Africans become our brothers.
Ayinla:	I have enough brothers already. Fifteen brothers and twenty-seven sisters.
Okon:	It means you can travel anywhere in West Africa and won't need a visa.
Ayinla:	I have no intention of going anywhere whatever. Everything I want is right here in Nigeria.
Okon:	It means we'll be able to sell Ibru Fish in Freetown and Odutola Tyres in Abidjan as well as 'Made in Nigeria' Peugeot cars in Cotonou.
Ayinla:	We don't need a union for that!
Okon:	It means we'll share our wealth with our brothers.
Ayinla:	I think, this country should adopt the same style as Chief Odutola. He doesn't go round telling everyone how much money he has and if anyone asks him for 'dash' he gives them work.
Okon:	You have to take a larger view. What is happening is that we are investing our short-term wealth for long-term benefits. In the long run, everyone will benefit but in the short term it may appear that we are doing all the giving.
Ayinla:	I don't believe in short term or long term. All I know is that what I have, I hold.
Okon:	That's selfish and shortsighted.
Ayinla:	If we are going to help our African brothers, what we must do is create a climate of ORDER here – so that everyone knows what he is required to do and next we create an atmosphere of efficiency, so everyone knows how he is required to do it. To my mind, that is the only way we'll ever reach the take-off stage that will transform us from an under-developing country.

Then we invite our African brothers to join us, one at a time.

Okon: You are missing the whole point of the union. It is a flexible union.

Ayinla: Look Ete Okon, when our African brothers start coming to Lagos to look for work, we'll be in trouble – unemployment will soar, accommodation will become even more scarce, rents will sky-rocket, our schools and hospitals are already over-crowded, and our 3rd Development Plan may even suffer considerable setback.

Okon: Your fears are exaggerated and in any case these dangers are only for the short term. What is far more important is that we should identify with our African brothers and each country would contribute its own special talents, skills and resources so that in the long term everyone does what they do best and we shall all benefit as goods, services, labour and ideas are able to move freely across international frontiers without self-imposed constraints.

It is not just an economic union. It is a spiritual union as well, and the Minister of Information should have gone round the country to explain what ECOWAS is all about. After all, Wednesday May 28 1975, the date when the treaty was signed could rank in historical importance alongside the creation of the 12 states and the cessation of the civil war.

Ayinla, you know the way things are in this country. If the Minister of Information tells people that ECOWAS is a good union, nobody will support it. However, if he tells people it is a bad union everyone will still disbelieve him and they will support the union.

Ayinla: In that case he should go round the country and tell everyone it's a bad union.

118

BUDDY, CAN YOU SPARE A PLANE?

[Continuing the story of OKON (LL.D) and AYINLA.]

OKON (LL.D) and his mate Ayinla set out on horseback from 'Rio de Ajegunle' for Ikeja to CONFUSE Mr Francis Obi, the General Manager of Nigerian Airways into letting them have one of his aeroplanes, which is up for sale, for FREE.

At Ikeja roundabout, the two riders find their progress halted by the approach of a police vehicle blaring its siren and carrying a warning – 'Road Closed' signifying that all traffic must stop to allow the procession of cars transporting the seven African Heads of State who had just launched the Economic Community of West African States in Lagos, to pass through the chaotic traffic unimpeded.

The last car in the procession was followed by another police vehicle carrying the sign 'Road Open' which triggered off a mad scramble among motorists, cyclists and pedestrians anxious to continue their journey.

Ayinla: I think it's about time the sign 'Road Closed' was changed to 'Road Confused'.

Okon: And change 'Road Open' to 'Road More Confused'.

Ayinla: If we ever build a new capital, I don't think we ought to tell anyone, otherwise we'll have so many visitors that the place will become just as choked up as Lagos. I think we ought to call it the SECRET CAPITAL.

Okon: Ayinla, with all due respect, I think you are a fool. How can you hide a whole capital? What we ought to do is build a sort of 'Western White House' like the Americans so that all our

119

important visitors can go there straight from the airport without coming into Lagos at all.

Ayinla: When we get hold of this plane, I think we ought to 'drive' it to all the West African countries and see the people in their own habitat before we decide whether they are suitable partners.

Okon: That smacks of arrogance and condescension. They are our brothers and the bigger the family the better. At any rate if you go there all you'll see is the same pattern of extremes of poverty and isolated cases of affluence. Believe me, there are parts of Abidjan and Dakar that are even more beautiful than Paris but they are surrounded by poverty that's even worse than ours.

Ayinla: Doctor, I don't believe you. Do they have people poorer than the people of Ajegunle?

Okon: Far worse. Take Dahomey for instance – in 1969 when Richard Burton and Elizabeth Taylor were making that film called 'THE COMEDIANS' the two film stars spent more money in three months than the whole country for the whole year.

Ayinla: But was it a good film? I mean was there plenty of action – Kung Fu and that sort of hot stuff.

Okon: That's not the point, look in one of those countries, I went to visit a Post Office Savings Bank. There was only one clerk to deal with a long queue of customers each brandishing his savings book. The clerk opened his cash box and dealt with the first six customers. He then displayed the empty cash box to those left in the queue and declared 'C'est finis'. Imagine not being able to withdraw your own money from the government treasury.

Ayinla: Doctor, you are making that up.

Okon: I swear it's true. I tell you something else. I

overheard a Dahomean student who had just been to Lagos for the University Games, telling an enchanted audience what a wonderful place Lagos is. He even told them that life in Lagos is so fast and wonderful that when people get knocked down by cars nobody stops to move the corpse to hospital. I was forced to ask him where he stayed in Lagos – it was Idi-Oro.

Ayinla: Tell me more.

Okon: In one of those countries, there are only three indigenous doctors and one of them is a Doctor of Divinity.

Ayinla: You mean General Gowon is right when he says Nigerians don't know how lucky they are.

Okon: Absolutely right!

Ayinla: But they put their opponents in detention?

Okon: That's another story. Look in some of those countries, there are more people in detention than outside. They don't even bother to conduct census – they just count the number of people in detention and multiply by two.

Ayinla: Then, why are we bothering to join them?

Okon: They are our brothers. What we are building is a cultural bridge and the economic foundation for mutual inter-dependence.

Ayinla: I don't understand all this. What I do know is that General Gowon is a fine soldier and a fine sportsman. It always makes me sad when I hear anyone has been put in detention.

Okon: He has done a lot for this country. Don't worry Ayinla, by October there won't be anyone in detention.

Ayinla: Are you sure?

Okon: Yes of course. It's quite simple. The Queen of England is coming here in October and I have a list of all the places she has visited since she ascended the throne and in none of those places do they put people in detention. Now, you know it is British tradition to preserve British tradition. In other words, the Queen would never break tradition by visiting a country that has people in detention.

Ayinla: Is that so?

Okon: Yes, absolutely correct, I agree with you, this country owes a lot to General Gowon and I can assure you he'll do the decent thing at the right time.

Ayinla: He's a gentleman.

Okon: To illustrate how much this country owes him, think back to those dark days of the civil war. At any moment, the country could have disintegrated. He held it together and he was only 32 years old.

Ayinla: That's right, doctor.

Okon: Now, think of all the people you know who are that same age. Is there any single one of them you could say to: You are 32 years old, you have no previous experience of government, these are confused times, but to you I bequeath this country of 80 million people, 250 tribes and as many languages, Northerners who don't know what goes on in the South and Southerners who don't even want to know what goes on in the North. Now run it.

Ayinla: I can't think of anyone except Alhaji Waheed. I know what he'll do – he'll award the running of the government to someone else on contract and collect his percentage.

Okon: Be serious Ayinla. The answer is no one. The General's record speaks for itslef. He restored discipline among the mutinous forces and gave us peace and security. He used force with extreme reluctance during the civil war and it was his policy that his opponents should not be regarded as the enemy but as dissident members of one and the same country. When he had at length put down their opposition he displayed complete honesty and good faith.

	There was no revenge.
Ayinla:	What really bothers me is what will happen when civilians come back to power. I feel certain that for every man detained under the Military regime, the civilians will detain a hundred.
Okon:	In other words you are saying that if we create an atmosphere of civilised tolerance now so that 'no man feels oppressed', a civilian government will have no excuse for behaving otherwise.
Ayinla:	That's correct.
Okon:	There is no point in worrying about what a civilian government will or won't do. There isn't going to be a civilian government in our lifetime.
Okon:	How do you know that?
Ayinla:	Simple. Last year the Minister of Information was telling everyone that the army would leave in 1976 but this was subsequently denied by the government. So now that the Minister of Information is telling everyone that the army will not leave in 1976, I know they WILL in fact leave; and invite civilians to run the government and keep a watchful eye just to be sure that the splendid work they have done is not wrecked.
Okon:	Amazing logic.
Ayinla:	I've heard that phrase before. Now I remember – it was when my townsman who is a Commissioner was explaining to me that the government has a fine record of solid achievements to its credit; but somehow it can't yet get across to the public.

Even in areas such as Foreign Affairs where you may think we have no policy at all, there is in fact a policy of caution and restraint. For example, we could easily have retaliated against Ghana and Zaire for deporting

Nigerians who had lived among them for generations.

A civilian government tempted to play to the gallery or show muscle-power may even have gone as far as military adventurism. Instead we acted with restraint and to-day we have excellent relations with both countries.

Okon: Enough talk for now. The traffic is a little less choked up now and we must hurry to see Mr Obi. Ayinla, call me 'doctor' once more.

Ayinla: Doctor!

HORSEPOWER

[Continuing the story of OKON LL.D and AYINLA]

The story so far
OKON LL.D and Ayinla set out for Ikeja Airport to persuade Mr Francis Obi, General Manager of Nigerian Airways to sell them a government plane for FREE.

Thanks to the chaotic traffic in Lagos, after two weeks of dodging crazy drivers, avoiding yawning pot-holes, swimming-pool size puddles, exchanging salutations with nude madmen – ('The Lord Mayors'), and placating extortionist beggars shoving repulsive sores and stumps at them, the two gentlemen finally make it to Ikeja Airport.

This gives the Minister of Information adequate time to ring Ikeja Airport and warn:
"FRANCIS, TWO CONFUSIONISTS ARE ON THEIR WAY. . . .'

Okon:	Ayinla isn't that a refuse disposal lorry?
Ayinla:	Yes Okon.
Okon:	I can't understand why instead of COLLECTING the rubbish it's littering the road – the lorry is overfull and all the rubbish keeps falling out.
Ayinla:	Strange things happen in Lagos. That lorry is full of milk, sugar and cement all stolen from the National Supply Corporation – they just use the rubbish to cover the stuff so they don't have trouble at the check-points.
Okon:	Jesus, Almighty!
Ayinla:	Jesus has nothing to do with it.

125

Okon:	What about that other lorry over there – the one with the funny carriage.
Ayinla:	That's where all the stink is coming from. Believe it or not – here we are in 1975 and human faeces are still being transported about in lorries in our capital. I've seen those lorries break down on the new Eko Bridge and even on Yakubu Gowon Street.
	The one on Yakubu Gowon Street was the result of a head-on collision with a Mercedes-Benz 280, and the contents were spilled all over the street. The stench was unbearable for miles around.
Okon:	This horse feels like a Mercedes-280 SL. I think we ought to re-name it 'Mercedes 280 SL'.
Ayinla:	I agree.
Okon:	I feel philosophical.
Ayinla:	Does that mean you are hungry?
Okon:	No, it means I'm trying to make some sense out of all the chaos around me.
Ayinla:	Go ahead – but I tell you, you are boring me and Mercedes 280 SL.
Okon:	Look at it this way. Running a country is in many ways like riding a horse. Any horse rider will tell you there must never be any doubt as to who is in charge otherwise you'll be heading one way but the horse will be pulling madly in the other direction.
Ayinla:	That's true enough. Surely, from time to time, you have to check that the horse has enough to eat and give it clean water to drink. Also, you must be careful you don't ride it too roughly otherwise it will start complaining and finally just refuse to go any further.
Okon:	That's what happened to the politicians.

	They rode the horse so badly and so many were struggling to get on the back of the same horse that the horse started neighing loudly but to deaf ears and finally the horse threw them off its back.
Ayinla:	The horse didn't throw them off – they were removed.
Okon:	Same thing.
Ayinla:	What's the answer to our problems?
Okon:	Horsepower.
Ayinla:	What do you mean by that?
Okon:	It means first you make sure your horse takes you in the direction you want to go and secondly, instead of everybody trying to get on the back of the same horse, each person gets his own horse. That way nobody complains.
Ayinla:	Are you sure? Who are the people complaining?
Okon:	The people who have no horses.
Ayinla:	Life is tough for people who don't have horses.
Okon:	I tell you something else. Do you remember when John Kennedy the American President died? Right in front of the funeral procession was a riderless horse.
Ayinla:	Yes, I do remember seeing the film.
Okon:	In Greek philosophy, the riderless horse was the symbol of despair and desolation as well as grief.
Ayinla:	How interesting. You know we have the same thing here. I remember when Herbert Macaulay died, the funeral procession was headed by a riderless horse. I saw them pass through Campos Square. The same thing happened when Sir Adeyemo Alakija died.
Okon:	So you see the riderless horse is a universal symbol.

Ayinla:	I get it. That's why we must never let Mercedes 280 SL think he is a riderless horse otherwise he won't take us where we want to go.
Okon:	You know in the British army the first thing you learn is horse-riding.
Ayinla:	That's not true.
Okon:	It is. An officer explained it all to me – leadership is like good horsemanship. In other words the essentials of good horsemanship such as balance, co-ordination, and control are the basic ingredients of good leadership.
Ayinla:	Okon, look over there. Isn't that your friend Abdullahi from Kano?
Okon:	It's him alright. Abdullahi! Abdullahi!

Okon embraces Abdullahi warmly and introduces him to Ayinla.

Okon:	I was just telling Ayinla that you walked all the way from Kano to Lagos.
Abdullahi:	That's true. Even in Lagos everywhere I go, I walk.
Ayinla:	You must like walking.
Abdullahi:	No, not all. It's a necessity. I feel sick whenever I get on 'Bolekaja' 'Kia-kia' bus or 'Danfo'. Those things are not meant for human beings at all. It's criminal to let them get away with packing people like sardines.
Okon:	Where are you off to anyway?
Abdullahi:	I'm going to work. I have a job as a messenger at the Ministry of Labour, Obalende. My number one problem is how to get there on time.
Ayinla:	Is it true that in order to get to work at 8 o'clock you have to leave home by 5 a.m.?
Abdullahi:	Believe me – it's worse than that. What I do now is that on Monday evening I set

128

	out for work and hope I get there in time
	for Tuesday!
Okon:	Abdullahi, your lie pass all lie.
Ayinla:	Why don't you come with us. We are
	going to see Mr Francis Obi.
Abdullahi:	Who is he?
Okon:	He is the most important man in Nigeria.

NEXT WEEK: ABDULLAHI, AYINLA AND DR OKON (LL.D Cantab.) CONVINCE MR OBI THAT BP (Bottom Power) PASS ALL.

. . . AND NOW FOR SOMETHING COMPLETELY DIFFERENT.

Last week's Lagos State Open Squash Rackets Championships was dominated by religion. The last three contestants were Patrick Ani (No. 1 seed), Tayo Sofoluwe (No. 1 A seed), and Bola Osinbowale (No. 2 seed).

Sofoluwe got down on his knees right in the middle of the court and prayed:

'God, as a practising High Church Anglican, I pray that Osinbowale breaks his leg.'

Osinbowale soon got down on his and prayed:'God, as a practising Black Muslim, I pray that Sofoluwe breaks his leg.'

Patrick Ani not to be outdone, raised both hands to heaven and asked God – 'As a non-believer, I ask you to grant the prayers of these two religious fanatics.'

Result: Patrick Ani won.

ABDULLAHI LIE PASS ALL LIE

THE story so far
Dr Okon (LL.D Cantab.) and his mate Ayinla set out for
Ikeja Airport with the declared intention of confusing Mr
Francis Obi, Chairman of Nigeria Airways into selling
them one of his planes for FREE. On the way they are
joined by their friend Abdullahi Wallahi, Northern
branch Manager of Confusion Ltd.

Ayinla:	Abdullahi, what do you think of Lagos?
Abdullahi:	Lagos is full of 'Jagudas' – 'proper jagudas'.
Okon:	You sound like a friend of mine, Chief Basewa of Lagos. After consuming six bottles of champagne and fourteen cigars at a party the other night, he announced to all present – 'Lagos is full of Jagudas, but BEFORE THEY JAGUDA ME, I shall Jaguda them.'
Ayinla:	What does 'Jaguda' mean?
Okon:	It means DAYLIGHT ROBBERY WHILE EVERY-BODY IS LOOKING.
Abdullahi:	Wallahi Tallahi, the most blatant case of proper jaguda I have ever seen happened last year on the very first day I arrived in Lagos.
Ayinla:	What happened?
Abdullahi:	Russian cement imported by the government was hijacked on the high seas and sold openly at the Apapa docks! Bisimillai, that sort of thing would never happen in the north and if it did – all the culprits

	would be publicly flogged.
Okon:	Things are more civilised in Lagos. After all, the hijackers did the right thing – they voluntarily agreed to sell the cement back to the government at only double the price! Do you realise that out of the 10 richest and most powerful people in this country SIX ARE WOMEN?
Ayinla:	Don't worry it's international Women's Year.
Okon:	I tell you, women are powerful in this country.
Abdullahi:	You Southerners think we are stupid – but that is precisely why we northerners keep them locked up.
Ayinla:	Abdullahi, have you met any interesting people since you came down south?
Abdullahi:	Yes. Last night, I was introduced to Chief Odutola.
Okon:	Did you like him?
Abdullahi:	Yes, very much.
Ayinla:	You know he is one of the very few Nigerian businessmen about whom you can say 'I can see where the money is coming from'.
Okon:	True, true – he has his own factories . He even gave his people a school and when he awards scholarships he doesn't take out a newspaper supplement to publicise it.
Ayinla:	Strange though, with all his money he doesn't own a Rolls-Royce.
Okon:	He doesn't need it, in fact he could buy 50 Rolls-Royces if he wanted to.
Abdullahi:	Strange also he doesn't go around puffing a large cigar and drinking Champagne.
Okon:	I tell you something else. That man worked hard for his money. You can hold as many public enquiries as you like, you won't find his name in any fraudulent

deals or customs evasion.

Ayinla: Abdullahi, who else have you met?

Abdullahi: Admiral Wey.

Okon: Where did you meet him?

Abdullahi: On a plane – between Calabar and Lagos.

Ayinla: You mean he was on an ordinary scheduled flight – no special plane?

Abdullahi: Yes, and what is more he was at the airport on time so as to avoid keeping the other passengers waiting.

Ayinla: Really. There is hope for this country yet.

Abdullahi: You know I was sitting right behind him and I kept thinking, this is the second most powerful man in the country and here he is being accompanied by only his aide-de-camp. He even took off his cap and much to the great amusement of the passengers, he declared: 'I'm the old man without hair!'

Ayinla: What about the air hostesses, did they make a fuss of him?

Okon: Of course they would. All the air hostesses love him.

Ayinla: Did he tell that famous story of his about 'Abdullahi lie pass all lie?'

Abdullahi: Yes – but I don't remember it too well. I think it's about a man who lent money to his friend Abdullahi, and every time he went to demand his money he always found Abdullahi praying. His patience got exhausted when he discovered that Abdullahi was a fake – he was only pretending to be praying in order to dodge his obligations.

Ayinla: Admiral Wey always looks content with life.

Okon: Yes. You know why – he's seen it all.

Abdullahi: I hear that his most prized possession is a photograph of himself and Earl Mountbat-

	ten.
Ayinla:	I hear that there is nothing he enjoys more than a drink with the boys.
Okon:	That's true. You know, he would sometimes get on board the 'NNS Nigeria' and jokingly announce to his officers 'everybody is under house arrest'. This is the signal for all present to have a drink on him.
Ayinla:	Who else has impressed you?
Abdullahi:	Brigadier Ekpo.
Okon:	Where did you meet him?
Abdullahi:	At the airport on the day he was being flown out of the country for medical treatment abroad. I've never seen anything like it – the airport came to a standstill. Everyone from messengers, porters and clerks to soldiers, nurses and doctors were praying openly for him. Some women even wept. It was as if all these people – many of whom had never met Brigadier Ekpo suddenly realised that he was one of the few good men left around and begged God to save his life.
Okon:	You know he has consistently said sensible things about freedom of speech.
Ayinla:	And the handing over of power to civilians.
Okon:	During the civil war he was one of the 'backroom boys' and when the war was over he readily went over to Kaduna as Commandant of the Military Academy – a job nobody else wanted.
Ayinla:	You know something, it wasn't just the medicines and injections which they gave him abroad that made him better. It was the simple prayers of people like you and me.
Abdullahi:	You see, you southerners are too

money-mad and power hungry to believe in God. I'll tell you why God made him better – it's because God has a special duty for him.

Okon: What is that duty?

Abdullahi: To put some sanity into our agricultural policy.

Ayinla: Is that why he was made Commissioner for Agriculture?

Okon: Yes.

Abdullahi: Someone told me that he bagged a law degree only three years ago and I couldn't help wondering what makes a man of 42 with such a senior rank suddenly decide to start attending university lectures.

Okon: There comes a time in a man's life when he suddenly realises 'I can do better than I'm doing'. This comes with the realisation that one has faculties and resources which are being left untapped. This country has to do the same.

Abdullahi: But Brigadier Ekpo let me down by announcing that the army, 250,000 strong, are not farmers and therefore would not participate in the agricultural programme.

Okon: Our situation is far too serious for any one group – be they soldiers, doctors, lawyers, accountants, engineers or whatever – to choose what they will not do. Everyone must be prepared to do more than their normal requirements.

Abdullahi: I agree. What is more, the army are probably better organised than any other group to mobilise men and resources and ensure that 'low yields, decreasing soil fertility with limited use of fertilizer, unimproved crop varieties, lack of credit, inadequate extension services and the use of very simple manually operated tools' are things

	of the past.
Okon:	They sure have the men. I'm sure if you said to someone like Brigadier Samuel Ogbemudia 'Sam, these are tough times. I know there is nothing you like more than sports and farming – but forget about sports for now. We are going to put food first. You can have all the men you want, and as for money, we've got it. We are going to stop all this nonsense about graduates in agriculture ending up as clerks. Sam, you know farming is a great life – the big outdoor, plenty of fresh air and no traffic hang-ups. We are going to have big farms – government farms and private ones. If there is any shortage of fertilizers or tractors, you know you only have to say the word and you'll get them.'
Ayinla:	It's the civil servants who won't let him.
Okon:	How do you know that?
	They'll first tell him 'right now what we need is colour television or Black Arts Festival'.
Abdullahi:	Or they'll just give him the treatment.
Ayinla:	What is the treatment?
Abdullahi:	Treatment No. 1 says: 'It can't be done.' Treatment No. 2 says: 'We are not ready for it yet.' Treatment No. 3 says: 'The last man who tried to do it committed suicide!'
Okon:	Ayinla, call me 'doctor' once more.
Ayinla:	'Doctor!'

WHO IS SORRY NOW?

Continuing the story of Dr Okon, Ayinla and Abdullahi

The story so far

Dr Okon, Ayinla and Abdullahi set out on horseback to confuse Mr Francis Obi, Chariman of Nigeria Airways into letting them have a government plane free. They finally made it to Ikeja Airport.

Ayinla:	Doctor! I think I left my wallet behind.
Okon:	Don't worry. You are not going to need it anyway – we are going to so completely confuse Mr Obi, he'll beg us to take the plane away!
Abdullahi:	Wait a minute. It's all very well being confusionists but I'm not ready to die yet. Look over there – the airport has been surrounded by soldiers.
Ayinla:	Me too, I'm not ready to die.

At this point, the confusionists are challenged by a soldier.

Soldier:	What is your business here?

The three confusionists immediately collapse with fear. Dr Okon is the first to recover.

Okon:	Officer. Please don't shoot. Please, please I beg you.
Soldier:	Answer my question.
Okon:	We were just having a stroll.
Soldier:	Bloody liar. It's the first time I've heard of three people having a 'stroll' on horseback.

Ayinla:	Officer, I beg don't shoot. We are con-fusionists.
Soldier:	Very good. You are just the sort of people we are going to deal with ruthlessly. We must have discipline in this country. We are going to put a stop to all this nonsense going on.
Abdullahi:	Officer, we promise – from now on, no more confusion.
Soldier:	We know how to deal with people like you. The people who pray hardest for peace are the very people causing confu-sion.
Okon:	Officer, as a political scientist I can explain that. You see, there are people in this country for whom peace and confusion are the ideal combination. When the country is confused, the situation permits them to steal as much as they can grab and peace permits them to enjoy their ill-gotten gains.
Soldier:	The new government is not going to brook any nonsense from the confusionists.
Okon:	Is there a new government? What hap-pened? When did it happen? How?
Soldier:	A bloodless coup took place in the early hours of this morning. General Gowon has ceased to be the Head of State.
Ayinla:	Bravo! I'm so glad it was bloodless.
Abdullahi:	He was not a wicked man – he just chose the wrong friends and got his priorities all wrong.
Soldier:	The new government has announced the postponement of the Black Arts Festival. And cancelled the 1973 Census figures.
Okon, Abdullahi and Ayinla:	Bravo!
Soldier:	Don't tell me you are surprised. Surely you must have been expecting a coup at any time during the past six months.

137

Okon:	I knew the end of General Gowon's regime was at hand when I heard that he had appointed Edwin Clark of all people as his Commissioner for Information.
Soldier:	As for me – I'm only an ordinary soldier but I knew his regime was finished when he announced publicly that he was. satisfied with the progress being made in building the Festival Village and that the houses would be completed in time for the Black Arts Festival. I had visited the village and observed that some of the contractors hadn't even started.
Ayinla:	I went there too and I remember telling Okon that even if you employed 80 million magicians, the Festival Village could not possibly be ready in time.
Okon:	When I heard him declare on October 1 that he had no intention of leaving in 1976, I knew that Tai Solarin was right. This was the beginning of the end.
Abdullahi:	As for me, I knew there would be trouble when I heard him announce that the 1973 census was 'the most thorough head count of human beings by human beings anywhere in the world'. I am a northerner and the figures favoured us, but I am also a Nigerian and I knew that the rest of the country would never accept those crazy figures.
Okon:	With the benefit of hindsight, my own conclusion is that what really finished the General was the Udoji Award. It was a crazy exercise in self-imposed calamity. It is the sort of error of judgement that is beyond rectification because it is now impossible to tell workers to go back to earning what they were earning before Udoji gave them fantastic increments.

Soldier:	There is still trouble ahead. Already, employers have started warning the government that the incredibly generous pension scheme granted by Udoji to civil servants is now being demanded by workers in the private sector. If the private sector should accede to this, labour costs would go up by at least 40 per cent and of course the employers would have to increase once more the prices of their commodities and we would start another round of 'push-me-I-push-you', inflation.
Ayinla:	I knew trouble was coming when Dr Adebayo Adedeji, the Commissioner for Economic Development announced the ₦31 billion Third Development Plan and promptly left to take up an appointment with the United Nations as Secretary of the Economic Commission for Africa.
Abdullahi:	I couldn't help wondering why he was leaving if things were going to be as rosy as suggested by the plan.
Okon:	Actually, the first hint of trouble was given by none other than Major-General Hassan Katsina, who declared that the whole country was corrupt from the top downwards. Now, you can't be more explicit than that without actually naming the Head of State.
Soldier:	That's true. Look here, I am a Regimental Sergeant-Major but I tell you, the day any of my men publicly suggests that I am corrupt, I'm sure going to deal with him firmly. For a start he'll be clamped in the guardroom followed by court martial and a reduction in rank unless he can substantiate his charges.
Abdullahi:	That was the turning point. Up till then, the public image of General Gowon was

139

that of a wide-eyed young man, who had the highest public office forced upon him yet remained firmly rooted to his Christian up-bringing. There was no chink in his armour and corruption was something for lesser men.

Ayinla: It was Hassan's revelation that threw the first brick at the saintly halo which the press, particularly the foreign press had hoisted on Gen. Gowon. For the public, this was a rude shock – he was no more the man who won the war and saved the country and waited for his reward in heaven.

Okon: You know something else – it was the Tarka-Daboh affair that gave the General's saintliness the knock-out punch. The public couldn't help wondering why he couldn't sack Tarka within 24 hours of receiving clearly well documented allegations of shady dealings in high places. If he didn't have anything to hide – why couldn't he call Tarka's boast that if he were to tell all he knew, he would bring down the Government.

Abdullahi: It was the Aper-Aku-Gomwalk scandal that provided the final rout of any claims to innocence by the General. Anyone with any knowledge of property values in Jos could have told the General point-blank that Governor Gomwalk was telling less than the truth.

Okon: The way the General took only two hours to absolve Gomwalk from the serious allegations made against him made people start wondering first whether the General was determined to drive the Chief Justice and other judges into unemployment; and secondly whether there was one law for

	the ordinary folk and a special one for powerful public figures.
Soldier:	As far as I am concerned it was the Governors who finished the General. Apart from the fact that the Governors ran their states as private empires, happily dispensing patronage and favours in exchange for 'tips', terrorising their subjects and exhorting the public to make sacrifices which they themselves had no intention of making, after eight years in office they still found one ploy after another for delaying their departure. In other words, it was for them to tell the General when they were ready to leave and not the other way round.
Ayinla:	What I found incredible was that they were even bold enough to tell the General that if they had been in office too long, so had he himself. Even, Ukpabi Asika, Administrator of East Central State who after all is a civilian, was quoted as saying that 'not even General Gowon knew when the governors would leave'.
Abdullahi:	Wallahi Tallahi – who's jiving who?

SWEET AND SOUR

Continuing the story of Dr Okon, Ayinla and Abdullahi

The story so far

THE Three confusionists set out to convince Mr Francis Obi, Chairman of Nigeria Airways to let them have a Government plane for free. Owing to the traffic congestion they decide to go on horseback only to discover that the Airport has been surrounded by Soldiers.

Soldier:	This is a Military area – What is your business here?
Okon:	We want to see Mr Obi.
Soldier:	What for?
Ayinla:	Urgent business. We want to confuse him.
Soldier:	You people are crazy – I have strict instructions not to allow any confusionists into the Airport.
Abdullahi:	I agree with you, Officer. These two are master-confusionists and I think the first thing the new Government must do is to retire them with full benefits.
Soldier:	I'm going to follow you wherever you go. You are dangerous people and I'm determined to put you under 24-hour surveillance.
Okon:	You mean you'll come with us to see Mr Obi. That's great – otherwise we won't be able to get in.
Soldier:	Let me warn you, and I want to say this with maximum emphasis, this Govern-

	ment means business and will deal ruthlessly with confusionists wherever we find them. We are determined to maintain a military posture in all our dealings with the public.
Okon:	That's okay with us but you may just as well shoot us now. We are confusionists and we shall continue to be confusionists no matter what government is in power.
Abdullahi:	This new regime has started well. For the first time in almost ten years we have a government.
Ayinla:	I like the way the crucial issues such as congestion on the roads and the ports, creation of states and inflation are being tackled directly or passed to panels for review.
Okon:	But what is the point in having panels without adequate representation from confusionists? I think there should be a quota, for confusionists on every panel.
Soldier:	My advice to all confusionists like you is TALK LESS, LISTEN MORE AND YOU WILL LEARN A LOT.
Abdullahi:	Enough talk – let's go and see Mr Obi.

The three confusionists then proceed to Mr Obi's office only to be told by his Secretary: 'Mr Obi says he is busy at a meeting with his new Commissioner. He adds that pressing matters such as a new plane, the Hadji pilgrimage, remuneration of pilots, Airport extension etc. prevent him from having time for confusionists.

Okon:	Better tell Mr Obi that unless he agrees to talk to us we shall have to retire him with full benefits.
Ayinla:	And with immediate effect.
Abdullahi:	I think retirement with immediate effect should be extended to the Private Sector too.
Ayinla:	I agree. I must however add that probes

would be meaningless unless you probe General Gowon himself. There is no logic in probing his lieutenants while exempting the man at the top without whose passive indulgence some of the political atrocities and financial plundering would not have been possible.

Okon: Unless the new regime is very careful – it could very easily find that General Gowon and what to do with him are its biggest problems.

Abdullahi: But he is not here.

Okon: You are taking a very simplistic view of the situation. You see, for nine years the foreign press devoted a lot of time and energy into projecting him as a God-fearing leader and even now, they are still determined to preserve that image. To leave that false image untouched is to cultivate a potential source of danger and a rallying point for disgruntled elements.

Ayinla: General Gowon should be asked to fill exactly the same assets declaration questionnaire that his lieutenants – the Governors, permanent secretaries etc. have been asked to complete.

Abdullahi: What is essential is that the break with his regime should be total and irreversible. The last thing we need is any semblance of a mere shuffling of the cards as if his going was a prearranged gentlemen's agreement.

Okon: We won't need to fabricate anything. In fact we'll give him credit for his humane conduct of the war, his genuine reconciliation policy thereafter, his creation of the twelve state structure and many more glowing contributions he made towards the preservation of national unity.

144

Ayinla:	At the same time, we owe it a duty to ourselves and to the world at large to set the records straight and declare with concrete examples what General Gowon's regime stood for – bribery, nepotism, aggradisement, arrogance etc.
Abdullahi:	I can't tell you how upset I was at the relevation that a supposedly God-fearing leader put Benjamin Adebekun in detention for no better cause than the crossing of telephone lines between a private citizen and his Head of State.
Ayinla:	Also, according to Chief Awolowo, the same God-fearing leader forced Mallam Gusau, his Commissioner for Development into resignation when the latter discovered that with the knowledge of the Head of State his signature or initials had been appended to a document which he hadn't ever seen.
Abdullahi:	Under the same God-fearing leader, journalist Bonny Kasayo Esinulo was detained on flimsy suspicion for 23 months in the most nefarious and rigorous solitary confinement. Augustine Ekweribe, Philip Bassey and Ramoni Bakare all died in savage detention.
Ayinla:	Similarly, the same God-fearing leader did not think fit to reprimand Governor Diette Spiff for shaving a journalist's hair and having him flogged.
Abdullahi:	All these people were ordinary citizens having wives, children and dependents – yet whatever decency, ambitions, hopes and self-respect they had were ruthlessly snuffed out.
Okon:	Abdullahi and Ayinla you are both very naive. The moment General Gowon declared jokingly that by the time he quit

145

office he would be too old to go back to the barracks, I knew he meant it. Let me add that I was never deceived about the true intentions of Gowon's Government.

He and his governors wanted to run the country as a private empire. The country was being turned into a Mafia racket with General Gowon as the Godfather, 'The Capo tuti de Capo', the boss of all bosses with governors as regional 'Capo regime', the only thing that saved us was that he was essentially a simple man without the ruthlessness to sustain his racket.

Ayinla: You are being very unfair. Surely not all the Governor's were terrors. I know for a fact that Brigadier Johnson never detained anyone.

Okon: I know what I'm talking about. Look at the way he and his governors carried on – they gave everything to their friends and sycophants. If you were a friend there was no favour too big or too small for you to have; but if you were not a friend or classified as 'not known', it didn't matter whether what you wanted was yours by right or merit – they just didn't have any time for you.

Ayinla: But surely, the General did a lot for the country.

Okon: If his argument that 'there are no bad rulers but bad advisers' is followed to its rightful conclusion, the credit for his achievement belongs to his advisers and not to him. If blame lies with the advisers so must also the credit.

Abdullahi: The same God-fearing man wanted to build a ₦20,000,000 palace for himself, in a country where 90% of the population live below subsistence level with an average

	per capita income of ₦130 per annum.
Ayinla:	The same God-fearing man sanctioned a budget of ₦300,000,000 for a perfectly useless exercise in cultural rape classified as Black Arts Festival. At the same time you and I are 'trying to try' to survive, the court-jesters and jokers were merrily planning to spend ₦90,000,000 on furniture for Black Arts Festival Village; ₦22,000,000 on street decoration for the duration of the Festival and ₦42,000,000 to fly food in for the consumption of our guests.
Abdullahi:	Not only that, the only little piece of greenery left in Lagos – the racecourse was hurriedly converted into an architectural monstrosity. Believe it or not, work was already half-completed on the racecourse before the public was told what the mad rush was all about. We just woke up to find the place covered with towering pyramids of sand. Then the Government advertised for tenders and designs to change the surrounding area to blend with the monster baby.
Okon:	The new regime should immediately announce that we care very much about international opinion but we are sorry we now have a serious government with a military posture – therefore we have no time for shows and regrettably have to cancel the Festival. Power is sweet but it will soon turn sour unless it is used for the rapid solution of pressing problems.
Ayinla:	As for the racecourse, we should cease further work forthwith and leave the site as a permanent reminder of Gowon's folly.
Soldier:	But that would be going too far.

Abdullahi:	Let us send a message to Mr Francis Obi that unless he agrees to see us immediately, our temper will soon turn from sweet to sour.
Okon:	Ayinla, call me 'Doctor' once more.
Ayinla:	Doctor.

THE VICs
(Very Important Confusionists)

WHILE waiting to see the Chairman of Nigeria Airways, the three VICs (Very Important Confusionists), Dr Okon, Ayinla and Abdullahi sent an urgent message to the Airways boss through their soldier friend. The reply from Mr Obi came over loud and clear via the airport loud-speaker: 'Ladies and gentlemen – all confusionists have been grounded and on no account will I agree to speak to them.'

Abdullahi: The problem is solved then – we'll just move over to the VIP lounge and drink all the champagne we can lay our hands on.

At the VIP lounge, there is champagne in abundance and the three confusionists help themselves freely to the first-class stuff.

Okon: I think we ought to offer our soldier friend here some champagne.

Soldier: Nonsense. No more of that champagne nonsense. This is a new regime – we are under strict orders not to drink champagne.

Ayinla: I thank God I'm not a soldier. This is a very good drink – I'm going to recommend it to all the poor people of Nigeria.

Abdullahi: When the politicians come back to power, we are going to campaign that champagne just like education, health services, water supply should be free.

Soldier: It's difficult enough dealing with you confusionists while you are sober but now

	that you are getting drunk, I'll have to shoot you. You are crazy.
Okon:	Wait a minute, officer. If you shoot all confusionists – how are you going to run the country?
Soldier:	We are determined to eliminate the confusionists wherever we find them.
Okon:	Actually, the military hold a very strong trump card. If they want to keep certain people out of politics, all they have to do is issue a decree that any civilian who is unwilling to submit to a probe of his activities and percentages during the last regime would be banned from participating in politics or publishing newspaper articles or giving public lectures.
Abdullahi:	I can't understand this pre-occupation with probes. We have more important things to do than wasting time on probes.
Okon:	Nonsense. Probes are a vital necessity. They are like purgatives – unpleasant but necessary for the purification of the body politic.
Ayinla:	Doctor, let me warn you – in your enthusiasm for purges, probes and retirement with immediate effect – just remember that there is a Yoruba saying that the same 'atori', (cane) that was used to whip the present wife will eventually be used to whip the mistress after the wife has been done away with.
Okon:	Look Ayinla – we must have probes. I'm an expert on probes.
Soldier:	You confusionists are experts on everything.
Okon:	I'm serious – I'm a specialist on probes. My doctoral thesis was on probes and it won me a distinction. Probes are not time wasting at all and I can demonstrate it.

Soldier:	How?
Okon:	First of all, give the person you want to probe one hour to write down all his assets. Any assets he hasn't put down by then is automatically forfeited.
Soldier:	What if the assets are abroad – how are you going to get hold of them?
Okon:	Simple, very simple. I don't want to say it out loud, you never know who might be listening but if you come nearer I'll whisper it into your ears.

The soldier expresses great consternation at Dr Okon's ingenious master-plan, which is conveyed to him in a whisper.

Soldier:	Which are you – genius or madman?
Okon:	Neither – just a confusionist!
Ayinla:	The major reason why I support probes is that they enable those who have not 'chopped' public money to redeem their reputation instead of being labelled as corrupt along with everybody else.
Abdullahi:	That's right. After all, Alhaji Ganiyu Dawodu who served as a Lagos State Commissioner for nine years declared publicly that he is ready to be probed at any time.
Ayinla:	Don't forget he is from 'H' Ward where people speak their minds freely. If they have cause to believe that he was just 'chopping' like the rest of them, they would just go to him and tell him face-to-face 'you are not our son anymore and no amount of money will make us vote for you'. H-Ward people are never afraid!
Soldier:	Instead of putting you people in detention, I'm going to give you a chance to do something useful. Would you like the exclusive contract for repatriating all Nigerian stolen money stashed away

	abroad in secret accounts?
Abdullahi:	That's really a heavy contract.
Okon:	I have just written a petition that all the people with illicit money abroad should form a joint venture to finance the Black Arts Festival, Trade Fair, Colour Television, the next Census, the building of the new Federal Capital as well as the Iron and Steel Complex. As a reward, the government should let them keep whatever is left plus free pardon.
Soldier:	Doctor! I'm appointing you as a consultant straight-away.
Okon:	You are a good man, officer. I hope demobilisation won't affect you.
Soldier:	Don't worry about me. I've been a professional soldier all my life. In or out of the army I will always be a soldier. I've seen action in Burma and Congo and I was right there with Federal troops at Ore.
	It is only civilians who can talk lightly about civil war. Every war is bad but civil strife is a terrible infamy – brother versus brother. Look, the war ended five years ago and even now when I think of all that blood that was shed – young lives, innocent lives wiped out I think I'm going to be sick. It's a mental picture of rotten corpse, infested injuries and vicious agony I know I'll carry to my grave.
	In war, there are no officers or men – you are all there to kill and be killed. That's why I can tolerate anything you confusionists do but don't ever start another war because if you do, the consequences will be terrible all round.
Confusionists:	(all together) – We promise.
Soldier:	Look for us soldiers – war is what is what we are trained for, so we can live with it

but for civilians its a different story.

During the last civil war, I was trying to get some refugees across a river in a canoe in an area where we knew that the enemy was within shooting distance. It was dark and the last thing we wanted was to give our position away. Unfortunately, a little child got so frightened she started crying. Its mother had to throw the child overboard otherwise the enemy would have been able to locate us. Till the day I die, I shall always carry the voice of that little child in my mind.

Abdullahi: Soldier, I think you should write a book about your war experience.

Soldier: Maybe after I leave the army. After I retire, I'm going to buy a small farm in my village and grow coco-yams, enjoy the fresh air free from traffic congestion, go fishing with my children and maybe write a book.

Ayinla: You don't seem to be afraid of demobilisation, officer.

Soldier: Those of us in the army know who the bad eggs are. They are the ones who at heart are not soldiers at all and they are as much an embarrassment to us as a potential source of danger to the relationship between the army and civilians.

Ayinla: Apart from demobilisation, the military still have to take a firm stand on probes.

Okon: The decision to be made by the new regime as regards probes involves more than listing assets. It is the far more important issue of determining what the texture and ethics of public life will be. You can be sure whatever style is set in the next two years will determine irrevocably what the pattern will be for the next thirty or forty years.

Abdullahi:	It is not enough to ask a man who has declared only eight houses out of ten to forfeit the two undeclared houses.
Okon:	You still have the problem of deciding what to do with the eight he has declared but which far exceed his honest entitlements. If you let him keep them – then there is no punishment or deterrent either for him or his successors.
Soldier:	I've decided to leave you confusionists to drown in your own confusion. Whatever, the government does you will still complain even if the government was run by Jesus Christ or Muhammed.
Okon:	Officer, have some champagne please but remember you don't have to be a saint to be a great leader. Which of the following were saints – Churchill, Lyndon Johnson, John Kennedy, Roosevelt, De Gaulle? None.
Soldier:	I can see right through your scheming – you are trying the same old game – first you try to corrupt me, next you will try to confuse me – just like you did with our last 'oga patapata'. Say your last prayers!
Abdullahi:	Please don't shoot.
Ayinla:	Okon, what is that degree that has just been conferred on you?
Okon:	RWFB.
Soldier:	So you are now Dr Okon 'LL.D'; RWFB (Retired with full benefits.)

DIAL 'T' FOR TROUBLE

THE government has just received a report which in a few days should render all the problems of the telephone user a thing of the past. At an impressive ceremony preceded by the inevitable 'cultural show', Uri Geller 'The mind bender' handed over his official report. Uri Geller is the young Jewish fellow who gained wild international fame in 1973 by performing miracles on British television.

Well, not quite miracles but he did all sorts of fantastic things like converting all black and white TV sets to colour transmission simply by winking at them; women who had for years battled with weight problems suddenly emerged from his cuddle with sylph-like elfin figures, short men became giants just by shaking hands with Uri Geller and ever the British Government was not left out.

For several months Prime Minister Ted Heath had been rehearsing his 'torn curtain' speech in which he would announce that the country was broke; the Chancellor of the Exchequer had fled with the ₦1000 left in the treasury; Christine Keeler had reluctantly accepted a peerage; the Trade Union Congress had released the country on bail; and the Atheneum Club would accept luncheon vouchers.

The annual horse racing showcase Royal Ascot would have to do without horses; the Chairman of the Confederation of British Industries had returned his Knighthood and was now living on the dole; Biggs the train-robber would be given a ticker-tape reception on Throgmorton Street for repatriating his stolen loot from Brazil; and would everybody please switch off their lights and get

155

ready for the end. Finally, BRIAN SILK would BE TIED HAND AND FOOT AND DEPORTED TO LAGOS IN EXCHANGE FOR OIL. Britain was saved by Henry Kissinger who successfully negotiated an introduction of the Prime Minister to Uri Geller. Simply by laying hands on the British Prime Minister, Uri made the country well again.

Rolls-Royce which had been on the verge of bankruptcy was back in business; oil was discovered on Britain's doorstep – the North Sea, and Arab oil money filled the treasury. The country was back on its feet – at least until Benn (not the big one) was released from detention.

At a secret session, Professor Uri Geller addressed Nigerian telephone engineers and told them all the things they already knew as follows:
"Gentlemen,

I have carried out a comprehensive survey of the telephones in Nigeria and the problem is simple and at the same time gigantic. It revolves around 'SYNCHRO-NISATION' otherwise known as 'SYNCHRO-SYSTEM'. What you have is a mixed-bag of Japanese head-sets, Canadian consoles, American monitors, British amplifiers, Hong Kong digitals, Russian buggers, French relays, Chinese mouth-pieces, Bulgarian cables, Swedish codifiers, Indian transmitters and Filipino pulsators.

It's like the United Nations – no one understands what anyone else is saying and each is out to destroy the other or at least sabotage it. For example, the 'Out of order' tone you are always getting is the result of the Russian parts issuing a communique against Chinese aggression; the 'not on seat' reply you get every time you dial a government official is the result of Irish parts testing their listening devices; and the 'Calabar lines are out of order' reply you get whenever you make trunk calls is the Hungarian Ambassador disguised as a telephone operator.

Or to put it more crudely, how would any of you like to have Japanese eyes, Chinese ears, American hair, British toes, Jewish hands, Hong Kong feet, Filipino knees, Russian necks ('red necks'), Egyptian tongue and Hungarian brains? The result is that you would become what the Americans call a 'nonfunctional person'. or what is known in some parts of Nigeria as 'USELESS MAN'.

During my short stay, I have observed the following frustrations and inadequacies of your telephones.

MUSIC WHEN YOU DON'T WANT IT

When you dial an Apapa number, you would nine times out of ten suddenly hear music after dialling the first three digits. This is the result of the Russian parts jamming the America transmitters.

THE LIE DETECTOR

Yesterday, I asked the telephonist in my hotel to tell Chief Arabise whenever he called that I was out. He had been bugging me too much for a contract. To my astonishment, the Chief was able to get through on to my extension direct without going via the switchboard operator!

THE LONELINESS OF THE LONG DISTANCE CALLER

Last Sunday, I booked a call to London. It took 23 hours before it finally came through. Every hour, the international operator called to say 'we are just about to connect you.' I dared not go to the toilet or bath or dining room for fear of missing my call. When it finally came through, I couldn't be heard at the other end! In that time, I could have taken a plane to London and back again.

THE BUSINESS WRECKER

Mr Salau of Agingbidi says he is totally fed up with complaining to the authorities that his business as an estate agent has been completely wrecked by his telephone. For example, yesterday he lost a big deal that would have set him up for life, because his client swore he spent three hours trying to ring him but to no avail – his line was continuously engaged, therefore he had to try another agency. Mr Salau swears that he did not make or receive a single call during the period concerned.

THE HOME WRECKER

Mrs Lakeru of Ibadan was calling a friend when she was startled by a familiar sounding voice. It was a crossed line and it was a shock to recognise her husband's voice obviously booking a room at a local new hotel for the week-end. She held her breath when she heard Mr Lakeru ask for a suite in the name of Mr and Mrs Lakeru. As she had never had cause to suspect her husband during ten years of marriage, she was sure he wanted to treat her to a special week-end away from all her household chores.

She nearly fainted when her husband announced that urgent business matters required him to travel to Abidjan for the week-end. He packed his suitcase and drove in the direction of the airport only to make a detour back to the hotel. In the meantime, Mrs Lakeru had made straight for the hotel. Mr Lakeru walked into the hotel suite accompanied by the 'assistant' Mrs Lakeru only to be confronted by the real Mrs Lakeru!.

THE EMBARRASSING INTERRUPTION

Prince Ukpasi of Onitsha was boasting on the telephone to his newly acquired girl friend that money was no problem – he would set her up in a new flat in Lagos, buy her a car etc. when the conversation was interrupted by the stern voice of the manager of the local bank who somehow managed to get through – 'Prince, I'm fed up with returning your bounced cheques'.

THE PRIORITY CALL

First thing Monday morning Mallam Alli was telephoning a girl he had just met to book a date for the following evening. At the same time Chike Enyamba was frantically telephoning his bank manager to please extend his overdraft for a few more days to enable him to clear his goods from the ports. The two telephone calls got crossed and in desperation, Mr Enyamba had to plead:

'Mallam, you are looking for a WOMAN, I am looking for MONEY, it's only Monday morning – don't you think I ought to have priority?'

THE SECURITY RISK

Mr Adesekun was speaking to a beer distributor at Abeokuta when he suddenly discovered that he was on a crossed line with DODAN BARRACKS!

THE ANSWER MY FRIENDS . . .

My report would not be complete if I did not at least offer a few solutions, but I'm afraid 'The answer, my friends, is blowing in the wind'. In the meantime if it is your misfortune to have to make a telephone call, carry out these steps:

1 THINK of the number you want.
2 Then DIAL the number you do NOT want.
3 You'll then get the number you WANT.
Try it – it works!

Signed
Professor Uri Geller – Mind-bender.

EDDIE MY LOVE

I know Mr Edwin Clark gets blamed for everything, but the Ministry of Information has assured me he is not responsible for the telephones and he NEVER said:

'I SAW TELEPHONES EVERYWHERE.' Neither did he say, 'THE TELEPHONES HAVE BEEN TOO FAMILIAR'.

DEATH BY TELEPHONE

Mathew Nathan, expatriate night manager of a new Lagos Hotel came off the night shift at midnight on a cold wet night. He couldn't ever get used to night work – he just couldn't get to sleep afterwards. He was stead-

159

ily becoming an insomniac. This agitated him terribly but he needed the money.

On getting home, he took FOUR sleeping tablets instead of the two prescribed by his doctor. He got into bed and waited for the tablets to work. At 2 a.m. just when he was beginning to doze off, his telephone rang. The caller wanted Miss Alice Ebong. Mathew answered politely:

'I'm sorry you've got a wrong number – there's no Alice Ebong here.'

He took FOUR more tablets and tried to go to sleep once more. At 3 a.m. the telephone rang again just as Mathew was about dozing off. It was the same voice again:

'Hi Alice, it's me Oladele.

Mathew really lost his temper this time. 'Bloody hell! It's 3 a.m. for Christ sake and I told you before, there's no Alice here.' Greatly agitated, Mathew took FOUR more tablets, adjusted the sheets and was really determined to sleep.

At 4 a.m. the telephone rang again. Wild with agitation, Mathew jerked the receiver off its hook but before he could bang it, he heard a sultry voice at the other end:

'This is Alice Ebong. I wonder whether you have any telephone message for me.'

This was really too much for Mathew, he banged the phone, smashed it up, jerked the connection wire and took SIX more tablets. By 6 a.m. Mathew Nathan was dead. Coroner's verdict – 'Death by misadventure while lying in bed.'

WHAT ELSE HAVE I MISSED?

ONE of the hazards of travelling out of the country is the risk of missing some of the most eventful happenings in the history of the country. The most sour complaint we have received so far has come from Alhaji Isangbetoh who was out of the country when both the first and second coups occurred.

Unfortunately for Alhaji, he was also out of the country when the 'change of Government' was effected on July 29. Needless to say, Alhaji Isangbetoh has immediately fired two complaints to ALHAJI MAITAMA SULE. Chief Commissioner of the Public Complaints Commission:

COMPLAINT NO. 1

Why were intending travellers not informed of the imminent change of government and given the opportunity to witness the historic events of July 29?

COMPLAINT NO. 2

Is it pure coincidence that all the people I want to complain about are members of the Public Complaints Commission?

While awaiting the reply to his complaints, Alhaji has been going round the country. He can't believe his eyes – suddenly everyone is so civil and mindful of right and wrong. Alhaji Isangbetoh could hardly believe this is the same country he left only three months ago. Consequently he has felt compelled to ask friends and foes alike – 'What else have I missed?' Here are some of the big news items he missed.

FIRST THE POLICE NEWS

A few days ago, a policeman arrested a very, very senior official of the present government for a traffic offence. The senior official (who was wearing civilian clothes) pleaded for leniency but the policeman would have none of it. Looking desperate, the official pulled out his wallet and offered the policeman ₦10 as a bribe.

The policeman shook his head and this prompted the official to double his offer to ₦20. The policeman shook his head once more and declared 'Look mister, this is Muhammed's regime. If you "chop", you "quench". I don't want to be retired. I'm afraid you'll have to come along with me to the police station for your summons.'

The policeman got into the car and instructed the offender to proceed to the station. The official was persistent and increased his offer to ₦30 with the remark 'If you don't take it, I'm sure your boss at the station will be only too glad to take it'. At this point, the policeman firmly declared 'That's where you are wrong mister. Things have changed – just as they are watching us, we are also watching them. Boss or no boss, anyone caught "chopping" is going to be punished.'

On getting to the station, the policeman handed over the offender to his boss who immediately pulled out his charge-sheet and was poised to issue the summons. At this point he turned to the offender and demanded his name. When the official gave his name, both the policeman and his boss started saluting 'six at a time'. The official immediately gave instructions that the policeman should be promoted to the rank of Inspector.

NOW THE EXAM NEWS

Mr Isa Wayo, Proprietor of Miracle Results in Science College entered seventy students for the WAEC exams. The results were published last week – all the students failed. Disregarding the fact that the school had neither science teachers nor laboratories; and students were fed on gari and dry fish three times a day (and nothing on

Sundays), Mr Wayo has complained to the Public Complaints by telegram:

'THERE IS SOMETHING SERIOUSLY WRONG WITH THE WAEC EXAMS!'

AND NOW NEWS FROM THE STATES

A newly appointed state Governor readily agreed to see a delegation of local businessmen who wished to 'pay their respects' at Government Lodge. They turned up in their fleet of Mercedes-Benz cars and treated the Governor to a generous dose of flattery.

The leader of the delegation wished him well and expressed regret that they had not called on him earlier. This they assured him was not due to disrespect on their part but rather to the Governor's stern demeanour in all his photographs so far published in the newspapers.

The leader of the delegation then sought the indulgence of the Governor to mention a matter that was close to their hearts. The Governor gave immediate encouragement only to discover that the subject matter was CEMENT, in respect of which the 'controlled price' of ₦2.60 had been announced by the Federal Military Government.

The delegation pleaded that the Governor should give them a few months to go on selling their stocks at the best prices they could get and make some profit for themselves before the Governor imposed the controlled price. The Governor cunningly declared that since like him they were all men of the world he didn't see why this could not be done.

The delegation was jubilant and as a mark of their appreciation, they made 'a donation' of ₦2,000 to the Governor as a 'token of respect'. The Governor thanked them warmly and assured them of his co-operation at all times. He left the money untouched in a tray, ordered a fresh round of drinks to be served and retreated to his bedroom from where he phoned the local army commander and requested the immediate despatch of twelve soldiers with horsewhips to join the party.

The local hospital has reported heavy casualty among the businessmen and added that any evidence of severe beatings from horsewhips is pure coincidence.

SPECIAL PRAYERS

Hundreds of people who have had to wait for months and even years before they could be issued with a passport if at all, because they were not 'well-connected' or 'properly introduced' turned up at a rally yesterday to offer special prayers and thanksgiving to Col. Joe Garba, the Commissioner for External Affairs who, apart from being the first public officer in the history of this country to declare publicly that every citizen of this country is by right entitled to a passport, has actually made it possible for hundreds of ordinary people to collect their passports without having to bribe anybody.

An elderly gentleman commented – 'Since 1914, successive governments of this country have used one ploy or the other to deny passports to ordinary people. I would never have believed I would live to see the day when the government would pay for newspaper advertisements to invite people to collect their passports.'

AND FINALLY THE PCC NEWS

(i) Chief Esha Sekonda has complained to the Public Complaints Commission that it is of paramount importance that it should be declared official policy that whenever anyone is compulsorily sacked for 'negligence, inefficiency, corruption or old age', a BETTER person should be appointed as his successor.
(ii) Following the setting up of the PCC, civil servants have started agitating for a civil service complaints commission to handle complaints by civil servants against the public!

NO MORE PAIN

A group of young doctors have declared their unequivocal support for Brigadier Haruna's call for a massive improvement in the attitude of those rendering service to the public via hospitals, post offices, airports, hotels, etc. They have however warned that if there's going to be a clean up of the medical service, it must start at the Ministry of Health itself.

The doctors went on to complain about inexcusable delay on the part of the ministry in sending out maintenance engineers to fix equipment that have broken down in the hospitals. As for drugs, the doctors say that the system of drug control is in complete confusion – either they have to wait for months to get basic and essential drugs or they suddenly find the hospital flooded with five years supply of drugs they don't want.

However, an official of the ministry has stated – 'I'm sick and tired of doctors complaining. They are as money crazy as the rest of us. The only people they are interested in are their own private patients.'

Anyway, there is no denying that the hospitals are in a mess. It is really appalling that there are reports that patients have to provide money for petrol before the ambulance would move; patients have to queue for up to three or four hours just to get registered; patients sleep on the floor; operations are cancelled at the last minute without valid explanations.

Water shortage and power failure are not infrequent; five times more babies out of every 100 die within the first month than in Sweden; the biggest rats are to be found in our hospitals; the food served by hospitals is invariably poor and of course it is generally believed NOBODY GIVES A DAMN.

THE LAST, LAST AND FINAL SALUTE

A HISTORICAL review of General Gowon's years of office clearly demonstrates that quite unknown to him, his administration was from the beginning set on a collision course against six easily identifiable groups. Right at the top of the list were the old politicians whose appetite for the excitement of party politics and the attendant, ethnic rivalry, intrigues, grass roots mobilisation and power-trading were entirely frustrated by Gowon's ban on politics throughout the nine years he was Head of State. As far as money was concerned, individually the old politicians had little to complain about. Most found lush pastures either by dealing in arms, securing juicy contracts and even accepting public office. For the most part, they made more money while out of politics than before but this was no substitute for the real excitement of politics which they craved. Even now, many of them openly admit that they 'are born politicians' and will die politicians. Particularly towards the end of Gowon's regime and with all the oil money floating around, the old politicians got increasingly impatient as the General followed one mistake with an even more damaging error of judgement. Among the old politicians there were many who genuinely felt that with the oil money, they would have been able to perform wonders and confidently drew attention to their past record. For example, they pointed out that with a budget of only ₦15,000,000, under the old politicians a particular state had been able to introduce free Primary Education, Housing Corporation, University, Teaching Hospital, first-class roads etc. The same state now has a budget of ₦300,000,000 and didn't seem able to get anything together – even what was there before was allowed to deteriorate. They were the first to conclude that not only did Gowon govern badly, he also didn't know how to handle money.

The second group was made up of the professionals who as magistrates, doctors, teachers, dentists, accountants, engineers, and technicians, had served the colonial government under a unitary administration.

For many of them, their careers had taken them on assignments to all the nooks and corners of the country. For example, five years – in Warri may be followed by three years in Benin followed by four years in Jos. Their salaries were generally low but they bore the inconvenience of shifting their families around and swopping respectable accommodation for dingy quarters with dignity. For them the real prize was the annual overseas leave spent in the U.K. at Government expense both before and after Independence. When oil money started flowing in, this group was astonished at being completely side-tracked just as it had been in the years immediately following independence. As a group they were not powerful. However, they had influence through their children who had been generally well-educated and held quite powerful positions in the Civil Service as well as within the professions.

The third group consisted of the ever increasing breed of educated young men and women who were split into two sub-groups. Namely those educated abroad and those educated at home. What united them was their common frustration. In the years immediately following Independence, to be a graduate meant an automatic ticket to a cushy job, mostly in the Civil Service with Government quarters thrown in. Under Gowon, it was not enough to be educated – you needed to be well-connected as well. This created a pool of disillusioned young men who spent months writing applications for jobs, attending interviews, and finally having to offer bribes to get jobs. It was shattering for them to discover that their not so well educated contemporaries were making money hand over fist from selling second-hand imported cars, bribing their way through Customs and throwing money all over the place and graphically telling them – 'see where your education got you!' Thus the educated group that had taken it for granted that it would be the succeeding elite quite quickly found that apart from looking for jobs, they had to pay extortionist rent mostly one year or two years in advance from salaries that were earned monthly. So they started their working life already in debt from having to borrow to raise advance rent.

The fourth group was made up of the large mass of the mostly rural people. They lived relatively simple lives close to the land and far from the complexities of city life. They placed great value on honesty, hard work, moderation and simple pleasures. Much of their lives centred around their family and their religion. Through education, they believed that whatever they could not have, their children could – therefore they were particularly diligent in educating their children, mostly through mission schools. To this end no sacrifice was too great. Ironically, General Gowon's father was an outstanding example of this group. When Gowon talked about millions and billions of Naira, this was the group that really couldn't identify with what the General was beating the drum about. They were far more interested in roads, electricity and water supply. In fact there are many who believe that Gowon started 'missing the road' from the day his father died.

The fifth group consisted of the 'Oilmen' – these were young graduates who had joined the Civil Service almost from the beginning of Nigeria's era as an oil producing country. Most of them were reared by Abdul Atta who was then Permanent Secretary, Ministry of Finance and handled oil affairs from the beginning. In determining oil policy and dealing with the oil companies, Atta gave his young lieutenants their head and encouraged them to use their own initiative. It was this group that was probably the first to realise that whoever controlled oil power had the greatest leverage in government. It was this group that were most bitter when under Gowon, they found that control of oil power lay firmly under the Ministry of Mines and Power reporting directly and almost exclusively to the Head of State. The hard-core of this group of young technocrats had moved to the Nigerian National Oil Corporation only to discover that oil policy was determined by the Ministry of Mines and Power; and the Nigerian National Oil Corporation with the consent of Gowon was itself, firmly controlled by the Ministry of Mines and Power.

The sixth group and by far the most powerful group were the young officers in the Army and to a lesser extent in the Navy and Air Force.

Most of them were only a few years younger than Gowon himself, but they regarded themselves as professional soldiers full stop. To them the indiscipline, drift and rot that had set in under Gowon were distasteful. They had been dyed in the best traditions of Sandhurst and other officer training institutions and to them Gowon's antics, his love of shows and vacillations were contrary to the best traditions of the Armed Forces. This group was sufficiently confident and didn't need the flattery of sycophants. Most of them joined the Army out of choice – mostly because their fathers or relatives were ex-servicemen. Not only did they realise that they were sufficiently bright to go to University if they had so chosen, many of them were well read in economics and politics and several of them qualified as engineers etc. within the Armed Forces. This was the group that was to supplant Gowon and put a brake on the drift. As a group they fit into the image of patriotic soldiers capable of guaranteeing law and order provided it is used to rescue the country.

There were in fact two other groups – the natural rulers, particularly the Northern Emirs who regarded Gowon and his lieutenants as 'upstarts' who didn't show enough respect and in certain cases (both North and South) were not, sufficiently knowledgeable about the traditions of the people they sought to rule. The last group was made up of housewives and wage earners who throughout Gowon's regime fought a losing battle against scarcity, shortages, and inflation – prices just went UP and UP and UP.

Beginning from January of this year, all these powerful groups were systematically driven to despair by the actions of General Gowon and the ridiculous utterances of his Chief Spokesman and No. 1 Worshipper, Edwin Clark, Commissioner for Information. In addition, it has been suggested in very high quarters that the last straw that broke the camel's back was Gowon's attempt to impose his appointment of Mr I. G. T. Ordor (formerly General Manager of the Port Harcourt Refinery) as the General Manager and Chief Executive of the Nigerian Nation Oil Corporation on the Federal Executive Council. Quite contrary to Paragraph 4, Section II of N.N.O.C. Decree dated 18 April 1971, which clearly states that the General Manager of N.N.O.C. could only be appointed on the recommendation of the Commissioner for Mines and Power and the approval of the Federal Executive Council, General Gowon made Ordor's appointment by Executive Order.

On 27 July, when General Gowon set off for Kampala to attend the 13th OAU Summit, all the powerful groups whom he had alienated were fully represented at the Airport. The crowd burst into wild applause when the General proceeded into the plane and the door shut after he had received three salutes from the Commander of the Brigade of the Guards – Col. Joe Garba. Incidently among the Military, that last salute is regarded as vintage stuff which was fortunately preserved for posterity by the television cameras.

There were many in the audience who knew that it was the LAST, LAST AND FINAL SALUTE and a signal for everyone to go home, say his prayers, wait for the official radio announcement and hopefully witness the beginning of another era without a single drop of blood being shed.

170

DECLINE AND FALL

THERE is a lot of merit in the assertion that General Gowon's fall originated at the point when he ceased to regard himself as 'a simple soldier' who happened to have been thrust into the glare of the highest public office in the country, but nevertheless anxious to get back to the barracks and camaraderie of the officers mess where he was easily liked and very much in his element.

His relish of the trappings of office and the flatteries of sycophants was too obvious and contradicted the austere bearing and disciplined leadership that would have been more in accord with the prevailing circumstances.

Not only should he have demonstrated his amusement at being hoisted as a world leader, he actively encouraged the adulation of the world stage at precisely the same time his popularity at home was gradually being whittled away.

In a matter of months, the response of the Nigerian public changed from hero-worship to passivity and finally boredom intermitted with total alienation. In fairness to him, not even his worst enemies could declare him wicked – he was just misguided. THE COUNTRY HAD SIMPLY OUTGROWN HIM.

This was inevitable – in nine years of being in office, Gowon had made little or no effort to understand the reality of basic economics or the political processes and machinery that sustained him. He became like the late Alhaji Tafawa Balewa the storekeeper who had no knowledge of what he was supposed to be safeguarding or from whom. If someone broke into the store, he could always count on his innocence to exonerate him.   It would have been more in keeping with his finer instincts if he had told those who saw him as a world leader – 'A joke is a joke – I have had enough trouble ruling a country with a population of at least 60 million out of which close to 30 per cent don't know whether they live in Dahomey, Chad, Niger or Cameroons. Millions even now don't know that the government has changed hands because they didn't know that the government existed in the first place.'

Instead, the pursuit of the mirage of world leadership became an obsession manifested by the eager grab of the Chairmanship of OAU, the hosting of ECOWAS; the mindless address at the United Nations; and the astonishing declaration of the Black Arts Festival as the pinnacle of our scale of priorities. It was to prove an expensive lesson – namely, any African leader determined to play the world leadership role is playing with fire.

Apart from the fact that African political processes are still in a state of flux, the governmental institutions are fragile imitations borrowed from other civilisations. Even more important, their own countrymen are far more concerned with the basic essentials – food and shelter.

In other words, a good leader is not necessarily the man who maintains the right posture on Vietnam, Apartheid, Nuclear Proliferation, or the Middle East conflict – these are merely 'extras'. For millions, a good government is one that builds roads, hospitals, schools, houses and provides food, water and electricity. A bad government is simply one that doesn't.

Apart from growing out of step with the country he ruled, General Gowon steadily lost touch with his immediate lieutenants who were much chagrined that not only were some of the most important national issues decided contrary to their advice but also they learnt of the decisions or indecisions for the first time from the radio, television or newspapers. With each growing crisis, rather than widen the channel of advice, he narrowed his vision and withdrew into himself.

A classic example was his inept handling of the

doctors strike. It was obvious that the doctors had legitimate grounds for rejecting the recommendations of the Udoji panel – and this was clearly recognised by Admiral Wey and Major-General Hassan who in negotiating with the doctors adopted conciliatory tactics and assured the doctors that their grievances would be properly examined by the government and appropriate redress would follow.

A potentially explosive situation was defused and the doctors were quite prepared to go back to work having made their point. To their astonishment, within hours Gowon adopted an aggressive pose quite contrary to the understanding the doctors had won from his lieutenants.

It was obvious that the General had overruled their advice. Instead he saw the strike as a challenge to his authority and went on to issue a fatuous order to the effect that if the doctors didn't immediately call off their strike he would obtain doctors from elsewhere to man government hospitals.

This was clearly a ridiculous threat – one thing you can't produce overnight are doctors. The result was predictable – the doctors called his bluff! The rest is history – Gowon had administered the wrong medicine, and the ensuing crisis rocked the foundation of his Government.

While the crisis was boiling, General Gowon chose to make official visits to Togo and Dahomey, thus the government was virtually paralysed while the Head of State was prancing to the cultural dancing, welcome addresses and comradely flattery of our neighbours.

What a lot of Nigerians found difficult to stomach were the constant reports and photographs of the Head of State receiving endless delegations, flying off to foreign lands and giving money away left right and centre when millions of our people are daily confronted with poverty, disease, hunger and illiteracy.

In other words international fame was the ultimate prize to be won at all costs even at the expense of urgent domestic issues. Many were astonished that at precisely the time that teachers in the South Eastern State hadn't been paid their salaries for close to six months, the General had on the spur of the moment grandly offered to pay the salaries of civil servants in one of the Caribbean Islands.

To crown it all, General Gowon committed the unpardonable offence of criticising his own people while abroad. When a Caribbean Island reporter asked him what effect our oil wealth had on the people of this country, the General minced no words and flatly declared that it had turned us into a nation of lazy people. This was a ridiculous answer because for a start, millions of Nigerians don't even know about our oil wealth.

For many, oil money in fact made life more difficult. Not only had prices shot up to astronomical heights, but their crops close to the oilfields had been destroyed and the ecology of their immediate environment rendered permanently beyond rescue by the leakages, overspills and waste from the oil fields.

The final disenchantment came when General Gowon announced, right in the middle of the Udoji crisis, at Chief C. O. Lawson's send-off party that the errors of his government should be blamed not on him but on his advisers because according to him there were no such things 'as bad rulers but bad advisers'.

This led many into wondering about who was really running the country. Was it the Head of State or his advisers and if the answer was his advisers – then why not turn the country over to the advisers anyway?

Even more damning was the view that the system of government had deteriorated to the level where ordinary people were beginning to wonder about the sense in doing honest work for modest wages when there was all this money around to be had for free from fraudulent deals and contracts which were not meant to be executed.

Policemen, teachers, postal clerks, and engineers and doctors began to query the sanity of working from morning to night when you could earn 100 times more by supplying cement or gravel to the government.

Further disillusion came with the harassment of the young editor of 'Newbreed' Magazine who had dared to print an interview with a Federal commissioner who clearly confirmed that he had deviously used his position to feather his own nest. By his own account, even though he started public life six years before with very modest assets, he was now worth a cool million.

Many had taken it for granted that a corrective regime did not allow such things to happen. Neither could the public stomach the flagrant 'hijacking' of government cement from the high seas. One would have thought that the fear of swift and certain punishment by the military would dissuade even the most hardened grab-bers.

Rather than face the grave social, economic and social issues, the General chose to lecture the nation that Nigerians hadn't learnt their lesson – therefore he would not quit the stage until the 'new Nigerian' had emerged.

The logical question of course was – who are the new Nigerians? Are they the sycophants or court-jesters or are they the cynics who with a shrug of the shoulders warned – 'Why worry, one chop-chop government will be followed by another. Praise God and wait for your turn?'

To compound his error of judgement, the General aged only 40 chose to arrogate to himself the title 'FATHER OF THE NATION' while the very foundation of the nation was being violently rocked by blatant corruption and stealing on the grandest scale. What was really amazing was the competitive greed of the main culprits.

When a public official who had swindled the government of ₦100,000 heard that a colleague had pulled-off a ₦250,000 masterpiece, he promptly decided that it was time for him to pull off a ₦500,000 deal just to keep ahead.

The last straw came when it was officially anounced that as his own share of the ₦31 billion Development Plan, the Head of State proposed a ₦20,000,000 State

House on Victoria Island, not to mention a ₦200,000 yacht for himself. The chicken finally came to roost when the Grand Khaddi, who in effect is the Chief Justice of the North re-echoed the words of Major-General Hassan Katsina that the country was corrupt from THE TOP downwards – this was really the drum beat for THE END.

NIGHT MUST FALL

AT the beginning of this year, General Gowon commissioned a firm of Auditors to write a comprehensive report on his administration since 1966. The draft report, beautifully bound, was handed to him on Sunday, 27 July 1975. Unfortunately, the General was in such a hurry to catch his plane to Kampala, he never got round to reading it. He was still carrying the report under his arm as he embarked the plane and had every intention of reading it en route. Even more unfortunate for the General, the constant interruptions from members of his delegation who continuously flattered and congratulated him on his wonderful running of the Government prevented him from opening the report. Unknown to the General, someone had stocked the plane with an ample supply of 'Gowon For Ever Champagne' which accounted for the general merriment and riotous bottom pinching on board. The plane that took the General to Kampala returned to Lagos on the same day. A casual search revealed that the report was still lying unopened and unread underneath the General's seat. Here is an extract (expurgated) from the Auditor's report:

GOWON & CO. LIMITED
(Report of the Auditors to the Shareholders of Gowon & Co. Ltd)

. . . We have now completed our audit of the above-named Company's performance from 1966 to 1975. During the course of our audit, we observed certain matters which we consider should be formally brought to your notice.

1. HEADQUARTERS (DODAN BARRACKS)

We had been misled into believing that the Company's headquarters was located in a barracks. After several vain attempts to locate the barracks, we gave up the search. We did, however, come across a big sprawling building located in spacious grounds that resembled something of a cross between the Taj Mahal and the White House. How the story ever got around that the Managing Director lived in a barracks is beyond our imagination.

2. CONTROL

We were never quite certain about who controlled the Company. There were several key areas where the Company had no policy at all or pursued policies that were neither consistent nor sensible. What was clear was that there was plenty of room for drift while vital decisions were either not made at all or made on an ad hoc basis only to be subsequently reversed. We found several instances where the Company had acted in clear breach of its Memorandum and Articles of Association particularly in the giving away of Company funds to foreign countries. Since there was no provision for such gifts in the Vote, we propose to surcharge the Managing Director as the gifts are clearly disallowable for Income Tax because they were not 'necessarily incurred for the benefit of the business'.

3. TURNOVER

We found the Managing Director guilty of acquiescing to the deliberate inflation of the Turnover (Census) figures. While the total figure was clearly dubious, the regional distribution was certainly questionable.

4. SECURITY

Security was entrusted to a member of staff designated 'Chief of Staff' – his performance both prior to his appointment and thereafter is the subject of another report marked 'secret'. Suffice to say that at no time did the gentleman in question enjoy the confidence of the security staff, the customers (public), or the press at whom he threw wild and ill-advised accusations of corruption. The same gentleman has been credited with a certain athletic feat (which we are unable to substantiate) which should surely earn him a place in the Guinness Book of Records (Cycling).

5. CAPITAL EXPENDITURE

We observed that contracts were awarded in a most haphazard manner. We have, however, been unable to confirm that in certain cases, contractors were specifically instructed that on no account were they to fulfil contracts for which handsome advance payments had been made. We did however, notice some instances where contracts on which advance payments had been made were cancelled for non-performance only to be followed by the same contract being awarded to the same contractor at an even higher figure.

Other strange events related to contracts in respect of which no one could remember who had commissioned them in the first place. We also found many instances where payments were made to contractors even before the contract had been awarded. Our random check revealed that three-quarters of the contracting Companies which we sampled and which had received heavy payments were either non-existent or had 'back-to-back; belly-to-belly' connections with senior officials of the Company. We would add that the country is littered with contracts that were never started at all or have been permanently abandoned half-way even though heavy advances in both local and foreign currencies had been made.

6. ENTERTAINMENT EXPENSES

We were staggered at the amount of money spent by the Company on entertainment. Apart from the huge amounts lavished on the Managing Director's Annual Birthday Party, Managing Director's Christmas Party; Managing Director's New Year's Party, Managing Director's Eve of Departure to U.K. Party; Managing Director's Safe Return from China Party, etc., there were astronomical bills for entertaining ECOWAS visitors, uncountable cultural shows, balloons etc. We were, however, never quite certain why the Black Arts Festival, ECOWAS, Friendship Games etc. each necessitated the purchase of a new fleet of motor vehicles. We would add that according to the official log book, the Managing Director persistently idled away valuable Company time receiving an endless stream of foreign visitors and home-grown contact men. We report on this and other related matters under a separate report marked – 'Operation Fantastic'.

7. ADVERTISING

We expended a considerable amount of time and effort on vouching advertising expenses and have concluded that less than 10 per cent of the advertising expenses was for the Company's products – the rest went towards advertising the Managing Director and projecting his image as a 'God-fearing father of the nation'.

8. CONSULTANCY SERVICES

It would appear that the recommendations of the Consultants (Udoji & Co.) completely confused the Managing Director and very nearly brought the Company down on its knees. It rapidly led to grave discontent among the staff and caused general industrial chaos.

While on the subject of consultants, we would mention an occasion when three Departmental Heads (Permanent Secretaries) who were supposed to be jointly controlling a project could not remember which of them had commissioned a consultant (who was charging the Company ₦100,000 per day) when he submitted his beautifully bound report. There was another occasion

180

when four different groups of consultants were paid for the same project and none of them knew that the other had been commissioned and certainly did not know who they were supposed to be reporting to.

9. SUBSIDIARY COMPANIES

We observed that the subsidiary Companies, otherwise known as Statutory Corporations were a law unto themselves. They neither reported to nor took any notice whatever of the directives from Headquarters. None of them showed a profit (not even the Company licensed to print money!) and they operated on the basis that it was too bad they were neither efficient nor profitable but they certainly knew how to make huge losses.

10. ACQUISITION OF SHARES

Through the Indigenisation Decree, the Company sought the participation of employees (Nigerians) in ownership of the Company's equity so that they could control the 'commanding heights' in industry! This is the subject of a separate report marked 'For your Ears Only'. Suffice to say that there were indeed some very funny goings-on in this regard. This prompted a certain gentleman to ask 'where would I be without my friends?' This drew the retort 'with a little help from your friends, you can own anything and everything'.

11. OIL REVENUE

It would appear that only the Managing Director and one other very senior official of the Company knew exactly how much the oil revenue was and how it was spent.

Finally, we wish to place on record our appreciation of the Managing Director's genuine contribution towards peace; to congratulate him on preserving the Company during the Civil War; to commend him for his statesman-like efforts at reconciliation thereafter; to laud him for opening twelve branches thoughout the country and finally to wish him well in his 'retirement with full benefits'.

It is unfortunate that the Managing Director allowed too many employees, particularly the Branch Managers (Governors), to act as if without them, the sun won't shine. But they forgot that sooner or later NIGHT MUST FALL.

Signed:................
ORIDOTA, ODENSON & CO.
Auditors:
'H' Ward
OKEPOPO

GOWON & CO.
THE BRANCH MANAGERS (GOVERNORS) AUDIT REPORT

'Peace is not the absence of strife
But the presence of social justice'

WE have had to refrain from including the above quotation in our official report. Nevertheless, we must place on record the fact that virtually in all the Branches we visited, the largest number of complaints from customers (the public) centred around serious allegations suggesting that almost without exception, the Branch Managers (Governors) ran the Branches single-handedly without any regard to social justice. Assets, funds and amenities were generally distributed, without any regard to fairness or equity. Over and over again, we found that with the exception of the western branch, the largest benefits were invariably diverted to the Branch Managers' area of origin. In all the Branches we visited, we observed that staff promotions, location of industries and the award of contracts had to have the blessing of the Branch Manager who gave or withheld approval according to his whims and caprices. Our examination of Branch returns revealed disturbing examples of squandermania ranging from staggering to piffling sums.

It is not our intention to single out any particular Branch Manager for approbriation but the performance of one of the Eastern Branch Manager brought virtually every member of our audit team to tears. It is our opinion that when an ethnic group has suffered so much from the ravages of civil war, they deserve to be treated with greater mercy.

We received persistent complaints that rather than heal old wounds, the East Central State administration festered new sores and infected the area with greed, selfishness and complete blindness to the legitimate demands of the customers. Head Office was continually pestered for funds which consistently found their way to private purses and crazy schemes. To put it crudely, it was as if this particular Branch Manager who, destiny had cast as his own people's Moses, had decided 'I HAVE FOUND MY OWN PROMISED LAND' and turned round to exhort his people 'NOW, YOU GO AND FIND YOURS . . . or wait until the second coming of Christ'.

Without any regard to propriety or moderation, Company money was lavished on Rolls Royce, Masserati, private mansions and exclusive retreats. We were unable to establish the purpose or justification for ₦500,000 of Company money as well as ₦1,200,000 of fertilisers etc., skilfully diverted into the Branch Manager's wife's private Company called 'Otu Olu Obodo Society Ltd' We had been deliberately misled into believing that it was a debt-collecting agency for the exclusive benefit of the Company. We were astonished to discover that the Branch Manager was engaged in a nefarious shake-down of Company staff by soliciting or turning a blind eye towards donations for the funeral expenses of the Branch Manager's father-in-law. This is a point that calls for further investigation because we could not understand why in spite of all the money already salted away by Branch Managers, they could not bury their deceased relations and in-laws out of their own pocket – rather they felt compelled to resort to Company funds, vehicles, food, drinks etc., or by organising collections from our dealers and contractors. This was a practice we found rampant in virtually all the Branches as well as Head Office. We also discovered that Company property (generators, blankets, etc.) valued at ₦500,000 had been siphoned away to in-laws as a belated bride price. In view of the above-mentioned highly fraudulent practices, we have no hesitation in confirming that the only thing that unites our Eastern customers is their intense hatred of this particular Branch Manager.

We have also examined the performance of another Eastern Branch Manager whose area of jurisdiction embraced virtually all the oil fields and report that he has been unanimously awarded the first prize for LAZINESS COMPOUNDED BY ARROGANCE MULTIPLIED BY SQUANDERMANIA AND STUBBORNESS. This Branch Manager, like his counterpart already referred to as well as their Western colleague not only failed to build badly needed roads for which they had collected handsome subvention but also allowed the ones already in existence to deteriorate almost beyond recognition. He boasted openly that he never got out of bed before 11.00 a.m. and by 3.00 p.m., he was to be found either on the golf course or gadding about in his private plane or carousing on his ₦500,000 yacht. To this day, we are still unable to fathom what he actually achieved in nine years in office. There is no single road, industry, office, hospital or school that anyone could point to as the handiwork of this particular Manager.

As for the other Eastern Branch Manager, it is no business of ours to comment on leaks suggesting that the Branch Manager's wife was subject to severe 'general beating of the body', (he is not the first or the last man to beat his wife). We were however, concerned about the damage to Company image by leaks suggesting that the Branch Manager had acquired an assistant wife without bothering to look outside his own domestic staff. We found that the Branch Manager re-instated the Branch Accountant even though the latter was caught with his hand in the till. We did however, receive an explanation from the Branch Manager. He declared, 'The Accountant is my friend'. Needless to add, we found convincing evidence that the Branch Manager had substantial interests in firms to which juicy contracts were awarded contrary to expert advice.

We were unable to visit the Western Branch owing to a combination of poor roads and traffic congestion at the Branch Office. We have, however, received reports from local auditors suggesting that the Branch Manager did not do anything for the branch and left it almost exactly as he found it. We have not yet been able to investigate newspaper reports suggesting that the Branch Manager privately acquired 20 square miles of farmland. This is a lot of land for one person. In fact, it is about 1/15,000 of the total land area in the country or just a little smaller than Lagos! It does appear though that the Branch Manager tried to grab control of the Company's training school (University) by tampering with its Memorandum and Articles of Association.

As for the Lagos Branch Manager, he started off with great promise and all indications were that he would do wonders for the Branch. Unfortunately, though a young man himself, he abandoned the company and advice of fellow young men and sought instead the counsel and camaraderie of the older ones who instead of guiding him, misled him, used him, confused him and were quick to abandon him when he hit trouble. He pursued a cosy but clearly unhealthy relationship with a particular distributor (tycoon) to whom he gave a large chunk of valuable Company land on Victoria Island (this is the subject of another report). We did receive reports that on numerous occasions, much to the annoyance of other road users, the Branch Manager drove against one-way traffic. As for reports that the Branch Manager built a road (out of Company funds) as far as his mother's house and stopped right there, we just refuse to believe that.

We observed that the Northern Branches were a law unto themselves and considered themselves completely independent of Headquarters. In fact they were the first to point out to the Managing Director that if he wanted to remove them he had better remove himself first. They generally took no notice of Head office instructions and publicly contradicted the Managing Director on several policy matters. We discovered that one of the Northern Branch Managers had committed the Company to some really odd swop-arrangements in respect of Company property much to the disadvantage of the Company but to the benefit of the Branch Managers and their friends. One of the Branch Managers claimed that 'tips' (bribes) were part of his legitimate remuneration; and another one built a magnificent palace (far better than Headquarters) for himself and spent the rest of his time building artificial lakes, zoos, amusement parks and game reserves. To make matters worse, the Northern Branch Managers generally treated prime customers (natural rulers) with thinly-disguised disrespect and sometimes contempt.

We can only conclude that the Company's decay owed its origin to the period immediately following the end of the Civil War. While the war lasted, our customers willingly suspended their rights and legitimate demands. However, once it was over, all the pent-up frustrations, aggravations and aspirations burst forth like a deluge. The Company completely failed to meet the challenge. Instead of overhauling Company policy to meet the changing circumstances, the Managing Director and the Branch Managers completely misread the mood of their customers.

Consequently, we have been flooded with petitions for the compulsory winding-up of the Company and the liquidation of all its Branches.

EVENTS AFTER BALANCE SHEET DATE

A powerful group has made a take-over bid for the Company and has submitted impressive dividend forecasts, cash flow projections, welfare schemes, injection of management by objectives, financial control, and public accountability. We are pleased to note that the take-over bid has been effected without bloodshed and recommend that all former Directors and Managers of the Company should collect their pensions with immediate effect and return all Company property (both here and abroad).

Signed: . . . .
    ORIDOTA, ODENSON & CO.

Auditors:
'H' Ward
OKEPOPO

OH KAMPALA!

FIRST THE GOOD NEWS

JUST before the last regime collapsed, Nigeria signed a special Technical Assistance Treaty with Uganda and accordingly our Commissioner for Information Chief (Dr) Edwin Clark quietly slipped out of the country to act as Consultant to 'Big Daddy' Idi Amin.

Initially, the Commissioner would be principally concerned with the public relations aspect of the OAU conference of African Heads of State to be held in Kampala and at which General Gowon would be the principal speaker.

On arriving at Kampala, the commissioner in his usual 'incisive and tactful' manner, and on being confronted by the world press, assured those worried about their personal safety by declaring:

'There is no country in the world where people don't disappear under mysterious circumstances. In fact, when I was in America last month, five million people disappeared.'

Asked about the future of Gowon's government, the Commissioner informed all present that each morning he personally opened 80 million letters from all over Nigeria asking the General to stay in power for ever. Bursting with laughter, the commissioner gleefully distributed free but entirely blank copies of his latest book entitled 'The Thoughts of Edwin Clark' as well as 'Gowon for Ever' flags.

Following recent events in Nigeria, 'Big Daddy' has now inserted a new clause into the treaty to enable Edwin Clark to remain in the post for the whole duration (50 years) of the treaty.

Alhaji Idi Amin commented: 'Me and Ed, we get along fine. He is an excellent choice – what I need is a man who speaks the same language and enjoys shadow boxing. As the current Chairman of OAU, I have officially informed all African territories which are saddled with leaders who want to stay in power for ever – SEND THEM TO KAMPALA AND THEY WILL MEET THEIR "KAMPALA" IN KAMPALA.'

THE MAN WITHOUT WHOM THE NEWS WOULDN'T BE THE NEWS

In answer to 'whether he dug his piles into cement hijacking and milk piracy' (Sunday Sketch), Chief Henry Fajemirokun, President of the Nigerian Chamber of Commerce burst into laughter and declared – 'when you people write all this rubbish, we laugh from this end. How is it possible to hijack cement on the high seas – with canoe or what?'

BLACK ARTS NEWS

At the Institute of Contemporary Affairs, Mallam Sangir Ketekete called for restraint in criticising the Balck Arts Festival. The eminent Mallam declared that it is not his intention to embarrass the government, but he felt compelled to warn that just as PRICES are beginning to settle down (or shall we say 'settle up') after the violent jolt from the Udoji award, they would almost certainly RISE again if the Government decides to go ahead and hold the festival anyway and undoubtedly, the sharpest rises would be in respect of FOOD and ACCOMMODATION.

The Mallam drew attention to the fact that some owners of incredibly dingy guest houses in Ajegunle are already advertising rooms to let during the festival (whenever it is held) at ₦200 per night. Their excuse is that 'well, if you can't make money during the festival, you'll never make it'.

Mallam Sangir added – 'The present build-up of traffic in Lagos is child's play compared with what is on the way during the festival. All those who had previously thought that the traffic couldn't possibly get any worse than it is now are in for a big disappointment.

Looking very glum, Mallam Sangir predicted that whenever the festival is held, schools and universities and even workers would have to go on compulsory holiday at a time when we should be striving for greater productivity.

He went on to complain that the timing of the Udoji Award was completely wrong because he felt that with a prestige project such as the festival only a few months away, it was crucial that nothing should be allowed to disrupt the economy or polarise worker/employer relationship.

Rather, all disputes should be quietly settled to ensure that the government and industry are not trapped into granting wild and inflationary wage demands as the price for saving the festival.

Finally, Mallam Sangir declared his astonishment at those who sought to justify the festival by arguing that if a small country like Senegal could host the first festival, there is no reason why we can't run the second.

The Mallam felt compelled to point out that Senegal is a SMALL and POOR country and could justify the festival as it focused the attention of the world on the country for a few weeks. Our case is different – we are BIG, we are RICH and we ALREADY have the attention of the world.

AND NOW THE SHIPPING NEWS

A few days ago, Television News gave generous coverage to a certain Chief who was launching his two 'new' ships, one of which he named after himself. An Ambassador who was present at the ceremony was seen bursting with laughter and was overheard when he whispered to his first secretary that he had never come across a case where a 20-year-old ship was not only being named after a prominent living personality but also launched in such a grand style.

A second observer who had partaken generously of the Chief's ample supply of Champagne declared that since most shipping companies write-off the cost of ships over 15 or 20 years and since the two ships being launched by the Chief were built in 1953 and 1954 respectively they would by now be completely written-off and therefore valued at nil.

This was quickly contradicted by an auditor who was within hearing distance – 'It would depend on the extent of the overhauling of the parts and refurbishments of the ships – and these could easily run into very large sums.'

A ship-broker interrupted with the comment, 'considering the present glut in the shipping market, there are many relatively new ships to be picked up at a bargain and I really can't understand why anyone would wish to buy these ancient ships'.

At this point, one of the Chief's assistants burst out in anger – 'That's the trouble with you book people. You think you know everything. Let me assure you, this is another example of the Chief's foresight and business acumen. It is not a diversion – rather it's based on sound economic vertical integration. The ships were purchased from a company which deals in motor car distribution, so we'll be in a position to offer shipping facilities for their imports as well as cater for our own import of building materials, engineering equipment etc., and of course we'll be able to load export produce for the outward journey.'

He was supported by a gentleman from the Inland Revenue who added: 'The Chief is on good ground, and provided he can support his purchase with the appropriate certificate from the Ministry of Industry's Inspectorate Division, he will be entitled to generous initial and annual capital allowances.'

A lady who watched the launching ceremony on television couldn't resist complaining – 'The Government-owned television stations should know better than to allow the NEWS to be used as free advertisement for the private business pursuits of individuals. You tell me – what is newsworthy about two old ships being launched?'

At this point he was reminded – 'Army go, Army come, civilian or military – for better or for worse, the Chief will continue to grow from strength to strength!' LONG LIFE AND GOD BLESS.

FIRST AGAIN!

Just as under the previous regime, the 'ungovernable West' was the first (and the only one to change governors) when Governor Rotimi replaced Governor Adebayo, last week the West scored another first when Captain Aduwo was replaced as Governor by Col. David Jemibewon.

INFLATION

BRIGADIER Murtala Muhammed has rightly declared INFLATION as the country's public enemy No. 1. However, let there be no illusion about one central fact – the war against inflation cannot be won in a year but it can certainly be lost in a year. As was amply demonstrated by the Udoji Award, you only need to put one foot wrong and the financial and economic superstructure comes crashing down. Most economic postulations are at best hazardous guess work but with inflation one is dealing with an equation where the variables are limited and are clearly subservient to the constants. Put simply, the basic equation is the ratio between supply and demand. In a perfect market situation the point at which supply and demand converge should be the price.

The equation can be broken down further by splitting demand into (i) demand by the public sector as evidenced by government spending and (ii) demand by the private sector as evidenced by the spending pattern of individuals and business units. Equally, supply can be split into goods and services or alternatively imports and our own production output. There is no denying that the sub-factors to be considered are the efficiency of the distribution network; the availability of substitutes (certainly not chalk instead of cement); and the money supply i.e. the amount of money in circulation – both genuine and counterfeit. Nevertheless, the basic equation remains firmly the ratio between the effective demand and supply.

This is the equation we can expect to read:

GOVERNMENT SPENDING AND PRIVATE SPENDING

VERSUS
IMPORTED GOODS AND GOODS PRODUCED LOCALLY (AND SERVICES)

Therefore, any course of action to be recommended must embrace a delicate balancing act between these four factors in order to achieve the desired result which is clearly a curb on inflation evidenced by either stabilising prices or actually forcing a downward trend. Thus we must either put a brake on either or both government spending and private sector spending or increase the quantity of goods and services available through importation or local production capacity.

There is no getting away from the fact that inflation has worsened over the last two years largely because by default, the government allowed the economy to get out of control. While we were busy patting ourselves on the back that 'after all inflation is a world-wide affliction', we should have rolled up our sleeves and done something about it. Clearly, the flood of oil money was strangling the economy and we didn't try enough to get to grips with it.

Now at the invitation of the government itself we have an opportunity to debate the issues and chart our course of action. It would be a disservice to the people of this country if we merely threw jabs at the monster of inflation instead of wrestling with it scientifically. I'm afraid, in dealing with inflation there is no such thing as a 'bloodless coup'. We had better be prepared to take a lot of strong medicine. Fortunately, the government has both the muscle and the sense of direction necessary to administer the medicine. A lot of sacred cows are going to get gored but there is hope because for the first time in almost ten years, the country is actually being governed.

By making a public issue of inflation, the Military Regime has by inference demonstrated that it is not out to protect the interest of any one section. To put it crudely, it would be short-sighted to isolate any section of the community from the treatment to be administered.

194

After all, soldiers in their public and private roles are individuals too with aged fathers to support, families to feed, and pockets that have developed leakages. Just like the rest of us, they have discovered that there is not much sense in earning double what you previously got if at the same time you have to contend with prices that have shot up three or fourfold.

We can therefore feel free to examine the pattern of spending by the government itself. Two facts emerge – the government through ministries, corporations, agencies etc. is clearly the biggest employer and is therefore in a unique position to influence the cost of labour. Secondly, the last budget left us in no doubt that over half of the budget would be committed to defence. From this emerges another interesting point which was publicly admitted by the last Commissioner of Finance – namely the largest chunk of military spending is by way of salaries to an army estimated at 250,000. This is money being pumped directly, (we have no reason to believe that a large slice of the salaries is being accumulated as savings) into the economy for consumer spending. This is bound to alter the supply and demand ratio because in purely economic terms, there is no corresponding increase in the supply of goods and this will be reflected in higher prices for whatever goods are available. We can therefore control the ratio by ensuring that instead of limiting the functions of a corps of 250,000 able-bodied, largely literate and disciplined men purely to defence, we capitalise on their talents, resources and high mobility to directly influence supply. We can do this by engaging them in providing a more efficient distribution network starting with the decongestion of the ports or active production through model farms or road-building programmes. Rather than stick rigidly to the dogma that 'soldiers are not farmers or road-builders', we need look no further than Libya to see how the special talents and resources of the army have been skillfully channelled to spearhead the drive against poverty, illiteracy and disease.

Secondly, there is the need to compensate soldiers and the rest of the working population not with meaningless increased salaries and rapidly deteriorating paper money but with better social amenities, education, housing, transportation and recreations which would result in higher real benefits.

We now move on to the other items on the government spending list. We don't want to cut the education budget – because we realise that our education programme represents an investment in skill and knowledge. We would however, need to keep a close watch on the Universal Primary Education scheme to ensure that not only do we get value for money in terms of hardware – buildings, equipment etc. but also that the scheme is guided towards our real needs, and that it is only part of a process that will lead to free university education in the shortest possible time. On health and transportation we know that we are not spending enough. Nevertheless we sharpen the scalpel just to ensure we are getting value for money at all levels. As for information, we can safely disregard all those who say all the information that needs to be disseminated has already been done by Mr Edwin Clark! Therefore apart from the saving that would ensue from our value-for-money programme, the areas calling for surgery are the non-essential items. This means the kiss of death to all the nonsensical prestigious spending. We only need to recognise that the public continuously remonstrated with the last government – 'the Black Arts Festival is a fine idea but is it worth all this trouble and what benefit do we get from it?' So we just keep the infrastructure and write off the rest as a bad loss – This is a serious government, we have no time for shows and pageantry.

We now take a look at the supply side of our equation and concentrate on its two main ingredients – imports and locally produced goods. In this regard, we have to bear in mind that local spending is inflationary when it does not lead to producing real wealth i.e. commodities which can be sold. Similarly, foreign spending is

196

inflationary when it brings non-productive commodities into the country at ever higher prices which would have to be borne by the consumer. Therefore our strategy must be two-pronged. At the local level, the keyword is self-reliance. This is translated into action directed at ensuring that local spending is geared towards producing for basic needs i.e. consumer goods and essential services. As regards foreign spending, the keyword is selectivity. This means we simply refuse to accept inflated prices by refusing to buy over-priced commodities. Furthermore, whatever we do spend should be on capital goods which are production oriented. This means that we put a full stop to the importation of envelopes, paper-clips, candles, pencils which are only poor examples of thousands of items which we are too lazy to produce ourselves.

If there is a need to justify the opposition to inflated prices, we have the classic example of motor-cycles and a host of other machinery which are sold here for three or four times the price in their country of origin. The difference is certainly not explained by freight, insurance and other direct increased costs. The unexplained difference is imported inflation. Our message to our overseas suppliers should be clear and unequivocal – 'we love you, but please keep your inflation to yourselves. We are not interested in absorbing other people's inflation.' The surprising thing is they won't mind it in the least – if anything, they'll respect us for it because they will discover we mean business. We should sit down with them and choose what we will buy and at what price. This is precisely what Russia did when it needed to purchase wheat from America last year.

In determining what price to pay for imported goods, OPEC has been advocating the gearing of increases in oil prices to increases in the price of imports. In effect, the oil producing countries decline to pay for imports as regards which prices are escalating faster than oil prices. Equally important in the fight against inflation is the need to build up a corps of our own technical experts

197

who are sufficiently knowledgeable to evaluate the purchases of hardware and the availability of substitutes. These are people who are able to report whether the capital equipment we do buy will be able to perform the functions for which they are required. Considering the acute shortage or absence of such a corps at the moment, the mind boggles at the amount of junk we may be buying for our telecommunications network, railways, television and radio, and agriculture.

In the war against inflation, we now shift to the home front in tackling the supply side of our equation. Here the key is agriculture. Put bluntly – we are simply not producing anywhere near enough food and unless we start doing something about it now, our situation will get progressively worse. Our strategy should be aimed at assuring the farmers and their children that they don't need to migrate to the urban centres in order to get their own share of the oil money. We have to tell them – 'stay where you are and the oil money will come to you'. Translated into action, this means accelerated rural electrification and pipe-borne water schemes. Our programme would embrace both government and private farms as well as co-operatives. The scope would cover the provision of subsidised seedlings, pesticides, and fertilisers as well as irrigation schemes. Agricultural policy would be directed at assisting and guiding the farmer right from the planting and harvesting stages right through to storage and marketing. We should aim at ensuring that within five years, the ugly spectacle of emanciated farmers carrying hoe and machete completely disappear to be replaced by farmers owning or sharing tractors and are content to stay on the land in the full knowledge that the only things they miss are the traffic jams of the urban centres.

In order to spread development on a country-wide basis, we would need to create secondary points of economic growth. So as to avoid uneven development by concentrating our energies on Lagos, Kano, Ibadan, Enugu, Kaduna, Benin or any of the state capitals, we set out to create a second tier of urban centres such as Ikorodu, Abeokuta, Kafanchan, Lokoja, Okene, Asaba, Abakaliki, Obudu, Katsina and Kontagora. This will enable food as well as industries, fuel and services to be more widely distributed.

In order to stimulate supply, we would have to recognise the urgent need for full agricultural revolution and mobilisation as well as vastly improved transportation and distribution infrastructure. For this purpose, we should feel free to draw on the readily available pool of labour from the armed forces, urban and rural unemployed as well as prisons, schools and universities.

Probably the most interesting aspect of our deliberations on inflation are the exciting possibilities of completely dynamising production levels of local goods. One of the most glaring contrasts between a developing economy and an underdeveloped one is that the former would be export-oriented while at the same time confining its imports to essential mass consumer goods. On the other hand, an underdeveloped economy would tend to be nonchalant about its exports while greedily absorbing imports of luxury goods. The lesson is clearly that we shall of course import but we shall only import those items which we cannot produce and which we feel will assist us in the fight against inflation – both imported and otherwise.

Impressive positive results could be achieved if the government and the business community would sit down and iron out policy about increased production. In this regard, it is important to bear in mind the interdependence between government on one hand and the business community – both indigeneous and expatriate. The message from the government would be that we want to work out mutually advantageous long-term policy. I have no doubt that this would be welcome by the business community because it would remove uncertainty about government policy that is often expressed as 'we don't know what the government is up to'. In other words, government would be saying that irrespective of who is at the helm of affairs, we have a policy that would survive changes and succession. Policy would no longer depend on the whims and caprices of any particular Minister. I feel sure that the business community would welcome a government that is both knowledge-able and open. On the other hand, the government would be quite firm in ensuring that there are no special exemptions or favours. Companies would get only what they are entitled to – no amount of bribery is going to change that. Any amendments to be conceded would apply to the business community as a whole and would not be based on special relationships between companies and government officials. More and more companies are beginning to realise their vulnerability if they have to give bribes to obtain concessions. They realise that once they start giving, they have to keep on giving. Secondly, whenever there is a change the successor would have to be courted with flattery and generous gifts if only to maintain the status quo. Even more damaging is the ever present possibility of blackmail by the employees who are used as intermediaries or possess evidence of wrongdoing by the company.

Government artillery in stimulating local production are wide and varied. For a start, government could offer preferential rates of tax. Instead of the present flat rate of 45%, income tax levied on companies engaged in manufacturing (not those merely assembling) would be fixed at a ceiling of say 30 per cent. Also, we could re-arrange exchange control procedures in order to ensure that there is a clear tilt in favour of companies that are directly involved in manufacturing. Here, it is essential to have clear definitions as to what constitutes a manufacturing company and in order to prevent abuse and corruption it should be possible for a company to appeal for a re-classification or have a competitor company re-classified if such a company has been given unfair advantage by unmerited classification as a manu-facturing company. As part of the package, the govern-ment would insist that any company manufacturing goods had better make sure their quality is first class or else serious penalties would follow if they fail to meet sensible quality standards. We would want to know why made-in-Nigeria matches flare in a manner that constitutes serious danger to the eyes. This also applies to textiles that shrink or fade after the first wash. Unless there is a rapid improvement we would have no option but to close such a factory because the war involves assuring the consumer that the home-made stuff is as good as the imported.

In fighting inflation, we would be guided by the knowledge that essentially its constituents can be narrowed down to four different components. The first takes the form of sharp new outside stimulus to prices e.g. Udoji award or congestion at the ports. The second element derives from attempts by the public to protect themselves from the effects of inflation which has already happened and further inflation which they consider inevitable. As they miscalculate, over-compensate and fight to preserve their illusory purchasing paper they would usually succeed only in creating an even bigger mess.

The third factor which can be highly disruptive arises when an economy tries to grow faster than its underlying resources will permit. The fourth element arises from the lop-sidedness of the economy e.g. overdependence on oil.

Nigeria as of now has the worst possible combination of low productivity both in the agricultural and industrial sectors and a rapidly rising cost of labour engaged in a 'push-me-I-push-you' struggle with the prices of scarce commodities. Fortunately, we are in an excellent position to begin work on the containment of inflation. We can draw on personnel from various fields to work out the details but they must be given specific briefs and close supervision because otherwise it would be only too easy for them to refrain from thinking on the basis of new definitions which are badly needed to wrestle with escalating inflation and poverty.

We can't even rule out the possibility that the Government may feel sufficiently uninhibited by orthodoxy and invite both employees, trade unions and civil servants to think again. The government's brief to them would be along the following lines:

'The Udoji Awards were a terrible mistake. Let's make a fresh start, the workers can of course keep their arrears but are the new wage rates realistic? If workers are willing to make wage concessions and industry is willing to lower prices while government is willing to give wide-ranging social amenities to workers that would result in real benefits,. maybe there is a basis for negotiating.'

Wallahi Tallahi, the struggle against inflation definitely continues – or else we revert to exchange by barter.

TIME WILL TELL

ALL IS WELL THAT STARTS WELL

A FEW days ago, the newspapers carried photographs of the Head of State's car stuck in the chaotic Lagos traffic. He was not preceded by a battalion of siren-blaring jeeps and Mercedes-Benz cars. This prompted a very senior government official to declare in all seriousness that whether Nigerians know it or not they are in for PHASE 1 – that is LEADERSHIP BY EXAMPLE.

If there are any hardship or inconvenience to be borne, we all suffer equally with no exemptions other than the sick, the disabled, or women in labour. He went on to add that while the measures adopted by the government have gone a long way to ease the traffic problems, the snags have by no means disappeared. In fact in some areas, the traffic problems have worsened – nevertheless, motorists and bus-users alike are bearing their suffering with patience in the sure knowledge that the government is actively and genuinely concerned with finding both short-term and long-term solutions.

The ancient Greeks demanded of their leaders that they should 'think more; know more and above all FEEL more than their followers'. Obviously they could not possibly feel more than their followers if they isolated themselves from the pressures and problems of the people they sought to lead. The logical corollary to PHASE 1 is PHASE 2: that is LEADERSHIP BY SACRIFICE.

If there are any sacrifices to be made then those who call for sacrifices would be the first to make them. The third is PHASE 3: that is LEADERSHIP BY ACTION. The problems are identified and wherever possible, immediate remedial action is taken – but failing this, the problem is thrown open to public debate and passed to the best minds for analysis and solution.

One might add that as regards both the purging of the old administration by retiring 'inefficient, old or corrupt' officers by giving them 'retirements with full benefits' and the appointment of new ones, one can point to one or two cases of officers against whom allegations warranting 'retirement' would be 'doubtful' – this is inevitable. It is simply the law of averages. Equally one can point to one or two cases who have miraculously escaped the purification exercise.

Incidentally, since the revelation that Brigadier Murtala Muhammed has no intention of exempting himself from the congestion on the roads, there have been other reports of the Head of State visiting Apapa Ports and attending Jumat Prayers unheralded; going into a post office unaccompanied and going into a bank to cash his own cheque.

As a matter of fact, two days after the coup, the Head of State was seen walking from his house to Dodan Barracks!!! Also, a few days after the coup, Col. Joe Garba, (the voice that first announced the change of government to a stunned audience on the 29 July), was seen hitching a ride on a motor-cycle on his way to the National Sports Stadium.

This is in sharp contrast to the style adopted by General Gowon who from his earliest days was preceded everywhere by armoured cars, sirens, saracens, and in later days employed the circus grand style of motorcade accompanied by sleek uniformed 'rev-rev' outriders. For the major part of his reign – Gowon was a prisoner in his own country and towards the end took to making clandestine nocturnal visits.

Brigadier Haruna's (Commissioner for Information) seven-point appeal to the press and the country can be summed up as follows – 'This is a government that is anxious to demonstrate that at every opportunity it should be seen to have a CONSCIENCE.' The public verdict is clearly – SO FAR SO GOOD, ALL IS WELL THAT STARTS WELL.

NOW THE HOME NEWS

i) On 28 July Mrs Ekodun Amuludun left home 'to visit her desperately ill mother at Abeokuta'. Instead she headed for Cotonou in a brand new Mercedes-Benz 280S in the company of a 'newfoundland'.

On 29 July, the Nigerian Dahomey border was sealed off following the 'change of government in Nigeria' – consequently Mrs Amuludun and her boyfriend were stuck on the wrong side of the border. On the same day, a worried Mr Amuludun fearing the worst, headed for Abeokuta only to find that his supposedly 'close to death' mother-in-law was hale and hearty and hadn't seen her daughter for six months.

ii) On Saturday 13 September, Mrs Asirititu was astonished to find her husband's name listed among the recipients of government land at Victoria Island. A quick visit to the site revealed that unknown to her, her husband owned a couple of duplex on which he had already collected five years advance rent.

iii) On the same day, Mr Iwo Jokobe nearly fainted when he saw his wife's name among the recipients of government land on the same Victoria Island. Grabbing his wife by the throat, he demanded the answer to three questions:

a) What service had she rendered?
b) To WHOM?
c) And how many times?

FUGITIVE OFFENDER

On hearing news of the coup, one of the Military Governors immediately set off for his well-stocked super luxury yacht with the intention of escaping to Cotonou. On seeing His Excellency approaching and carrying two heavy suit-cases, obviously containing cash, the captain of the yacht immediately put out to sea thus frustrating His Excellency's attempts to get on board. Over the yacht's loudspeaker system the captain coolly announced: 'Your Excellency, now is the time to face the music.'

A MAN FOR ALL SEASONS

Dr Godwin Daboh LL.D Chairman and President – General of the Nigerian Anti-Corruption League is on the warpath again. Having liquidated his erstwhile bosom friend and 'brother' Mr Joseph S. Tarka (former Federal Commissioner for Communication) by revealing damaging evidence of 'corruption in high places' thereby forcing General Gowon to call on 'JS'(Tarka) to resign and sing his 'Nunc Dimitis' (let thy servant now depart in peace) even though 'JS' would have preferred to sing hymn 593 'Abide with me', Daboh has now threatened to reveal the names, addresses, bankers, assets, girl-friends, gambling debts, compromising photographs, bounced cheques, property deals and sharp practices of the 60 million Nigerians who 'chopped' public money.

At a packed press conference, Dr Daboh informed the press 'I am no saint but I know who the crooks are'. A gentleman in the audience suggested that for his troubles, Daboh should be given a bullet-proof vest, an armoured car, police protection 'by land, air and sea' as well as ten per cent of all the money recovered as a result of information given by him.

THE FOUR JUST MEN

The Lagos State Ministry of information a few weeks ago announced that all those whose property on Victoria Island ('crown land') has been acquired by the Government should forward their claims for compensation to the specially appointed panel consisting of four gentlemen.

On the same day, 'Radio Lagos' announced that all those who did not have the good fortune of having crown land allocated to them in the first place and thereby missed out on the opportunity to make substantial 'windfall gains' via contractor finance are also entitled to compensation. Their claims should be forwarded to the same panel marked:

'FOR THE ATTENTION OF THE FOUR JUST MEN.'

AND NOW THE EX-NEWS

General Yakubu Gowon the ex-Head of State was till last week living in a mansion in Bishops Avenue, (Millionaires' Row) Hampstead, London. In his garage – a gleaming Rolls Royce. A few days ago, Mrs Gowon went shopping – the bill was a cool £38,000 (Sterling). i.e. ₦64,000 (Four times his last annual salary even after Udoji).

Not bad for a retired soldier. Maybe life really begins at 40!

Fortunately, Reuters have checked the story and declared it untrue.

IT WON'T HAPPEN SIR

ACCORDING to Professor Janduku, Nigerians suffer from a national affliction known as the 'It won't happen sir!' disease. The professor diagnosed it as the ability to leave crucial duties unperformed while at the same time relying on absurd optimism and hoping that by an act of fate the obvious disastrous consequences will somehow not happen.

This affliction was again highlighted by Governor David Jemibewon (fondly called 'Bamibewon' by his people) who when he visited a hospital was incensed at discovering that a nurse who should have been on duty was nowhere to be found. This was the result of a mix-up over the duty roster.

When the Governor castigated the officials of the hospital and drew their attention to the possible grave consequences of their carelessness, he was coolly informed 'It won't happen sir!'

The same treatment was given to Governor Adekunle Lawal when he made a surprise visit to the Lagos General Hospital and discovered that out of eight doctors who should have been on duty only one was present. When the Governor raised the alarm and ordered an immediate investigation in order to emphasise the serious consequences of such dereliction of duty by reminding the officials that if doctors are not on duty when they should be, patients would die, wrong medicines might be prescribed and those requiring urgent treatment would not get it, he was also coolly reminded that 'It won't happen sir!'

Similarly, when Gowon and his lieutenants were enjoying the sweet life – they were warned that to completely ignore the serious problems while turning the country into a 'Champagne Republic' would make a coup inevitable, they coolly replied – 'It won't happen!'

All the iniquities and inefficiency of public services which Brigadier Haruna, Commissioner for Information, highlighted by drawing attention to the appalling service meted to customers at railway stations, hospitals, airports, post offices, banks, etc. are all the result of 'It won't happen sir' disease.

For example, when Mr Edun Ebiokosa called at his local post office to draw ₦5 from his savings account in order to purchase drugs for his sick child, he was kept waiting for two hours. When he complained that his child was close to death, the post office clerk replied coolly 'It won't happen sir!' and went off for her lunch.

Under rather different circumstances, Mrs Elizabeth Fuyomare could hardly control her rage when on getting home, she discovered that her housemaid had left the gas cylinder open thereby causing poisonous gas to escape. When she yelled at her housemaid – 'You could have killed all my three children as well as yourself', the housemaid simply replied 'I beg madam, it won't happen'.

A close examination of Brigadier Haruna's speech reveals that he is questioning the ability and willingness of Nigerians (be they post office clerks, stewards, bus-conductors, ticket-officers, doctors, nurses, dentists, immigration officers, etc.) to treat each other with respect and consideration. It looks more and more as if anyone who is not wearing army uniform or is not easily identifiable as a V.I.P. cannot expect prompt attention at the bank, post office, customs, hotels, or the airport.

The Brigadier's complaint is also a reminder of what Professor Janduku once said – 'Nigerians are very good at carrying out simple instructions but hopeless when it comes to handling complex ideas or situations.'

T.V. NEWS

Television viewers are in for a surprise. Tomorrow on

NBC-TV 'VIEWPOINT'. They will see Chief Jerome Udoji advocating MASSIVE IMPORTATION OF GOODS as an answer to inflation. The dangers inherent in this policy are:

(i) Our port facilities are clearly inadequate and will remain so for some time;

(ii) In the alternative we would have to rely on port facilities available in neighbouring countries and we could end up clogging not only our own ports but also Cotonou, Lome, Accra all the way up to Monrovia, Freetown and Bathurst with our imports;

(iii) The only reason why our neighbouring countries are willing to let us use their ports is because they are relatively poor, their ports are under-utilised, and they need our money which we gladly hand over as rent and port charges;

(iv) In the event of any of our neighbours discovering oil or enjoying a sudden boom, they themselves will want to use their own ports and you can be sure they won't hesitate to throw us out;

(v) By relying on massive importation, Nigeria will become a dumping ground for all sorts of imports produced cheaply abroad against which locally manufactured goods would not be able to compete. Local industry will just collapse and when oil money is over — where would we be?

(vi) The only reason we are able to pay for the imports is our massive oil revenue and in the event of a collapse of or reduction in oil revenue we would be stuck;

(vii) Surely, instead of letting oil money strangle the economy, we should aim at controlling it, to ensure greater productivity in both the industrial and agricultural sectors while at the same time controlling the quality of our products and ensuring a better distribution network;

(viii) However, success depends on involving the whole community AT ALL LEVELS by getting the Ministry of Information to highlight the problem and publicise government efforts to deal with it and getting employers as well as the trade unions to contribute to and evaluate guidelines laid down by the government.

(ix) We shall of course import, but we must be SELECTIVE by insisting that we get value for money and importing only items which we really need in the fight against inflation.

TOO GOOD TO BE EMPLOYED

Once in every generation, a man of extraordinary brilliance turns up. One such person is a young doctor – Dr S.F.K. who amazingly finds himself unable to get a job with the Lagos Medical School at a time when we are crying out for more doctors.

His qualifications are clearly impressive. Aged only 31, he is married with two children. He attended King's College, Lagos, followed by College of Medicine, University of Lagos where apart from winning the Entrance Prize in 1964 for the student with the best entrance qualification, on graduation he won ALL the distinction prizes in Anatomy, Physiology, Bio-Chemistry, Pathology, Surgery and Medicine.

He also attended University of Rochester School of Medicine, U.S.A. and did post-graduate work at Royal Post-graduate Medical School, Hammersmith Hospital; University of London; and Pritzter School of Medicine, University of Chicago. Consequently he holds B.Sc. (Hons) Pathology and Medical Bio-Chemistry; M.B., B.S. (Hons), M.Sc. (Clinical Pathology) M.R.C.P. (U.K.), and Ph.D. (London).

He is also a Gold Medalist in medicine, Surgery, Pediatrics and Anaesthesia. His fellowships are (i) Predoctoral Fellowship Commonwealth Fund of New York; University of Rochester; Post doctoral Scholar, University of Lagos; Commonwealth Scholar and he is presently a Clinical Fellow (Endocrinology) University of Chicago.

I don't see how we can expect to be taken seriously if a man of such distinction cannot get a job in his own country.

NOTHING WILL EVER BE THE SAME AGAIN

THE FIRST 100 DAYS

The new regime has now completed its first 100 days in office. It would be dishonest to pretend that it has done EVERYTHING that needed to be done. What is beyond doubt is that in the short period since it came into power, the regime has moved with almost dizzy speed to overhaul The Machinery it inherited from The Old regime. The purge has reached all corners and communities of the nation and the revelation of corruption, abuse of office, extortion, rip-offs, and gross negligence grow more and more nauseating. One could be forgiven for wondering about what would have happened had General Gowon chosen his own successor – A PERMANENT SEAL WOULD HAVE BEEN PUT ON THE DECAY! The public would never have known who did what or for that matter WHO GOT WHAT AND HOW. This has prompted Chief Eyiwa Leni-Kosinkan to urge the Constitution Drafting Committee to declare as its cardinal principle – 'No government shall have the right to choose its own successor.'

Perhaps it is true to say that the most staggering and traumatic effect of the on-going exercise is to be felt in the 'retirement' of public figures, some of whom held the highest and most sensitive positions in government. This is not the place to report the highly damaging leaked stories about very senior officials who have been retired but whose conduct, and reputation had generally been thought impeccable. Naturally one would be hesitant to accept such stories at their face value but it is difficult to resist the conclusion that there is no smoke without fire.

213

In the last 100 days, many things to which we had reconciled ourselves as permanent fixtures have been liquidated; persons we had hitherto regarded as unshakable from public life have been removed and many things which we had hitherto believed would not happen in our own lifetime are in fact happening albeit not as quickly nor as extensively as we would have wished – but at least we have made a start. If in the process, there are still people who are able to point out those who have perpetrated acts which should have earned them immediate retirement but have somehow escaped, we can only concede that that is a fair point. Equally, we can accept as fair comment those who with some justification are able to point out minor, unwilling or genuinely mistaken actors who have been punished while the lead players have got away.

ONE MORE STATE

Alhaji Sule Sugomu has sent off an urgent telegram to the Creation of States Panel, under Justice Irikefe urging the panel to create an extra state to be known as the 'RETIRED STATE', meant exclusively for those who have been 'retired with full benefits'. In view of the large number of public servants who have been retired, the state would not only be viable but would have more than adequate supply of 'retired' policemen, soldiers, customs and excise personnel, doctors, judges, commissioners, civil servants and possibly a retired Head of State.

RETIREMENT NEWS

Professor Carl Kemmel-Whyle came into town a few days ago and quietly booked into a Lagos Hotel. He is the world's leading expert on the psychology of retirement and he is here under the auspices of one of our universities. The learned professor has devoted the last 25 years to carrying out extensive research into the subject of retirement which he classifies as:
  i) Planned retirement and
  ii) Sudden retirement.

According to the professor even with planned retirement there are problems. Even though there may be no financial problems, the retired person may face serious psychological problems during the period of adjustment to a slower pace or due to having too much time on his hands. Difficulties may also arise where a wife finds that her husband who had previously spent much of the day out of the house suddenly becomes a permanent fixture.

The problems are even more serious where retirement occurs suddenly either through industrial redundancy or otherwise. This is particularly so where retirement occurs at a relatively early age. The main problem is invariably that of finding something worthwhile and challenging to do. Apart from that, the retired person would usually feel a mixture of emotions ranging from that of having failed, to being unappreciated. The loss of power and status compounded by a dwindling circle of friends would inevitably build-up a reserve of resentment and frustration which uncontrolled could lead to alcoholism, rapid loss of weight and even more serious consequences.

FIRST: THE MATERNITY NEWS

Alhaji Wahala Npayon nearly collapsed at the Lagos Island Maternity hospital, (the 'baby factory') when he learnt that his wife had just given birth to triplets. He pleaded with the doctor on duty 'Mr Surgeon-General, I know that ONE of them is mine. Please ask my wife who the father of the other two is.'

THEN THE PATERNITY NEWS

During a paternity suit against army sergeant Samuel Kurekure, the mother of the disputed baby pleaded with the presiding judge, Chief Eshin Owewu: 'please sir, take a look at the baby's shoulder. It has three stripes as birth marks on both shoulders. It is definitely his baby.'

HERE COMES THE JUDGE

While dealing with a hotly contested case, a magistrate

declared in open court: 'Justice must not only be done, it must also be seen to be done. I have therefore, decided to refund ₦250.00 (Two Hundred and Fifty Naira) out of the ₦750.00 (Seven Hundred and Fifty Naira) given by the plaintiff to my messenger, without my knowledge. I am reliably informed that the defendants have also without my knowledge given ₦500.00 (Five Hundred Naira) to the same messenger. Let me emphasise that there is no question of my being anything but fair and impartial.'

HERE GOES THE JUDGE

A magistrate whose messenger had been over zealous in 'collecting' gifts (without the magistrate's knowledge of course!) suddenly found his name among the list of people retired with immediate effect by the new government. Magistrate Kosisishe Kosaishe promptly instructed the messenger to refund all such gifts 'with immediate effect'.

THE HONEYMOON IS OVER?

On Monday – The electricity was off the whole day. On Tuesday both the electricity and water were off. On Wednesday, electricity was back but the water was still off and the telephone was dead. On Thursday, the telephone was still dead but the water started trickling and the electricity started playing games by coming on and then going off every fifteen minutes.

On Friday, there was NO FUEL for the car, the electricity was off; there was no water, the phone was suffering from 'suspended animation', no mail, and then the sewage pipes burst. Thank heavens the electricity came back on just before the 9 o'clock only to show newscaster Mike Enahoro suffering from severe hiccups while reading all the bad news – he gave up at exactly the same minute the lights went off.

ALHAJI 'FIFTY-FIFTY'

Alhaji 'Fifty-Fifty' the well-known ex-smuggler, money-doubler, conjurer, counterfeiter, con-man now turned 'business tycoon' has publicly declared his support for the new military regime. However, on hearing that the present clean-up campaign would go on till 1979, Alhaji fired off a complaint to the Chairman of the Public Complaints Commission, Alhaji Maitama Sule as follows:

'I have thoroughly examined the list of the new Governors and Commissioners – I don't know any of them. I urge you to implore the new regime to declare a moratorium between now and Christmas to allow people like me to finish off all our "deals". After all, I'm too old to learn a new trade and how are people like me going to survive while all this cleaning up is going on? Is it true nothing will ever be the same again?'

THE FIRE NEXT TIME

IT would be misleading to suggest that when Murtala ordered 'quick march', the whole country was solidly behind him. The preceding years of drift and aimlessness within the government had firmly entrenched apathy and cynicism in the minds of the public. Apart from those who privately moaned that 'Murtala's government won't last more than six months', there were the stream of powerful public figures who loudly declared their support for the new government but nevertheless did their utmost in private to discredit the government by spreading stories about Murtala's private wealth, and its source. Wherever possible, this group gave the new government only minimum and grudging support while doing whatever they could to wreck government policies and exploit its inexperience. It is ironical that much of the praises showered on Murtala after his death came from the hypocrites who did their hardest to discredit him and sabotage his efforts while he was alive. In fairness though, it must be stated that there was another group who believed that Murtala's government was marching in the wrong direction and attacking the wrong targets. There were also those who believed that Murtala was trying to do too much too quickly and that he paid too little regard to their advice to temper his reforming zeal with patience and compromise.

Nevertheless, by the time he died Murtala had won the grudging respect if not the adulation of those who initially opposed him. This is not to say that they were unable to fault him as regards his appointment of public officers which to any impartial observer were clearly not entirely devoid of favouritism and hints of ethnic preferences. The same could be said as regards the retirement of public officers. Even those who doubted Murtala were compelled to give him credit for the remarkable success the new government had achieved in decongesting the ports; the creation of states; the cancellation of the dubious 1973 census figures; the vigorous pursuit of respect for the black man in international affairs; the handling of the cement crisis etc.

Whatever success Murtala achieved was to a large extent due to the wide support he drew from the masses who readily identified with him and recognised him as their champion. This of course, raises the question of how sincere was Murtala's concern for the 'common man'. No doubt he had charisma and an over-powering personality to which the public at first re-acted with fear followed by subdued affection. Throughout Murtala's reign there was little evidence of public adulation by way of banner-carrying processions or wildly enthusiastic mobs. These only happened after his death!

From all available evidence, Murtala's concern for the 'masses' or 'common man' was genuine and heartfelt. For our most convincing evidence, we have to go as far back as 1963, when he was only a newly commissioned officer, a 2nd lieutenant in the Nigerian Army, he was then assigned to Ibadan as aide-de-camp to the then Administrator-General of Western Nigeria who was quartered at the sumptuous Government House. Murtala would come back from his not infrequent visits to the local market at Dugbe and exclaim in despair – 'The government must do something for the common people.' He was genuinely appalled at the poverty, the filth, the frustrations and the total hopelessness of the ordinary people he saw at the market who eagerly sold the product of months of toil to the affluent and powerful 'nouveau rich' who had no inhibitions at displaying their big cars, their dazzling jewellery and conspicuous cash.

Also, it is a pity that not many people know that Murtala was one of the earliest advocates of the full reabsorption of the Ibo's into the mainstream of the nation after the civil war. This was in sharp contrast with the unfortunate reputation he had gained during the war as a ruthless blood-thirsty commander determined to wipe out the Ibo race. It is on record that it was Murtala who confronted Gowon and told him in no uncertain terms that unless Gowon was prepared to welcome the Ibo's back into the fold, he, Murtala, could not go on with the liberation of the Eastern States.

Furthermore, this is something that many are going to find difficult to believe – but it is true that when Murtala visited the Eastern States after the civil war – HE BROKE DOWN IN TEARS! He knew how much money The Federal Government had poured into that area in the months that followed the war in order to rehabilitate the Ibos. Millions had been poured in but the greed and corruption of the Administration of the Eastern Region and its functionaries had left the roads unmended, the war damage was still in evidence everywhere, and there was little to show for the huge funds that had been allocated for the welfare of the Ibo's. The money had simply disappeared! Murtala was genuinely appalled at the conditions of the roads and the poverty of the people.

In order to understand Murtala's role in the July, 1966 counter-coup – one would have to remember that in the January, 1966 coup, the two people he admired most – The Sarduana of Sokoto and the Prime Minister, Sir Abubakar Tafawa Balewa had both been assassinated. To Murtala's mind their death could not go unrevenged.

Those who are determined to fault Murtala have cast doubts about the sincerity of his government's stance on foreign policy. They argue that there was nothing in his background to support the dynamic stand Nigeria had suddenly adopted on Angola, Namibia etc. The insinuation is of course, that he was merely reading speeches prepared for him. This is totally incorrect. Murtala was genuinely concerned about the suffering of the blackman in South Africa and elsewhere and truly believed that as long as black people were oppressed by minority rulers, no blackman, (even those who were running their own country) could lay claim to any respect. The best confirmation of this is probably to be found in a film of the last OAU Conference. Leopold Senghor, President of Senegal was addressing the conference. He was preaching dialogue and accommodation with South Africa. By watching Murtala's reaction one could easily detect his revulsion at the policy Senghor was advocating. He was clearly upset and agitated and perhaps under different circumstances where Senghor would not be protected by protocol, Murtala would have interrupted him!

However, I think Murtala himself would have been amused by the attempt by all sorts of strange people to confer strange labels on him. He never claimed that he was a revolutionary or socialist or anything else for that matter. Our best approach is to regard him as a man who came home only to find that the house was on fire and went ahead to do whatever he could to save the house before it was burnt to the ground. He got hold of water and doused the fire and it is only history that will tell how well he succeeded in putting out the fire. One thing is certain though – he didn't stand by and watch the house burn down. The only trouble though is that there are far too many people who were too blind to notice that the house was on fire.

We had all better watch out for the fire next time.

DON'T LET THEM DIE YOUNG

THE Military Tribunal set up under Major-General Abisoye to investigate the guilt or otherwise of those arrested in connection with the abortive coup, has completed its assignment but there is some unfinished business left. Perhaps the most disturbing aspect of the last coup attempt was the complete abandon with which so many young men, regardless of their responsibilities to their wives, children and parents, committed their young lives to a cause so bloody and unnecessary, particularly when they could not have been in any doubt that the price of failure would be their own death. In order to prevent a re-occurence, it is crucial that the government should carry out a thorough enquiry to find out why these young men eagerly committed themselves to such a desperate cause and how they were able to hatch their plot virtually in the open without being apprehended before they could carry out their dastardly act.

Even if one was willing to write off B. S. Dimka as a crackpot obsessed with beer and women, surely this could not apply to all the other participants. Apart from army demobilisation, the reasons given by Dimka are too flippant and ridiculous to be the real reasons behind the coup attempt. I flatly refuse to believe that the ex-Governors could have been re-instated. Similarly, Gowon would not have survived more than a month as Head of State second time round without killing or detaining thousands of Nigerians.

It is quite clear from the manner of Murtala Muhammed's death and the number of bullets pumped into him, that his assailants wanted him dead very, very badly. Had Dimka & Co. succeeded in killing the other top army officers on their guest list, the consequences would have been too bloody to be contemplated. Literally, there would have been 'blood everywhere'. It would have been an orgy of political massacre. There are many who believe that when Dimka announced the imposition of a curfew from '6.00 a.m. to 6.00 p.m.' that was precisely what he meant (and not 6.00 p.m. to 6.00 a.m.) as this would have provided him and his fellow murderers ample time to kill all those who might constitute a threat, in their own homes in broad daylight! I can't quite put my finger on it – but there is something about Dimka's evidence (at least that part of it that has been made public) that just 'doesn't hang together'. There is a missing link which has triggered off speculation that apart from the 'major's plot' which was headed by Clement Dabang and Lt-Col. Dimka's plot, there must have been a third group' the identity of which was skilfully concealed by Major-General I. D. Bisalla from Dimka. The logical deduction from this is that Bisalla's strategy would be to lie low for a couple of days until the killing of senior army officers was over and then do an 'Ironsi' by emerging as the most senior surviving army officer – and then in the name of 'law and order' proceed to declare himself the new Head of State. It is even conceivable that he would then proceed to arrest Dimka and Dabang for treason and as the *coup de grâce* he would have declared Gowon a 'wanted person' rather than return him to power!

The participants in the coup are such a motley crowd glaringly lacking in cohesion of interest and idealogy that one is prompted to enquire whether they were in fact members of a secret cult. This is a real possibility in view of the fact that Dimka & Co. were apparently ready to carry out clearly illegal orders without asking even basic questions such as:

 i) What support and protection would they get;
 ii) What was their reward for success; and
iii) In the event of failure how would they escape?

It's rather strange that Dimka was quite satisfied with nothing more than a nod of approval and vague promises of protection from Bisalla.

One other strange observation about the coup plotters is the very stunning facial resemblance between B. S. Dimka, Yakubu Gowon and Joseph Gomwalk (especially the front page photograph published in the 'Sunday Times' of 16 May, 1976). This has led to speculation that the gentleman who was spotted in Togo three days before the coup and was thought to be Gowon was in fact Joseph Gomwalk!

Of all the coup plotters, Bisalla's participation was the most surprising because as the Commissioner for Defence, his duty was to defend the government rather than turn himself into the Commissioner for attack. Besides, he was a long-standing friend of Murtala even though in recent years their relationship had not been as intimate as it used to be. While Murtala had made little effort to conceal his contempt for Gowon, Bisalla had been more accommodating and had never shown any direct disloyalty to Gowon. Furthermore, Bisalla, Murtala Major-Gen. Shuwa and Major-Gen. Haruna had joined the army on the same day and had been together at the army training school at Teshi followed by Sandhurst. Apart from Murtala, none of Bisalla's coursemates had superseded him. His claim that he was frequently sent out of the room when important decisions were being made by the Supreme Military Council of which he was a member just doesn't ring true.

One strange fact that does emerge, is that in spite of his seniority in the army he was generally regarded as a 'weakling'. He would never have had the guts to stage the coup himself – someone else would have to do it – this was true to his character. A colleague of Bisalla has remarked that Bisalla 'always wanted things done for him. So much so that if he met a pretty girl at a party, he could not date her himself. He would send someone else to do the chatting up.'

Stranger still is the fact that on the eve of the coup and

in the presence of several people, Bisalla had warned Murtala of the need to tighten security! This was of course 'camouflage' – because Bisalla already knew that within a matter of hours, the coup attempt would be made.

Murtala died young, and – so also did Col. Taiwo and Lt Akinshehinwa (Murtala's aide-de-camp). The plotters executed were mostly young men who had everything to live for.

Take Dimka – here was a young man who joined the army only in 1967 during the civil war and secured a field rank. Even though he only read up to class four, by 1975 he was a full Lt.-Colonel in the army. He had plenty of money to spend; he was never short of women; he travelled where and when he liked within the country and overseas; none of his mates had been promoted above him and his position was secure and in fact he was the only Lt.-Col. who flew a flag on his staff car. This was a status symbol to which as head of the physical training corps he was entitled. Yet all these were not enough. He was certainly not motivated by ideology or idealism.

We have a problem – we must find out what propels these young men to yield to madness and the naked grab for power even when it means not only killing other young men but also playing Russian roulette with their own lives. It was Field Marshall Bernard Montgomery who once declared: 'IN WAR, THERE IS OFTEN A PLACE FOR MAD PEOPLE.' But we are not at war – or are we? Somebody had better go and talk to these young men – DON'T LET THEM DIE YOUNG.

THE GOOD, BAD AND THE UGLY

FIRST THE BAD NEWS

WHILE commenting on the plight of two accident victims who had been taken to the General Hospital, Lagos at about 1.30 p.m. only to discover that there was no doctor on duty, a worried nurse remarked: 'IF IT WERE THE EXPATRIATE DOCTORS, THEY NEVER FAIL TO BE ON DUTY.' This prompts one to ponder whether if we are still faced with this sort of situation fifteen years after 'INDEPENDENCE', maybe it is time to give Independence back to the people who gave it to us. On the other hand, it may be that the expatriate doctors are so backward that they haven't heard of the extinction of the 'Humanitarian doctor' so loudly announced by Dr Ekpo Eyo – 'President – General and All-in-all' of the Nigerian Medical Association.

CRIME AND PUNISHMENT

The Gondola Bar Association has sent a telegram to Chief Magistrate Chief (Dr) Utuk Utuk XV urging him to set free Mr Ekeete Zulu, a well-known bicycle thief and award him a medal of honour instead. The Bar Association apparently feels very strongly that there can be no justification for sending a man to jail for stealing a bicycle in a society where eminent citizens steal millions of public funds and are told they can keep 50 per cent of the loot 'on compassionate grounds'; or where powerful Chiefs 'hijack government cement on the high seas' and nothing happens!

STRANGE NEWS

Last week, Chief the-more-you-look-the-less-you-see

226

D.S.O. drew the attention of the Press to the fact that as a result of the probe into the performance of contractors responsible for building houses at the Black Arts Village, the Government had cancelled the contract awarded to a company of which a Nigerian Doctor-turned-businessman was until recently the Managing Director. In addition, the company was ordered to refund ₦4,000,000 of tax payers' money and its equipment on the site were seized. This action was contained in the Government 'White Paper' and was widely publicised. Believe it or not, the following day's newspaper showed a photograph of the same Doctor-turned-businessman 'dining and wining' with very senior government officials while hustling a book about the late General Murtala Muhammed. Someone even got conned into paying ₦250.00 for a copy of the book.

The Chief's final comment was – 'it can only happen in Nigeria'.

IBRU NEWS

Chief Michael Ibru (the business magnate) has this week been receiving an endless stream of well-wishers at home. Also around was his brother Felix who when asked to comment on recent events in the country stated flatly 'Absolutely no comments'. He did however, confide to a friend that now he knows who his real friends are. Our latest report is that he is off to Kainji for a rest.

If you like champagne go and visit the Chief. He imports the stuff wholesale; it's first-class quality and a more generous man will be hard to find.

VERY SAD NEWS

It has been reported that the Irish-born wife of one of the military officers executed for their part in the abortive coup of 13 February died last Sunday. All the available evidence suggests suicide. It is reported that in the note which she left behind, she declared that she could no longer carry on since her friends had abandoned her; and she and her children had been totally ostracised on account of her husband's part in the abortive coup.

LATE NEWS

Last year a governor (now retired) decided to spend a few days at the Obudu Cattle Ranch in the Cross River State. The ranch is beautiful by any standard and as a holiday resort it certainly provides refreshing and calm relaxation. However, it is way up in the 'MOUNTAINS' and the only way to get up there in the past was to follow a tortuous meandering route up the mountain by land-rover. The Ex-Governor was half way up before he decided that the route was too dangerous for him and chose to turn back. The only trouble was that the route was too narrow to allow the land-rover to turn round. Answer: He got his large entourage to lift the land-rover up in the air and turn it round!

PASSPORT NEWS

A bald-headed gentleman caused work to come to a halt at the passport office yesterday. On his passport application form he had filled against 'colour of hair' that his hair was black. Confusion broke out when the passport officer insisted that since the applicant's head was clearly shiny and completely barren, the correct answer to the question about colour of hair was 'NOT APPLICABLE'!

VERY BAD NEWS

It looks as if armed robbers are back in business in the Ikeja area. One of the worst hit areas is Oregun Village where the latest victim, Alhaji Supo Adetona described how a gang of robbers numbering at least 30 turned up at 1.00 a.m. at his house and made off with valuable property. The following night they came back to complete their unfinished business. According to the Alhaji, numerous complaints to the police have so far produced ZERO result.

STUDENT POWER

A few days ago Brigadier Shehu Yar'Adua announced

that the 26,000 University Students taking part in 'Operation Feed the Nation' would be paid a monthly allowance of ₦96.00 for 2½ months (that is ₦6,240,000). An observer has commented that unless the students are paid the same rate as the ordinary farm workers they would not appreciate the plight of farm workers. On the other hand Alhaji keep-your-mouth-shut called a press conference and announced that the participation of students in OPERATION FEED THE NATION (OFN) was an excellent idea and that in order to produce concrete results and at the same time deal with students unrest, the students should not be allowed to go back to their Universities until they have produced food worth at least THREE TIMES WHATEVER MONEY the government pays them, (that is ₦18,720,000.00 extra food!)

OPERATION HOUSE YOURSELF

Commenting on the amazing squalor in which millions of Nigerians live Chief I-Bow-and-Tremble urged the Federal Government to launch Operation House Yourself. According to the Chief, who has just returned from the Habitat Conference, the housing problem in Nigeria can never be solved by the government unless it is able to organise groups of people to build their own houses in turn by pooling labour and materials. Particularly in the rural areas, the results could be spectacular China did it and that is why in China (population 700,000,000), there are no slums.

WE HAVE TO GO ON STRUGGLING.

CUSTOMS & NONSENSE

ALHAJI Shehu Musa, the ex-Permanent Secretary at the Ministry of Health is an excellent choice as the new boss of the Customs and Excise. He already has a well-earned reputation for efficiency and straightforwardness and there is absolutely no question about his integrity. When he starts reading the files and investigating the performance of his predecessors in office, he will no doubt submit a list of people who should be declared 'CONTRABAND'.

A few days ago, when the Alhaji went on his first official inspection tour of the Customs and Excise procedure at Ikeja Airport, he was accompanied by a reporter who made the following observations:

HAVE YOU ANYTHING TO DECLARE?

Monsieur Pierre de Marchrand, General Manager of a Lagos based Oil Company was suddenly summoned to an emergency meeting at the Paris Head Office. He set out from his office to head homewards to pack a few things but he was held up for three hours in the traffic. Realising that he was in serious danger of missing the last flight to Paris he decided to head for the Airport instead. Fortunately, he already possessed an unused air ticket. At the ticket counter, Monsieur was assured that the flight was fully booked and there was no chance whatever of his getting a seat on the plane.

Monsieur pleaded passionately – 'I've got to be on that plane. I have a very important meeting at 8 o'clock tomorrow morning in Paris.'

'In that case why don't you send Head Office a telex message to send the Concorde to pick you up?' suggested the ticket clerk. At this point, a helpful uniformed customs and excise officer came to the rescue. 'There is no need to be so rude to Monsieur.' He then turned round to Monsieur Pierre and whispered – 'I think we can sort this out amicably sir. As a customs officer I'm not allowed to receive bribes but being a Nigerian I know that a "dash" of ₦50 could suddenly find you a vacant seat.' Monsieur Pierre though grateful for the advice protested that he didn't have as much as ₦50 in Nigerian currency but he could offer French francs.

'Beautiful. I don't trust naira, anyway,' declared the ticket clerk and promptly gave Monsieur a boarding pass.

Monsieur Pierre nearly collapsed when on frantically getting into the plane he discovered there were only two other passengers on board all the way to Paris.

As soon as the meeting was over, Monsieur made for Orly airport and without any trouble at all was booked on a flight back to Lagos. But his troubles were not over yet. On landing at Ikeja Airport he was put through the drill by a Customs and Excise Officer.

'Have you anything to declare?'

'Nothing at all – I have no luggage,' replied Monsieur.

'What do you mean by you have no luggage?', demanded the Officer.

'Simple. As you can see from my passport and ticket I was away for only one day.' he replied.

'I see. But didn't you buy any presents?'

'None,' replied Monsieur Pierre.

'You mean no presents for Madame?'

'None,' replied Monsieur Pierre.

'Very interesting – I'm sure though you didn't forget to buy me a present', declared the customs officer, coolly.

'Of course not – I'll be a fool to forget. Here it is,' whispered Monsieur Pierre, handing over an extra large bottle of his wife's favourite perfume.

DANGEROUS NAIRA

Mrs Cynthia Macksmith, wife of the General Manager of

Lukman Corporation 'breezed' through Kano Airport a few days after a short but splendid holiday in Toremillinos, Spain. Everything was fine until she got to the Customs and Excise desk. She was suddenly jolted from her reverie about Mario whom she ahd met on holiday and who had stood in for husband Peter (who 'due to recent events in Nigeria' couldn't make the trip).

The Customs Officer was astonished to discover that the entire contents of Cynthia's suitcase was a pair of bikinis. His suspicion now thoroughly aroused the officer decided to poke further only to discover a few naira notes tucked away in a corner of the suitcase.

'Aha!' exclaimed the delighted officer 'You know this can land you in jail. It is a contravention of the currency regulations to take Nigerian money outside the country.'

Cynthia replied coolly 'Sorry, Officer. The only reason I always take a few naira notes with me whenever I leave the country is so that on my way back in I'll have enough money to BRIBE THE CUSTOMS OFFICERS.'

DUTY FREE

Alhaji Wontobe arrived on Nigerian Airways flight from London after being away for 15 years in 'search of the golden fleece'. As he came through the Customs Hall, Alhaji was overwhelmed with embraces and huggings from relatives. In the pandemonium, he put the duty-free bottles of brandy and whisky on the floor and promptly forgot about them.

It was not until he was halfway down Ikorodu road that he remembered. He decided that owing to the traffic congestion, rather than turn round he would return to the Airport the following day.

Next day, he went straight to the office of the most senior Customs officer and complained that he had left his duty-free brandy and whisky in the Customs Hall.

Officer bursting with laughter – 'I know you've been out of the country a long while, but you don't mean to tell me you left your property in the Customs Hall and you expect to find it 24 hours afterwards?' By this time the

Officer was laughing so much his face was streaming with tears. However, he invited Alhaji to follow him to his assistant's office. Alhaji repeated his complaint and straight away both officers were rolling with laughter only to be joined by other officers who on hearing the complaint burst into even greater laughter.

Officer: 'Alhaji, in 12 years of being at this Airport I have never heard such a complaint. Anything can disappear in this Customs Hall. Whenever the Head of State is returning to the country, I always have to personally lead my boys just to be sure none of his luggage disappears.'

PERSONAL EFFECTS

Mrs Ase-Belaiyeri holds a doctorate in psychology as well as being married to a doctor, so she's quite used to being treated with respect and deference.

On arriving at Ikeja airport after 18 years away in America, she was carrying only her American Express card but no cash. This was quickly discovered by the customs boys who then proceeded to inspect all her personal effects one by one. To her astonishment, all her suitcases were emptied leaving the Customs Hall strewn with her personal effects right down to panties and bra. Her ordeal prompted her to declare:

'It seems Customs and Excise provide ready work for all sorts of queers and creeps.'

DUTY EVASION

Chief Enila Seunla imported six exquisite chandeliers (valued at ₦2,000 each) from Rome. On the customs form, he however declared that they were worth only ₦50.00 each. Unfortunately for the Chief, while the chandeliers were in the custody of the Customs, they were damaged. Consequently, the Customs have accepted liability for only ₦300. The Chief is however insisting on getting ₦12,000 i.e. the full cost of his damaged chandeliers and has instructed his lawyer to write to the Customs and Excise and point out that he was merely AVOIDING duty – not EVADING it.

THE MADAME

A vigilant Customs Officer went through Madame Boleya Koya's luggage and discovered that she was carrying £2,000 (sterling) and 3,000 dollars in excess of her travel allowance. He confiscated it and sternly warned madame that she could either insist on collecting a receipt for it in which case she would be prosecuted for smuggling currency out of the country or to quietly forget it. Madame assured him that she didn't want any trouble and would rather forget it. Madame Boleya Koya burst into great laughter as her plane took off. Her hand luggage consisted of £10,000 sterling and 15,000 dollars! The currency confiscated by the Customs Officer was all counterfeit.

AND NOW THE NONSENSE

Mrs Adunni Igbalaiye is stunning and she knows it. A few days ago, when she came through the Customs Hall at Ikeja Airport with 18 pieces of luggage, she was charged customs duty of ₦4.300 by a rather zealous officer. Coolly, she winked at a star-studded superior officer who came walking past and nearly keeled over on receiving such a welcome invitation from the beautiful young lady in distress. He promptly waved a disapproving finger at his junior officer and said – 'The lady has nothing to declare.'

'Thank you, Officer' whispered the lady and followed up with a kiss on the cheek.

The officer couldn't believe his luck and demanded her address which she readily gave. 'Can I come and see you tonight?' he demanded. 'Yes of course, come at midnight,' she replied.

'Why midnight – isn't that rather late?' he enquired.

'Don't worry, my husband will be home alright. He's a wrestler and judo expert – just tell him you are the gentleman from the CUSTOMS & NONSENSE and he'll show you my bedroom.'

SO WHAT??

FIRST THE GOOD NEWS

THE Public Relations Department of Customs and Excise announced a few days with great fanfare that a tunnel via which millions of naira worth of goods had been spirited out of Apapa docks warehouse by criminals had been discovered by vigilant Customs and Excise Officials.

NOW THE BAD NEWS

My spy at Apapa docks greeted the news with uncontrollable laughter. According to him, the existence of the 100-metre tunnel has been the best known secret in Apapa for several months and he was rather perplexed at the pretence by customs officials that it was a sudden discovery. According to Chief Man-Pass-Man, the existence of the tunnel was so widely known by customs officials that for several months they had been openly referring to the tunnel as 'SHEHU MUSA AVENUE' – named after Alhaji Shehu Musa, Permanent Secretary, Federal Ministry of Health, who was deployed by the Government to go and clean up the Customs and Excise but gave it up as a bad job and wrote a one line report back to the Public Service Commission – 'This is Mission Impossible.'

QUESTION TIME

For several months the residents of South-West Ikoyi have been continuously irritated by the antics of evangelical revivalists who every night hold frenzied prayer meetings at which the slogan 'CHRIST IS THE ANSWER' is yelled over and over again right through the night. One enterprising soul whose house overlooks the prayer ground has installed a tape recorder that repeats over and over – 'WHAT WAS THE QUESTION?'

SURPRISING NEWS

A few days ago, the Federal Military Government announced its surprise on learning that the French Government had decided to go ahead and supply South Africa with nuclear reactors, thus posing a serious threat to the security of BLACK AFRICA.

I AM SURPRISED THAT THE GOVERNMENT IS SURPRISED.

The consequences of South Africa developing atomic weapons are too staggering. It would completely alter the balance of power in Africa and tempt South Africa into a pre-emptive strike against militant black nations who are committed to the liberation of Africa.

STRANGE NEWS

It seems that once again the Ghanaian Government is determined to expel 'aliens'. The recently promulgated Investment Policy Decree No. 329 provides that 'no person other than a Ghanaian shall sell or be concerned with the sale of anything whatsoever in any market'.

Inevitably, Nigerians who have lived and traded within the borders of Ghana will once more find themselves denied employment and livelihood. This of course means that they will be forced to head for home.

Decree No. 329 is clearly against the spirit of ECOWAS Ironically, it was Nigerians who were the first settlers of Accra back in the 17th century. They were the Ga people from Ile-Ife and have up till today retained some of their Nigerian *traditions* evidenced by their celebration of 'HOMOWO' Festival, known as the 'TWIN' festival; they still have Chiefs styled as 'NEE' (or Oni), 'sango' shrines are still to be found in some *traditional* Ga areas of Accra; and there are several prominent Accra families who bear Nigerian names such as Adegbite, Akinwunmi etc., etc. The growth of Accra itself as a city in the 19th

236

and 20th century owes quite a great deal to the efforts of a Nigerian, Chief Brimah who hailed from Ilorin and was responsible for the development of areas such as Cow Lane, Tudu, Adabrika and Lagos Town (now known as Accra new Town).

SECRETARIAL NEWS

After the admission by United States Congressman Wayne Hays that he had an affair with his secretary Elizabeth Ray – who says she was 'purely a mistress and couldn't type, file, or even take phone messages' – several other secretaries on Capitol Hill (where Congress is located) are now wearing buttons that read: 'I ONLY TYPE.'

EXTERNAL NEWS

Our Ministry of External Affairs spends considerable sums on grooming our would-be Ambassadors in the delicate aspects of their jobs such as etiquette, decorum and protocol. However, I hear that a little while back, one of our Ambassadors posted to Europe was ever so anxious to demonstrate his newly-acquired skill at dancing the waltz. He was attending a state occasion but all his attention was concentrated on a tall, elegantly dressed lady seated on the other side of the room. On hearing the band start playing what sounded like a waltz, our Ambassador could hardly wait to get the lady in question into his arms and waltz away. He walked across, bowed charmingly and asked for a dance! There were a lot of red faces when the 'lady' announced in a very masculine voice – 'Mr Ambassador for wherever-you-come-from, first I think you are drunk; second that was our National Anthem; and third I am the Cardinal.'

INTERNAL NEWS

Commenting on the spate of investigations into various Government Agencies now going on in the country, a U.N. observer told a crowded press conference at Murtala Muhammed Airport, Ikeja – 'The real trouble with

Nigeria are the "Chiefs" and "Alhajis". They are deeply involved in every racket – They are the people causing all the confusion. If anyone introduces himself to you as "Alhaji (Chief) . . ." just take cover.'

MONETARY NEWS

At the recent UNTAD conference in East Africa. The Chairman of the Committee on 'shipping and Naval matters' was surprised to see the delegate from land-locked Central Africa Republic.

CHAIRMAN: 'What are you doing here – your country has no ships and no navy?'

CHAD DELEGATE: 'What's that got to do with it? The BRITISH Chancellor of the Exchequer is here and he is Chairman of the Finance Committee – Lord knows Britain doesn't have any money either!'

MONKEY SENSE

If there's any insult that really upsets Nigerians, surely it must be when they hear themselves being referred to as 'black monkeys'. However, how does one explain the fact that large sections of the aluminium barriers on the Lagos 'EKO BRIDGE' which should protect motorists from instant death have been DELIBERATELY removed by some crazy characters even though it is quite clear that by stealing those barriers they are exposing human lives to serious danger.

Equally, how does one explain the fact that in spite of the Government's tireless efforts to reduce the price of cement and thus make housing cheaper for everybody, it is Nigerians who go all out to frustrate the government by creating an 'artificial shortage'. There is abundant cement in the country but thanks to the activities of some criminal middlemen who hijack cement from the ports, cement is now selling at almost ₦5.00 per bag in some parts of the country instead of the controlled price of ₦2.50 per bag.

PS: DON'T MIND NIGERIANS; BUT FEAR THEM!

FOR BETTER FOR WORSE

THE ancient Greeks, were the first to declare August the most propitious month for marriage. It was a month for gestation and blissful communion with nature that augured well for the future happiness of newly-married couples. The most eminent astrologers by common assent declared SATURDAY, 23 AUGUST the ideal day to get married. It was the 'Eve of Saint Agnes'. The patron saint of maidens who on that day at the stroke of midnight would knock on the doors of the brand-new brides to offer her blessings. Here are extracts from St Agnes' report for this year:

LONDON

Alhaji Mio Gbagbere who had already spent 15 years in London declared that at 42 he was old enough to admit that (i) there was no hope of his ever passing his accountancy exams; (ii) he would never be able to persuade an English girl to marry him and (iii) the only course open to him was to ask his mother to send him a wife from his village.

Alhaji Mio had no qualms about such an arranged marriage but he laid down three conditions. First the wife must not be (i) deaf (ii) have a hunch-back (iii) suffer from lameness. Having received cast-iron assurances from his mother that the three conditions had been scrupulously fulfilled, Alhaji Mio turned up at Gatwick Airport on Saturday, 23 August carrying a photograph of the wife who was being 'posted' to him. The last passenger off the Nigeria Airways flight was the bride for whom he had paid a generous dowry.

He nearly collapsed with embarrassment, clad as he

was in a three-piece pin-stripe suit with pocket handker-chief to match when he discovered that his bride WAS NOT WEARING ANY SHOES! His first instinct was to disclaim her and demand his money back but the British Immigration Authorities would have none of that. Alhaji Mio couldn't get out of the airport quick enough and without saying a word, he rushed her into a taxi and off to the nearest Bata Shoe Shop. The shop manager welcomed them with proper civility as if nothing at all was amiss and asked the bride Wosilatu what her size was. As Wosilatu had never worn shoes in her life, she had no idea at all what size would fit her. She pointed to a pair of black shoes and asked for the price.

'That's a size FOUR, the price is SIX pounds, madam,' answered the shop-manager.

Wosilatu looked around and pointed to a bigger pair of the same shoes.

'That's a size NINE, it's also SIX pounds, Your Excellency,' replied the shop-manager.

Wosilatu leapt with excitement at the sound of a bargain and insisted on having the size NINE shoes with the comment: 'I'M NOT GOING TO LET ANY WHITE-MAN CHEAT ME.'

BENIN

Miss Eremeya Mosadebey, the first lady barrister from Akpakava confessed to her mother that Saturday, 23 August last year found her on board a ship returning from Liverpool to Lagos. According to her, on the first day on board, the captain of the ship wished her an enjoyable voyage free of sea-sickness; on the second day, he asked for her name; on the third day he complimented her on her beauty and chocolate-brown skin complexion; on the fourth day he invited her to join him at the captain's table for a sumptuous dinner and champagne; on the fifth day he let her know that he had a spare key to her cabin; on the sixth day, he propositioned her; on the seventh day, he told her that unless she said YES, he would sink the ship along with its crew of 100 and 500 passengers'.

At this point her mother interrupted – 'So my dear – what did you do?'

'M'am, I SAVED SIX HUNDRED LIVES.'

LAGOS

GOD SENT HUBERT TOWRY-COKER!

YESTERDAY, (Saturday, 23 August), at a fantastic wedding ceremony, EX-BACHELOR, Dr Olanrewaju Hubert Towry-Coker (LL.D) was joined in matrimony with EX-MISS Olabisi Adetoun Ogunbanjo. Shortly before the wedding, the bride's father confronted the bridegroom:

'My daughter is the finished product of loving care and excellent education. What makes you think you have the right to take her away?'

'G.S.M. Sir.'

'What is G.S.M., young man?'

'God Sent Me, Sir.'

KADUNA

On the thirteenth anniversary of his marriage, Mallam Gumi Ado decided that since he had had nothing but trouble from his wife Sikirat, it was time to consult the most renowned fortune-teller in Kaduna – Alhaji Tefi Mona.

Alhaji Tefi Mona tok a long pensive look at Mallam Ado's palm and after solemn deliberation declared: 'You have been frustrated and miserable for the last thirty years.'

'I know that,' the Mallam quickly interrupted 'it's the next thirty years I'm worried about.'

Alhaji Tefi Mona comforted him with the words: 'YOU'LL CONTINUE TO BE FRUSTRATED AND MISERABLE. BUT DON'T WORRY – YOU'LL GET USED TO IT.'

ABA

Last week, Chief Uguata Simeon Oguata, of Aba wrote off to a marriage counsellor in one of the Women

241

Magazines to lodge a complaint against his wife and seek advice.

His letter was a one-liner:

'I AM FED UP WITH BEATING MY WIFE.'

THE EX-MILLIONAIRE

The axiom that 'no condition is permanent' has received further confirmation from Dennis Blake, the self-made millionaire who has turned a personal fortune 'of ₦8,000,000 two and half years ago into admitted debts of ₦6,000,000'.

In 1967, Blake had formed the Standard Tyre Company which made huge profits from tyre and battery distribution business. He sold his company for a huge sum to motor parts supplier Quinton Hazell, which in turn was bought up by Burmah Oil. Blake ended up with a large block of Burmah Oil shares, which he sold and invested the proceeds to buy a controlling interest in Brown Brothers & Albany another tyre distribution group, 'which under his direction made a disastrous ₦8,000,000 investment in motor car distributor Henlys late in 1973'. Within a matter of months, Blake had lost ₦3,600,000 of his investment in Brown Brothers; ₦1,800,000 in a bed and breakfast share deal; ₦1,600,000 in Contractors' Services Group; ₦500,000 in a washing machine venture; and incurred income tax liabilities of ₦800,000.

HE IS NOW WORKING AS A ₦120 A WEEK CAR SALESMAN.

THE EX-FATHER-TO-BE

Last week, while Captain Lawal, the new Military Governor of Lagos was making his first official visit to the baby factory – Island Maternity Hospital, every effort was made to keep him away from the labour room. Commotion had broken out on account of a certain Mr Nwankwo Udenicha. Just before Mrs Udenicha went into labour, her husband waving a determined finger in her face firmly reminded her – 'BETTER MAKE SURE IT'S A BOY.'

After three hours of waiting, Mr Udenicha grew impatient and demanded to know from the staff nurse what was delaying the arrival of the baby. He was politely informed: 'We are very busy here – please be patient.'

After two more hours, Mr Udenicha went up to the nurse again, 'Look madam, I don't even care if it's a girl for Christ's sake tell her to hurry up.'

After three more hours, the impatient husband informed the nurse 'Madam, please tell her I'm giving her five more minutes to have the baby or else I'm leaving. After all, when my other wife had her baby at Umualaka Herbalist and Native Care Centre, it took only 20 minutes.'

Precisely five minutes afterwards, the gynaecologist who had been attending Mrs Udenicha emerged from the labour room: 'Mr Udenicha, I must speak to you privately.' The father-to-be followed him into his private room only to be told 'look old boy, don't take it too badly, I'm sorry it's a phantom pregnancy.' 'What does that mean?' demanded Udenicha. 'It means that what made your wife's belly swell up so much was merely AIR.' 'Mr Surgeon-General, don't talk nonsense,' shouted Udenicha taking off his trousers and displaying his manhood – 'What do you think this is? A BICYCLE PUMP?'

UPSIDE DOWN

FIRST THE GOOD NEWS

IN Columbia, the United Nations backed programme to control the birth-rate scored a great success with the distribution of free TV sets to villagers. Parents watched and the figures dropped dramatically.

NOW THE BAD NEWS

Greatly encouraged by their success in Columbia, United Nation Officials rushed to India and repeated the same experiment. The result was a complete disaster. The children were sent to watch TV while the parents got busy making more babies.

UNUSUAL NEWS

As late as the early years of the 20th century, it was traditional for women in upper Egypt to terminate unwanted pregnancies by lying face down on the railway tracks and allowing the next scheduled train to pass over them.

BAD ADVICE

Lagos motorists are perplexed at how it now seems that there is no foolproof device to stop car burglars from getting into their cars. It seems nothing will stop the car thieves – if they want your car, they'll get it, irrespective of your car alarm, twin-lock, interlock etc. In desperation, motorists have turned to the Police for advice. The Public Relations Department of the Police have accordingly distributed leaflets and placed adverts containing the following advice – 'Rig a charge of plastic explosive to your car before you leave. If a car thief gets past all your alarm systems, you'll lose your car, but there will be one less car thief running around. Of course, if you forget to unhook it . . . just start playing the first verse of 'Lord, I'm coming home . . .'

MISTAKEN NEWS

An agency hired by a Lagos hotel to send thank-you letters and Xmas cards to former guests of the hotel mistakenly thanked the wrong mailing list and threw hundreds of households into turmoil. The hotel was flooded with demands by irate husbands and wives demanding either more information about their spouses' recent patronage or assurances to one spouse that the other hadn't stayed there. According to the embarrassed manager, 'we got a lot of calls from women who said now they knew where their husbands spent their lunch hours'. One pregnant woman who received a letter tearfully said her husband was furious and doubtful about whether the baby was his. A United Nation's observer who was staying at the hotel at the time of the mammoth crisis commented: 'Husbands and wives don't trust each other much these days – it's a serious problem which could easily start the Third World War.'

BIBLE NEWS

Rev Keith Armstrong who is himself a 'hippy' has just launched a hippy version of the Bible which he claims he has translated to reflect the way people actually talk these days. Sample quote: 'Psalm 23' which used to be 'My Lord is my shepherd, I shall not want . . .' now translates as;

'Though I walk the valley of death,
I fear no evil
Because, I am
The biggest, baddest bastard of them all.'

CONSTITUTIONAL NEWS

Yesterday, I talked to a member of the Constitution Drafting Panel (not Dr Kole Abayomi) and enquired about the progress made so far. I got a very cynical reply as follows:

'We are holding the ropes of the boxing ring ready for the politicians to step into the arena when they have agreed on the rules of the fight – outside the ring.'

CONFUSED NEWS

The venomous nature of the Senegalese attack on Nigerian leaders coupled with the suggestion that we don't have 'common sense' caught many of us by surprise largely because we have failed to appreciate the depth of Senegalese jealousy of our oil wealth. Maybe they are right in thinking that if only they had one-tenth of our wealth, they would do wonders. At any rate, instead of offering platitudinous apologia and diplomatic niceties, our Ambassador Mr Kadiri should have cut out the waffle and told the Senegalese the honest truth as follows:

'We are confused alright, but we are not as confused as the Senegalese.'

KENNEDY NEWS

An American newspaper has published some well documented astonishing revelations about the sexual prowess of the late President John F. Kennedy. According to the newspaper Kennedy's sexual appetite was insatiable and if the paper is to be believed, he went to bed with a different woman every day and he had no inhibitions about swimming nude surrounded by pretty girls in the White House pool. The newspaper also quotes a certain Mrs Exner who had a 'close relationship of a very personal nature' with the President. Apparently, the relationship was so close that Mrs Exner was a regular visitor to the White House while the President's wife was away on cultural tours, and shared hotel rooms with him on numerous occasions. Mrs Exner is reported to have recalled how on one occasion, Kennedy was campaigning in her neighbourhood, but took only 20 minutes to get off the campaign trail, knock on her door, get into bed with her, make his exit over her back door fence and get back on the campaign trail. On another occasion, the President is reported to have suggested to Mrs Exner and another lady that they both go to bed with him at the same time!

These revelations of President Kennedy's sexual antics have thrown a new light on the mystery of who really killed him. It seems that Lee Oswald (who was not really Lee Oswald but a planted Russian agent) was not the murderer. Rather, Kennedy was shot by a jealous husband whose self-control was shattered when his wife phoned him in the office to announce:

'I've just had the PRESIDENT for lunch, you'll have to fix your dinner yourself.'

UNBELIEVABLE NEWS

I simply refuse to believe a report credited to the Rating Department of Lagos City Council to the effect that one of the Senior Officers of the Lagos State Government who was sent on compulsory retirement owns 166 houses (repeat one hundred and sixty-six houses!) in Lagos.

UNITED NATION NEWS

Quote from the report of United Nation's Secretary-General Dr Kurt Weildstein after his brief visit to Nigeria – 'Nothing works in Nigeria; everyone owns a Mercedes-Benz 280 "Air-conditioned, no hand signals"; and EVERYTHING IS UPSIDE DOWN.'

ALL THAT GLITTERS

THE GOLD RUSH

PERHAPS the most chilling report to emerge from war-torn Beirut concerns the activities of Nigerian business-women, known as 'Alhajas'. Apparently, right in the midst of the chaos into which Beirut was plunged by its civil war and the consequent shortage of food and other basic necessities, Nigerian women traders lured by the prospect of cheap gold were prepared to risk their lives. They eagerly took food, drinks etc., to Beirut and greedily exchanged them for gold trinkets, bracelets, and assorted jewellery which the desperate Lebanese readily parted with at rock-bottom prices. Really and truly, we are a money-mad society.

THE COMPLAINTS' BUREAU

While addressing newsmen at Murtala Muhammed Airport, Chief Ole'Ntele Afa called on the Federal Military Government to disband the newly established Public Complaints Bureau because according to the Chief, the Bureau encourages the public to complain about the government instead of complaining about themsleves. Looking very angry, the Chief declared, 'The trouble is not with the government but with the people themselves'.

Urged by the press corps who insisted on talking about specifics rather than generalities, the Chief elaborated: 'Look, the government is committed to cheap housing. Every effort has been made to reduce the cost of building materials. In particular, the price of cement was fixed at ₦2.5 per bag because there is sufficient supply available from local sources augmented by massive importation. However, the reality is something else. Thanks largely to the activities of middlemen and black-marketeers there is an artificial shortage of cement and in many parts of the country, you have to pay ₦5.00 per bag – if you can get it.' Really and truly, we are a money-mad society.

At this point, Dr Kurlhein Walt an engineer seconded by the UN to assist Nigeria with its Rural Electrification Programme, interrupted the Chief and added his own observation: 'I don't know much about the cement business, but I do know that in Anambra and Imo States our copper wires for electrifying the rural areas for the benefit of all and sundry have been so massively depleted by constant raids by thieves that we may have to abandon the scheme. It's a constant battle – no sooner do we receive a consignment of copper wires after long delays at the ports than our stores are raided. Even the wires we manage to put up get swiped. It's so frustrating for us to discover that your people use these copper wires as jewellery or spare parts for motor cars! There is an active black-market in stolen copper wire. Really and truly, even your best friends are forced to tell you that you are a money-mad society.'

Mallam Bala Gongola could not resist adding his own comment: 'Look at the new Eko Bridge in Lagos. Millions of tax payers' money went into building it. Little by little the aluminium barriers have been yanked out by thieves who sell the aluminium at a fantastic profit on the black-market. Those barriers are meant to protect motorists and save lives, yet fellow Nigerians rip them out for a quick sale. How can you possibly deny that really and truly, we are money-mad?'

THE UNKNOWN SOLDIER

The tomb of the 'Unknown Soldier' (known as 'Soja Idumota') is an unmistakable landmark at Idumota. For years, residents of Lagos have been puzzled by the inscription of 'Dogo Yaro' on the tomb. 'Dogo Yaro' which translates as 'Tall Man' was presumed to be the name of the soldier portrayed by the statue. The history of the statue is not exactly clear but it would appear that there is general agreement that it was built to commemorate the Nigerian soldiers who died in the First World War (1914–18).

However, an ex-serviceman has pointed out that (unlike the Second World War when soldiers were properly identified and screened before being recruited into the army), during the First World War, recruitment was so hastily done that soldiers, most of whom came from up-country were just given names and numbers on the spur of the moment by the British Officers. Consequently 'Dogo Yaro' was probably no more than the physical description of the soldier in recognition of his immense height. This partly explains the preponderance of such names as Lance-Corporal 'One-eye'; Sergeant 'Fat Belly'; Regimental Sergeant-Major 'No Shoes' and Corporal 'Missing Fingers' as well as the occasional 'Strongman', 'No-fear', 'Never wash', 'Deaf and Dumb' etc.

THE AFFLUENT SOCIETY

I think, Dr Majibu Bokassa, an eminent sociologist was quite right to describe Obalende as the 'Melting-Pot' of Lagos. Obalende is only a small area right on the doorstep of Dodan Barracks and it is sandwiched between the affluent south-west Ikoyi and the axis of Keffi Street, MacGregor Canal, and the near-side of the even more affluent Victoria Island.

Obalende is a paradox of elegant houses right next door to the most filthy slums occupied by a weird assortment of tradesmen, prostitutes, dope-peddlars, beer parlours, 'Ogogoro' (illicit gin) sellers, a few clerks as well as the slummy Police Barracks which is dirty and poorly maintained. Strangely enough, St Gregory's College, a Catholic School, which used to be one of the best schools in Lagos is situated there. Talk of evil influences on young minds! There is hardly any tribe in Nigeria that is not represented in Obalende.

Quite unknown to the majority of dwellers in Obalende, the area is still classified as 'Crown Land'. Just after the First World War, the land adjoining the Obalende Military Barracks was carved into plots and given to ex-servicemen who needed somewhere to settle in Lagos instead of going back up-country. All the plots were on leasehold and the occupiers were required to pay a nominal rent of 'one shilling'. For quite a long time, Obalende was in fact called 'Hausa Settlement' since it was predominantly occupied by Hausas. Thereafter a brisk trade in plots developed and many of the plots have changed hands several times. Sooner or later, the government will have to do something to arrest the decline of Obalende and it is inevitable that in the attempt to deal with the problem, the government would have to re-establish its claim and disillusion those who have bought plots in the area believing that they were buying freehold.

THE MONEY GAME

While commenting on the creation of Commodity Boards to replace State Marketing Boards, Chief Kojojibiti Kojojamba declared that the government's intention to assist farmers by fixing reasonable prices for their produce is admirable. However, according to the Chief who has just retired from the Western State Marketing Board after 30 years of service, the problem has always been how to put more money into the hands of farmers and ensure that the funds are ploughed into the expansion of their farms. The Chief recalled the experience of the old Western State which chose to do this by granting generous loans. However, this only led to large scale fraud and virtually all the loans were irrecoverable due to false identity, wrong addresses and massive collusion. Also, government spent considerable sums of good money trying to chase bad money. The Chief has therefore, called on the government to remember the axiom that when you are dealing with farmers, it is sometimes cheaper to give them money (via subsidies) than to LEND them money.

HERE COMES THE JUDGE

RECENTLY, when the Supreme Military Council directed that all judges should declare their assets, there was much grumbling among holders of this exalted office and there were muted complaints to the effect that the exercise was 'unconstitutional'. However, much of the sting in the judges' bow was neutralised by the Supreme Military Council's decision that its own members would also declare their assets.

It now appears that those judges who either because they were dismayed by the exercise or through fear of being discomfited by embarrassing revelations decided to leave the bench were quietly told – 'Declare your assets first'.

One interesting development is that quite a few judges are themselves startled at the extent and size of assets – mostly property and shares which are said to belong to fellow judges. If there is any truth in some of the stories now circulating, several judges are virtually property millionaires with sizeable chunks of houses, office blocks, blocks of flats in prime locations as well as extensive farmlands. Also, it is common knowledge that quite a few judges benefited generously from the 'Indigenisation Decree' through privileged acquisition of shares in expatriate companies on a scale denied to ordinary citizens. Apparently, some companies even sold their property to judges without first advertising them on the open market.

I think it is only fair to remind ourselves that first, only a minority of judges were involved. Secondly, many of the present judges ran highly successful and lucrative law practices before becoming judges and in some cases, elevation to the bench meant considerable financial sacrifice. In addition, judges like any other citizen do have a right to own property.

What is questionable however, is the means and 'muscle' with which property and shares were acquired by judges either in their own names or in the names of their wives. Also, it would appear that a small number of judges are engaged in property development of a highly speculative nature. The bone of contention is whether such extensive dealing in property and shares would in any way compromise judges in their onerous duties as regards which they must at all times be seen to be 'free and fair' in the dispassionate deliverance of justice. This raises the question whether a judge may not find himself hearing a case involving a company in which he is himself a substantial shareholder.

It was the late Chief Justice of Lagos, Mr Justice J. I. C. Taylor who declared that 'corruption does not consist entirely (or exclusively) of taking money'.

HOME NEWS

Among the guests at the recent marriage of Miss Loretta Akpani of 'FESTAC' Secretariat to Mr Richard Smith of IBWA Ltd was Brigadier 'The voice of 29 July' Joseph Garba, Federal Commissioner for External Affairs. The presence of his wife did not inhibit Brigadier from getting up and declaring before the microphone that his association with Miss Akpani was of a long-standing 'close personal relationship', going back to 1967. According to him, the relationship was so close that he had had considerable difficulty in persuading his own wife that it did not go beyond that of 'a sister and a brother'. Confirmation came by way of Mrs Garba's merry participation in the ensuing general laughter and applause.

Just for the record – the brand new Mrs Smith struck a blow for 'Women's Lib' by getting up to make a thank-you speech and correct some minor details as regards her husband's recollection of their first meeting. As far as I know, this is the first occasion when the bride got up to speak at a Lagos wedding. Most brides happily keep their mouth shut, at least for the first day!

Also for the record – the bride looked truly radiant, gorgeous and glowed with happiness. Here's wishing the newly-weds a long and joyous marriage. (PS. Mr Smith has denied any connection with the Smithsonian Institute.)

TRAFFIC CONTROL

Professor Ye Paripa who was commissioned to write an in-depth investigative report on traffic congestion in Lagos has now completed his daunting task. His major recommendation is that at peak hours, the government should create a fast lane restricted to buses, taxis, and cars carrying at least four passengers. Furthermore, women drivers, bishops, money-lenders, dentists, contractors, military vehicles, FGN cars, trade unionists, university lecturers, magicians, lawyers, accountants, money-doublers and astronauts should be restricted to the slow lane irrespective of the number of their passengers.

UNWANTED GUESTS

For the fourth time, the World Bank has had to postpone their inspectors' visit to London to check their customers' books and ensure that the huge loans advanced to Britain are still safe in spite of Joe Gormley, Tony Wedgewood Benn, Michael Foot, Harold Wilson, Lady Forkbender, Margeret Thatcher, Robert Relf, Enoch Powell and the several other prominent names who have featured in the heavy voting for the 'most disliked man in Britain' as well as for the 'most liked man in Britain' depending on your point of view.

The British Minister of Information has been at pains to explain that the outbreak of racial and other forms of violence is no more than 'summer madness' on account of the unbelievably hot summer. However, a spokesman for the World Bank has complained that 'it's all rather odd. Whenever we set out to check on our money it's either IRA bombs are falling or there's trouble over racial violence or there is a strike at the airport.' But for the fact that there is nothing funny at all about violence, one should be forgiven for thinking that if nothing else, it at least keeps the creditors away.

AND NOW THE GOOD NEWS

The Nigerian Government has been urged by Chief (Dr) Jagri Jagon to follow the example of the Australian Government by reviewing the Income Tax structure in order to 'fulfil the objective of getting the Government's hands out of tax-payer's pockets'. This would confirm that 'individuals attach considerable importance to their own command over their incomes and their ability so far as possible to spend those incomes as they see fit.' The Australian Government was very mindful of this when it recently announced its 'TAX INDEXATION' programme whereby tax deductions are related to the inflation rate prevalent in the country.

CONDITIONAL NEWS

As if to remind me that 'no condition is permanent', my car still shows a severe dent inflicted by the boot of one of Gowon's splendidly uniformed outriders accompanying him to the airport on his journey to Kampala. It never crossed my mind that three days afterwards – he would lose his throne or eight months thereafter, he would be declared 'A WANTED PERSON'.

SO WHAT?
ON BEHALF OF MYSELF AND MYSELF

THE ALHAJI

I HAVE known Alhaji Jagri Jagon since 1914, and as any of his friends would confirm, the Alhaji drinks too much, smokes too much, snuffs too much (and too noisily) and worst of all he talks too much and much of what he says is anyway pure unadulterated nonsense.

Yesterday, at the Institute of Contemporary Affairs, Victoria Island, Lagos, the Alhaji delivered a virtuoso lecture under the aegis of the Director of the Institute of National Affairs. This time, the Alhaji really surpassed himself with his studied illogicality and abrasive but twisted recollection of the history of this country.

He started off by declaring: 'Ladies and gentlemen, there are many people in this country who specialise in telling whatever government is in power how wonderful they are. On behalf of myself and myself, I wish to assure you that I do not belong to that club. In fact, I have never got along with any of the successive governments of this country, going back to 1914.'

He went on to add, while frothing at the mouth, 'when the British were here, I was always in trouble with them. I was always agitating for one thing or the other. However, I always acted alone, so there was no way they could charge me for conspiracy. The worst that ever happened to me was getting sacked as a Treasury clerk. They threatened to draft me into the Army, then changed their mind and instead wrote me off as a madman "suffering from delusions of grandeur and self importance". In fairness to them, they always treated me with great tolerance thereafter.

'I was a regular petitioner at every Commission of Enquiry. In 1928, I caused great laughter and merriment when I went before the Cathart Commission of Enquiry and demanded equal pay for blacks and whites in the civil service. In 1936, I was severely reprimanded by the Selwill Commission of Enquiry for observing that the cream of the British Civil Service were normally sent off to India followed by Sudan in second place and the rest only reluctantly accepted service in the "whiteman's grave" – West Africa. In 1949, I nearly went to jail for agitating for pipe-borne water, electricity and free public toilets for the whole of Nigeria, at the Mullberry Smith Commission of Enquiry. But for the intervention of the late Ernest Ikoli and the persuasive influence of Sir Martin Hilchapp, I would have been convicted for advocating the death penalty for anyone caught urinating in public, or anyone failing to take anti-malaria tablets or defecating walls by pasting "Post No Bills".'

At this point, the Alhaji digressed to reminisce that in those days, in spite of his troubles with the British, they always made a point of inviting him to the Governor's Garden Party, King's Birthday Party etc. In those days, people from all walks of life, from headmasters, to doctors, clergymen, lawyers, and produce merchants would be invited. It was quite unlike now when the only people who get invited to state parties are contractors, civil servants and diplomats. Alhaji Jagri Jagon went on to add that, 'In those days, the telephones worked perfectly – in any case, there were only two telephones in Lagos. One belonged to the Governor and the other belonged to the Chief Secretary. Neither was there traffic congestion. In fact, the fellow who built Carter Bridge, in Lagos, was sacked for making the bridge dual carriage instead of one lane!'

Taking absolutely no notice of the astonishment and disbelief prevalent among the audience, the Alhaji went on to recall that in 1960, just before Independence, he had gone over to see the then Governor-General and had cautioned him – 'Don't do it. All these politicians you want to hand over the government to – I don't trust the whole lot of them.'

The Governor-General was really taken aback but with cool self-control had demanded:

'What can I do if I don't hand over to the politicians?' The Alhaji's reply was – 'Simple. Just hand over the government to me – after all, this country used to be ruled by just one person.'

The astonished Governor-General refused to let himself get angry and coolly demanded – 'Just how do you propose to run the country?'

Alhaji: 'My plans are very simple. First of all, I'll put all politicians and would-be politicians on the farms to grow more food. Second, I will prohibit all exclusive all-white areas such as Ikoyi etc. I shall insist that irrespective of race, religion or tribe, we must all get together. I shall compel every white man to have at least one black man living under his roof (but not in the Boys' Quarters). Also, any white man who divorces his wife must, within six months marry an African wife. In addition every white man must speak at least one major Nigerian language and can stay as long as he likes in Nigeria without any hassle about expatriate quotas. In addition, all Nigerians who have more than one wife will be allowed to acquire extra wives, mistresses and girl-friends only if such women come from a part of the country at least five hundred miles away from the man's home town or village. Furthermore, anyone who travels by Nigerian Airways should be paid automatic damages of ₦500. Also, I would never have allowed oil exploration. If God wanted oil pumped – he would not have buried it in the ground.'

The Governor-General without displaying shock or discomfiture, informed the Alhaji – 'I dare say, old chap, your plans do sound jolly interesting. I shall convey them to the Home Office.'

Continuing with the lecture, Alhaji Jagri Jagon went on to add – 'That was the last I saw of the Governor-General. To my great astonishment, he went ahead and handed over to Dr Nnamdi Azikiwe on 1 October 1960. I reluctantly attended Dr Azikiwe's inauguration but I have to confess, I didn't understand a word of his speech – too much grammar and too many big words and scholarly quotations. Look, here we are nineteen years after I warned the British Government. If they had listened to me, we wouldn't be in such a mess now.'

At this point, the Alhaji offered to answer questions from the audience. The first questioner was Professor Ye Paripa who enquired – 'Surely, Alhaji not all governments are bad. The present Government is doing a good job. Wouldn't you agree?' The Alhaji replied – 'Of all the governments that this country has had, the present Government is the one that has given me the least trouble and the least cause for complaint. However, there is one issue on which I do not see eyeball to eyeball with the government. It is the question of "Natural Rulers". To my mind, the government is trying too hard to please the Obas, Chiefs and Emirs. To preserve "Natural Rulers" is to logically accept that there are such people as "Natural Followers". I just don't accept this because as long as your people are natural followers there is no urge for them to do anything beyond what they are told. It follows that there is no drive to acquire technological skill to blaze new frontiers and for as long as that is the case, we shall forever remain rooted in poverty.'

At this point, the audience walked out in protest. Undeterred, Alhaji climaxed by declaring 'On behalf of myself and myself, I apologise to myself and my departed listeners for my ignorance, illogicality and stupidity. For those who are unable to attend, free copies of my lectures are available from the National Broadcasting Corporation of Nigeria.'

CRITICAL CHOICES

THE GOVERNMENT AND US

THE present Government is now three years old. It has been a period crowded with far-reaching decisions and while it would be premature and even misleading to talk in terms of 'revolution', there is no denying that some crucial and fundamental restructuring has taken place. A lot of changes which we had hitherto thought could not possibly take place in our lifetime have come to pass. The consequent applause has been passionate; the disappointments may well be severe but they have been muted – at least until recently. This is not the time for cheap flattery or wild encomiums. Rather, it is the time for deep reflection on how much we have achieved and how very much more there is to do.

More than at any other time, it is now self-evident that this IS A DIFFICULT COUNTRY TO RULE AND THAT WE SURVIVED FOR SO LONG IS FURTHER CONFIRMATION THAT WHILE WE MAY NOT LOVE EACH OTHER – at least 'somebody up there' loves us. We have been very lucky. Famine, floods, plagues, volcanoes, tornadoes, earthquakes etc., are remote from us. We have wealth which we didn't really have to work for – it was generously endowed on us by nature. What we have never quite managed to do is to decide what to do with it. Our basic handicap is that we are a nation rooted in SELF-CONTRADICTIONS. This is the time for us to get to grips with and eliminate those inhibiting contradictions. We must evaluate the options OPEN TO us and decide on our CRITICAL CHOICES.

It is vital that in making these decisions we should not allow ourselves to be lured by the soft options or be hamstrung by convention, tradition or orthodoxy. The best results are often achieved by bold initiatives, radical mutations, and unfettered imagination. For example, at the 1968 Olympics, the crowning glory belonged to a little-known American high-jumper called Fosbury (the architect of what is now known as the 'Fosbury Flop'). For centuries, every high-jumper jumped feet first, facing the bar, culminating in the 'Western Roll'; the 'Eastern Cut-off'; 'Straddle'; the 'Scissors' etc., Fosbury did the opposite – he jumped head first with his back towards the bar and yet he soared above everybody else to emerge the undisputed champion among the cream of the world's athletes. Today, every front-ranking high-jumper has adopted the 'Fosbury Flop'. There is a lesson for us all in this. Yesterday's 'Madness' is today's fashion. We are the only people qualified to determine our own limitations. If we set our standards too low, we may succeed in ambling along but we shall achieve only correspondingly low results. Our limitations and inhibitions are self-imposed.

THE GOVERNMENT AND THE PRESS

The government has achieved much to its credit and has been duly commended by the press. The relationship between the government and the press has been far from cosy and this is as it should be. Relatively speaking, the Nigerian press enjoys 'freedom' to an extent that is unequalled in Africa minus one or two exceptions. It is gratifying to note that the government and the press have each belatedly come to appreciate that the survival and success of one does not depend on the destruction or control of the other. We are a nation of about 80 million people – consequently it is futile to postulate that we should all think alike on any one issue. If 1000 of advocate a particular policy, no damage is done if two or three or more think it is nonsense and say so! My observation is that so far the present government has been willing to accept press criticisms as long as it is convinced that such criticisms are not motivated by 'mischief' or desire to adulate the performance of its pre-decessor.

THE GOVERNMENT AND CORRUPTION

There are millions of Nigerians who didn't believe that they would live to see the day when members of the Supreme Military Council would voluntarily declare their assets – but it's happening right now. However, this is only a step in the right direction. The far more gigantic task is to educate the public and raise the level of their consciousness to a degree whereby they are able to see corruption for what it is – a fraud perpetrated on the public by the public itself. Everybody is scrambling for a 'piece of the action'. Right now, the only people crying out loud against corruption are those who are not yet in a position to benefit from the 10 per cent rake-off directly. Consequently, one should be forgiven for wondering whether their condemnation would not be muted or non-existent once they themselves start benefiting from the system of 'chop your own and shut up'.

THE GOVERNMENT, THE ARMY AND THE CENSUS

There is no doubt in my mind that the present leaders are determined to hand over to civilians in 1979. Already, there are indications that some of the leading spirits would be only too pleased to hand over before then. However, sooner or later the Military Government would have to accept that perhaps the greatest legacy it can leave for posterity would be to streamline the army without compromising its efficiency; and secondly carry out a free, fair and credible census. These are no small tasks. The real problem is that if the Military Government does not take on these two onerous tasks, there are serious doubts about whether a civilian government would have a hope in hell of either streamlining the army or carrying out an acceptable census without precipitating a crisis. The naked truth, however painful, is that without an accurate census, virtually all our economic and social planning would be pure guess-work at best or more likely, inspired fiction. How do you begin to plan the right number of houses, hospitals, schools, factories, new towns, new capital etc. when you don't even know the number of people you are planning for?

THE GOVERNMENT, NATURAL RULERS AND LOCAL GOVERNMENT

If there is one area of government about which I have serious reservations, it is as regards the baffling readiness to entrench natural rulers and the preoccupation with local government reform. The extremists have already pointed out that it is a contradiction in terms to advocate an 'EGALITARIAN SOCIETY' while at the same time paying obeisance to natural rulers. To them, natural rulers are only one stage removed from feudalism and to seek to enhance their prestige or enlarge their influence is to turn the hands of the clock backwards. It is the sacrifice of expediency for logic. They argue, quite rightly that the unsavoury squabbling and dangerous intrigues as well as rioting, that invariably attend the choice of a successor when a natural ruler dies (particularly in the south) are unnecessary distraction from our true goals. In addition, it is arguable whether the concept of natural rulers as 'fathers' of their people, the fountain-head of wisdom, incorruptible and impartial custodians of law, order and tradition is more of a myth than reality. For these reasons, there are those who advocate the phasing out of natural rulers! That is, the government should decree that on the death of a natural ruler – no successor should be chosen. Anybody who wants to rule should stand for election and be answerable to those over whom he rules. This is dynamite! As for local government elections, the government's sincerity is not in doubt and its efforts to begin the restructuring of the *status quo* by reforming local government and involving the grass roots is well meaning and commendable. What is questionable is the methodology. As far as I am concerned, to hold local government elections or any elections for that

263

matter without lifting the ban on party politics, is like playing tennis without a net. If in addition, there is no proper census – then our plight becomes more compounded. We would be playing tennis without a net and without a ball!

THE GOVERNMENT AND THE PEOPLE

There is an urgent need for the government to reappraise its true functions. At present, the government is taking on so many tasks, particularly at the Federal level. To my mind – most of these tasks are best handled at state level primarily and beyond that by the local communities. Because the government is so willing and anxious to take on all sorts of onerous duties – there is the danger of our rapidly becoming a nation of morons, ever ready to let the government do everything for us. This is precisely why our streets are dirty – the gutters stink; water supply is unpredictable; electricity supply is unreliable; our telephones are mere decorations; our mails are a joke; and our traffic is a shambles – precisely because everybody is waiting for someone else to do the job.

Government must begin to tell the people that the tasks ahead are far too big to be undertaken by the government alone. Every community must be told clearly and unequivocally that whatever they want, it is up to them to take the first steps. Thereafter the government will come to their aid and supplement their efforts.

THE GOVERNMENT AND FOREIGN POLICY

We really ought to start making sure that our stance and pronouncements at the international level are a reflection of our own internal cohesion. It is futile to break our neck trying to appear bigger abroad than we are at home. Anyone who is foolish enough to accept at face value our claims to being the true leader of Africa only needs to take a look at our slums, the stench of our cities, the paucity and poor quality of our production and the primitiveness of our agriculture!

It's easy enough to hire an ambassador, dress him in a

three-piece suit plus a chauffeur-driven Rolls-Royce and have him rant and rave about justice, morality and threaten retaliation and boycott. All this would be meaningless unless we have 'something' to back it up. That 'something' is not oil at all – recent events have shown that when we put up the price of oil 10 per cent, they jerk up the price of fertilizers by 30 per cent – the joke is on us. What is missing is our ability to face our problems head on – to produce more goods; grow more food, approach our difficulties with imagination; acquire technological skills; and insist on making our efforts at tackling our own problems instead of letting somebody else do it. Above all, we must identify our true self-interest and marry our international postulation to it. How can our threats be taken seriously when the weapons, ammunition and the other wherewithal are all going to be purchased from the very people we are threatening?

THE GOVERNMENT AND THE GOVERNED

I firmly believe that those who run the affairs of this country and expect gratitude are likely to find that their optimism is misplaced! In fact, the only thing we have mastered so far is how to kill our leaders.

FIRST THE MAIN ITEMS

FIRST THE BAD NEWS

Dr OLU ONAGORUWA (LL.D) has declared President Jean-Bedel Bokassa of tiny Central African Republic as the holder of the 'unbeatable record for cruelty'. According to him, the President once removed the eyes of his rival and powerful cousin, Jean-Baptiste Mounoumbaye in the presence of his wife and children before ordering him to be shot.

The previous record-holder was none other than 'Big Daddy' Idi Amin of Uganda who according to the London 'TIMES' – 'had more success than any other NCO's in the periodic confiscation that took place of spears belonging to a tribe of rustlers (cattle thieves) in the North-Eastern Uganda. Amin simply lined the tribesmen up, made them stand with their private parts on a table and threatened to cut them off with a machete unless they told him where their spears were hidden.'

NOW THE MAN WITHOUT WHOM THE NEWS WOULDN'T BE THE NEWS

In an interview published in 'SPEAR' magazine, Chief Henry Fajemirokun, President of the Nigerian Chamber of Commerce declared:

'Banks are not charitable institutions. A banker is a businessman and if he must give out money on loan, he wants to be satisfied that he will get his money back.'

AND THEN THE EX-NEWS

An ex-Governor whose vast property empire has been

confiscated by the new regime, has been telling friends that all is not lost and that he is well on his way to his second fortune. According to him, he has just secured the exclusive distribution rights for a new drug called 'Genseed' which when taken with alcohol produces incredible sexual potency for the over 50s. Genseed was first discovered by the Chinese who used it for centuries to treat drug overdose without realising its full potentialities. The ex-Governor reports that business is so good he is thinking of opening branches in all the ECOWAS countries.

U.N. NEWS

While addressing a United Nations sub-committee currently investigating the relatively low life expectancy in under-developed countries, Dr Paul Weiken declared *inter alia* . . . 'One of the penalties of a double life appears to be that you only live half as long. It is not adultery that kills, it is the alibi.'

THE HOME NEWS

It's quite a few weeks now since Mr Ejuyitche, the former Head of the Civil Service and Secretary to the Military Government publicly declared that his integrity and honesty were never compromised during his 30-year career and threw a challenge to the public to provide evidence that he used his high office to line his own pockets.

It seems that contrary to popular belief, there are still a few people who enjoy a first-class reputation. Some of the names being suggested are Mr P. K. Tabiowo (Central Bank, Foreign Exchange) and Mr T. A. Tugbogbo (Deputy Permanent Secretary; Federal) who could easily have become millionaires if they had engaged in the 'ten per cent' or 'fifty-fifty' business while holding highly sensitive posts.

DYING NEWS

This morning, at a crowded press conference, Alhaji

Lakuregbe announced to a sympathetic audience – 'My wife has died. When I woke up this morning and put my hand out to wake her, she was as cold as a wet stone. She was alright last night. She made my soup, and it was very good soup. SHE NEVER TOLD ME SHE WAS GOING TO DIE.'

DIPLOMATIC NEWS

During the Nigerian Civil War, our Ambassador in U.K. was confronted by a hostile British Press who took him to task. In desperation, the flabbergasted Ambassador declared: 'How many times do I have to tell you that this is no religious war? It seems I can keep on denying it until I'm BLUE in the face – and you still won't believe me.'

BLACK ARTS FESTIVAL NEWS

It seems there is no end to the Black Arts Festival saga. I think we ought to deport the expert who took a look at the festival village and declared – 'The buildings have been put up without any regard for environmental blending. The houses come in all sorts of colours and hues. There are no telephones and the water supply is unpredictable. The houses have been built too close to each other. In seven years' time, the whole place could degenerate into another slum unless immediate remedial action is taken.' What a mess.

THE RACECOURSE NEWS

The same expert took a look at the Lagos Racecourse and yelled 'Christ Almighty! Can you imagine what the public outrage would be if the British Government built such a crazy monstrosity as this in Hyde Park, or if the Americans tried it with Central Park?' He was gently informed that nobody seems to know what is actually going on the racecourse. Lagos residents just woke up one morning and found the whole place covered with sand and cement. The next day, the bulldozers, cranes etc. moved in and work started in earnest. In fairness to the contractors, they worked day and night. It was only at that stage that word leaked out that the Government was determined to bulldoze the only open space left in Central Lagos. Towering solid concrete structures sprang up. Somehow, the whole thing did not blend with the surrounding buildings – High Court, Supreme Court, King's College etc. The Government then paid for advertisements inviting the public to come up with suggestions as to what is to be done with the surrounding area! The expert has concluded: 'These structures are so solid that it will cost almost as much money to knock them down as it cost to put them up!'

CONGESTED NEWS

In its efforts to decongest Apapa ports, the Nigerian Government has been diverting incoming ships to Accra, under an arrangement with the Ghanaian Government. The goods are off-loaded at Accra and transported by road through Togo and Dahomey, and transit duty of $2\frac{1}{2}$ per cent is levied at each of the borders. Businessmen who are only too willing to co-operate with the Government are now complaining that under this arrangement, it is costing them almost double the landed cost to bring in essential machinery and spare parts. Apart from the avalanche of additional paper work, it seems that part of the problem revolves around the unavailability of lorries for transportation. Instead of relying on the Ghana State Transport Corporation to provide the lorries (which together with spare parts are in short supply in Ghana anyway), we should ourselves provide the lorries through government agencies or private contractors.

ECOWAS NEWS

Under Dr Busia, Ghana passed the Alien's Act, the sole purpose of which was to expel Nigerians from Ghana and deprive them of their property. Anyone who has witnessed the appalling plight of hitherto quite prosperous traders, farmers, technicians etc., suddenly turned into refugees and beggars cannot but wonder at the insensitiveness of an African country in its determination to inflict suffering on fellow Africans. These refugees were never paid compensation for their property which they either lost entirely or were forced to sell at ridiculous prices. Apart from a few noises here and there, the then Nigerian Government hardly made any protest on behalf of its own citizens. If the euphoric concept of ECOWAS is to have any meaning, this is the time to re-open the issue and obtain fair compensation.

Wallahi Tallahi – where do we go from here?

LET'S DO IT AGAIN

AT a crowded press conference held at the Institute of Contemporary Affairs, Chief Pantija Wereja declared his whole-hearted support for the Government's determination to return to civilian rule and party politics by 1979. According to the Chief, there is just no substitute for the excitement of party politics and the attendant intrigues, back-stabbing, hypocrisy, manipulation, horse-trading, juggling and power grabbing – 'That's the stuff that makes the juices run.' After dealing with the usual round of inane questions and insipid observations by the press, Chief Wereja led a mammoth placard-carrying procession singing 'Let's do it again' to the British Embassy, the American Embassy and finally Dodan Barracks. Before the procession broke up, Chief Pantija Wereja distributed free 'Let's do it again' badges and announced that next week at the Ikoyi Hotel he would launch his party, but of course in view of the present ban on political parties he would not call it a party. Instead it would be launched as 'The National Club' to deliberate on the choice of a 'Lingua Franca for Nigeria'.

A Senior Civil Servant who was asked to comment on the launching of the National Club burst into laughter and asked 'who do they think they are fooling?' Let me ask you – can you think of a more political issue right now than the 'Lingua Franca' business with its hints of tribal domination? A Senior Police Officer who was asked to comment declared: 'Chief Pantija Wereja is one of our regular customers. Every government that has come into being in this country whether military or

271

civilian has had to detain the Chief for one reason or the other – ranging from sedition to embezzlement.'

THE GOOD OLD DAYS

It is now ten (10) years since the politicians went out of business but many still recall the events of those heady days particularly when it came to sharing the booty among 'party members'. Here is a sample: Chief Nkot Bassey's new Mercedes-Benz car was delivered to his hut on a Friday. It was a gift from the government as reward for his staunch loyalty to the party and his astuteness in rigging the last elections. During the elections, opposition members were suddenly missing, their houses were set on fire, their shops were looted and their children terrorised. Ballot papers dropped into the box for the opposition turned out to be massively ink-stained and were consequently nullified. Needless to add that the Government's candidate won by a landslide even bigger than the number of registered voters.

In order to reward Chief Nkot Bassey, the government had awarded him a ₦100,000.00 contract to build a new road in Okoto Creek Town. While thanking the Minister for Works and Roads, the Chief reminded the Minister: 'Honourable Minister, Okoto town is built on creeks. All our houses are on stilts – it is impossible to build roads here.'

The Minister told the Chief not to worry – 'The Government likes to show its appreciation to party stalwarts like you. Of course, we don't expect you to build any roads. You don't expect any miracles from us – neither do we expect any miracles from you. Is that understood?'

'Yes, Mr Honourable Minister,' said the Chief.

'Now, Chief, the money is for you to do whatever you like with. You can even buy a car like mine, a Mercedes-Benz, so that your people will really know that the Government looks after its supporters very well,' declared the Minister.

'Yes, Mr Honourable Minister, I'd like a Mercedes-Benz. It looks so big and beautiful,' said the Chief, 'But where shall I drive it? There are no roads in Okoto – we all travel by canoes.'

At this point, the Minister getting irritable, drew the Chief aside and whispered:

'CHIEF, we are not talking about DRIVING the car – we are talking about your people SEEING what the government can do for them.'

For the next five years, the car stood idle in front of Chief Bassey's hut.

POLICE NEWS

A few days ago, Mr A. Cudjoe, a cameraman employed by the Ministry of Local Government and Information, was driving along Araromi Street, Oke-Padi, Ibadan, when a four-year-old boy who attempted to cross the road, narrowly escaped being hit by the car. Mr Cudjoe came out of his car and decided to take the child to the police station but was attacked by the crowd that had quickly gathered. 'The cameraman was brutally beaten and his head battered.' All over the country, there have been incidents in which motorists who have stopped to assist injured victims have been given severe beatings which in some cases have resulted in the death of the motorists.

There is therefore an urgent need for the police to offer clear and unequivocal advice to motorists in this regard. Should the motorist involved in an accident stop to assist his victim at the risk of putting his own life in peril particularly when he has not been guilty of dangerous driving? Or should he drive straight to the nearest police station and leave it to the police to arrange for first-aid and conveyance of the victim to a hospital? The danger of leaving the victim and rushing off to the police station is of course that the victim would have been denied immediate assistance which could have been provided had he been conveyed directly to a hospital.

TRIBAL NEWS

At the risk of stating the obvious, we need to remind

ourselves that the greatest obstacle to the stability and development of this country is tribalism. If you put an Ibo man at the head of an organisation, in a matter of months, he will surround himself with his 'townsmen'. The Hausaman will do the same – and ditto the Yoruba-man, the Efikman, the Ijawman etc. The tragedy of it all is that tribalism is based largely on fear and above all ignorance of our true origin and history.

Only recently, at the Olorogun Adodo – Chieftaincy dispute, it was disclosed that the Olorogun Adodo Chief-taincy family in Lagos came originally from Ikokogbe royal compound in Benin. Other traditional Chiefs that originated from the same compound include the Erejuwa of Warri, the Obi of Onitsha and the Obi of Arochukwu. This is the sort of information that every schoolboy in the country should know.

Incidently, considering that we know so little about ourselves, how can we justify the expenditure of such huge sums on the FESTAC jamboree on the pretext that we want to make 'black people all over the world aware of themselves'?

OLD NEWS

Ever since Chief Obafemi Awolowo commented at Mur-tala Muhammed Airport that 'when young people say they don't want old politicians back in the field, I always have a feeling that they are afraid of these old men', there has been considerable debate about whether or not the government should impose an age limit when we return to civilian rule. A panel appointed to look into the problem has come up with a formula that should be acceptable to all. The panel insists that every case should be treated on its own merit and the formula should take into account the candidate's height, weight, colour of hair, formal education, teeth formation, eye-sight, diet, service to the nation, financial resources, number of wives, number of children, religion, tax receipts, smoking and drinking habits etc., etc. In the case of Chief Awolowo, his age limit works out at 128 years.

274

THE PROFESSOR

YESTERDAY, Professor Okon (LL.D.) was given a 30-minute standing ovation at the end of his annual 'State of the Nation' address to an impressive and obviously impressed audience at the Institute of Contemporary Affairs. One of the points made by the Professor is that we are basically a nation that is 'anti-hard work' and to illustrate this, he drew attention to the familiar pattern of Engineers donning three-piece suits plus pocket handkerchiefs and staunchly declaring their preference for the cool comfort of an air-conditioned office to dirtying their hands on construction sites. He went on to add that his dealings with Nigerian contractors had convinced him that Nigeria is the only place in the world where on being awarded a contract, an indigenous contractor would not only believe that he has immediately struck it rich but would immediately proceed to spend the profit without waiting to finish the job. This was hotly contested by Chief Ejo Ngboro, a prominent businessman who declared that what is happening is nothing other than a vicious circle – those who are prepared to work hard, do not get rewarded, so they have stopped bothering and surrendered themselves to the benevolence of Allah.

The learned Professor declared himself a contemporary of Professor de Bono at Cambridge University and had been one of the earliest converts to 'lateral logic' which he wrongly claimed to be conclusive proof that for every complex problem, there is a weird and baffling but nevertheless simple and logical answer. In confirmation of this, Professor Okon, guided by 'lateral logic' offered the following comments in response to questions about matters of the day. Here are a few samples:

UNIVERSITY STUDENTS

University students are not a problem at all. The trouble lies with their teachers! Many of the research officers cannot even remember what they are supposed to be researching. The Universities have been turned into hot-beds of politics, tribalism, intrigues, and even oath-taking and sexual licentiousness. You'll be amazed when I show you the list of university teachers with secret Swiss bank accounts! I tell you many of those people who run the Universities should never have been allowed beyond the visitors' car park in the first place. (This is nonsense, of course – our University lecturers are simply magnificent.)

HOSPITALS

The fault is entirely with the PATIENTS – too many of them actually expect to be cured.

CENSUS

This is no problem at all – after all we have an army estimated at 250,000 made up of largely literate people. We don't need to spend another ₦20,000,000 on a new census. We would just order every soldier to write down the full name, age and address of everyone he knows. Then the data would be fed through a central computer and pronto – you'll have the exact population figure. (This sounds crazy.)

OIL

Oil money is clearly the work of the devil. By now, nobody should be in any doubt about our inability to control it or spend it wisely. It is choking us and strangling the economy. Look at the congestion at the ports, multiple hold-ups on the roads and giant-sized inflation. We should stop all oil production immediately and leave the oil in the ground until we are ready and capable of managing it. (Is this Prof. an enemy or a friend?) Anyway, what is worth remembering is that A LOT OF MONEY WILL NOT LAST A LONG TIME, IF YOU ARE DETERMINED TO WASTE IT.

THE BAN ON POLITICS

It is impossible to ban politics in Nigeria – you only succeed in driving it underground. At best, group or ethnic interest, and self-preservation will simply replace party politics. The English talk about their weather, the French talk about their food; the Germans are crazy about efficiency; and the Americans talk about their dollar; and for exactly the same reasons, Nigerians talk about politics all the time.

When you see two or three Nigerians gathered – you can be sure they are not talking about the weather, they are talking politics. If you want to feel the political pulse of the country, go to Ibadan. It is there you'll hear precisely what the Government is going to do or won't do.

DR NWAGWU

His advocacy of 'zero-party' politics is conclusive proof that he is not the first genius to completely fail to understand what democracy is all about.

PRESS FREEDOM

The press has never been free; is not free and certainly can never be free. (Maybe he has a point.) Anyway, apart from worrying about the laws of libel, editors prefer to sleep in their own beds rather than in detention.

THE CONSTITUTION

Drafting a Constitution is no problem at all. You can do it in one month, one year or five years or decide to do away with a written constitution altogether. The problem is with the people who are going to run the constitution. The moment you appoint an executive president, you can be sure it will be only a matter of time before he puts the leader of opposition behind bars, suspends the constitution and declares himself President for life together with the right to choose his own successor. (This Professor is the Prophet of doom.)

THE THIRD NATIONAL DEVELOPMENT PLAN

This is not a plan at all. It is merely a shopping list prepared by the last Government. All it tells you is how much money the Government plans to spend on various projects. If you look through the document, there is no consistent rhyme or reason. It is just a jumble of figures. Here and there, are vague optimistic targets for the private sector without any clearly spelt out and mutually agreed guidelines and penalties. There is no political or administrative machinery whereby those responsible for implementing the plan can monitor the performance of the States or ensure that the States actually spend the funds made available to them directly on the laid down projects. If any State fails to perform Phase I of a project, you cannot withhold the funds for Phase II! Let's face it – the Third Development Plan is more of a political document than an economic strategy. Purely as an economic plan, it is not worth the paper it's written on. (The Professor has obviously not read the plan.)

EXECUTIVE PRESIDENT

The problem is not so much about what powers the President should have. The real problem is how to devise a system whereby the chances of a Kanuri man, Ibibio woman, Itsekiri Chief, Ijebu 'Alagba', a Hausa 'Mallam' or Ijaw man becoming President, are roughly the same – all things being equal.

CAR PARKS

The plan by Lagos State to build a multi-storey car park in Central Lagos will only lead to further confusion on the roads. It will merely encourage more and more motorists to bring their cars to town. The long-term plan should be to discourage car owners from bringing more cars into the already choked traffic. We should provide car parks on the outer perimeters and introduce mass transit system so that having left their cars in the car parks, motorists can get into town in comfortable buses, monorails etc.

FOREIGN POLICY

1 We should simply let Israel know that its declared policy of 'An eye for an eye' is relevant only in the country of the blind.
2 We should support the Chinese application for the Coca-Cola franchise at the United Nations.

CREATION OF STATES

There is no reason why we can't have as many States as we want. The real issues are (i) how to monitor and supervise what goes on within the State in order to ensure fair play and justice in the distribution of amenities, industries and infrastructure.

(ii) How much autonomy would each State have? If you push the subject or autonomy far enough, it is conceivable that you may have one State opting for Socialism within its borders while its next door neighbour may choose to go Communist, Capitalist or declare itself a Moslem or Catholic State.

PORT CONGESTION

Considering that the congestion at the ports is principally due to the avalanche of cement ordered by the last Government, we have no option but to invest in a new American invention called the 'Decongester'. It's fully computerised and works by radar. Its operation is the ultimate in simplicity. You simply choose whatever location (within a radius of 35 miles of Apapa Ports), where you want the cement landed and pin-point it by radar. Next you press a button which automatically releases the cement and drops it at the chosen location. The only inconvenience is that residents of Lagos may find cement bags flying all over the place.

TRAFFIC CONGESTION

A thorough survey has revealed that out of every ten cars on the roads, four are driven by women and two are military. It is obvious that if you ban cars driven by women and military vehicles, the problem is solved. Alternatively, you could order all women and military drivers to keep to the right, while the rest of us keep to the left. (This is the recipe for guaranteed confusion.)

CHOICE OF A NEW CAPITAL (Lagos: Leave It or Love It)

Those who wish to move the capital out of Lagos are hereby informed that WHEN A MAN IS TIRED OF LAGOS, HE IS TIRED OF LIFE. Anyway, even if you take the capital out of Lagos, you can't take EKO out of Lagos. (Obviously, the Prof. does not know what he's talking about.)

RACIAL DISCRIMINATION

Order everyone to pray for a White Christmas.

WHO IS FOOLING WHO?

THE PARTY MANIFESTO

AFTER reading through all the Party Manifestoes at present in circulation, Alhaji L.P.O. sent off an urgent telegram to the Federal Electoral Commission, better known as 'FEDECO'. Consequently, any day now, 'FEDECO' will make an official announcement directing all party manifestoes to be clearly stamped 'RUBBISH' before being distributed.

However, it looks as if Fedeco has adopted a realistic approach by granting exemption from this onerous directive to the manifesto issued by 'THE PARTY'. After going through the manifesto, I could not help supporting Fedeco's decision to grant exemption to 'The Party' in this regard. Not only is the manifesto a literary gem – it is also clearly the product of clear thinking and unfettered imagination bridled only by a fiercely intelligent perception of our present situation. However, what is hard to understand is the lengths to which Dr Bolaji Akinyemi (Presidential candidate) and Dr Umar Eleazu (Vice-Presidential candidate) have gone to deny any association with 'The Party'.

THE COVER

For a start, the cover of the manifesto carries in bold type the party slogan – 'THE ONLY THING THAT UNITES US IS OUR IGNORANCE OF EACH OTHER!' Full marks for that.

FIRST PAGE

Secondly, on the first page of the manifesto, the party policy on the sharing of political posts is clearly stated –

All party posts must be shared strictly in ALPHABETICAL order. None of this nonsense about sharing posts on the basis of state of origin or north/south!

THE EMBLEM

Before I forget, I must mention that instead of the usual dreary palm tree; hoe; oil rig; sun; cocoa pod; etc., 'The Party' has chosen as its official emblem – a full-blooded voluptuous 'Page 3 Girl' from 'The Punch!'

RELIGION

In matters pertaining to religion, 'The Party' has vowed that it shall be guided by the wise words of Imam Ali's 'Nahjol-balagha'. 'Remember, Malik, that among your subjects there are two kinds of people: those who have the same religion as yourself and they are brothers unto you and those who have other religions than yours and yet are human beings like you; men of either category suffer from the same weaknesses and disabilities that human flesh is heir to; they commit sins and indulge in vices, either intentionally or foolishly and unintentionally without realising the enormity of their deeds. Let your mercy and compassion come to their rescue and help in the same way and to the same extent that you expect God to show mercy and forgiveness to you.'

EDUCATION

Without a doubt, 'The Party' has got the right policy on Education. The manifesto is loud and clear in declaring that since oil is the very basis of our wealth and political muscle – every student must learn all the basic essentials about oil. e.g. its organic origin; its chemical properties, etc. Furthermore, no student would be granted admission to any University or Institution of Higher Learning unless he passes an examination paper covering oil economics; energy consumption; production and refining of oil; importation and exportation of oil etc.

As for FREE Education, 'The Party' is unequivocal in its policy – anyone expecting 'Free' education or 'Free' anything else should get ready to leave the country! What the party is interested in is to ensure that at least 80 per cent of the adult population are able to read and write within the next ten years. Through a well planned massive literacy programme, every able-bodied illiterate adult would be compelled to attend evening classes continuously for three years. The levy would be 5 per cent of his taxable income and if he can persuade his wife to go to literacy classes with him, the levy would drop to $2\frac{1}{2}$ per cent. On completion of the three-year course, all those graduating from literacy classes must make their services available to teach at literacy classes for at least one year.

HOUSING

According to 'The Party', any Government attempt to embark on low-cost housing is doomed to fail as long as architects', engineers' and quantity surveyors' fees are based on the cost of the houses. In other words the more costly the houses, the higher their fees! A realistic approach suggests that the Government should immediately embark on massive luxury homes for all and sundry.

AGRICULTURE

The Party has quite rightly pointed out that agricultural output will continue to decline unless we do something really drastic to arrest the inverse ratio between income levels on the farms and in the towns. There is no reason why a farm labourer who is on the farm from dawn till dusk should earn less than the messenger who sleeps all day in the office.

NEPA [National Electric Power Authority]

There is no point in having a policy on NEPA. It is beyond redemption. Power cuts have come to stay. Better get used to them or write your will now.

NIGERIA AIRWAYS

The Party on assuming power will set up a high-powered Commission of Enquiry to find out whether it is pure coincidence that every time Nigeria Airways buy a new plane, they promptly crash an old one!

LOCAL GOVERNMENT REFORMS

The Party is firmly commited to giving Local Governments a bonanza in spite of the fact that 100 per cent of the money is bound to go down the drain. The policy of the Party is to pump so much money into Local Government that no one will need to travel more than three kilometres in order to commit a major fraud. If things work out okay, you should be able to stay in your own village and steal millions of Naira of public funds instead of hearing or reading about what your brethren are sharing out.

PARTY TIME

To anyone who is a friend of Alhaji L.P.O. it cannot come as a surprise that New Year's day found him in a state of deep comatose, otherwise known as 'category 4' among doctors. Alhaji was recovering from the night after the night before stretching all the way back to Christmas eve. What is now puzzling the experts is how come Alhaji has suddenly switched to 'TOP' beer. Considering he has an established reputation as a 'connoisseur' of the stuff (beer), Alhaji's endorsement has resulted in the quadrupling of sales of 'TOP'. Suddenly everyone wants to share the Alhaji's joy. In fact on television recently, he admitted that he always carries a bottle of the stuff in his 'Agbada' because according to him it is his secret weapon against indigestion, headaches, depression, malaria, migraine, traffic regulations 'men in uniform', bad plumbing, JAMB; Nigeria Airways; NEPA; and party manifestoes.

NEW SOURCE OF REVENUE

Without breaking the trance to which he had abandoned himself, Alhaji started recalling how the night before he had been at a party given by a former classmate who is now in the military. You know how among friends you can really let your hair down? Anyway, this senior officer who is well known for his zany sense of humour really went to town with his 'missiles' – very 'risque' jokes about politics, military officers, sex, bishops, ambassadors etc.

There was one story about how after all this talk by politicians about 'new sources of revenue', the Government decided to find out whether the new source actually exists. Well, the Government needs the money! So, all available data were fed into the brand new massive computer recently installed at the Federal Ministry of Finance. After a lot of flashing of lights, grinding of levers and gurgling, the computer gabbled out the following print-out – 'Since all other sources have been exhausted, all there is left is Indian hemp!

REGISTRATION OF PARTIES

There was another story which I consider even more 'risque'. Apparently, a big time contractor who is involved in 'heavy' military contracts was asked on TV:

Question: 'Sir, what party do you belong to: GNPP; NPP; PRP; UPN or NPN?'

Answer: 'I belong to "NA". Indeed, I am a firm supporter of "NA".'

Question: 'But sir, that is not one of the parties registered by FEDECO. Anyway, what does "NA" stand for?'

Answer: 'It stands for Nigerian Army and whether FEDECO likes it or not it will have to register NA. After all NA has provided the last four "Presidents" – beginning with General Ironsi!'

OPERATION FEED THE NATION

A little while ago, a Military Governor was challenged by his own people as to why he passed over his own 'townsman' (who had a PhD in agriculture) from Harvard University in choosing his Director of Agriculture. Instead, he had chosen someone who had had thirty years' experience in farming. His reply was brief and clear: 'Gentlemen, what does "PhD" mean? It means Doctor of Philosophy. Well, "philosophy" will not grow yams, vegetables, fruits, cassava, millet etc. and that's what I need for my people.'

THE DOCTORS

Recently, when the doctors threatened to go on strike and paralyse the hospitals, an 'SOS' message was sent to all doctors in government establishments to abandon their desks and proceed to the nearest hospitals in order to take over the saving of lives in case the doctors decided to go through with their strike. Somehow, the message got through to the 'Daily Times' marked for the attention of Dr Patrick Cole (PhD – Government); Dr Oguniyi (PhD – Economics); Dr Olu Onagoruwa (PhD – Law); and of course the irrepressible Dr Stanley Macebuh (PhD – Logic). That took a lot of explaining!

THE GHOST

Many years ago, there was this military chap who was very good at conjuring up the ghost of famous soldiers – Alexander, Montgomery, Ho Chi Min, Eisenhower, De Gaulle etc. Anyway, one day in the Officers' Mess, he was asked to conjure up the ghost of Adolf Hitler. This he promptly did. However, his commanding officer insisted on asking:

'Are you really the ghost of Adolf Hitler?'

Answer: 'Ja!'

Question: 'Do you have any message for the world? You can consider it an order.'

Answer: 'Ja!'

Question: 'What is the message?'
Answer: 'Tell the Jews – NEXT TIME, I'm not going to be
          so nice!'

THE MESSAGE

An army commander was truly astonished that in spite
of a very urgent message to Headquarters, no reinforcements had turned up. Just when he was about to abandon a very crucial part of his campaign strategy, he
decided to obtain a copy of the message from his signal-
man. He was shocked to discover that instead of the correct message – 'We are advancing stop of utmost importance you send reinforcements immediately,' the message that was actually sent was:
'We are going to a dance stop of utmost importance you
send three-and-four-pence immediately!'

THE GENERALS

Unknown to the rest of the world, one of the factors
responsible for Israel's reluctance to sign the Peace
Treaty with Egypt is the question of what to do with
Israel's array of Generals once peace is established in the
area. President Carter has of course made it clear that he
is willing and ready to give anything to get the peace
treaty signed. However, even he was astonished at the
latest Israeli demand. Israeli Prime Minister Begin has
cabled President Carter as follows:
'OK Mr President we'll give you six GENERALS but you'll
have to give us GENERAL Motors, GENERAL Electric,
GENERAL Consolidated and three other GENERALS
quoted on the U.S. stock Exchange.'

MR PRESIDENT, SIR!

IT is quite interesting to watch the part played by Time and Chance in the affairs of nations. So many events that have led to fundamental changes in the history and relationship of mankind owe their origin and indeed fruition almost entirely to time and chance. As one watches the frenzy of activities which are now emerging as we hit the road that would eventually lead to civilian rule, there are still so many 'ifs' and 'buts' that it is now quite clear that success will to a large extent depend on time and chance. We are certainly going to need all the luck we can get – otherwise we may succeed in electing a President but there may not be a country to rule! This was the gloomy prediction of Alhaji L.P.O. Needless to say that I disagree with him entirely – everything is going to come up roses!

According to Alhaji L.P.O's survey, the more the present Administration declares on television; radio; newspapers and by word of mouth that it is on its way out, the more people are determined to believe that due to circumstances beyond its control, the military have come to stay! Even if they go away – it will be only for a short vacation. The politicians will see to that. This is a very sad state of affairs because by word and deed the military have done more than enough to convince us all of their determination to ensure an orderly and permanent transfer of power. This is something one would expect all reasonable people to accept – but then we are not reasonable people.

In the same vein, in spite of the considerable trouble

which both Dr Bolaji Akinyemi and Dr Umar Eleazu have gone to deny any political ambitions, the votes still keep pouring in. It is beginning to look as if the more emphatic they are in educating the public that they are civil servants without any interest in holding office, the more feverish public support for 'THE PARTY', (which has firmly nominated the two gentlemen for the Presidency/Vice-Presidency), has become. Indeed, it seems the public is determined to abide by Plato's exhortation in 'The Republic' that power should only be entrusted to those who least desire it.

According to the Alhaji, there are some extremists who are going around telling people in the villages that the country is not yet ready for a full-scale return to party politics. I cannot make much sense out of their argument that a leopard cannot change its spots. They are adamant that once party politics get into full swing, the thugs and the mobsters will be back in business. The alternative they are advocating is an 'interregnum' – a salutary interval of two years between military rule and party politics. They claim that the interval would provide the newly formed parties ample time to mature (and if necessary disintegrate in order to reform) under clearly established leadership and ideology.

This seems to be the main reason why they are supporting the Dr Akinyemi/Dr Eleazu ticket in such large numbers. As an insurance, they are already suggesting that in case the two gentlemen refuse to answer the call to national service, then we shall have to fall back on the PRESIDENT of the Federal Court of Appeal (at least he has had some experience as President), with the Director of the Corrupt Practices Bureau as his Vice-President.

One can understand the general apathy about party politics. Broadly speaking, those who are ice-cool about the return to party politics divide into three groups. The first group is headed by contractors etc., who have done extremely well for themselves financially under the military. The second group consists of those who can clearly discern the same old traits and rituals being demonstrated by those who have lined up to take over from the military. The third group, and by no means a minority, are those who have adopted the position that it does not matter who is in power, nobody cares about them. However, there is another group who can be safely ignored. These are the ultra-extremists who maintain that when the British governed us, we were not satisfied; we have been governing ourselves for eighteen years – we are still not satisfied – it's all grumble, grumble. Therefore, now is the time to outlaw politics and allow the country to rule itself and everyone should be his own President. As far as I am concerned this is a clear invitation to anarchy! They insist that even at this late stage it would be cheaper for the Government to invite all the political aspirants to a round table conference; offer to refund whatever expenses the politicians have incurred so far (subject to the auditor's certificate of course); tell all of them to forget about politics and let's have some peace, please.

It is easy to share some of the anxiety of those who are not keen on the return of party politics, because it is human nature to fear change. Also, there are those who are suggesting that the antipathy is due to the generally low level of awareness of the Nigerian public. However, I cannot see much that the Government can do about it. You can hardly expect the Government to whip up public enthusiasm for party politics by telling the country – 'after us, the next lot are going to be a hell of a lot better!'

Like it or not we have to go on with the return to party politics. This is not the time to listen to the chicken-hearted. We have our credibility to think about. We have told the world we are going to do it – so we have to go ahead and do it or else no one will believe us next time (if there is a next time).

If you want clean politics and a President who is not offering any magic cures – the sensible thing to do is to vote for 'THE PARTY'.

THE REAL EMERGENCY

I HOPE it's only coincidence but the last three nation-wide TV broadcasts by the Head of State have been interrupted (at least in my area) by instant power failure somewhere between the completition of the National Anthem and the introduction '. . . Fellow countrymen . . .' Alhaji L.P.O. has come up with suitable comfort – not to worry, 'Top' Beer tastes better in the dark anyway!

I however gather that on his last TV appearance the H. of S. announced the lifting of the 'State of Emergency' and all the other things that go with it. Also, as if to prove that Government does have a sense of humour, the C. of S. (SHQ) and the I. G. (Police) were simultaneously vested with wide – sweeping detention powers!

I had quite reconciled myself to this state of affairs until Alhaji L.P.O. turned up as one of the guest speakers at the Dinner to mark the 25th Anniversary of the 'Sunday Times'. Unlike the other guest speakers who provided ample pleasure for the Daily Times/Sunday Times establishment by showering praises on the paper and recalling its glorious past, Alhaji L.P.O.s chose to make a completely irrelevant speech the main thrust of which was . . .

'Ladies and gentlemen, the lifting of the State of Emergency is the beginning of the REAL EMERGENCY''. The Alhaji then went on to explain that more than at any other time, the relative peace and tranquility, if not prosperity which we have come to take for granted will come under severe strain. The orderly transfer of power from a military to a civilian administration, by the very fact that it is unprecedented, will severely test our tolerance level. Salvation and hope lie in the willingness of each and every one of us to surrender the very things we value most in the national interest. That is the true sacrifice – not the sacrifice of the expendables but the sacrifice of the invaluable.

This is necessarily so because the base on which we have sought to build a nation is a very narrow one. Its main ingredients are our vast ignorance of each other combined with an equal dosage of our undeclared but feverish mutual suspicion of each other. Look around you. How many Hausas do you see living under the same roof as Yorubas? How many Ibos are in partnership in business with Efiks, Kanuris or Idomas? How many university student union elections are held on non-tribal lines? In how many Local Government elections were non-indigenes voted in? Today, if an Ibo and Yoruba get into a fight at Tinubu Square, you can be sure that every Ibo who happens to be at the scene will automatically support his fellow Ibo and the same goes for the Yoruba – without any attempt to enquire about what started the quarrel in the first place. You would get exactly the same result if an Ijaw and a Hausa got into a fight.

As of now, it is truly premature to label the political groupings that have emerged as national parties. All that has happened is that each state (apart from one or two exceptions) has formed its own party and then gone shopping for alignment with whatever other group looks like a winner. How else can on explain Mvendaga Jibo and Chief Udoji being in the same party – certainly not after that memorable television debate?

The irony of the history of political development in Nigeria is that we are told that the Army intervened in 1966 as a strike against (i) corruption and (ii) tribalism. I am not qualified to render an expert opinion on whether or not corruption and tribalism are on the wane. We can leave that to Dr. J. A. Adegbite of the Corrupt Practices Bureau. What I do know is that the politicians and would-be politicians have now introduced an equally destructive element – religious chauvinism of the worst order. Make no mistake about it – this is the beginning of the REAL EMERGENCY.

FEDECO GETS TOUGH

One of the most eagerly awaited documents is the Federal Electoral Commission's list of people who are barred from contesting the next elections. According to Alhaji L.P.O. a very reliable source has confirmed that FEDECO has taken a really tough stand and has decided that:

(i) We must make a fresh start.
(ii) There must be strict regard and adherence to law and order (otherwise we can forget about having free and fair elections).
(iii) Consequently, all those who in utter disregard of the then existing ban on political activity, were in anyway connected with the formation of political parties before 21 October 1978 are automatically barred from contesting the next elections!

The obvious result of this decision which has won the support of the Government is that it has eliminated virtually all the contestants, thus leaving the Presidency at the mercy of Dr. Bolaji Akinyemi/Dr. Umar Eleazu whose party is now known in official circles as "THE PARTY". You had better join now before all the party posts get filled up.

H.E. AND THE C.J.

A FEW days ago, Alhaji L.P.O. solemnly declared – 'There is nothing more inspiring than watching a professional at work.' He was referring to Mr. Alex Nwokedi, Press Secretary to H.E. Alhaji had just returned from a press briefing at Dodan Barracks and he was full of praise for the Press Secretary's Professionalism –" he really knows how to handle the Press".

Beginning with his speech at Jaji, H.E. has on several occasions expounded lucidly on the 'qualities of a good leader". In response to hundreds of readers who have written to ask for concrete examples of the qualities mentioned by H.E., I pleaded with Alhaji L.P.O. to urgently obtain from the P.S. (Press Secretary), examples of good leadership which could be used to support a statement recently credited to H.E. in which he again stressed that a good leader should be guided by among other things '. . . compassion, common sense and a good sense of humour.' The P.S. is yet to grant audience to Alhaji L.P.O. – he can afford to keep him waiting but we cannot afford to keep you waiting. So, here goes:

COMPASSION

In 1975, when the present H.E. was the deputy H.E., he was in his office at Dodan Barracks when the then H.E. burst into his office. Obviously in a rage, the late H.E. declared – '. . . just look at this!'

It was a report concerning the indiscretions of a judge. This was at a time when judges were being retired left, right and centre all over the country and even the then C.J. (Chief Justice) was one of the first to go. The Deputy H.E. coolly appealed for calmness and compassion. He quietly pointed out that the judge involved was in a London Hospital still recovering from surgery. He rightly pleaded for compassion because the trauma of the drastic disciplinary action (removal) contemplated by H.E. could send the judge to an early grave. Why not wait until he had been discharged from hospital when he could be given an opportunity to clear his name? Indeed, only a few days before, a very senior civil servant had taken his removal from the Public Service Commission as such a severe personal humiliation that he had died suddenly under very mysterious circumstances (that had triggered off wild rumours of suicide).

In the end, compassion won the day – that judge is still rendering very useful service to the country.

COMMON SENSE

Just before FESTAC, the traffic situation in Lagos had truly deteriorated to clearly chaotic proportions. The city was slowly grinding to a standstill as the familiar pile up of cars on both major and feeder roads had stubbornly defied all solutions.

The situation was bound to get even worse as at least 100,000 overseas visitors were expected to attend "Festac". On top of that, the buses specially ordered for the festival, which was only a few days away, had not arrived because of a mix-up at the Central Bank which had delayed the release of the appropriate letter of credit to the German suppliers of the buses.

Undoubtedly what saved us was the 'ODD/EVEN' edict which was promulgated only a few days before the opening ceremony of FESTAC. Since then, many have wondered about how the edict, which restricted traffic to cars with even or odd first digit on alternate days, came about. Was it the brain-wave of a university professor? The recommendation of a consultant? The product of a high-powered panel? Or the divination of a first-rate magician?

Even though the edict clearly inconvenienced many people, particularly those who were forced to buy a second car and in some cases two or three extra cars, it was certainly effective and the credit for it belongs to none other than the present H.E.!

At a memorable meeting at Dodan Barracks, all those connected with Festac arrangements, Lagos State Officials as well as the Police and Army top brass were assembled. In the chair was H.E. himself and the number one topic was – Lagos traffic. It was a very tense meeting and it was beginning to flounder in frustration as it became more and more obvious that none of the suggestions being offered would have any appreciable impact on the traffic problem. The atmosphere was becoming really charged and it certainly did not help matters when traces of a long-standing feud between the Army and the Police began to emerge. At one point, H.E. had to appeal to both sides for calm and restraint – and reminded them that they were both 'members of the Armed Forces' and that the meeting was not an occasion for washing dirty linen in public. A senior female Police Officer (who has now retired) quickly pointed out that the Police were not members of the Armed Forces – otherwise how come they were getting such a raw deal as regards the preferential treatment given to the Army in respect of conditions of service, equipment, facilities etc. Also, some of the traditional functions of the Police such as traffic control had been usurped by the Army. Obviously, no responsible newspaper would want to publish matters that may cause disaffection between the Army or Police. For that reason, we shall not disclose the comments of the 'Inspector-General of the Military Police' which caused so much displeasure among the top brass of the Police. Anyway, the important point is that H.E. was quick to grasp the highly explosive direction in which the deliberations of the meeting were heading. Common sense took charge and H.E. skilfully re-addressed the meeting to dealing with the problem at hand – Lagos traffic.

Once again, all sorts of ideas (including creating a special lane for buses, taxis, ambulances, military vehicles etc.) were considered and rejected.

As the hours wore on, it was beginning to look as if the problem would not be solved. Suddenly, H.E. (who had obviously taken great trouble to thoroughly read every paper submitted on the subject) quietly made a suggestion that no one had thought about – 'why not find a solution that would halve the number of cars on the road? Perhaps restrict traffic on Mondays to cars with numbers beginning with odd numbers and Tuesdays even numbers and so on . . .'.

Even those who like Alhaji L.P.O. have a store of stories relating how those responsible for enforcing the edict were quick to strike profitable deals with offending motorists, have now realised that without that edict traffic during Festac would simply have been deplorable beyond imagination. As far as I know, the credit for it has not previously been accorded to the person to whom it belongs.

HUMOUR

Recently, the P.S. had to issue a press statement denying a story carried prominently by a newspaper. It had erroneously been alleged that H.E. in a speech at the University of Nigeria, Nsukka had castigated members of the Constituent Assembly as being more interested in collecting their allowances and making business contacts than in producing a first-rate Constitution. It was Alhaji L.P.O. who first drew my attention to the fact that the way the denial was craftily worded, left you in no doubt – even if H.E. didn't say it, we certainly wish he had said it!

Actually, Alhaji L.P.O. carried out a poll at the Assembly and discovered that 30 per cent were truly dedicated to serving the nation; 10 per cent did not know why they were chosen or what the Constitution is all about; 5 per cent came to see the 'Seventh Wonder of the World' – the Eko Bridge (they just wouldn't believe that cars could travel in the air!); as for the remaining 55 per

297

cent, they truly felt that the country had been taking them for a ride for the last twenty years and this was their chance to get even!

AND NOW THE C.J.

The present Chief Justice of the Federation is certainly a refreshing example of how one can attain the highest rung of ones profession and still add a little more dignity to an already dignified post. It is no mean achievement that even though he served for many years as a judge in the 'wild, wild, West' – the old Western Region, there was never any dent to his reputation. He went on to serve in the former South Eastern Sate (now known as the Cross River State). His Chairmanship of the recent Judges Conference was another testimony to his good judgement and humour. His handling of the 'Sharia' was a combination of skill, subdued good humour and patience.

Since he became the C.J. he has been consistent in his concern about the congestion in the courts and the attendant problems of suspects kept in custody for unduly long periods.

Last night, Alhaji L.P.O. was at the Annual Convention of the National Union of Alleged Criminals Pending Trial (NUACPT) at which the following resolutions were passed and telegrammed to the C.J.:

  (i) Let us all out.
 (ii) Give us the chance to look around.
(iii) Let us back in again, if we don't like what is going on in the country!

WHO IS GOING TO RUN THE COUNTRY?

I MUST confess to being an inveterate observer of the present Head of State and I feel sure that many are overwhelmed by the modesty with which he carries his exalted office while at the same time upholding its dignity. What is clear though is that he shows no particular appetite for the intrigues that necessarily appertain to the office nor a relish for the trappings and flatteries that go with the position. We can therefore safely conclude that come 1979, all things being equal, he will take his graceful bow and make a dignified exit – another duty completed.

This leaves us with the very interesting question – who is going to run the country after 1979? Already, the main actors are flexing their muscles. The bold and the brave have volubly declared their stand while the cunning have publicly reserved their position while discreetly and deviously shovelling up their support privately.

In trying to forecast the eventual winner, we must perforce choose between the 'old politicians' as against the 'new faces'; the Northerner' against the 'Southerner' – this is not a reference to tribalism but an evaluation of where the candidate would most likely draw the bulk of his support; or whether the winner would emerge from the 'Institutions' e.g. the Universities; the Public Corporations; the Civil Service; the Armed Forces; or the Business World.

I think we can safely assume that any candidate who can draw a good deal of support from the Northern States (he may not necessarily be of Northern origin!) must start off with an in-built advantage. This is because the distribution of seats (and the creation of states) is for the main part anchored on the 1963 Census figures.

Most pundits are now generally agreed that assuming that we do have 'free and fair elections' in 1979, the candidates left at the final hurdle will almost certainly be men (or women!) with very strong vote-pulling muscle at the state level. It follows quite logically from this that the sort of voting pattern that will emerge nation wide will probably follow the pattern reflected in the recent American elections. It looks very likely that the final result will show a very strong regional voting bias. Most Americans have come to accept the verdict of a prestigious newspaper which announced the American election result with the headline: 'The South Launches Carter to the White House (Presidency)' In our own case, the geographical reference is likely to be the reverse!

It only remains to cast a nation-wide net and try to evaluate the main contenders. The obvious starting point is Chief Obafemi Awolowo who has never made a secret of his political ambitions. For a man of 73, he is truly amazing. However, the dice is loaded against him. Apart from his age, the creation of states has fragmented his political base. Furthermore, by the very character of Chief Awolowo's political life, he has made as many enemies as he has made friends.

From the old Western State, one could pick an endless list of possibles – Mr Richard Akinjide, (I find his advocacy of or endorsement of quota system at University level most disappointing); Chief A. M. A. Akinloye; Chief Akin Deko; Chief Akin Olugbade; Mr Bola Ige; Chief G. B. A. Akinyede; the formidable Mr Kehinde Sofola; and of course Chief Sobo Sowemimo who enjoys a solid 'Egba' base as well as having numerous Northern friends. Chief Harold Sodipo – astute and very much his own man cannot be counted out. Also expected to make a strong showing is Mr Gani Fawehinmi who has not succeeded in convincing impartial observers that his stance on 'Free Education' and on Ondo Chieftaincy is entirely unrelated to political ambitions.

In Lagos State, there is a strong possibility of a straight fight between Alhaji Femi Okunnu ex-Federal Commissioner for Works (his handicap is that of being too closely identified with Gowon) and Alhaji Ganiyu Dawodu who got a clean certificate of 'good conduct' from the Assets Investigation Panel. Chief Adeniran Ogunsanya and the indefatigable Chief T. O. S. Benson are expected to feature either directly or as 'King-makers'. Had Mr Rasheed Gbadamosi behaved differently while he was Lagos State Commissioner for Economic Development, he would be the natural rallying point for the 'youth vote' which will probably now focus on the articulate and versatile Professor Ayodele Awojobi, who not only holds very strong views but unfortunately has earned a reputation for not being an easy person to get on with – a major weakness in a candidate for political office.

In Bendel State, the front runners at present are Chief Dennis Osadebay who used to be President of the Senate and in fact acted as the Head of State on several occasions; Chief A. Y. Eke, who was cleared by the Assets Investigation Panel, Chief Anthony Enahoro – that man loves trouble; Prince Solomon Akenzua (the present Bendel State Commissioner and heir-apparent to the Akenzua of Benin); and no one should be surprised at seeing one of the Ibru brothers (with strong business support) turn up. Also not to be forgotten is Chief Omo-Osagie (who by all accounts endured much suffering under the Ogemudia regime) and Professor Tam David-west who abandoned the 'Ivory Tower' of academics at University of Ibadan to accept political office as a Commissioner in Bendel State.

In Kwara, J. S. Olawoyin the seasoned politician will almost certainly feature. Incidentally, those who have been watching the activities of Dr. Sola Saraki, the Turakin of Ilorin suspect there must be something in the political wind.

The Imo – Anambra States axis will readily support the last President of the country Dr Nnamdi Azikwe but his advocacy of 'Diarchy' i.e. army/civilian rule must make many wonder whether or not this contributed in a large measure to confirming Gowon's belief that Nigerians were generally reconciled to indefinite military rule. Certainly not to be ruled out is the self-effacing, Mr Raymond Njokwu who almost unnoticed was a Federal Minister for a hefty 12-year term. You are all warned not to overlook Dr K. O. Mbadiwe, the man of 'timbre and calibre' and of course Dr S. G. Ikoku who certainly knows what politics is all about.

Rivers State seems reluctant at showing its hand too early but the personable Chief Dappa Biriye is no light-weight. Dr Nabo Graham- Douglas (Ex-Federal Attorney-General – did he endorse all those obnoxious Decrees by Gowon?) and Mr Wenike Briggs (he now runs a highly lucrative law practice) are still full of running.

In Cross River State, Dr Okoi Arikpo, long-term Commissioner for External Affairs under Gowon is still very much around; but who can overlook the popularity of Mr Michael Ogon who in spite of his long-term in politics (he entered Parliament at 21) is still bursting with youthful vigour.

From the old 'Benue-Plateau' Mr Aper Aku, the Gboko businessman who was detained by Gowon (and humi-lated by Governor Gomwalk) but was subsequently vin-dicated following Gowon's downfall is something of a hero but is yet to make a national impact. There are many observers who swear that Mr Joseph Tarka the Ex-Federal Commissioner for Communications (and no friend of Mr Godwin Daboh!) is the man to watch.

As far as the Northern States are concerned, there are many who believe that a single formidable candidate with solid regional support will probably emerge. The probability is that the ever-forthright Alhaji Aminu Kano will lead an equally formidable splinter group but relying more on country-wide support albeit thinly-spread. He is expected to by-pass the Emirs in the North and instead appeal to the masses for grass-root support.

The names being mentioned as standard-bearers of the

North are first and foremost Alhaji Inua Wada, uncle of General Murtala Mohammed, the late Head of State, and the strongman (jointly with the late Alhaji Ribadu) of the Balewa Cabinet. However, age is not on his side and this leaves room for such contenders as Alhaji Shehu Shagari (ex-Federal Commissioner for Finance) and Alhaji Shettima Ali Monguno (ex-Federal Commissioner for Mines & Power) who both emerged from the Gowon regime with their integrity intact. One other name that has been given prominence is that of Alhaji Waziri Ibrahim as regards whom observers have wondered whether his eager launching of the 'National Club' is merely a warm up to the launching of a national political party!

However, the more discerning are quietly suggesting that the man to watch is Mallam Mamman Daura who recently retired as the Managing Director of 'New Nigeria' (which is by any standard a first-class newspaper – next to the 'Punch' of course!). Apart from the fact that it is rather odd that a man who has retired so early (he is still in his forties) has given no indication of his future plans, he certainly has a lot going for him. His age; education (he holds an M.Sc from Dublin University); the humiliation inflicted on him by Gowon (Mamman Daura was detained at Kirikiri Prison, famous for its 'made-in-Nigeria' giant mosquitoes); and his political guts, (bordering on stubbornness) are all plus factors. Besides, he is highly regarded in press circles where his highly successful term of office as Managing Director of 'New Nigeria' has not gone unnoticed. He is even suspected of being 'Candido' ('the face behind the mask'), the columnist. Also, because of his close association with Mr Adamu Ciroma, Governor of the Central Bank, who was his mentor, big business will readily endorse his candidature. The only reservations that one could possibly offer against him is that under him, the 'New Nigeria' sometimes appeared unduly over-zealous in protecting what it considered to be 'in the interest of the North'.

One sector that cannot be ignored is of course is the

Armed Forces itself. As already announced by the Federal Military Government, any member of the Armed Forces who wishes to seek political office must first resign his commission. It follows from this that whatever candidate emerges from this sector must have star appeal – i.e. he would probably be one of the 'heroes' e.g. Retired Brigadier Benjamin Adekunle, the 'Black Scorpion' (but he is too unpredictable); Major-General Shuwa (he has enough problems with the insurance companies!); and Col. Babangida who commands the crack Armoured Brigade and was definitely the hero of 13 February, when the late Head of State, General Murtala Mohammed was assasinated (he is not interested). This leaves us with Brigadier Joseph Garba, ('the Voice of 29 July' when Gowon was toppled) who is at present Commissioner for External Affairs, and who apart from one gaffe (Nigeria/Angola/Brazil axis) has pursued his duties with great vigour and energy and has certainly eclipsed all his predecessors in this particular office. Any suggestion that Brigadier Shehu Yar'Adua, Chief of Staff Supreme Headquarters and the 'de facto' Prime Minister may seek political office is pure speculation.

Looking at the broad spectrum, there is no gainsaying that an entirely fresh face would not eventually emerge as the next President. What is certain is that we all have a part to play in the choice of the next President. POLITICS IS FAR TOO IMPORTANT TO BE LEFT TO POLITICIANS ALONE. Roll on 1979!

ADVERTISEMENT FOR THE PRESIDENT

I AM truly amazed at the number of people who like Alhaji L.P.O. really cannot fathom why anyone should want to be the next President. Their thinking is that once you discount the raw basic human greed for power – being President is not only a thankless job, it is also a high risk assignment. If you doubt it, ask your insurer to quote you the premium!

One is reminded of the observation by a senior member of the last Government who after several bottles of champagne solemnly declared: 'Whoever comes after us will certainly not have as much power or money to throw around.' Even if he has the power, he won't have the money; and if he has the money, he won't have the power to do whatever he likes.'

I suppose it's true that the President will be an obvious target for continuous public speculation about his houses; money stashed away in Switzerland; his business interests; his mistresses; his vested interest in various government projects; his tribal loyalty; and of course the genuineness of his commitment to ideology and the advancement of the true interest of the nation.

On top of all these, he'll never know who are his real friends or who are plotting against him. He won't be able to go about as and when he pleases – he would become a virtual prisoner in the Presidential Palace. He would have to deal with a restive Civil Service who would offer only grudging support to his policies but would be ready to disassociate themselves from policies that prove either unsuccessful or unpopular. Above all, there is the ever constant threat of a coup – a smoking gun directly pointing at his head.

The determination of the Military to hand over to a Civilian Administration has now reached such a pitch that one should be forgiven for believing that if it were possible, they would hand over today. Clearly, ruling this country is no easy matter. However, the trouble is to whom should they hand over? It seems obvious that it is naïve to believe that the present Government has no interest whatever in the quality or nature of its successor. Why else would the Government go through with the implementation of its political programme, with far-reaching consequencies, in its efforts to ensure an orderly transfer of power not only to its immediate successor but also hopefully to those that would come after? The Military intervened to save the country from a crisis – so how does it make sense to hand over to a successor who is determined to drive in reverse gear straight back to the same crisis? Much better to stop the first man you come across in the street; ask him 'Do you want to rule the country?' and if he says 'yes' – then drive him straight to the Presidential Palace and declare him the President.

Anyway, we are still left with the problem – of who is going to be the next President. I cannot say that I am entirely surprised that Nigerians have with their usual ingenuity solved the problem beautifully. What has happened is that much to the consternation of the Federal Electoral Commission, Nigerians have already started voting for the next President without bothering to wait for election day. Their argument is that since the politicians did not wait for the ban on politics to be lifted before launching political parties left, right and centre – the electorate are equally entitled to start voting before the election.

Surprisingly, most of the votes so far received by the Federal Electoral Commission have been solidly in favour of the Dr. Bolaji Akinyemi/Dr. Umar Eleazu ticket. For the benefit of those who do not know, Dr. Akinyemi is the Director-General of the Nigerian Institute of International Affairs while Dr. Eleazu is the Director of the

'Think Tank'. I can see why this combination is so popular with the voters. First of all, both of them have untainted reputation so there is no question of either of them being disqualified under section 207 of the new constitution. Secondly, their integrity is undoubted. It is totally inconceivable that either of them would stoop to hiring thugs, tampering with ballot boxes or having their opponents locked up on trumped up charges on election day.

Above all, the name of their party is "THE PARTY' and they have come up with a slogan that is sure to become a big vote-catcher – 'The only thing that unites us is our ignorance of each other!'

Next time you run into either Dr. Akinymei or Dr. Eleazu – treat them with a little more respect – you may well be talking to the next President or Vice-president!

GAMES END

ACCORDING to 'unreliable sources' – namely Alhaji L.P.O., this year's Republic Day (1 October) is going to be a very sober affair. No celebrations, no banquets, no flowers and certainly no champagne. All those, particularly diplomats and out-of-work journalists, who were eagerly looking forward to the usual fiesta will have to settle for an evening devoted to watching TV (N.E.P.A. permitting of course).

It seems that the 'Think Tank' has persuaded the Government that Republic Day should be devoted to a critical review of the Nigerian economy. I daresay the thinking of the 'Think Tank' on this score is faultless. Their 'position paper' is emphatic that particularly with the feverish politicking going on and the Government's determination to hand over to civilians next year, everything rests squarely and firmly on our immediate economic performance and long range projection of our revenue generating resources. Already, the economic indicators suggest that tough times lie ahead.

Right from the beginning of the year, the Government itself has been at pains to educate the public on the seriousness of our financial plight. At one point, it was publicly announced that Government revenue this year could drop by as much as 40 per cent below what it was last year. In simple arithmetic, this means that for every one thousand naira that was available for spending last year, there will be only six hundred naira this year. When you compound this with the sharp escalation in prices/inflation triggered off by this year's budget, the result is that even the remaining 60% would buy a good deal less than what it did last year. The obvious conclusion is that things are going to be tough all round.

The latest reports suggest that our oil production is rising again almost to the same level as last year. However, the questions that remain to be answered are first of all – at what price will we be able to sell our oil; and secondly, even if we are able to sell at fairly good prices, can we absorb the inevitable 'short-change' since oil prices are quoted in United States dollars at a time when the dollar is under considerable pressure on the international market. The financial experts are already agreed that it is almost inconceivable that the dollar could survive this year without being devalued. In fact, there are some who insist that for all practical purposes, the dollar has effectively been devalued already.

What this means within the context of the Nigerian economy is that the Federal and State Governments will have a good deal less money to spend. Furthermore, since the Government is easily the biggest spender, the chain reaction of the severe constraints as regards Federal revenue will automatically be reflected throughout the financial network. Government would almost certainly insist on much longer credit from its suppliers (both goods and services); and as contractors and suppliers find themselves having to wait several months before they can recover their outlay while at the same time having to finance higher interest charges, it is inevitable that there would be a decline in capital formation and investment as well as employment.

Substantial domestic deficits and international borrowing would be carried over to the succeeding civilian administration. The next President and Governors would almost certainly have to make drastic cuts right across the board – both at Federal and State level. In effect, rosy promises made at election time may have to be quickly jettisoned. As is usual in such circumstances, the first victims will be projects either still on the drawing board or those in respect of which not much progress has been made. The civil service is also an obvious target for severe curtailment of allowances, fringe benefits etc.

The ongoing debate about car loans and allowances is only the tip of the iceberg. The pessimists are already forecasting that at least a third of the civil service and probably as much as half of our embassies scattered all over the world will have to do a quick march to the chopping block.

Of course the problem of inflation will still be very much around. According to Dr. B. U. Ekong, Chief Economist of the Central Bank of Nigeria, 'inflation was slowed down from 33.5 per cent in 1975 to 22.1 per cent in 1976.' Rough calculations suggest that it is on the rise again and is probably between 33 and 35 per cent at present.

However, the optimists led by Alhaji L.P.O. are adamant that all is not lost. They insist that apart from the fact that the economy is merely going through a predictable trough – the economic cycle, what is required now is a critical review of our priorities and a change of strategy. They have pointed out that rather than abandon the massive Government housing programme which is not only very expensive but extremely difficult to control, the shift should be towards encouraging more and more people to build their own houses through not only Building Societies but also by Government providing housing estates with Government participation being limited to the provision of basic infrastructure.

It is a slower process but salvation lies in the hope that the houses and flats previously occupied by the new house-owners will become available to those on the lower rungs of the economic ladder.

I have it on good authority that the 'Think Tank' has already sent out invitations to the heavyweights – the Heads of Economic Departments in all the Universities; Commissioners of Finance in all the States; the 'Captains of Industry'; the Labour Leaders; the big-time farmers; bankers; and of course the President of the Chamber of Commerce, who will almost certainly point out that the only trouble with government is that there is too much of it.

310

No doubt about it – the discussions should be lively and illuminating. I congratulate the 'Think Tank'.

BEFORE WE SAY 'GOOD-BYE'

We have it on good authority that the 'Think Tank' has recommended that before the Military hand over power to civilians, the prison system should be dismantled if we are to combat the rising crime wave. Apparently, what the 'Think Tank' has in mind is a gradual phasing out of all punishment for crime. This is clearly a logical deduction from the fact that the system of imposing punishments on offenders has been tried for thousands of years and has completely failed to eliminate crime.

Alhaji L.P.O. has obtained the following denial from the 'Think Tank':

'Even though we accept that prison sentences have in no way acted as a deterrent, the suggestion that prisons should be abolished represents a minority opinion. It is ridiculous – these do-gooders should all be locked up'.

BIG MAN LIVES HERE!

I MUST confess that I am truly amazed at the sudden popularity and proliferation of 'BMLH' signboards which have sprung up all over Lagos and various other parts of the country. For the benefit of those who may not know – 'BMLH' stands for Big Man Lives Here! The man responsible for it is none other than Alhaji L.P.O.

The origin of 'BMLH' goes back to the time of President Jimmy Carter's visit to Nigeria. At the party given by the American Ambassador (an excellent host), I found myself only a few feet away from the President – arguably the most powerful man in the world – at least when the dollar is not tumbling; or when he can be sure that his United Nations Ambassador, Chief (DR) Andrew Young is not going to say precisely what he was authorised not to say. Two things immediately strike one about the President – he is not a tall man (even though Americans probably have the highest average height in the world). Secondly, he shakes hands warmly, looks you straight between the eyes and even though it's all over in seconds, one is left with the message – 'I may be the President but you are a big man too'. He leaves you with the feeling that he sincerely hopes you would meet again even though you both know that the chances are that you will never meet again. It is a feeling that one associates with sitting next to a complete stranger on the plane. For the first few hours of the flight, you are silent partners. Suddenly, in the last quarter hour of the flight a chance remark triggers off some strange mechanism. You both discover that you are not really strangers – you have common interests – sports; literature; business; architecture; urban congestion; fear of flying; juvenile deliquency etc. You both get off the plane and in a sudden panic, you frantically exchange addresses when you discover you are going different places. You promise to write but both of you know that you are never going to write and you are never going to meet.

Anyway, it was a really enjoyable party. Over to my far right I could see Alhaji L.P.O. truly in his element among the army of United States press corps (two plane-loads of them!) who were covering the President's visit. The press corps were heartily engaged in what they call the 'DED'. Apparently, 'DED' means 'Drink the Embassy Dry' and it is a tradition that whenever the United States Press Corps cover a Presidential visit, the President cannot leave the host country until the 'DED' exercise is completed! Furthermore, any pressman who comes on board the press plane without clear and convincing evidence of a massive hangover is promptly ejected in mid-air!

As the official hour for the end of the party approached, the Ambassador for one of the Scandinavian countries came dashing through, obviously in a panic. He was profuse with apologies for his lateness – the trouble was that there was no water, not a drop at his Ikoyi residence. In fact the only reason he came at all was because his wife had threatened instant divorce if she missed the opportunity of being introduced to President Carter. Would the President mind tarrying a few more minutes while he fetched his wife from the car? The ever smiling President was only too willing to oblige, but an aide whispered into his ear – 'Sir, there's no vote in this!'

After the excitement had subsided, the unfortunate Ambassador was surprised to find himself being accosted by Alhaji L.P.O. – 'Your Excellency, it is really amazing that Ikoyi, the choicest part of Lagos, is without water.'

The Ambassador declared that for the past nine months he had been paying ₦120 every week just to have water delivered in tankers to his official residence. In spite of rigorous complaints at the highest level, nothing had been done to remedy the situation.

However, there is a happy ending to the story. Alhaji L.P.O. persuaded the Ambassador to hire him as his 'consultant' with fees payable in advance in foreign exchange.

The Alhaji's consultancy report was brief and unambiguous – 'Your Excellency, just hang a BMLH signboard outside your house. That way everyone would know that A BIG MAN LIVES HERE!'

The result was truly dramatic – from the day the signboard went up, the Ambassador has had a full and uninterrupted supply of water; electricity; gas; milk; sugar; flour etc. Everything gets delivered at his doorstep! Well there you are, in Nigeria if you want to be sure of getting things and getting things done for you – you let everybody know that you are A BIG MAN.

THE HOLY BUDGET

MY good friend Alhaji L.P.O. has described the 1978/79 Budget as the "HOLY BUDGET' because it creates as many new (if not more) holes as the old holes which it sought to fill!

Apart from the Budget, Alhaji has been moaning about the newly promulgated Land Use Decree which vests ownership of land in State Governments; and the Decree on Professional Practice which has severely curtailed private practice by Professionals – Architects; Engineers; Accountants etc.

What a package – the Land Use Decree; Professional Practice Decree and then the Budget all within the same week! An overdose of bad medicine?

Alhaji L.P.O. was particularly galled by the Land Use Decree which was announced by the Head of State himself on the eve of President Carter's visit to Nigeria. He was quick to point out that the irony of the timing of the announcement was not lost on him – 'If President Carter was to go on TV in America and announce that henceforth all land belongs to the Government, HE WOULD NOT LAST TWENTY-FOUR HOURS IN OFFICE!'

I don't think I made much impression on Alhaji when I suggested that the promulgation of the Land Use Decree provides further confirmation that the Military are determined to hand over power to civilians next year. This is so because I find it hard to believe that any administration that wants to hang on to power would promulgate a decree the ramifications of which are so complex that it could bring Government itself to a standstill. So much energy and effort (and of course money!) would have to be devoted to making it work that there would be little time for actually governing the country. Can you imagine the thousands (if not millions) of people whose full-time occupation would become the pushing of paper – all in search of the tantalising 'CERTIFICATE OF OCCUPANCY'! It would certainly be easier for a succeeding civilian government to accept that the Land Use Decree as it stands at present is a manifestation of the GOOD intention of the Military regime to stop land speculation/monopoly.

It is unlikely that a civilian government would scrap the Land Use Decree in its entirety. What is more likely is that the civilian government would create plenty of elbow room for itself i.e. selective application of the decree. The cynics are already proclaiming that PARTY MEMBERS would be granted automatic exemption; whereas the unfaithful – the members of the opposition, they would face the full brunt of the Decree! Of course the immediate effect of the Land Use Decree is that anyone wishing to buy land would have to pay twice – first to the original owner and then negotiate with the State Government for 'Certificate of Occupancy'.

In assessing the Government's Policies on recent issues, one cannot help thinking that the Government's major problem is that it has laid itself wide open to harassment from all and sundry each with conflicting demands and interests. In addition, much of the energy of the Government is already committed to the maintenance of law and order. This has resulted in considerable in-built frustration because armed robbery; vehicle snatching; and (in certain areas), kidnapping and general disregard for the law are very much in evidence.

Consequently, there is very little time and energy left for creative legislation whereby problems are carefully analysed; dispassionately discussed; and the consequencies of remedial action are carefully thought out within the context of clearly stated objectives.

The Government deserves much sympathy for its present plight particularly when one remembers that when the present administration took over in 1975, the ports were congested; inflation was rampant; and the economy was being slowly but surely strangulated. All these were vigorously tackled and for quite a while the attendant relief was self-evident. This makes it even more difficult to understand why the same administration should now announce a budget, the immediate effect of which is a pronounced and irreversible rise in prices. Basic needs – foodstuffs; clothing; transportation and housing will certainly cost more. The hardest hit will be those already living a precarious existence – the poor. Thanks to N.E.P.A. and its 'load shedding' together with its erratic power supply; and the increased cost of raw materials plus higher taxes – we shall probably face a slump in production which will inevitably result in higher unemployment. Once again, the hardest hit will be the poor/low income group.

Alhaji L.P.O. has been going round the country lamenting that he can no longer practise his profession (he is a money-doubler) thanks to the Professional Practice Decree; he has to pay 50 per cent of his profits to the Government; and even his land no longer belongs to him! Haba, Alhaji who have you offended?

Alhaji was on TV a little while ago. On that occasion he overwhelmed the audience by declaring:

'The only thing that keeps me in this country is STAR BEER – it's not just a drink. It's more a way of life!'

I think it is correct to say that the Professional Practice Decree has not seriously addressed itself to tackle the main reason why professionals – doctors, engineers, architects, accountants etc. have been deserting the Civil Service in large numbers. More and more of them are finding themselves permanently at the losing end of the unabated conflict and struggle for power between the Administrators and the Professionals within the Civil Service. Even in minor and basically routine matters such as the recommendation of drugs for purchase, a doctor may find himself overruled by the Administrator who knows next to nothing about the merits or demerits of the drugs. At another level, professionals find themselves most frustrated and maligned when say a professional engineer or architect recommends a consultant or contractor for a particular project. Without any regard for or evaluation of his professional judgement, it is immediately presumed that the professional must have collected substantial bribes from those he has recommended!

I have had the benefit of personal contact with those connected with drafting the budget and giving advice on recent policy decisions. There is no doubt that they are dedicated, sincere and hardworking. They are also subjected to considerable pressure to deliver advice at incredibly short notice. However, what is clear as regards recent major decisions is that in the frantic attempt to reconcile basically conflicting ideas and interests, insufficient attention has been given to all the available options and the primary objective has been lost sight of. The Budget has not done full justice to the considerable talents of the team of Government advisers. There is certainly a case for reviewing the Budget now before it wrecks further havoc with the economy.

WHO IS AFRAID OF THERESA BOWYER?

I HAVE known for a long time that my good friend Alhaji L.P.O. has a big hang up about THERESA BOWYER, the formidable woman journalist. When in the early sixties, Mrs Bowyer quit the 'Daily Times', Alhaji went on hunger strike for three weeks passionately pleading with his favourite journalist to withdraw her letter of resignation. As far as I know, Mrs Bowyer never replied to any of his letters – certainly not the one in which Alhaji categorically declared: 'Without Theresa – the "Daily Times" is finished!' It is a matter of history that since the day Mrs Bowyer wrote her last column for 'Daily Times', Alhaji has not bought or read a single copy of the paper.

I was therefore not in the least surprised a few years ago when Mrs Bower resumed writing again – but this time for the 'New Nigerian'. Alhaji L.P.O.'s response was predictable. Bursting with excitement as if he had just won the pools, Alhaji plunged into my office waving a copy of 'New Nigerian' with Mrs Bowyer's maiden article in it. He feverishly declared: 'Theresa is back – all hope is not lost!'

I would add that Alhaji's flat is literally plastered with blown up photographs of his favourite columnist. On display are photographs of Theresa as a schoolgirl; Theresa at the Independence Ball; Theresa at the Republic Dance; Theresa at a school prize-giving ceremony; Theresa full of gaiety at a swinging party – she had her shoes off; Theresa giving a lecture to the Young Women Christian Association; Theresa getting married (to someone other than Alhaji – fancy being called Mrs L.P.O.!) and more recent photographs of Mrs Bowyer at a meeting of the Board of Directors of New Nigerian Newspapers and another one of her as a member of the panel appointed by the Federal Military Government to look into the administration of Teaching Hospitals all over the country (incidentally, what became of that report?).

I was just recovering from an all night party when first thing on Saturday (April 15) morning my phone rang. This was a minor miracle – considering the phone hadn't worked for at least nine months! Really, I can't think of who else to bribe to get the phone fixed! Anyway, it was Alhaji L.P.O. on the phone. Without bothering to exchange greetings – Alhaji straightaway declared . . . 'Salvation is at hand – you simply must read Theresa's column in today's New Nigerian. If it does not win her the "Journalist of the year award", I shall surrender my citizenship.'

I assured Alhaji that I would read it and I did. I had to admit that 'Not so Good, Gentlemen' was a very good article indeed! First-class stuff – even though it was nearly ruined by an unnecessary and harsh reference to Miss Sienne Allwell-Browne (who says anything is All-well in this country?), the TV newscaster. Good manners prevent me from suggesting feminine bitchiness. Sienne may not be exactly Angela Rippon or Barbara Walters but she is certainly the best thing going on Nigerian Television – with or without her 'mouth . . . a little wider'. O.K.?

Anyway, back to Mrs Bowyer's article. Her opening jab on the Federal Government Budget was a direct hit – 'IT WAS A VERY BAD BUDGET'. Then, she went on to deliver the good news (for the rich!). 'The rich always survive and there will be enough for those who have money to buy'. But for the poor – it's bad news all the way. 'If you are poor, you have had it. You have no hope. Your ₦60 or ₦70 or ₦80 a month does not permit luxuries now. Soon you will not be able to afford necessities'. She then went on to polish off the unfortunate Mr B. D. W. Mafeni, the Federal Commissioner for Agriculture '. . . this portfolio is always given to someone nobody has or ever will have heard of'. The final *'coup de grace'* (to make sure he does not have peace in his own home?) follows with a desperate appeal over his head (to his wife).

'In the meantime, would Mrs Mafeni, if there is one, please have a word with her old man and kindly explain a few basic facts about housekeeping'. To quote Alhaji – 'What is the budget about if not housekeeping?' He is firmly in support of Mrs Bowyer's assertion that '. . . the highest policy making body (the Supreme Military Council) contains no female member. Had the weaker (indeed!) sex been represented there, we might have had a more sensible budget . . .'.

With characteristic crazy sense and upside-down logic, Alhaji L.P.O. added the profound paradox that women are in fact the 'fathers of the nation'. I was rather baffled by this but Alhaji went on to explain that when Gowon declared himself the 'father of the Nation', it was not the sentiment that was wrong – rather it was the concept that was misplaced. According to Alhaji, in order to be truly the 'Father of the Nation', a great leader would have to do what women (at least the sensible ones) do everyday – plead (when they are in fact ordering); give (when they are fact taking); exercise patience (when they are in fact in a hurry) and above all, care for all.

Alhaji was quick to point out the recent occasion when the Head of State had to deal with a highly explosive situation – when 87 members of the Constituent Assembly walked out over the Sharia issue. Rather than order the MCA's back (in true Military fashion) and run the risk of his order being defied, he chose the pose of the 'Father of the Nation' and appealed to BOTH sides for fairness, tolerance and understanding in the interest of the nation. To drive his points home, he added that if the MCA's chose to plunge the nation into a crisis, the rich and the powerful would be the first to flee leaving the poor as 'common fodder'. It worked!

It is arguable whether in an all male set-up there is an

in-built tendency to deal with a crisis by meeting force with force and thereby escalating violence. Alhaji has been telling everyone who would grant him audience that had the same 'Father of the Nation' approach been adopted in dealing with the University students' protest over the sudden increase of tuition fees from ₦150 to ₦500 per session, eleven students would not have died of 'gun shot wounds'. Most fair-minded people are still dazed with the horror of such wanton killing of unarmed students.

Much criticism has been levelled against two of the principal actors in the students riots – Col. Ahmadu Ali, the Federal Commissioner for Education, and Dr Aminu Jibrin, Secretary of the National Universities Commission. The painful irony is that this pair should be the last people to be involved in an event that smacks so much of callousness. Apart from the fact that both of them are doctors by profession (and of course went to University themselves), Col. Ali is generally regarded as humble, accessible (contrary to the 'Daily Times' editorial) and a liberal with a lively interest in Arts and Literature. Dr Aminu is to this day regarded as a brilliant doctor and certainly one of the best students ever of the University of Ibadan Medical School.

According to Alhaji L.P.O. part of the problem with this country is that we know so little about our history. In ancient times, rather than revolt against an unpopular ruler, the subjects through their elders and chiefs would offer the ruler the hand of a woman who they considered wise, gentle and endowed with common sense to save the errant ruler.

Alhaji, are you suggesting that we should offer 'Dear Theresa' to the Head of State? 'No. Not literally – but she should certainly be co-opted into the Supreme Military Council'.

Personally, I think that would be going too far. (There may be problems about what rank to give her.) I would be quite happy to see her appointed as a Federal Commissioner. Alhaji L.P.O. was quick to suggest a title –

'Commissioner for Agriculture!'
  To a great lady – I salute.

OPEN LETTER TO MEMBERS OF THE CONSTITUENT ASSEMBLY

FOR the first time in his life, Alhaji L.P.O. has been looking gloomy. He was clutching an official letter from the Nigerian Institute of International Affairs inviting him to deliver a lecture on any topic of his choice as long as it concerns a major international issue. I could not help asking Alhaji what the problem was. His answer was very testy:

'First of all, I have no interest whatever in international affairs – all our troubles are right here at home. Secondly, I may be misquoted by the Press and thirdly for the first time in my life I have to admit that I do not understand this country anymore.'

I had to remonstrate with Alhaji – 'Surely, you can't turn down such an invitation. It's a great honour. Just imagine the number of newspapers which would carry bold headlines headed – "Full text of the lecture delivered by Alhaji L.P.O. at the Nigerian Institute of International Affairs!"'

Alhaji was still obstinate and declared 'I have learnt my lesson. Look only a few days ago, Professor Ayodele Awojobi distributed copies of his twenty-page observations on the recent student crisis to all the major newspapers but each one attributed a different conclusion to him. One Newspaper declared that the Professor had blamed the Federal Military Government while another stoutly claimed that he blamed it all on the Vice-Chancellors while yet another stoutly proclaimed that the Professor had announced that the real culprits were the Federal Commissioner for Education and the Secretary of the National University Commission. One newspaper even printed a headline that suggested that the

Professor was blaming the students. If they can do that to a Professor, what chance do I stand?'

When I pointed out to Alhaji that he would be offending Dr Bolaji Akinyemi, Director-General of the Institute of International Affairs by not accepting the invitation, he was very curt: 'I am sure he is a very nice man with a pleasant sense of humour otherwise he would not be going round the country complaining about not getting donations from the multinational corporations in order to finance his institute to publish reports on how to control the multinationals!'

There and then, Alhaji L.P.O. decided that he would much rather write an open letter to members of the Constituent Assembly on issues of the day and he wanted me to prepare the draft. He insisted that the letter must be headed 'I DON'T UNDERSTAND THIS COUNTRY ANY MORE'.

Dear Sirs,
SHARIA

Even now I still do not understand why you fellows (and ladies) wanted to break up the country over what is purely a religious matter. You seem to have forgotten that in order TO BE A GOOD MOSLEM YOU NEED TO BE A GOOD CHRISTIAN AND VICE-VERSA. One religion says 'Fear thy God' and the other says 'Submit yourself to the will of Allah' – so what is the difference? Personally, I am in favour of Sharia but against all judges, courts and lawyers. Law and order should be administered by natural rulers who are well versed in business, stock exchange and property development.

O F N (Operation Feed the Nation)

This programme is in serious trouble – it has soaked up millions of naira with little to show for it. It urgently needs a man with dash, dynamism and charisma to head it. I cannot think of a better personality than our much travelled Commissioner for External Affairs – BRIGADIER

JOSEPH GARBA. No two ways about it – Joe is the man for the job. From his extensive travelling, he is sure to know how in other countries food production is given top priority as the backbone of the economy which is the ultimate backbone of foreign policy.

LAND USE DECREE

I fully support the Land Use Decree because after all, the land belongs to the PEOPLE; the Government belongs to the PEOPLE – therefore the land and the Government and the PEOPLE are all the same. 'Q.E.D.' the land still belongs to the PEOPLE! In fact, the Decree should be retroactive to 1960 (when we became independent)!

STUDENTS' PROTEST

I am quite astonished that virtually nothing was said at the Constituent Assembly about the loss of lives at Lagos University and Ahmadu Bello University, Zaria following the confrontation between students and law enforcement agencies. Even if it is too much to expect the Assembly to adjourn for a day or observe a minute's silence at the loss of such young lives, surely at least one MCA should have pointed out the cardinal principle – every Nigerian life is valuable. Our culture abhors bloodshed – the guns should point outwards not inwards. I am not sure about the validity of the Government's posture – that the students should not have protested in the first place therefore the consequences were entirely of their own making. Perhaps it is too much to expect the Government to apologise but surely it takes a great man to admit that an error of judgement has been committed and that the guns started blazing too soon. Is it any wonder that we fell prey to the London 'Telegraph's' headline which described the shooting as 'Nigeria's Soweto'? This is a great country but we all owe an obligation to make it GREATER. We all make mistakes – the Government makes mistakes; blind people make mistakes; deaf people make mistakes; poor people and rich people alike make mistakes – shooting is not the answer.

HIGHWAY TOLL

I am definitely against any attempt to charge tolls on highways (which no one asked them to build!) paid for with tax-payer's money. The only sensible compromise is to levy tolls on motorists who use the expressway and give rebates to those who undertake not to use the expressway!

PRESS FREEDOM

I am one hundred per cent against press freedom. All newspapers should be controlled by U.A.C. and I.T.T. should control all TV stations!

SMUGGLING

I want to place on record my total disagreement with the powerful lobby who insist that smuggling should be enshrined in the Constitution. These jokers are going round the country telling everybody (at least those who will listen) that the smuggler is the poor man's ultimate saviour from oppression. He is the only man willing to let you have a commodity which your government does not want you to have at a price you are willing to pay! Their argument is that the smuggler is just like every other professional. He takes risks – there is always the danger of being caught. But then every professional has to take risks – the doctor knows that his patient may die (before he can pay the bill); the lawyer knows that his client may go to jail; the architect knows that the building may collapse; the banker knows that his debtor may pay him back in counterfeit notes or take off for Timbuktoo; but THE SOLDIER TAKES THE BIGGEST RISK OF ALL.

As for the Constitution maker, he knows that even if he drafts a lousy Constitution, he is sure to be invited next time round to re-draft the same constitution and make the same mistakes all over!

As they say in higher circles – HAPPY DELIBERATIONS!

Yours sincerely,
Alhaji (Chief) Dr L.P.O.

STOP IT – I LIKE IT

HERE COMES (OR EXITS?) THE CENSOR

ACCORDING to Alhaji L.P.O. the most hilarious aspect of the debacle over whether or not the Government decided to censor the Press (following the wide coverage given to the students' protest and the ensuing confrontation with the Police/Military) was Dr G. B. Leton's vigorous but unconvincing defence of the Government. Alhaji was quick to point out that the Press conference given by the honourable Commissioner for Information should not have lasted more than two minutes. All he needed to say was: 'Gentlemen of the Press, my name is not Edwin Clarke! I shall be perfectly frank with you. Obviously the Government was under considerable pressure during the students' crisis. Apart from the totally unexpected turn of events, the Government was getting a very bad Press. One newspaper even published damaging photographs of Police brutality. You are all mature people I hope, and you would be deceiving yourselves if you cannot accept that one of the options open to the Government was to consider Press censorship. However, on sober reflection the Government decided not to go ahead with it. In the meantime, one or two State Governments had jumped the gun'. End of story (and roaring applause).

In case any pressman was sufficiently drunk or impudent to ask 'Honourable Commissioner, has the Government completely abandoned Press censorship or is it that the time is not yet ripe?' The Commissioner's reply should have been:

'I think you have answered your own question; I can however tell you that as far as the present Government is concerned, there are far more pressing problems than Press censorship. As to what may happen in the future – you just wait till the civilians take over. If I were you, I would start looking for another job now!'

The other aspect of Dr Leton's speech that amused Alhaji L.P.O. was the Honourable Commissioner's choice of words. He was quoted as saying that the furious attack on the Government by the Press over censorship was 'a case of giving a DOG a bad name'. The Alhaji almost interrupted the audience to remind them of an occasion when reporters had tried to verify a very sensitive news item by calling at the office of a very senior member of the previous administration. One of the reporters had simply asked:

'Sir, we have come to hear from the HORSE'S mouth . . .'. They were caught completely off-guard by the violence of the response from the official – 'who be horse? You be horse – and your mother and father too. And ditto your Editor'.

LET THERE BE LIGHT

It is common knowledge that since the Nigerian Electric Power Authority (N.E.P.A.) started its load-shedding programme, blackouts have become the order of the day. Alhaji L.P.O. has taken it upon himself to go round the country (he says it is his civic duty) and tell everyone who would listen that contrary to what N.E.P.A. says, there is ample electricity in the country. His punch (!) line is:

'It is pure coincidence that many offices and factories are discovering that the lights go off at opening time and come on at closing time!' As far as Alhaji is concerned, the whole thing is a conspiracy between N.E.P.A. and the Candle Manufacturers who have been making a killing from the incessant blackouts.

According to Alhaji, the Candle Manufacturers have got so bold that they have instructed N.E.P.A. as follows:

'Give us a little more light so that we can increase our

production in order to cope with the demand for candles'.

What irritates Alhaji about blackouts is that he does not like praying in the dark (you may not be able to see the person to whom your prayers are directed!) unless there is someone else who wants to pray with him. Dear Alhaji – you are mixing prayers with pleasure!

CRAZY CHOICE

Quite unknown to the Nigerian public, the Constituent Asembly was equally divided as regards whether we would have an Executive President or a Non-Executive President. In his role as Special Consultant to the Assembly, Alhaji L.P.O. rushed to the Assembly Hall. He got a standing ovation when he solemnly counselled the Assembly that in the interest of peace and national unity – the Assembly should incorporate two Presidents into the Constitution. One President would be Executive and the other would serve as the Non-Executive President.

A member of the Assembly (who does not want his name revealed) congratulated Alhaji warmly and wondered aloud why members had not themselves thought of such an obvious and sensible idea. According to him there is no end to the attractive permutations of such an arrangement. For example, we would have an Executive President from the South while the Non-Executive President would come from the North (or vice versa) and they could change places every other day! Equally, we could have a woman as the Non-Executive President while a man would be the Executive President. We could do the same with Moslems and Christians; or civilians and military (!) – that way nobody needs to feel cheated.

THE PROFESSIONALS

LAST Friday Alhaji L.P.O. was a guest at a luncheon hosted by the National Policy Development Centre – otherwise known as the 'Think Tank' at the ultra modern and ultra expensive (and ultra no telephone; no water; no electricity and no service?) Eko Hotel. Considering the prices charged at the Eko Hotel, it is not surprising that the only people who can still afford to eat there are members of the 'Think Tank'.

The drinks flowed freely and I was not in the least surprised that Alhaji L.P.O. exceeded his brief – which was simply to introduce Dr Eleazu, Director of the 'Think Tank' to the august (actually it's September now) audience. While the Alhaji is still recovering from his hangover, I offer my sincere apologies to Dr Eleazu for the embarrassment inflicted upon him by the Alhaji's comments particularly as the Alhaji's opening remarks were:

'I think the idea of having a 'Think Tank' is just fine. However, I find I think much better and much more clearly with the assistance of 'Top Beer'. So gentlemen, my question is how can you justify the setting up of a 'Think Tank' when there is an acute shortage of beer?'

He then went on to declare that he felt very strongly that it was a waste of everybody's time to introduce Dr Eleazu since everybody knows him anyway. After all, his name and picture are in the newspapers every day and he is on television every night. What else do you need to know – his blood-type or his National Pension Fund number?

He went on to announce that rather than introduce Dr Eleazu, he would much rather comment on a policy matter which the 'Think Tank' has been urging the

Government to consider. Apparently, the 'Think Tank' has advised the Government to confer special 'National Professional Merit Awards' on deserving Nigerians and expatriates (and institutions) on the 18th Anniversary of our Independence – 1 October. Naturally, the Government was worried about whether this would not amount to a duplication of the annual National Awards – Order of the Federal Republic of Nigeria; Order of Niger etc. However, the 'Think Tank' was quick to point out that while the emphasis of the National Awards is on 'Public Service', the 'Professional Merit Awards' would be specifically directed towards excellence in whatever profession one has chosen to pursue. The 'Think tank' has also buttressed its case by suggesting that it is all very well for the Government to complain about the performance of professionals as regards not only ethics but also the quality of advice they offer to the Government, what is even more important is to recognise outstanding professionals as models for the generations that would follow.

It was in this spirit that Alhaji L.P.O. went on to nominate the following professionals:

MEDICINE: (posthumous) Dr Oladele Ajose for his services to public health.

RURAL MEDICINE: The doctor from Bendel State whose name Alhaji could not remember but NTV screened a documentary on him a few months ago. Apparently, without any assistance from the Government, this good doctor and his wife have built up their own hospital in one of the rural areas of Bendel State.

INTERNATIONAL MEDICINE: Dr Modupe Norman-Williams for being the first Nigerian to be seconded as an adviser to the World Health Organisation.

CHEMISTRY: Dr Somorin (Department of Chemistry) Lagos University for his recent internationally acclaimed success in research. Do we have to wait for other international bodies to honour him?

AVIATION: To the Nigerian Pilot who has been flying for twenty-two accident-free years.

JUDICIARY: Chief Justice Sir Darnley Alexander for his

tireless efforts to decongest the courts; and Justice Omo-Eboh – the first Nigerian lady to be appointed a High Court judge.

DIPLOMACY: Brigadier Joseph Garba, former Commissioner for External Affairs – not for his creditable performance on the international scene. It is the little things that count. His citation is for liberalising the issuing of passports and ensuring that passports are not the privilege of a few. Never mind that Nigerians chose to undermine the policy by cashing in on the foreign exchange racket with fraudulent passports.

ARCHAELOGY: Mr Richard E. Leakey (a recent visitor to Nigeria). A few years ago he led the team that unearthed in Kenya the nearly complete skull of a creature called 'Homo habilis', a protoman who flourished some 2 million years ago. The citation is for his excellent newly published book – 'People of the Lake'. Sample quote:

'Sharing, not hunting or gathering as such is what made us human. We are human because our ancestors learned to share their food and their skills in an honoured network of obligation.

CIVIL SERVICE: Malam Liman Ciroma – Secretary to the Federal Military Government – for his outstanding services to the former North-Eastern State Government; Mr T. A. Tugbogbo – for being a shining example of the incorruptible civil servant; and Alhaji A.O.G. Otiti now a Director of the Central Bank but formerly head of the Foreign Exchange Control Department where he survived with his reputation undented.

ARCHITECTURE: The team of architects who recently completed the master plan for the new Federal Capital at Abuja.

ENGINEERING: Mr Adegboye – Project Manager (since its inception) of the Nigerian Steel Development Agency.

ELECTRONICS: Mr Imo Otite, Managing Director of Bizcontact Electronics Limited for successfully launching the manufacture of Zenith TV and radios in Nigeria.

GOVERNMENT: C. of C. (ShQ) for skilfully detonating a potentially explosive situation – the doctors' strike.

LEADERSHIP: H. E. The H. of S. – for his 'Jaji Declaration'; his speech at Khartoum; and his intervention when the Sharia issue triggered off a major crisis at the Constituent Assembly. Also for sparing us South American style or Idi Amin's version of Military Rule – tortures, interrogations, mysterious disappearances etc.

POLITICS: Dr Namdi Azikiwe – 1st President of the Federal Republic of Nigeria.

SCIENCE: The Nigerian (from Imo State) who was interviewed recently on American television. Apparently, he is one of the highest ranking scientists on the United States aerospace programme.

MILITARY: Major-General Martin Adamu, the poet – soldier, who is the highest ranking officer to retire from the army voluntarily; and Colonel Ibrahim Babangida – the hero of 13 February 1976. Also, the leader of the Nigerian Peace-keeping force in the Lebanon; and the 'unknown' soldier who rescued the victim of a motor accident, took him to hospital and handed over ₦6000 in cash which he found at the scene of the accident.

THE POLICE: Citation withheld until they rid the streets of armed robbers!

OFN (Operation Feed the Nation): To the Headmaster of the Oyo State School which has now become a model for others – all the food consumed by his students is grown on the school farm.

EDUCATION: Mr P. H. Davies, (formerly the Principal of King's College Lagos and now the Principal of Federal Government College Warri) who has been connected with education in Nigeria for almost thirty years. Also, Dr Tai Solarin for his pioneering work at Mayflower School, Ikenne.

HIGHER EDUCATION: University of Nigeria, Nsukka

for its efforts to rehabilitate a whole generation of students whose studies were disrupted during the Nigerian Civil war.

FINANCE: Mr G. O. Onosode, Chief Executive of Nigerian Acceptances Limited on successfully floating the ₦20 million Bendel State Loan Stock, 1988 – the first of its kind.

ACCOUNTANCY: Mr Akintola Williams for being the first Nigerian Chartered Accountant to set up his own practise; Mr C. O. O. Oyediran for being the only Nigerian ever to win first place in the final examination of the Institute of Chartered Accountants, England and Wales; and Mr L. C. Parker, Senior Partner of P. M. C. E. & Co, who is retiring after 25 years in Nigeria.

JOURNALISM: Alhaji Lateef Jakande ('Nigerian Tribune') for his report on the 1977 Hajj; and Malam Mohammed Haruna of 'New Nigeria' for his coverage of the Constituent Assembly; and of course to Alhaji L.P.O. of 'Sunday Punch' for his contributions to the rubbish published in Nigerian newspapers!

Alhaji L.P.O. rounded up his speech by reminding the guests of the 'Think Tank' that recently, 'Candido' of the NNN called on the Federal Military Government to follow the example of the United States and Britain where all cigarette packets carry the warning:

'The Surgeon-General says smoking is dangerous for your health'.

The suggestion is that in the case of Nigeria, the warning should read:

'The Director-General of the 'Think Tank' THINKS smoking is dangerous for your health.'

THE INNOCENT COUNTRY

WHOEVER was responsible for inviting Alhaji L.P.O. to appear on yesterday's edition of 'Face the nation' (the popular TV programme from Kaduna), must be bitterly regretting it.

Apart from the monumental discourtesy of not allowing the other participants to have their say, Alhaji L.P.O. started by holding up a copy of the 'New Nigerian' in which the weekly columnist 'Candido' had lavished fulsome praise on Dr Pius Okigbo for his contribution to the Constituent Assembly debate on the report of the panel on Revenue Allocation headed by Dr Aboyade of Ife University.

The moment Alhaji L.P.O. launched his attack on 'Candido' I knew there would be trouble. From personal experience, I know that no one in a position of authority or influence takes kindly to criticism. Certainly, when you start firing shots at a prominent columnist like 'Candido' – 'The man behind the Mask – you are inviting a lot of flak and you may even trigger off a Press war.

I have since read 'Candido's' comments and find nothing wrong with his generous commendation of an outstanding economist – Dr Pius Okigbo.

However, Alhaji L.P.O. took a completely different view. To quote him – 'For such a widely read columnist to shower praises purely on the skill and eloquence of one prominent economist to vilify a group of fellow professionals while forgetting the substance and issues raised by the report itself, is to adopt a singularly simplistic approach'.

If 'Candido' was so anxious to daub Dr Okigbo our all-time economic 'guru', what would have been more meaningful would be to examine Dr Okigbo's track record based on his performance as our Ambassador to the European Economic Community; the benefits or otherwise of the terms of the Treaty that emerged; and even more on his term of office as the nation's Chief Economic Adviser. (He may well have strongly advised against some of the very costly economic mistakes made by the government).

To do otherwise is to confirm that we are truly an innocent country. If Abdullahi Aminu (the Editor of New Nigeria) has anything to do with that column – then he has plenty to answer for.

On this score, I do not share Alhaji L.P.O.'s views at all. First of all, I think for once the Alhaji has lost his sense of humour. Candido's comments in fact follow logically from his earlier joke about 'one-handed economists' to which Dr Okigbo had referred in his contribution to the Constituent Assembly. The joke was about a king who was fed up with his economists who kept qualifying their forecast and options by adding – 'on the other hand'. In desperation, the king decided that henceforth he would only listen to one-handed economists.

Furthermore, it is entirely true to say that Dr Okigbo held the Assembly spellbound while he tore into the soft underbelly of the new Revnue Allocation formula proposed by Dr Aboyade and his team. To quote a member of the Assembly – Dr Okigbo made a football of the basic contradictions and abstractions of the report and in the end, he succeeded brilliantly in making the report look like a horseradish (and that is putting it politely).

I know for a fact that there are two people, who are greatly admired by Alhaji L.P.O. for their ability to critically examine issues without any regard for fraudulent ethnic interests. They are Dr Bala Usman (of Ahmadu Bello University) and Aminu Abdullahi. I also know he has framed Abubakar Rimi's excellent contribution to the Sharia debate (published in the 'New Nigerian').

Alhaji has also preserved in a bound volume Candido's comments about natural rulers in which he went out on a limb to question the established order which natural rulers hold as sacrosanct. That article must have made the founding fathers of the 'New Nigerian' turn in their graves!

I am not sure how much merit there is in Alhaji L.P.O.'s broadside – 'Nigerians are cursed with an incurable sense of high dramatics. They must always have someone they are praising to high heavens (Dr Okigbo) and of course someone they are condemning to the fiery depths of hell (Dr Aboyade).''

I must however add that it is quite easy to observe that whether a particular Nigerian leader is being showered with praises or being condemned as the personification of evil has less to do with critical analysis of their performance in office – rather it has more to do with whatever point of view happens to be fashionable. For example, Alhaji Tafawa Balewa, the first and indeed the only Prime Minister we have had was unquestionably an honest decent man.

What we cannot, however, overlook is that his simple approach to burning issues cost us dearly. He was totally unable to outflank either the Sardauna, his party leader or Alhaji Ribadu, the 'Strongman' and Minister of Defence. What is often forgotten by those who have cast Sir Abubakar in the role of 'the voice of the Sardauna' is that both he and the Sardauna had a major force to contend with – Alhaji Ribadu who was simply not prepared to 'brook any nonsense' from anyone, the Saudauna and the Prime Minister included.

The Prime Minister being the modest man he was, he quite happily accepted the role of the 'golden voice' and even at crucial points when a drastic change of course was required e.g. when he was warned about the coming avalanche, he simply declared: 'There is not much I can do, whatever will happen will happen.' It is a testimony to his generous spirit that he was very tolerant of criticism.

Even when certain civil servants were singled out for 'liquidation', he refused to join the bloody-minded. He stoutly declared: 'I know that some of them can see nothing good in what the Government is trying to do, but as for betraying their country – never.'

As for the ladies, Sir Abubakar was certainly a hit. The names of the women who wormed their way into his heart and his bed reads like a roll call of Lagos high society.

The other case study centres on Major-General Ironsi, who following the assassination of Alhaji Tafawa Balewa became the Head of State. Contrary to the fashionable role of the 'blustering drunken buffoon' foisted on him, he had one enduring quality – he was an equal match for his advisers. He developed a compelling grasp of quite complex issues by employing a 'grass-root' approach reminiscent of what one often encounters in the villages – 'don't think that just because you have a chain of university degrees, you can confuse me.'

Ironsi lasted only six months but to quote one example, he once overwhelmed an audience of top civil servants by challenging them on a top policy matter 'when you go to a place like Australia, what their planners talk about is not just how much to vote for fertilizers but the concrete results to be expected from utilising X quantity of fertilizer', the crop yield; and of course the consequences of not doing so. Gentlemen, LET's HAVE A DRINK!'

Actually, part of Ironsi's problem was that he was only partly Ibo. His father was Mr Ironside Johnson, a Sierra Leonian who worked for many years as a customs officer and was based at Opobo. Consequently, Ironsi fell easy prey to those who openly taunted him into trying to prove that he was a true Ibo man.

The result was that in trying to prove his loyalty, he was trapped into following dangerous policies that identified him firmly with a particular ethnic group at the expense of others. This was to cost him dearly.

Personally, I am very sceptical about the usefulness of this business of 'criticise your leader'. In fact, I think

Alhaji L.P.O. is guilty of the same offence which he claims others are guilty of – his analysis is too simple!

THE INNOCENT COUNTRY (PART II)

I WAS numb with disbelief when I heard that Alhaji L.P.O. had been invited to make a second appearance on 'Face the Nation'. Considering that his appearance last week on the same TV programme was a total disaster, one has to be persuaded that those who run the programme operate on the thesis that even the devil deserves a second chance. It was obvious that Alhaji had come to the studio straight from his favourite drinking bar. In fact he was still wearing his now famous badge with the inscription – 'Top is not just a beer – it's a way of life!'

Alhaji's theme was that whatever is wrong (and there is plenty wrong) with the country now did not start today. Rather, the seeds were sown twenty years ago as the country prepared itself for Self-Government and eventually Independence (1960). When the British handed over, it was already obvious that plenty of trouble lay ahead. Back in 1958, Nigeria had inherited a first-class and highly disciplined civil service manned by Nigerians. Idealistic, highly-motivated young men were in abundance and there was plenty of talk about 'accelerated development' and 'pulling the country by the scruff of the neck' to drag it out of poverty, disease and ignorance. Also, the judiciary was in excellent shape – bright young lawyers had no hesitation in accepting appointment to the bench, even when it meant giving up their fabulously lucrative private practice. In addition, the country was blessed with a dogged, fearless and articulate press not to mention its embryo professional class of lawyers, architects, accountants, engineers, doctors etc. who had truly imbibed the ethics of their various professions and were severely mindful not only of their individual rights but also of their personal discipline as well as social obligations. Also very much in evidence were teachers who sincerely believed with missionary zeal that teaching was their true calling; plus of course farmers who could not see themselves doing anything other than farming – the close communion with the earth was all.

Even the most innocent observer cannot now insist that nothing has changed. It took us less than ten years to destroy all those fine qualities that confirmed the promise of an emerging country – a star in Africa, destined to show the way to others not by the extravagance of its hospitality but through skilful management of its resources and solid social as well as scientific achievements. How did we do it? Was it by an act of God or was it through wilful self-destruction?

For the answer, we have to go back to 1958 – when the politicians first tasted power. Once the date for Independence had been set, the British were on their way out and the steam had been taken out of all the vituperations that had previously been directed at the British. The fight turned inwards – the fragmentation became obvious and self-interest ran a close second to tribal interest (disguised as party interest). At first, the politicians were unsure of themselves – but by the time Independence came in 1960, they had come to relish their power and their importance which rested firmly on their power to say 'yes' or 'no'. The confrontation with the civil service was inevitable. The civil service truly had difficulty in accepting the new ruling class as their 'political masters'. Clearly, the civil service was the better educated class when compared with the politicians notwithstanding the sprinkling of lawyers who stoutly maintained that law and politics were inseparable twins. One gave you knowledge, the other gave you power and of course both gave you money! The civil service with pardonable arrogance made no secret that they felt it was supreme irony that they had to sign letters with the flourish – 'your obedient servant', when the politicians to whom the letters were addressed were for the most part erstwhile school teachers, second-rate traders, transporters, cocoa merchants, village scribes, produce buyers and second-hand dealers. To crown it all – some of them could neither read nor write English!

The politicians tasted power and loved not only its sweetness but also the trappings – English private secretaries; big cars; posh houses in hitherto 'European Quarters'; overseas travel etc. As far as the Ministers were concerned, it was not their secretaries (civil servants) who deserved the title 'permanent' – it was they the ministers. Priority number one was to put the civil servants in their place. All these 'Johnnies' from Oxford; Cambridge; Fourah Bay and of course Ibadan (then only a college) universities had to be put in their place. Consequently, the first casualty of the politicians' consolidation exercise was the civil servants. They were given plenty of time and paper to draft their long memos but when it came to 'yes' or 'no', it was the politicians who called the shots. The civil servants reacted quickly – idealism made a quick exit and disillusion set in rapidly. They quickly saw through what the political game was all about. 'Yes' or 'no' depended primarily on what the party stood to gain (not related to its last election promises but with an eye to the next election); and secondly on the self-interest of the Minister himself. As for the welfare of the people who had lavished their hopes on them or of the country as a whole – this was a matter of coincidence!

Having been raped of its idealism, the civil service quickly learnt the art of survival. For the majority of them, subservience to the wishes of the Minister was easy. They simply anchored their hopes for advancement on their clansmen. However, for the minority who found it degrading and distasteful, danger lay ahead. If you did not join the majority in singing the praises of the Government and its Ministers, then you constituted a threat. There was no place for you in the Civil Service – 'anyone who was not for the Government was certainly against the Government.'

Once the politicians had tackled the civil servants, the other groups were relatively easy game. The professionals quickly learnt their lesson – success had as much to do with competence as patronage. Even if you were not a party member but were outstanding in your profession, some of the crumbs would still drop you way but the moment you got identified with the opposition, the tap was turned off. Hence, the audit and legal briefs of Government Corporations changed hands readily the moment the loyalty (to the Government or the party) of the incumbent became suspect.

As for the judiciary, there was little need for DIRECT interference. These judges who proved adept at throwing out government – sponsored lawsuits or prosecution of members of the opposition quickly found out that their route on the promotion ladder was incredibly slow. Salvation lay in accepting secondment to some foreign land – either a newly independent former British colony or the Hague.

As for the Press, the Official Secrets Act provided a ready answer and the police were more than willing to provide the constant hassle and locking up of errant journalists. The more truthful the publication, the greater the danger that the editor would be accompanied by his reporter on a quick march to the police cells for a rendezvous with hardened criminals, sexual perverts, marijuana-junkies etc.

The teachers plucked from the blackboard were easy prey. What glory was there in teaching if at the end of thirty-five years of teaching all you had was a miserable pension; leaking shoes; rheumatism (from too many hours of standing); zero bank credit etc.? Rather than bask in the glory of your ex-students who owned big cars, big houses, voluptuous women and commanded respect from their bank managers, you too could have all these things. All you had to do was become a party stalwart and since you could read and write, your next promotion could be – yes, Minister of Education!

The slowest group to get the message were the farmers even though some of them had fathered politicians, engineers, university lecturers, bank cashiers not to mention soldiers and policemen. Farmers were easily fooled by the vagaries of the weather and the same trusting faith made them easy game to be fooled by their new masters. Independence did not mean 'market' or realistic prices for produce – rather it meant surplus funds built up by the marketing boards (at the expense of the farmers) for easy plunder by the party and party stalwarts. For the farmers who wanted to be saved, the party was ready with the bait – loans you did not have to repay (you did not even have to sign for them and it was alright to give a fictitious name); sponsored overseas travel to watch agricultural shows; appointments as 'Minister without portfolio' (you got paid a Minister's salary but you did not have to perform any duties – just turn up on pay-day and your cheque was waiting); and free seedlings and government equipment and labourers to till your farms.

Thank God, the end of the programme came just in time – it was beginning to look as if Alhaji L.P.O. would go on for ever. Personally, I do not agree with his views – his observations are based on very narrow analysis of a very complex and multi-faceted period of this country's history. Secondly, he has been unduly harsh with the politicians – surely, they deserve some credit for the new roads; the schools, the hospitals; etc. which they built not to mention the villages and towns which first tasted clean water and electricity when the politicians were in power. Many of the critics are in fact graduates of the universities set up by the politicians.

Also, Alhaji's views about civil servants is unduly romantic. There is ample evidence that some civil servants were no less adept at feathering their own nest and protecting their self interest as the politicians. One only needs to examine the list of Swiss bank accounts opened by Nigerians or the distribution of free government plots in Ikoyi, Victoria Island, Bodija and other 'Government

345

Reservation Areas' scattered all over the country, to realise that when it came to sharing the booty, it was an even match between the civil servants and the politicians.

It should also be pointed out that there is no empirical evidence to support Alhaji's claim that the civil servants were a better educated class than the politicians. After all, among the politicians you had the heavy-weights such as Dr Nnamdi Azikiwe; Chief Obafemi Awolowo; Chief S. L. A. Akintola; Dr Russell Dikko; Dr K. O. Mbadiwe; Dr Jaja Wachukwu; Chief F. R. A. Williams; Dr Michael Okpara; Dr Okoi Arikpo etc. Equally, among the top-flight civil servants, you had people such as Mr Michael Ani who clearly owed their position not to a chain of university degrees but to uplift through diligence, solid administrative experience, masterful grasp of the intricacies of government, loyalty, probity and above all an unequalled ability to get on with everyone irrespective of tribe or religion. It is no accident that Mr Ani though an Efik was for several years the secretary of the Yoruba Tennis Club, Lagos.

Also worth mentioning, is the fact that in the Northern areas, there were very few graduates in the civil service. Not only were people like Mallam Ali Akilu and Abdul Atta (who served in Lagos) exceptionally gifted – they were rare gems. Not to be forgotten are two top flight civil servants whose reputation and devotion to duty have remained unassailable – Mr S. O. Wey and Mr H. A. Ejueyitchie.

THE INNOCENT COUNTRY (PART III)

I REMEMBER vividly the first time I went to see Alhaji L.P.O. when he was a senior ranking civil servant. I had to fill one of those visitors' forms. Against 'purpose of visit', I had filled 'Alhaji, I have brought you your commission!' and insisted that his secretary take it in straightaway. I was ushered into a huge office with soft carpets, at least six inches deep. The office was so big, I couldn't help suggesting to Alhaji that he should either take up 'office golf' or install traffic-lights in his mammoth-sized office. There at the far end was Alhaji seated at a king-sized desk, frantically filling his football pools coupon. Just above his head was a plaque with the inscription – 'What you say here, What you see here, What you hear here, Let it stay here, When you leave here.'

The next time I went to see Alhaji, he had been 'relegated'. Not only did he not have a secretary, his office was so tiny that if he stretched his legs, they stuck out in the corridor. Also, there was a huge hole where his air-conditioner used to be. I could not help asking him what he had done to deserve his non-status. His answer was:

'Politics, inside politics. I fouled up somebody's deal. The Permanent Secretary can't get rid of me without going through the Public Service Commission. So, short of turning me into the gateman or coffee-boy, this is the next best thing.'

Alhaji then went on to deliver a long-playing monologue about the Civil Service and the Government. According to him, the Government NEEDS advice but

347

does not want it. It's all a fool's game. In the Caribbean, they call it the 'Pappy show' – plenty of noise and rhythm but no substance. On and on he went with his tirade against the government. Amongst other things, he claimed that long before the various symposia (with an impressive list of university professors), are set up, the Government would already have made up its mind. That is why all those hefty papers presented at symposia, commissions etc. have zero impact on government policy.

I was only too ready to dismiss Alhaji's allegations as no more than the rumbling and nattering of the disgruntled. Even though I have on several occasions heard it said that 'some of those advising the Government are those who are determined to see the Government fail', what shocked me was Alhaji's even more serious allegation that even among the top civil servants, there are those (like Alhaji) who have given up trying to correct the Government even when they realise that it is about to pursue wrong policies. They have taken the extreme position that what is happening is merely a continuation of a course that was embarked upon nearly twenty years ago!) They maintain that it has nothing to do with whether we have a civilian or military government. According to them, we are set on a course that is guaranteed to lead us to doom and the quicker the doom the better – then we can start afresh! To attempt to save the country before it hits the bottom is only to prolong the agony.

To my mind, not only is this view startling, it is also Machiavellian. It could be justified only if the government is totally irresponsible (it is not); or blood-thirsty (whatever bloodshed has occurred in Nigeria, it has certainly not reached the proportions of Ethiopia, Uganda or Chad). However, it does provide an explanation as to why certain strange policies have somehow managed to go through the whole machinery government without being thrown out even when such policies are clearly detrimental to the nation's interest and would certainly undermine the economy. Perhaps a good example is the 'Udoji Award'. Is it pure accident that rather than focus on the positive aspects of the Udoji Report, and pare down its unrealistic recommendations, the top rank of the civil service chose to fuel economic chaos and self-inflicted inflation by recommending (and persuading the government to accept) the payment of fantastic salary arrears and a pension scheme the generosity of which, (and the burden to the government) is unequalled anywhere in the world? The forecast is that even in twenty years time, Nigeria may still not have recovered from the severe damage done by the Udoji Award.

I asked a very senior government official for his comments. He declared: 'Alhaji L.P.O. and his clique are professional confusionists. I used to have a lot of time for them – trying to explain to them that the Government was not as bad or beyond redemption as they thought, and that we should all work together as a team to build a great country. All to no avail. If the Government comes up with any idea, all you get from Alhaji L.P.O. is a long list of why it should not be done and why it can't be done. For example, when there was an acute shortage of electricity and water, the Ministry approved a plan whereby generators would be installed in the houses of top government officials and similarly water would be delivered to their homes by special tankers. Can you imagine, Alhaji wrote me a long memo bleating that the scheme was 'elitist' as the top people would be insulated from the hardship suffered by the rest of the people and that we are only laying the foundation for a communist take-over! He even argued that the reason why the railways are in such a deplorable state is because top people do not travel by train! When I told him that there was no way communists could ever take over Nigeria – the country is too big for a start and every Nigerian is a natural capitalist, he was adamant and insisted on reminding me that 'The Chinese ruling class thought the same. Is Nigeria bigger than China? After all, Chairman

Mao had only six thousand supporters on his Long March." Look, as far as I am concerned, these people who talk about communism don't know what they are talking about. They would be the first to run if we ever were to become communist. Communism means tanks, armoured cars, tommy-guns, barbed wire and long queues for bread, milk, oil and sugar as well as exit visas and rigorous press control. One other thing, I have been involved in some of the trade negotiations with some of the East European countries and I can tell you that when it comes to hard bargaining, the communist countries are even more capitalist than the Western EUROPEANS OR Americans! Take the case of Ethiopia who are getting a lot of military hardware from the Russians. The Russians were insisting on cash (hard currency) against delivery and now they have got an even better bargain – Ethiopia's coffee output for the next five years has been pledged to the Russians in exchange for arms. You don't need to be a capitalist to know that the price of coffee is rising all the time on the world market. Look my friend, all this talk about the ideal society is nonsense. To quote Kingsley Amis – 'God was pissed when he made the world and he's had a screaming hangover ever since'.

I relayed all this to Alhaji, but he was not in the least ruffled. Instead, he opened his drawer and showed me his latest memo to his boss.

It read as follows:

'It is quite clear that even a journey of a thousand miles begins with the first step. When I think of the events of the last twenty years and what is going on now, I am reminded of the character (Tantalus) in Greek mythology – the grapes were always swinging out of reach and the stream sank whenever he bent down and tried to drink out of it. Nigerians love to moan and gripe about being exploited but have you ever heard of a country being exploited unless it was willing and ready to be exploited? We simply refuse to learn from our past errors – the same mistakes are being repeated over and over again. Let's go back to 1958 when we first disco-vered oil in this country. We have to overlook Dr Jaja Wachukwu's subsequent performance as Foreign Minis-ter (did his Ministry really need two Cadillacs?) – but he was certainly the first to warn that Nigeria appeared determined to waste the opportunity of utilising its newly-found source of wealth for the welfare of its people 'not through wickedness but through care-lessness and ignorance.' When the report of Professor Hollingsworth, who was hired by the Government itself, is made public it will lend powerful support to the alarm raised by Dr Wachukwu. Subsequent events have proved him right.

One is reminded of Alswin's story about three people who are trying to cross a swamp. They proceed slowly but there is a gap of 300 metres between them. The first man disappears into a ditch, unknown to the second man who even though he can no longer see the first man proceeds without stopping to think of what may have happened to the first man. The result is predictable – he ends up in the ditch. The third man who can no longer see the first two similarly does not stop to think and he too ends up in the ditch. Inside the ditch, just before they get eaten up by a crocodile – they start blaming each other!

Nigerians love to kid themselves that they are the leaders of Africa (because Time Magazine says so?). If leadership depended on size; population; force-feeding of diplomats at lavish cocktail parties and banquets for numerous Heads of State; monetary gifts and loans to bankrupt regimes, then Nigeria would have claimed vic-tory long ago. In fact in terms of availability and effi-ciency of basic infrastructure we lag behind Kenya and Zambia; as regards ideological commitment, we are behind Algeria and certainly when it is a question of the citizens identifying with the government, we trail behind Tanzania. As for oil and mineral resources, we rank behind Angola and Gabon.

One would like to believe that there are not many

people who share Alhaji's views. He has since quit the civil service to set up as a 'Consultant' – no business is too big and none too small. According to him, when he was a civil servant, there was nothing he found more frustrating than drafting a policy paper only to find that on several occasions the paper would have been thoroughly disembowelled by the time it got to the decision making level. It was not unusual for the paper to be so completely chewed up by his boss that it represented the reverse of what he set out to say. For example, he had seriously queried the wisdom of increasing the number of universities from seven to thirteen instead of expanding the facilities of the existing ones. As regards the Trade Fair, he had pleaded that the exhibition should be limited to Agricultural Machinery and Scientific Equipment. His paper advising caution in the planning and execution of the U.P.E. programme was shredded and discarded as an impudent irrelevance. As for the Kainji Dam – Alhaji actually submitted a paper in which he categorically stated that the location chosen for the dam was entirely wrong!

The problem posed by people like Alhaji L.P.O. is quite serious – their rallying call echoes Virgil – 'Troy is doomed.' If we are to disappoint people like him, then there is an urgent need to take a close look at the civil service – particularly how 'minority' or 'unpopular' opinions get smothered. Udoji merely scratched the surface. How can the civil service be a vehicle for democracy when it is itself undemocratic and intolerable of criticism within its own ranks? Alhaji is adamant that if we are truly, anxious not to repeat past mistakes, then it should be possible for those within the Government who hold minority opinion to state their case at the highest level. According to the Alhaji, the military have simply taken over where the politicians left off. In effect, there has been no real structural change in the machinery of government. In fact, when the military tried to purge the civil service by massive retiring of 'inefficient, old or corrupt' civil servants, the top rank of the civil service were bursting with glee. It gave them an opportunity to settle old scores; get rid of those who did not share their enthusiasm for particular programmes (which they considered wasteful) and generally rid the service of those who were known to hold minority views irrespective of whether such officers were competent or committed to the advancement of the country. One other unsavoury result of the purge is that most of the victims quickly joined the middlemen – the 'compradors'. Many of them are still reeling with shock and disbelief at how easy it is to make money by cashing in on their contacts both within and outside the various ministries and corporations. Some of them have been known to write love letters and offer sincere felicitations as well as gratitude to those who were responsible for their getting the boot!

Alhaji L.P.O. has been quick to point out that when President Julius Nyerere of Tanzania visited Nigeria, he was shocked by what he saw and even though he was anxious not to offend his hosts, he could not help observing that 'any African country that is so clearly anxious to blindly follow the Western pattern of spending and consumption is asking for trouble'. Added to this is the pitiful state of affairs whereby there is virtually no serious on-going study of the social problems and economic frustrations generated by oil money in such places as Venezuela and Iran. Even nearer home, how can one explain that there has been virtually no official effort to critically examine why five very Senior Federal Civil Servants (Permanent Secretaries in charge of some of our most sensitive Ministries) have decided to quit at the same time.

If we are to make a serious effort at dealing with our economic problems and deflate the escalating social tensions, there is certainly a case to be made for taking another look at the civil service. The civil service should be a vehicle for rational selection from alternative options – certainly not for the squashing of minority opinion or the unleashing of personal vendetta. It takes patience and determination to reach the desired goal.

353

One of the hottest issues being debated by the minority within the civil service is FERTILISERS. Why are we buying so much of the stuff; are we getting the right price; is it the right type; how is it distributed; how much of it is allowed to rot away; are we getting any real benefits? Is the 'Cement armada' going to be followed by a fertiliser deluge?

If one were to list the major Government programmes that have turned out to be disruptive or wasteful or have had to be abandoned) e.g. the takeover of schools, or the abrupt increase in Excise Duty, one would find that somewhere down the line, some government officials though representing a minority opinion had accurately predicted the consequencies of the action proposed. These dedicated, committed but independent-minded officials are still there – though not many. We have ignored them for far too long.

Lastly, Alhaji L.P.O.'s favourite quotation:

> 'Some things in life are too important.
> That is why there are some things one has to think about. Carefully.
> In case anything goes wrong.
> Advice is not the easiest thing in the world to give someone. Real advice is a tender thing.'

Amen.

MAGIC, BLOODY MAGIC

LAST night, the Nigerian Economics Society held its Annual Dinner at the Eko Hotel, Victoria Island. Unfortunately, the Guest of Honour – the Federal Commissioner for Finance was unable to show up owing to pressing matters not entirely unconnected with the state of the Nigerian economy.

Rather than allow the disappointed audience of bankers, accountants, lawyers, businessmen, university lecturers, tax-dodgers, and magicians to disperse without savouring the delicious dinner for which they had already paid, Alhaji L.P.O. much to everyone's annoyance insisted on making the following speech:

'Ladies and gentlemen, I sincerely implore you to enjoy your dinner. In six months time when the full effect of the budget begins to bite, not many of you will be able to come here for dinner. Either the food will not be available or the cost will be so high, you will have to bring your bank manager along with you to let him watch what you are spending your overdraft on.

'If you think things are bad now, you wait till six months time. The shops will be empty, unemployment will reach treble figures and as for the battle against inflation – just surrender and write your will. Scarcity and hoarding will become the order of the day. We could have been saved all these tribulations if only the Government advisers had remembered the cardinal rule in preparing a meaningful budget – THERE ARE LIMITS TO WHAT PEOPLE WILL STAND.

'As a result of the budget, for the fourth year in succession (since the Udoji Award), real wages (i.e. what your naira can buy) will fall. This is sure to cause major social and political problems. Many firms will be driven into bankruptcy and of course massive unemployment will follow.

'In fairness to the Government, we must admit that it has made a brilliant analysis of our present plight. The trouble is with the remedy it has opted to apply. Neither is there any doubt about the genuineness and sincerity of the present military administration in its determination to hand over a viable and thriving economy to its civilian successor. However, we are now faced with soaring prices of virtually every commodity in our markets.

'I beg your indulgence to quote my good friend Alhaji C. C. Ozurumba of Sokoto who in a telegram sent to the "New Nigerian" commented as follows:

'"The Budget has produced negative results due to the fact that it was based on mere assumptions which have no relevance to the reality of our economic situation."

'Briefing the nation recently, on the rationale behind some of the startling provisions in the Budget, the Director of the Nigerian Institute of Scientific and Economic research, Professor M. A. Onitiri (who is here with us on the high table) made the following astonishing assertions:

(i) He believed that the restriction on the importation of food would generate increased local food production especially with the new decree on land use which has removed all constraints on the acquisition of land by anybody who wants to farm.

(ii) He believed that the removal of some consumer goods from the list of controlled items would put an end to the hoarding of these items and also force down prices in accordance with the text-book laws of supply and demand.

(iii) He also believed that investors would re-schedule their investments in view of the new and attractive relief offered by the government to investors in the agricultural sector of our economy – some of which are reduced tax on equipment, raw materials, profits etc. and easy availability of land.

'We are also witnesses to the fact that NONE OF THESE HAS HAPPENED! As has already been pointed out by Dr Yaya Abubakar, Permanent Secretary (Special Duties – Political Division) who is also here with us on the high table, the deployment of effort and resources into agriculture is as much an economic input as a political choice.

'I agree entirely with Alhaji Ozurumba who has rightly pointed out that:

'"It is most unfortunate that the budget of a nation has to be based on grossly unrealistic beliefs. It is hasty, if not improper for the government to believe that the benefits of the controversial land use decree would be realised during the current financial year. Moreover, no sane investor would venture into any project on land acquired by virtue of the Land Use Decree – a promulgation which is yet to find its way into the constitution of this country. Investors would prefer to wait."

'We are all witnesses to the fact that the removal of some items from the price control list has failed to produce the desired result – the prices of these items have further sky-rocketed by more than 50 per cent.'

At this point, Alhaji L.P.O. was interrupted by N.E.P.A. (who inflicted instant blackout) and by the President of the Nigerian Economics Society who declared:

'After that stupid and uninformed speech by Alhaji L.P.O. I don't feel like eating anymore but one thing is for sure – I'm taking my dinner home! It will take magic, bloody magic to convince me that this budget was designed to make life more abundant.'

TOMORROW WILL BE TOO LATE

I THINK I can honestly say I am not addicted to television. Generally, I find television boring – it's always the same faces you see day (or night) in day out. It's either some grovelling interviewer stammering some nonsensical questions at some big wig (who of course does not understand the questions and certainly does not know the answers). As for the newscaster who always ends with the cliche 'bla–bla–bla–. . . TOMORROW is another day – . . .', I have news for him – he is slowly driving Alhaji L.P.O. crazy.

According to the Alhaji, the trouble with us is that we keep leaving everything till tomorrow instead of dealing with the problems today. For a start, we must face certain unpalatable truths – sample:

SELF-RELIANCE

It may be comforting to keep preaching self-reliance but what is there to rely on? Is it N.E.P.A; Nigerian Airways; the telephones; the schools (without teachers and without classrooms); or the postal service?

INDISCIPLINE

It is equally untrue to claim that Nigerians are undisciplined. Those who keep asserting that we are undisciplined obviously have their eyes glued on Lagos, Ibadan, Kano, Kaduna, Calabar, Port Harcourt and the other big towns where indiscipline, bred by frustration rooted in appetites that have been whetted by false promises, does reign supreme. But what about the millions of Nigerians in the rural areas who live their lives in simple expectation, surrender to disease, poverty, and death with unconditional faith? Must we keep maligning them? They walk miles to reach the nearest hospitals, spend hours patiently waiting for treatment and go back to their homes to be afflicted with the same infections all over again.

They hear of the big contracts being awarded, they cheer when the government officials with appropriate fanfare promise a new road, a new school, a new factory, a new hospital . . . all of which they know will never be built.

They do not go on a rampage, or allow envy to poison their lives. Rather, they say their prayers and till the farms from dawn to dusk even when they know that the harvest will be meagre. Nine months of waiting to sell a few crops – buy a cotton dress (which must last till the next harvest), a new gas lamp and perhaps another hoe.

Can you imagine their sense of outrage when they hear themselves being slandered as undisciplined? To quote them – 'what more does the government want from us?'

HOUSING

Whether we like it or not, we have to face the fact that we have a massive housing problem – but we do not have a coherent housing policy. To get back to basics – housing involves far more than providing four walls and a roof. It involves careful and critical ascertainment of objectives, plan execution and above all maintenance. In other words, if your housing programme is not in concert with the people for whom the houses are meant, you will end up creating brand new slums! You have to spend time and effort on educating the people and giving them the economic wherewithal to maintain (and feel proud of) the houses provided for them. Otherwise, you will end up with the situation that is already evident now – the government would move a poor family into a brand new house but in a matter of weeks, the family would find that they simply cannot cope with their new environment. They are separated from their friends, they have to pay more for transportation, food etc. and find new schools for their children. It is only a matter of time before they start smashing up the furniture even if only to use as firewood (when there is no gas or electricity). As for the toilets – you should see the state in which they are in simply because the occupants have no money for toilet paper!

In Nigeria, there is no such thing as LOW COST houses. You only need to compare what it costs the government to build a bungalow with what it would cost you to build the same thing.

What is happening is that we have collectively given free rein to destructive judgement by substituting assertion for reason. Reason demands that we accept that you cannot deal with the housing problem in isolation. In addition to housing, people require employment and many other needs that must be accommodated in a community. Education, health, social, cultural and administrative services as well as provision of food and other goods, require facilities conveniently near to dwelling places.

A STRANGER IS WATCHING

THE scene at the Institute of International Affairs, Victoria Island last night was truly fantastic. Lagos had simply never witnessed anything like it – at least not since the funeral of the much beloved Herbert Macaulay – and that was 30 years ago! The traffic jam was five kilometres long and those who had difficulty in believing that some people had actually queued overnight, in order to be sure of getting seats, found themselves confronted by the largest turn-out in the history of Lagos. The overspill resulted in the cocktail party going on next door (at the Metropolitan Club) having to be abandoned. Those who could not get into the lecture hall had taken over the club and had quite reconciled themselves to listening to Alhaji L.P.O.'s lecture on radio.

In his usual grand fashion, Alhaji L.P.O. rose to the occasion by declaring: 'Ladies and gentlemen, I am not here to praise Dr Bolaji Akinyemi, the Director-General of the Institute of International Affairs, who is right here beside me. Neither am I here to bury him. In fact what I would like to do before going to the main theme of my lecture is to appeal to the Federal Military Government to accentuate its economy drive by merging the Institute of International Affairs with the Federal Ministry of Works and Town Planning! You may well wonder about the rationale behind the merger. Well, it is quite simple. Apart from annoying Dr Akinyemi, the merger would save us a lot of money because Dr Akinyemi has himself admitted that he and his colleagues at the Institute are merely 'Observers' and not 'Advisers' as regards the foreign policy objectives being pursued by the Government. Therefore, it makes sense to merge the Institute

361

with another very eminent group of 'Observers' – the Ministry of Works, the true masters of the art of observing our roads being destroyed; our ecology being ruined; the environment being polluted and of course they don't plan any towns – they just watch houses sprouting up all over the place.

The second subject I would like to comment upon – albeit briefly, is the Land Use Decree. I have no hesitation in declaring that 'If everybody in the world had an acre of land, there would be no more wars'. However, I do know that there are many among you who would counter by insisting 'They would want two acres!'

At this stage, a considerable percentage of the audience started leaving but were persuaded to stay when Alhaji promised to go directly to the real subject of his lecture – 'THE STATE OF THE NATION'.

He declared: '1978 is a watershed in the history of this country. We have come to the end of an era. To quote the famous words of Dr Thomas Jeffer – 'It is essential to know when one phase of your life is over. As a country, we must abandon the old before it abandons us'. The starting point is to recognise and accept that our economy is in a mess. Our problems derive from the fact that productivity in our factories and on our farms is low, very low. The acute shortage of qualified managers and skilled technicians is obvious while we are rapidly acquiring a cumbersome and inefficient bureaucracy which is unwilling to provide encouragement but appears to be jealous of the incentives and rewards of private industry. We cannot honestly claim that corruption has disappeared or is even on the decline.

It is quite clear that for many years we have been spending too much money too fast and this has resulted in our present economic plight. According to a United Nations report – 'The boom which followed the quadrupling of oil prices in 1974 did lead to severe overheating in the economy. It also led to bad planning and unbalanced growth resulting in shortages of essential foodstuffs; lack of water; power failures; and insufficient development of communications and port facilities'.

Alhaji L.P.O. went on to declare 'Right now, the country is in spiritual disarray. The reason is obvious – you cannot have spiritual salvation without economic salvation. In other words, even though the Government is right in wanting to liberate us spiritually – we should love all black people (Festac); we should support our brothers in their fight for freedom (Angola; Namibia etc.) – the fact remains that the universal law still applies – you have to save people financially before you can save their souls'.

The stranger who is watching us should be forgiven for bursting with laughter at what African countries interpret as economic advancement – Idi Amin flies in plane loads of whisky; President Mobutu collects castles; President (or Emperor) Bokassa orders his own coronation and empties his treasury to the *haute couturers* of Paris – God! The list is endless. And nearer home, the things we do . . .!'

Maybe there is some truth in what the stranger said '. . . Watching Africans Countries spending money is like putting a blind man in a fast car and telling him to drive where and how he likes'.

Needless to say, by the time Alhaji finished his lecture the audience had walked out – which is not surprising. After all, the Greeks used to kill messengers who brought bad news. The logic was that by killing the man, you kill the news.

There was only one person left in the audience – THE STRANGER, staring with his intense gaze but believing nothing.

WINNERS AND LOSERS

The only thing that is certain about the imminent elections is that whatever party Alhaji L.P.O. supports is sure to lose! It is equally certain that the Alhaji's prediction about the result of the election is bound to be wrong. According to the Alhaji, and contrary to the fantastic claims being made by various party leaders, no single party is likely to win more than eight states. We had better get ready for a good deal of horse (or cash!) trading.

WOMEN AND POLITICS

The other false prediction made by the Alhaji is that the women's vote is going to be crucial. This must make it very tempting for one of the parties to try and capture the women's vote (since they outnumber men) by putting up a woman as its Vice-presidential candidate. I understand that the search has been frantic but unfruitful. However, a word of caution here – to quote Alhaji – 'The only people who think that women will vote for a woman are MEN.'

IF YOU 'TARKA' ME . . .

I have to thank Dr (why not chief as well?) Joseph Tarka for this vignette. Giving his reasons for his split with his erstwhile 'friend and political associate', Alhaji Aminu Kano, Dr Tarka alleged that this was triggered off by Alhaji Aminu's 'incessant agitation and protestion'. He has therefore warned the nation that: 'If Alhaji Aminu Kano is elected President today, you will see him on the streets tomorrow carrying a placard calling for the removal of the president before he realises that he is himself is the President!'

Well, you can hardly expect the President to be more democratic.

WILD, WILD, WILD . . .

In days gone by, the 'West' (the old Western Region with its capital at Ibadan) had secure tenancy of the title – 'Wild, wild West'. It appears we now have a new contender – Kano. According to a report carried on the front page of a national newspaper, supporters of the National Party of Nigeria (NPN) and the Peoples Redemption Party (PRP) 'clashed fiercely' last weekend.

If you are planning to come to Kano soon, and you

wish to enjoy 'laissez-passez', remember that the 'password' is 'PRP Nasara Amin'!

I do not wish to argue with Alhaji L.P.O. who has been telling everyone that come next month, we shall begin to witness the roughest election tactics ever experienced in the history of this country. It seems that the Party Leaders have still not got over the psychological shock generated by the determination of the Military to hand over power. Somebody had better tell them to COOL IT. The success of the election does not depend on the number of broken heads!

TRUE OR FALSE?

I have anxiously been waiting for official denial of a statement credited to one of the presidential candidates. He is quoted as having '. . . promised that if he was voted into power, he would be led by the electorate INSTEAD OF LEADING THEM!' Good gracious! THE PRESIDENT IS SUPPOSED TO LEAD – that is what the new constitution is all about.

CHILD'S PRAYER

Overheard;
> 'God bless Mummy. God bless Daddy! And God, please make the GOVERNMENT change its mind about the INCREASE IN THE PRICE OF PETROL before the whole country grinds to a standstill.'

THANK YOU VERY MUCH

An unprecedented event occurred this week. For three nights running, the Head of State was on network television in a special interview. I suppose it was inevitable that the 'Red Matador' of Kakawa Street would be one of the interviewers! I gather that it was pretty good – both questions and answers. The response from the public has been very favourable. This is the first step towards public 'account-ability' — *i.e. the ability to juggle figures*

THANKS TO N.E.P.A. — I did not see any of the interviews!

WHO SAID THAT. . .?

I am grateful to Chief (Dr) Lai Ogunsola for his definition of the FOUR TENENTS OF ZIKISM (the political philosophy of Dr Nnamdi Azikiwe) as:

(i)Spiritual Balance
(ii)Mental Emancipation
(iii)Economic Determinism
(iv)Political Resurgimento

Really! Will someone kindly let Alhaji L.P.O. know what all these mean.

NOW CHECK THIS

A national Sunday paper last week quoted a natural ruler, The Alafin of Oyo, Oba Lamidi Olayiwola Adeyemi as saying:

'The public should at least give us natural rulers the benefit that some of us are not imbeciles!'

NOW CHECK THAT

Also last week, on network television, a very, very senior government official let loose on contractors (both genuine and 'emergency') with very heavy artillery. His Excellency declared that:

'There are so many things he (the contractor) builds into his contract. He builds 'variation'; he builds infla-tion; he builds all sorts of things. So he never loses. He could afford to hire a house on Victoria Island (the choicest part of Lagos) for ₦40,000 a year because the first thing we do when he gets a contract is to give him 20 per cent to 25 per cent mobilisation fee.'

Following an official complaint from Alhaji L.P.O. (who has reminded us that the government itself has by Decree imposed a maximum rent of ₦28,000 per annum for a house on Victoria Island), we investigated the discrepancy between the ₦40,000 quoted by His Excel-lency and the maximum of ₦28,000 per the Decree.

We were shocked to discover that even though the Decree clearly states that anyone found collecting or paying more than the official ₦28,000 would be executed – wait for it – on Victoria Island (otherwise known as 'The Bar Beach Show'), what seems to be happening is that tenants on Victoria Island do in fact pay ₦28,000 per annum. However, in addition they pay:

(i) ₦2000.00 for the use of the garden;
(ii) ₦3000.00 for the use of the garage;
(iii) ₦4000.00 for the fence around the building;
(iv) ₦2000.00 (non-refundable) for the keys, and
(v) ₦1000.00 as 'traditional gift'.

BAD ARITHMETIC

Following the official disclosure that in the last six months, the Nigerian Army has been drastically trimmed down from 250,000 to 180,000, Alhaji L.P.O. has written to complain that at the rate of 'geometric progression', there will be only twelve people left in the army by 1st October when the civilian government takes over. According to the Alhaji, that will not even be enough to form the Presidential Guard!

CHECK THIS TOO

According to the story carried on the front page of 'THE PUNCH' on Saturday, 27 January, Dr (why not 'Chief' as well?) Alex Ekwueme was selected by a political party as its Vice-Presidential Candidate. However, the story continues:

'. . . he was then asked what he was prepared to give to the party as a TOKEN of his commitment to its ideals. He gave an undertaking to underwrite the Presidential Candidate's expenses to the tune of ₦1,000,000 (one million naira)'. The story is clearly false.

'FEDECO' AND THE COMMUNISTS

Last night on television, the leader of the Nigerian Communist Party enlightened viewers on why his party did not bother to register with the Federal Electoral Commission ('FEDECO') According to him, Communists do not context elections – THEY JUST ARRIVE!

'FEDECO' AND THE 'ABOLITIONISTS'

We have it from usually reliable sources that among the parties which 'FEDECO' refused to register was the 'ABOLITIONISTS' Party. Among the party's aims and objectives is the abolition of:

  (i) Schools;
 (ii) Hospitals;
(iii) Farms;
 (iv) Villages;
  (v) Air travel;
 (vi) Oil exploration;
(vii) Alcohol and gambling, and
(viii) Newspapers.

Furthermore, the party insists that the Nigerian Army should be placed under Schedule III of the Nigerian Enterprises Promotion Decree, 1977. Also, according to the party manifesto, the official Slogan is:

'If you can't ban it; Zone it!
Ah well, it takes all sorts.

CHECK THIS 'NEW NIGERIAN'

We have today received an angry letter from Alhaji L.P.O. suggesting that the 'New Nigerian' newspaper should be closed down because it has failed the nation by not publishing the comments of Dr (why not 'chief' as well?) Bala Yussuf, (who is his favourite political commentator) on the forthcoming elections. Aminu Abdullahi (editor), take note!

The second point raised in Alhaji L.P.O.'s letter is that it is 'unconstitutional' for the 'New Nigerian' to announce that the articles of his favourite columnist – Mrs Theresa Bowyer, will in future be published on the 'third Tuesday' of every month. Is this 'Banning' or 'Zoning'? Obviously, Mrs Bowyer's popularity is well deserved – remember that article on the last budget in which she asked the poignant question – 'what does this Government wish to be remembered for?'

The point raised by the Alhaji L.P.O. is that how are we supposed to remember the third Tuesday of the month – or does the 'New Nigerian' have advance information that the Government is planning to declare every third Tuesday of the month a public holiday?

Mrs Bowyer – Welcome Back!

'MISCHIEF'

I was really amused the other day to observe that one of my favourite columnists captioned his weekly contribution with the screaming headline – 'Mischief thou are afoot!' As far as I am concerned, to talk about mischief in this country is to state the obvious, almost the inconsequential. Or as our learned friends would say – it is a 'non sequitur'. It is like reminding us that today is Sunday; or that Nigeria should be spelt with a capital 'N'. The whole country is full of mischief.

I am not in the least surprised that Alhaji L.P.O. has sent an urgent telegram to the Secretary to the Military Government insisting that as part of the Budget announcement, every ministry, government – owned corporation; and university must be compelled to open a 'mischief' file. I confidently predict a lot of bulging files!

While still on the subject of mischief, isn't it the ultimate irony that probably the two most popular decisions made by the present military Government – namely, the creation of states and the programme for the transfer of power to freely elected politicians have turned out to be a bonanza for the mischief makers? Both the creation of states and the holding of free elections were specifically aimed at eliminating the fear of tribal ('ethnic' if you insist) supremacy and wasteful acrimonious rivalry. But what are we witnessing right now? The mischief makers are busy promising new states even though they know that when those new states are created, they will have to be further split for precisely the same reasons they were created in the first place. As for the prospects for 'free and fair elections', the mischief makers are adamant that the only way we can be sure of an outright winner – is to allow the Presidential elections to be rigged!

THE IDLE PRESS

I am truly astonished at the allegation of 'idleness' levelled against the Nigerian Press by the World-wide Press Institute. Apparently, quite a while ago, a very senior government official publicly declared that is was misleading for Nigerians to talk of 'returning' to 'democracy' because even under the civilian government, Nigeria could not be described as democratic. This is a fine point indeed – plenty of room for semantics here! According to Alhaji L.P.O. had the Nigerian Press been truly alert, this argument should not have been allowed to be lost by default. The Press should have pointed out that at present, (and thanks be to God), we do not have torture chambers; exit visas; mysterious disappearances of public figures; private executions; strict press censorship; and all those other nasty things practised by military regimes elsewhere – but none of these alter the fact that we are still under military rule. Personally, I think is it rather unfair to suggest that what interests the Press is not deep analysis but obituaries; silly rumours; sterile apologia and stupid stories about what to do about the 'other woman'.

THE 'LIBERATION' PARTY

Wonders will never cease! It has now been officially confirmed that one of the political parties which applied to the Federal Electoral Commission ('FEDECO') is the self-styled 'Liberation' Party. Fedeco refused to grant it registration because the party would not disclose 'who' or 'what' it wanted to liberate the country from; or 'how' it proposed to do it. In addition, the party manifesto (page I) declares its commitment to the holding of another 'FESTAC' on 1 October, this year!

370

THE UNLUCKY CITY

Ibadan, capital of Oyo State, must surely rank as one of the unluckiest cities in the world. In the past few months, it has been buffetted by collapsing buildings; ravaged by massive floods; and its largest market has been razed by fire; and on top of all these, it has a major refuse disposal problem on its hands. In addition, through fate and human design, virtually all the major roads are being dug up for reconstruction ALL AT THE SAME TIME! The inevitable disruption of life and the consequent traffic crisis together with public agony and suffering need to be seen to be believed.

Yet the city remains unbowed in its hour of tribulation and undaunted by its gigantic social/economic problems. According to a recently completed United Nations report, what keeps Ibadan going is POLITICS. Apparently, the taps may run dry, the telephones may be in permanent slumber; and the petrol queues may be six kilometres long but as long as there is Politics, they (the people of Ibadan) will manage somehow.

What I do find disturbing though is the section of the UN report which predicts that for a long time to come, Ibadan will continue to have serious sanitation and drainage problems unless the inhabitants change their eating habits. According to the report, leaves play vicious havoc with the drains because leaves used for wrapping food end up not in dust-bins but in the gutters. Believe it or not, 'Amala'; 'Oka'; 'Moyin Moyin'; etc. taste a good deal better if you eat them fresh from the leaves. I swear!

THE VICE-PRESIDENTIAL CANDIDATE

Following the publication in one of the national newspapers that Dr Alex Ekwueme offered a very substantial donation to the political party that nominated him as its Vice-Presidential candidate, several 'old boys' have been adamant that no 'Kings College boy' would do a thing like that. They have been proved right – Dr Ekwueme has denied the story in its entirety.

It may be worth mentioning that Dr Ekwueme was a brilliant student and by the very fact that he was just as good in science subjects as well as arts, he could easily have gone into any profession. He ended up by becoming an architect and prior to the civil war, he ran probably the biggest indeginious firm of architects. It says a lot for his industry that following the end of the civil war, he was able to re-establish his practice within a very short time – once again, it's one of the biggest firms around.

EXIT OF A CIVIL SERVANT

With very little pomp and pangeantry, a very senior civil servant retired from the Civil Service a little while ago. His name is Mr Gilbert Obatoyinbo and he was the Permanent Secretary (Political) at Cabinet Office. For a man holding such a key position, very little was known about him outside the civil service. I wonder how many people know that the Nigerian Indeginisation Decree was his 'baby' even going back to the time of Gowon.

WITH YOUR EARS TO THE GROUND

It is becoming increasingly clear that in the absence of reliable pollsters, you really have to place your ears very close to the ground in the hope that you can pick up the sounds that would enable you to decipher what is really going on present day politics. There are simply too many things that just do not make sense; too many factors that simply do not hang together. For a start, there are too many people who are clearly in the wrong party. You have to ask what is so and so doing in that party? All logic suggests that he should be in the other party! What is truly amazing is how even among those whom the newspapers lavishly daub as 'party stalwarts', 'party chairmen'; 'state leaders' etc., many are busy negotiating how they can abscond to some other party without too much loss of face! Apparently, what is important is to be in the party that looks as if it's going to win.

HARD WORK PAYS OFF

It is quite interesting to observe that a particular Presidential Candidate is winning coverts by the thousands not necessarily because he is a saint but rather because more and more people are beginning to say: 'that man works really hard'. Everything he says no matter how controversial is clearly thought out. He leaves you in no doubt that he has done his homework. Purely on merit, more and more people are becoming convinced that he is the best candidate.

Certainly, whoever becomes the next President is going to inherit plenty of problems. Our salvation rests firmly and squarely on his ability to handle the tough economic problems that lie ahead.

Gentlemen, this is not the time for sitting on the fence. Every right thinking Nigerian should realise that he has a non-negotiable interest in ensuring that the next government is the right government. Vote for Alhaji L.P.O.!

THIS MAN WILL NOT LAST

It is a pity to hear people refer to one of the presidential candidates sarcastically as 'THE SAFE BET'. It seems that the impression has been firmly established that this particular candidate has a very slim if not remote chance of becoming the next President. Furthermore, it has been concluded that even if by some miracle he got elected as President – he simply will not last.

Tacitus on the Emperor Galba comes all too readily to mind 'omnium consensu capax imperii nisi imperasset' (had he never been Emperor no one would have doubted his ability to rule).

ARE WE SAFE?

According to a recent report in the 'Daily Times', an Awka doctor and his wife were scared into hiding when a gunman appeared at their home and took aim.

Dr Nwonye Otue of the Community Hospital and his wife were resting in their sitting room at noon when the man showed up, brandishing two pistols and started firing.'

THE WITTY HEAD OF STATE

The Ghanaian High Commission has been at great pains to deny a sizzling story currently circulating in diplomatic circles. According to the story, when the Ghanaian Head of State, Lt.-General Akuffo visited Nigeria recently, he was asked why only a few days before he left his country he had banned all the old politicians in his country from participating in the next round of politics which hopefully would lead to the return to civil rule in Ghana.

His answer was: 'Ghana is a poor country. We had to ban the old politicians because we do not have any money to waste on State Funerals!

THE HEAD OF STATE AND THE WORLD PRESS

Alhaji L.P.O. has just drawn my attention to something I had previously overlooked. I suppose it was predictable that following the Nigerian Head of State's marathon TV interview (shown on network television for three consecutive nights at prime time), various demands should now be made on His Excellency to take on the World Press. The Alhaji has reminded me that if we are really interested in inviting the World Press we will have to discount any well thought out programme for return to civil rule; development of agriculture; transfer of technology etc. What would guarantee the interest of the world press would be for us to arrange a crisis over the elections or better still, precipitate civil war either on account of tribal conflict or religious bigotry. That is what is sure to get the world press here in a hurry. Even if we did not invite them, they would smuggle their way in.

K. O. IS THE MAN

Whether or not you agree with Dr K. O. Mbadiwe's

brand of politics, there is no denying that for about 30 years now, 'K. O.' has been the darling of the Nigerian Press. He has consistently been the sure fire saviour of editors desperate for an eye-catching front or back page. 'K. O.' can always be relied on to provide something to send heads spinning and tongues wagging. Indeed, no one other than 'K. O.' would dream of inviting the world press to explain why he is not going to be the next President! If the world press does show up for the press conference, the first thing 'K. O.' would have to do is to distribute free copies of his special dictionary of 'Juggernaut English'!

WHERE IS FLORA?

Alhaji L.P.O. really floored me the other day when he suddenly asked me – 'where is Flora?' He was of course refering to the First, Nigerian First Lady – Mrs Flora Azikiwe, wife of the First President of Nigeria, Dr Nnamdi Azikiwe. Irrespective of one's political inclination, even Dr Azikiwe's most hardened critics were forced to admit that his wife went about her official duties with dilligence and dignity. The opening of schools; the laying of the foundation stone of hospitals; The Red Cross; Girl Guides etc., got plenty of her attention. The point that Alhaji L.P.O. was trying to make is that this is an ungrateful country. How else can one explain how now that Dr Axikiwe is back on the hustings, no one has bothered to ask – 'where is the First, FIRST LADY?'.

HELP

FIRST THE BAD NEWS

AN American doctor was having trouble getting through passport control at Murtala Mohammed Airport when a Senior Immigration officer came to his rescue by ordering his junior officer to let him through since Nigeria is so badly in need of doctors. However, the junior officer insisted on checking the doctor's credentials and demanded – 'What sort of doctor are you anyway?'

Answer: 'I'm a chiropodist.'

Senior Officer (Interrupting,) Enquired: 'What sort of doctor is that?'

Answer: 'I'm a doctor of the FEET."

At this point, the Senior Immigration Officer declared loudly: 'forget it. In Nigeria, the problems we have are not with our feet but with our HEADS.'

'MADE IN NIGERIA' NEWS

Chief Alfred Eset-Idero who has just bought a 'MADE IN NIGERIA' car was showing off his new car on the Eko Bridge and telling his passengers how wonderful the car was when he changed into third gear. Lo and behold – the gear-stick came off in his hand!

DIPLOMATIC NEWS

Following his very narrow escape from being assasinated when a hand-grenade was lobbed at him, Field-Marshal Idi Amin of Uganda warned that a full investigation had been launched to ascertain foreign involvement in the plot to kill him. He went on to add that if evidence linked any of the diplomats resident in Uganda with the plot, they would face the firing squad – AND HE MEANT IT.

U.N. NEWS

The United States last Wednesday night vetoed a security council resolution recommending the admission of Angola into the U.N. The United States was protesting against the presence of Cuban troops in the former Portuguese Colony. According to the American Ambassador Albert Sherer – 'There is no justification for such a large presence of Cuban troops in a truly independent African State.' Thank goodness a member of the Nigerian delegation was smart enough to remind the American Ambassador that if membership of the U.N. was related to the extent of 'foreign presence' within the member state, Nigeria would be disqualified because of our expatriate population; so would Britain because of its West Indian, Pakistani and Indian population; and even the United States itself would be disqualified due to its large immigrant population of Italians, Germans, Scandinavians, Mexicans and of course the 'Superspades' all of whom are armed to the teeth in order to survive in America!

The irony of the American position is that America is opposing Liberation Movements (in Africa) who are doing exactly what America itself did 200 years ago in order to free itself from colonialisation. This is particularly poignant because this is America's bicentennial year.

HOME NEWS

The remarkable success of The Committee headed by Dr Olulonyo in easing traffic congestion in Ibadan is further proof that instead of flying all over the world looking for 'experts', most of our problems can be solved by our own efforts and initiative. What is more, the work carried out by the committee cost the Oyo State Government virtually nothing.

LOCAL NEWS

Since it now looks certain that the ban on political parties will not be lifted before the Local Government elections, Chief Dumb Dumb declared at a crowded press conference that 'Holding elections without lifting the ban on political parties is like playing tennis without a net.'

HOLIDAY NEWS

Yesterday, Alhaji Dan Abdul Zukal was spotted at the departure lounge of Kano Airport. At the security checking-point, the Alhaji was asked:

'ARE YOU GOING ABROAD ON BUSINESS?'

Answer: 'No.'

Question: 'Are you going for a holiday?'

Answer: 'No. I'm just going away for a few days to watch people behaving normally. With so many crazy people in this country, I need to get out once in a while just to remind myself what normal people look like.'

STOLEN NEWS

It's quite interesting to observe the number of people who insist on using the prefix 'Chief (Dr) . . .' before their names. As a matter of fact, when 'Doctor' Oyenusi, the armed-robber was executed, he was carrying a business card with the notation 'THIEF (Dr.) OYENUSI.'

AND NOW FOR SOMETHING COMPLETELY DIFFERENT

There is a story circulating among diplomats in Lagos that God once asked for volunteers to level a mountain. A smart American turned up carrying dynamite; a Ghananian had the good sense to turn up with a Caterpillar; but a Nigerian turned up carrying a spade and demanded a contract plus 10 per cent 'Mobilisation' fee!

THE DAILY TIMES: STANLEY 'M' AND THE REST OF US

I HAVE for long been puzzled by why Stanley Macebuh provokes such aggressive reaction. His latest contribution – (Daily Times 15 March), – 'Letter to my cousin' provides the answer. Stanley's three card trick is to display the catalogue but not to deliver the goods! On any issue, Stanley's intellectual vigour is such that he could argue for either side and still win; but that is only in verbal discussion. When it comes to putting it down on paper – it is a different story. Go back through his writings – where does he stand? Is he for capitalism or socialism; liberalism or repression (see his remedy for armed robbery); is he for regional primacy or centralisation; is he for intellectualism, or pragmatism? Does he favour military rule to civil rule? You will have to ask Stanley in person to find the answer.

It would clearly be unfair to suggest that Stanley does not hold any strong views at all or is simply looking over his shoulder out of fear of upsetting someone. What I discern is that he sees his role as a journalist is simply to bring to the public the options available by providing the pros and the cons. This presumes that the public is willing and able to weigh both sides of the argument dispassionately and make a choice based on the merit of the argument. How wrong! As Stanley himself rightly points out – major decisions are arrived out not so much on the basis of merit but rather 'on the basis of the sentiments of powerful members.'

One of the unkindest remarks I have heard expressed against Stanley's writings is that if you asked him to drive a car, the first thing he would do is to shift the gear into neutral! He certainly provides ample ammunition for such opinions when he says – '. . . as to which of them (Presidential Candidates) you might be willing to vote for. It would indeed have been ideal if we could merge the personalities of the five candidates into one', Chicken!

I ask you to read 'Letter to my cousin' again, but substitute 'Awo' for 'Zik' and vice versa – there is no difference whatever in the conclusion to be drawn! This does not necessarily detract from the quality of Stanley's writings. The consistent thread that runs through his contributions is his compelling anxiety to be 'fair' to both sides even at the risk of obscuring logic with polite understatement. For example, he says about a candidate 'it was (he) who once came up with the theory that tribalism can be an effective force in nation building.' [No comment?] 'That it is he who constantly harps on the concept of diarchy.' [Still no comment?] How sharply this conflicts with the charge often levelled against Stanley that his views are 'highly personalised'.

As an essayist, Stanley's style is hooked on the pattern – first the preamble; next a few paragraphs in favour of 'Z', next a few paragraphs in favour of 'A'; but sadly the conclusion is missing. Maybe this is a throw-back to his days as a sixth former at Kings College, Lagos when his essays were regularly read out to the class as a fine example of superb command of language; clarity of thought; etc. and above all 'for being fair to the other side'.

It could well be that he needs to make a fine distinction between his role as a 'journalist' as opposed to a 'columnist'. A journalist can aim at being neutral; but as Calvin Mellfall puts it – 'a columnist makes his mark by the vigour and robustness of his opinion which he actively offers for public consumption'.

As for Stanley's command of language, he has no equal; what is dangerous is his application of language in explaining away the unacceptable deeds or misdeeds of the government. One can understand why Chief (Dr) Olu Akaraogun (also of the Daily Times) was provoked to such perplexing anger by Stanley's use of language! Olu's charges of 'mischief' cannot be entirely unfounded. I remember that Stanley once suggested that Nigeria was in danger of 'being developed out of existence!' To my mind this only provides sweet comfort for the indolent – an encouragement for those charged with our development to feel smug and self-satisfied.

Now Stanley has come up with another one – '. . . staccato functionality of military culture . . .' Functionality indeed! What is happening to the telephone; electricity supply; Nigeria Airways etc.?

One must really ask Stanley in the familiar parlance of Aba (where he grew up and about which he wrote so brilliantly) – 'Which one una deh self?' i.e. On whose side are you?

QUOTE FROM ALHAJI L.P.O.

(i) Stanley does not tell you to turn right or turn left. He just lets you know that there is a roundabout fifty kilometres ahead!

(ii) The only conclusion to be drawn from 'Letter to my Cousin' is that the difference betwen Dr Azikiwe and Chief Awolowo is that one of them can dance – the other can't!

SO THEY NOW CALL US RUSHIANS!

I sat next to Alhaji L.P.O. at the Nigerian–American Chamber of Commerce luncheon at the Eko Holiday Inn. It was a very distinguished audience with Mr David Rockefeller as the Guest of Honour. Alhaji whispered: 'The only reason I came is to see what a billionaire looks like. As for the food here – it has improved tremendously. It used to be very bad, now it's just bad!' (I don't agree with Alhaji – the food was excellent).

The truth of the matter is that Mr Rockefeller does not look like a billionaire. I'm not even sure what a billionaire is supposed to look like. It is common knowledge that he was very much involved in packaging the jumbo-sized loans raised on the international market by the Federal Military Government. I rather liked the story by an American gentleman who whispered that the raising of the huge loans was no small achievement. It was a very tough operation and in the money market it was code-named 'The Rushian operation'. Apparently, we are now known as 'RUSHIANS' because we are in a rush for Iron and Steel; in a rush for a new Capital; in a rush to have new seaports and airports etc. We are even in a rush to hand over power to the same old breed of politicians!

BAD ARITHMETIC

Alhaji is a real illiterate when it comes to the simple task of doing a little arithmetic. YET HE HAS NO EXCUSE – he did not even go to a U.P.E. school! His latest gaffe occurred last night when he declared on television that there is no way the next Presidential election can result in an outright winner on the first ballot since the President is required by the Election Decree to win in at least thirteen states. The Alhaji's thesis is that since there are five aspirants and presumably each one of them would at least win in one state (his own 'catchment area'), that means that really there are only fourteen states on offer. If any party is unable to carry at least one state, then it should not have been registered by FEDECO or how else could it have qualified on the basis of 'grassroot support'. The vital point then is that in order to become an outright winner (by winning thirteen states), the President would have to win TWELVE out of FOURTEEN available states. According to the Alhaji, there is only one conclusion – 'NO WAY!'

I.T.T. AGAIN!

The I.T.T. dinner for the Press held at the Federal Palace Hotel was really something. Naturally, Alhaji L.P.O. who believes that a FREE press means having free dinners and free booze was there. Chief M. K. O. Abiola, the Chief Executive of I.T.T. Nigeria was in great form.

Overheard at the dinner:

(i) The telephone is the white man's black gift to the black man and there is no way the black man will ever understand it. Every race is entitled to its own black magic.

(ii) It is not true that the Chief gets letters addressed to 'Chief I.T.T. Abiola' (his correct initials are M. K. O.).

THE PERMANENT CONTROVERSY

Anyone who has taken he trouble to go to Abuja, where the new Federal Capital is being built, cannot fail to be impressed by the progress made so far. Thanks to the energetic leadership of Mr Ajose-Adeogun, the Commissioner for Special Duties, who has direct responsibility for the new capital. If things go according to plan, by 1986 the new capital should be functioning. The only trouble is that whether we like it or not, the building of the capital is going to be a source of controversy both before it is built and certainly after it is built. The politicians have already fired the first salvo by arguing about the site; the cost; and its ranking in our order of priorities. Fortunately, one of the presidential candidates has come out firmly in support of the new capital. In fact he has promised to pay for it out of his own pocket!

THE DICTATOR

The other day, Alhaji L.P.O. declared that what Nigeria needs is a dictator and that the Military should stay in power until the new capital is completed.

UP N.E.P.A.

The Public Relations Manager of N.E.P.A. (National Electric Power Authority) has taken great pains to deny the story currently circulating about how when the General Manager of N.E.P.A. was collecting his National Award, the band in attendance at the impressive ceremony started playing N.E.P.A.'s favourite tune – 'All the best things happen in the dark'.

POLICE WARNING

The latest victim of the armed robbers is the Chief Medical Officer of Niger State. Dr S. Shar who was shot dead at Oworoshoki on the Lagos – Ibadan expressway at about 6 a.m. Dr Shar, a Pakistani was in Lagos on Official duty; the robbers escaped with his official Volvo car.

Perhaps the time has now come for the Police to give serious consideration to giving guidelines to the public on what to do in case you run into armed robbers. Far too many people have been killed because they did precisely the very things they should not do in their moment of panic when confronted by armed robbers.

An even more gruesome aspect about the spate of armed robberies is that in several cases, people who put up no resistance whatever have been killed in cold blood and in certain cases the robbers did not even bother to take any property – they were content with either severely beating up or raping their victims.

This has prompted an eminent sociologist to suggest that what the armed robbers are trying to do is really to intimidate the Government. They are determined to ensure that by the time the next Government assumes power, the robbers would be in such a powerful position that the government would have to deal with them. In exchange for peace and some semblance of law and order, the next government would have to turn a blind eye to the 'Syndicate's' more lucrative business – drug trafficking; prostitution; smuggling etc. If this happens – we would be launching our own chapter of the MAFIA.

IF IT'S DEAD, DON'T BURY IT

IT is self-evident that the Nigerian Press is still in a state of euphoria about it's recent success in effectively scuttling The Nigerian Press Council Decree No. 31 which was recently promulgated by the Federal Military Government, (by formally launching its own Press Code). Like it or not – history has been made! What makes it more remarkable is that the Press pulled off this remarkable 'coup' not by aggressive confrontation with the Government but through pre-emption – by putting it's own house in order rather than hand over the keys to civil servants or their appointees. Whatever may be the merits or demerits of the Government's case, there is a lesson for other professions in the tactics successfully employed by the Press; albeit the press has a certain amount of advantage in that it enjoys 'possession' if not 'control' over the machinery of propaganda.

I suspect that the Press quickly realised that petitioning the Government would be a useless exercise. For the first six months of the life of the present administration, petitions were fashionable and quick results were guaranteed. Not so anymore! The Government has simply been flooded with petitions – Chieftaincy titles; boundary adjustments; abandoned property; promotions (both private and public); social amenities; ownership of schools etc. you name it and the files are bulging with petitions.

The other aspect of the Press Council Decree is that the Press had come to accept that whatever went wrong was not entirely the fault of the Government itself but that of the civil servants who rightly or wrongly are suspected of 'mischief'. The civil servants obviously know that the

Government's 'achilles heel' is its appetite for controlling things and everybody. They know that they only need to whisper to the Government – why not control inflation?; why not control schools?; why not control this and that? – They know they have a ready audience.

All things considered, the real victor is not the Press – rather it is the Government for showing mature restraint instead of allowing itself to be drawn into a pointless and distracting confrontation with the Press. As far as I know, no journalist even the ones employed on Government owned newspapers, television, radio etc. has been harrassed for taking part in the launching of the Nigerian Institute of Journalists' Declaration.

As for the Press Council Decree, it's dead but there is no need to bury it.

MR ERNEST IKOLI

Particularly with the 'hotting' up of the political campaign to elect the next Government, this seems a fine time to remind the present Nigerian Press that it is the fortunate inheritor of an admirable legacy from those that have now passed on. Pre-eminent among the forefathers of Nigerian journalism was Mr Ernest Ikoli. What a fine man! His powerful pen was matched by an overpowering personal dignity and integrity. Straight from conducting a fierce argument or writing a pungent editorial, there he was at the bar of the Lagos Island Club, firmly esconced in his favourite corner, like a Greek god – white hair sprouting all over and feet clad in open sandals dangling from the bar stool – dispensing wit, charm and hospitality in equal measure to friends and foe alike.

MR MOBOLAJI ODUNEWU

When the history of Nigerian journalism is written, a special place of honour must surely belong to Mr Mobolaji Odunewu, the elder brother of 'Allala-de', (Alhaji Alade Odunewu). Wracked by physical pain and a host of ailments for much of his later life, he never ceased to be what he was all his life – patient, kind to a fault, totally incorruptible and incredibly well-read but soft-spoken. Even the severe disappointment of being passed over for the top job at the Federal Ministry of Information was not enough to subdue his compassion; his excellent intellect; his generosity; his dedication to duty; his good humour and ready accommodation of other people's views. For a man who wrote some of the most incisive editorials and was a leading participant in arguing many of the controversial issues of the day, it is the ultimate accolade that no one can remember him ever saying an unkind word about anyone.

THE COMMISSIONER

Perhaps there is some truth in the claim by journalists that their work brings them in continuous contact with an aspect of humanity which is probably unknown to others – one day it's dinner with kings and princes but next day you are assigned to a story in the most fetid slums. Truly no condition is permanent. It is therefore not entirely surprising that Mr Abimbola Odunlami, a seasoned journalist (and formerly Lagos State Commissioner for Information) but now the 'Deputy-Governor' of Lagos remains totally unaffected by his high office. He must be one of the most unassuming and accessible Commissioners around.

DEATH OF A POLICEMAN

A few days ago, a very distinguished Nigerian quietly passed away in his sleep. He was Chief Louis Orok Edet O.F.R.; C.B.E. He was 65 years old and he was the first Nigerian to hold the top job in the Police – Inspector General of the Nigeria Police Force. He was given a fitting burial in Calabar – in fact it was a State Funeral, with all the top brass of the Police in attendance. There is not much that one could add to the glowing tributes paid to him by Chief T. A. Fagbola formerly the Deputy-Inspector General of the Police.

My first recollection of Chief Edet goes back to the

days when he lived next door to us at Ricca Street, Lagos. Those were happy days – our street was not even tarred! His cousin who as Admiral Akintunde Wey was later to head the Nigerian Navy lived just round the corner and at that time worked for the Royal Marine. At week-ends you could hear the sing-song from the Edet household – 'Give me that old time religion' was obviously a favourite. At Christmas and Easter – 'Ekpe' (the Efik masquerade) would show up to pay his respects. Even long after he moved to Ikoyi, Chief Edet kept an active interest in the births, marriages etc. at Ricca Street and in fact all his own children were born in that street.

Following his retirement from the Police, Chief Edet was the Commissioner for Home Affairs in the former South Eastern State and later on became a Director of Arbico and U.A.C. of Nigeria. However, it is certain he would most like to be remembered not as, The Inspector General or as a Director but rather as a devout Catholic and a Policeman. May his soul rest in peace.

ONE SINGS; THE OTHER DOESN'T

It is truly amusing and amazing to watch the righteous indignation of politicians in their response to His Excellency's categorisation of Nigerian Politicians into two classes. According to His Excellency, 'the first group comprises those who do not know what they are talking about but merely talk out of ignorance. They deserve to be pitied. The other set comprises those who know what they are talking about but deliberately mislead and misinform. They are mischievous.'

Of course it is a matter of considerable interest to wait and see which of these two groups ends up inheriting the reins of power from the present administration. Hurry up – 1 October!

On the other hand, since our politicians are so sensitive about such matters, when His Excellency's interview is shown on German television network (for which the interview was in fact recorded) my good friend Alhaji L.P.O. assures me that the edited version will categorise

the two groups of politicians as follows:
  'One sings; the other doesn't!'

PANEL; WHAT PANEL!

I think most fair-minded people (Alhaji L.P.O. is not one!) would agree that in the absence of freely elected representatives or referendums, the present government has made liberal use of the next best thing – panels and the results have generally been an acceptable compromise between excellence and pragmatism. The panels have invariably been headed by distinguished personalities, mostly judges and have not spared themselves in ensuring that their basket of views and opinions reflect the broad thinking of the various sections of the country. The panel on the creation of States (Chief [Dr] Patrick Dele Cole was its Secretary!) and the panel on the location of the New Capital produced a useful framework for subsequent policy decisions by the Government. However, the reports of the Land Use Panel and the Revenue Allocation Panel were anchored on more controversial terrain.

Anyway, whether panels are useful determinants of policy decision is open to debate. However, one panel that is not getting too much enthusiastic support from the public is the latest baby – The Panel on the Protection and Maintenance of Public Property. It appears that the general feeling (at a time when armed robbers have taken over our major cities) is 'who cares about property – it's lives we care about!

I think there is a good case for urging the Government to set up a panel to look into the problem of armed robbery. However, Alhaji L.P.O. was quick to ask the poignant question – 'WILL THE ARMED ROBBERS AGREE TO GIVE EVIDENCE BEFORE THE PANEL?'

BREAKFAST WITH A DIFFERENCE

Two months ago, a friend of mine who lives at Apapa, Lagos had a very narrow escape from armed robbers who demanded his Volvo car (right outside the Nigeria

Airways Office). It was only 8 p.m. and he had been working late in the office. He has since given up any thought of working late in the office; going to the cinema; or attending parties. The 7 o'clock news always finds him at home before his television set securely barricaded (or fortified?) behind the whole arsenal of security guards; burglary-proof windows and doors; stout iron gates; burglar alarm etc.

Last week, the burglars struck again – they came on Saturday – at 9 o'clock IN THE MORNING! My friend who was having breakfast with his wife just could not believe his eyes – the cool easy assurance of the robbers and the unhurried pace with which they helped themselves to cash, jewelry, stereo (and also the TV!) was really too much. On top of all that, his pregnant wife was subjected to a severe beating and humiliation which have resulted in her having a miscarriage.

My friend's only comment on the incident was: 'Do you really expect me to go out and vote for ANY GOVERNMENT?

CLEVER DOG

It looks as if Alhaji L.P.O. is on to a good thing. He is now in the security dog business. His fierce looking dogs are specially trained to let everyone – armed robbers, tradesmen, creditors, N.E.P.A. officials, census checkers etc. into your home. The only trouble is – once they get in, they cannot get out. The dogs won't let them!

'UDOJI HOURS'

It's a great pity that even though Chief Jerome Udoji clearly did not recommend shorter working hours, his report has somehow come to be linked with the 40 hour working week and the consequent compensation for those who have to do night-shift or 'anti-social hours'. It now appears that armed robbers have caught on to this and are demanding 'extra pay' for doing night-shift!

The other night, Dr Kola Aishegun was going home after twelve hours on duty when he was stopped by armed robbers at the junction of Isolo and the Badagry Road Expressway. He quietly handed over all the cash he had on him. It amounted to only ₦11. The robbers burst into laughter. The gang-leader coolly declared 'Doctor, I'm sure you don't really think we have been waiting here all night just to collect eleven lousy naira!'

DESPERATE ANSWER

The trouble with Alhaji L.P.O. is that armed robbers or no armed robbers – he just won't stop going out at night. He has now taken to driving around at night in a car labelled – 'ARMED ROBBER.' Apparently, armed robbers have their own code of ethics – THEY DO NOT ATTACK OTHER ARMED ROBBERS!

WEDDING DAY SPECIAL

YESTERDAY, Saturday, 19 May 1979 was a very special day for me – I got married! Right in the middle of my speech, at the point where I was about to say '. . . my wife and I . . .' to be followed by predictable rapturous applause from the audience that had defied the heavy rain, Alhaji L.P.O. came charging into the reception at Federal Palace Hotel, Victoria Island.

Much to everybody's astonishment, the Alhaji announced:

'Ladies and Gentlemen, we have a new President! At this very moment he is being sworn in and I have the bridegroom's permission (not true!) to relay the president's speech over the loudspeakers. I am sure you all appreciate that the president's speech is far more important than whatever my good friend the groom has to say.'

Right away, we could hear the unmistakable voice of the new President coming over loud and clear:

'Fellow countrymen, (do they always have to say that?), I know that during these past few months, those of you who have actively watched the campaigns, the intrigues, the double-crossing, the cheating, the lying etc., may have good cause to wonder whether we were about to choose a new President or whether we were merely putting up the country for sale.

All that is over now (not true!) and I as your President appeal to you all to forget the past. I enjoin you all to join hands with me in the task that confronts us. Let me make it abundantly clear that our most important consideration at all times must be UNITY. If you believe in the unity of the country, then it follows that you must be willing to WORK for it at all times.

Let me also add that if Nigeria fails – it is the failure of Africa. Remember, EVERY FIFTH MAN IN AFRICA IS A NIGERIAN (did somebody forget to rig the census?) Wherever you go in Africa, they look up to Nigeria for guidance. How can we lead when our own house is in disorder?

THE PRESIDENT AND THE PRESS

More than at any other time in the history of this country, it is crucial that the Press should be reminded of its sacred duty – to emphasise the things that unite us rather than what divides us. It is not for me to accuse the Press of irresponsibility – but when I think of some of the things published by the Press in the last few months, I often wonder whether some of our newspapers have determined that the disintegration of this country is their sublime goal.

Those who write so recklessly about tribalism and religion need to be reminded that there is no hamlet or village throughout this country where a stranger cannot knock on any door to ask for water to drink or be denied assistance (if his car broke down) either on account of tribe or religion.

THE PRESS AND RELIGION

As far as I as your President am concerned, the Nigerian Press has let the country down by its handling of the Sharia controversy. This was one imbroglio the country could have done without. The politicians knew that Sharia had very little to do with religion – it was about POWER! The Nigerian Press almost without exception missed the point entirely.

THE PRESS AND THE STUDENTS

The Press together with the students should be the conscience of the nation. What we find is entirely different. Rather than patiently seek to educate students on the wider dimensions of issues and problems, the Press regularly plunges for sensationalism. How come the Press did not feel any need to mobilise student opinion (nationwide) on declining agricultural productivity; urban poverty; rural stagnation; the plight of refugees forced to flee foreign lands where they had established their roots etc.?

Instead, the Press plonked for 'Educational imbalance' between the North and the South. Now, wait a minute. At no point were we enlightened as to what precisely this 'Education' is. Surely, education goes beyong literacy – reading and writing. It must surely embrace the ability to use your hands to make tools; agriculture and food production are part of it; language and culture are part of it. Religion and tolerance are certainly part of education. Can it be true that any one part of the country is at a disadvantage in ALL these aspects of education? We are relying on the Press to prove it!

YOUTH AND DUTY

I sincerely implore all our young men and women to make a conscious effort to shift from negative to positive action. I challenge each one of them to do SOMETHING SIGNIFICANT before the age of thirty. It does not matter what – write a book; set up your own farm; run a literacy school; build your own plough; design a new canoe; learn a language other than your own; run your own newspaper; build your own house etc. When you have done that – you would have earned the right to criticise your elders'.

PS.

By the time the President finished his speech, all my guests had left. I must check with FEDECO to find out whether the President has the right to interrupt my wedding! Surely, if the President is going around interrupting other people's weddings, there are not going to be many weddings this year.

THE PRESIDENT'S DIARY

THE President was sworn in on Saturday, 19 May. Within twelve hours, he had made his first major mistake – he appointed Alhaji L.P.O. as his special adviser! The Alhaji's duty is simply to keep a diary of the President's activities. I am dismayed at the appointment, but I dare not tell anyone. The Alhaji is excellent as a boozing companion – but as a Presidential Adviser, forget it. I know for certain that he is going to be either a disaster or a catastrophe.

I quote from the Alhaji's diary:

'The swearing-in of the President is only an hour away. It is a fine morning and the crowd at Tafawa Balewa Square is the largest single gathering in the history of this country. The President himself is clearly fatigued – the celebration at the Lagos Island Club had gone on all night and clearly in breach of all the rules of protocol, the President was one of the last to leave the party. However, our first problem is the "First Lady" – the President's wife. She is yelling at everyone (including the President). I think it is something to do with the sudden discovery that the President has a new wife! This is news to me – certainly the Press ever ready for red hot gossip know nothing about her. Anyway, the First Lady makes it quite clear that should the new wife show up at the swearing-in, only one of them would leave the ceremony alive!

What an incredible change. The President's wife who was always at the President's side throughout the long drawn out hours and rigours of campaigning suddenly collapses – she is not going to the swearing-in after all. She had been a tower of strength and inexhaustible fountain of comfort but for her victory is neither sweet nor soothing. She is already cursing the President – 'Just as you betrayed me, so will you betray the country!'

The President is truly shocked. The anguish is clearly visible but self control triumphs and he gives the order for the procession to commence its journey. The Commandant of the motorcade gives a smart salute and the gates of the State House are thrown open. Never mind, the President had promised during the election to forego the State House and the motorcade!

The procession is impressive – gleaming limousines; official flags; guards with their automatic rifles at the ready; sirens blaring; the outriders with their specially "souped-up" Suzukis', the princes of the motorcycle world; the Press corps are there with their air of "deja-vu' – they have seen it all before. This is a show. Certainly, this is not the time to bow to guilt feelings about poverty, misery, illiteracy and disease.

In a few minutes, the procession reaches Tafawa Balewa Square but it takes a whole hour to get the President through the surging crowd. We are running well behind schedule. By some strange coincidence (or oversight), the Presidential swearing-in was scheduled only an hour before the public execution of condemned armed robbers at the "Bar Beach Show".

Finally, the President makes it to the Presidential box. He is clearly preoccupied. It is so evident that he is merely going through the motions. His moment of victory is only a myth. There is plenty of trouble ahead – how do you set about solving the problems of 80 million people?

Mechanically, the President inspects the Guard of Honour – those rifles are they loaded? I am suddenly reminded of the memorable words of a cynic – "All that the President is required to do is to inspect Guards of Honour and sign documents."

In a few minutes, the President returns to his seat. Suddenly, it is time for the Presidential address. Panic! The microphones are dead – no electricity, thanks to

N.E.P.A. There is going to be further delay. The crowd is getting restive, the time for the Bar Beach Show is fast approaching. A voice from the crowd suddenly yells – "I have never missed any of the public executions and I do not intend to make an exception today!" The crowd begins to dwindle, everyone is heading for the spectacle of the public execution of the condemned robbers.

In a matter of minutes, Tafawa Balewa Square is virtually deserted. The President is still in his box he is too busy making last minute adjustments to his address to notice the rapid decimation of his audience.

By the time electricity has been restored and the microphones are functioning again, the audience has dwindled to a handful. The President gets up but changes his mind – the enormity of his task overwhelms him. He has inherited big problems – the aspirations of eighty million people have been hoisted on him.

The President is a dedicated sincere man – but where is he going to start from? Is it education; health; food; water; housing; or transportation? The equation has jellied – rising expectations versus declining revenues.

The weary President turns to me and demands:

"This is a strange country – WHY DO PEOPLE PREFER WATCHING THE EXECUTING OF ARMED ROBBERS to listening to their own President address them on the problems of the country and the plans for solving them?"

Well, search me!

CAUGHT BY SURPRISE

LONG before the Presidential election, most political pundits had reluctantly reconciled themselves to the obvious – there would be no outright winner on the first ballot. Within 24 hours of the end of the voting, it had become an indisputable fact. A 'Run-off' was inevitable. The final verdict was a total surprise. Even the eventual winner was caught by surprise – his elation at the mammoth crowds that attended his rallies had been quickly succeeded by despair as the election results trickled in. But now – sweet, sweet victory!

It has been a hectic week for the brand new President – the 'Think Tank' made sure of that! The President was continuously subjected to a deluge of memos and 'position papers' – all clearly illustrating why the President would not be able to deliver any of the 'goodies' he had promised the electorate. The top brass of the Civil Service have been quick to provide irrefutable confirmation. The Head of Service with all due deference cautions the President against any attempt to 'go for glory' in the 'First Hundred Days' (Kennedy Fashion).

In fact, all this week I have been able to see the President for only five minutes and even then he was preoccupied with the parting words of the Head of Service – 'The ignorant see miracles everyday'. Right away, I can see we are going to have big problems with the Civil Servants. In the six months preceding the elections – the civil servants had abandoned any attempt to make any decisions. All files were meticulously marked 'B/U – ATE' – meaning 'Bring up – after the elections'.

The growing tension between the President and the

Head of the Civil Service is further worsened by the discovery that one million copies of the President's five-year plan titled 'Planning with Care' have to be destroyed. The Government Printers somehow managed to get the wrong title. The result is that the plan was wrongly titled – 'PLANNING FOR CHAOS'! The President is livid and alleges sabotage while the Head of Service quietly blames it all on the 'Printers' devil'.

For the first time this week, Alhaji L.P.O. allows me to have a look at his 'Presidential Diary'. I see that eight presentations of 'Letters of Credence' are recorded. We are obviously a nation to be reckoned with – why else would so many countries be falling over each other to send the cream of their Ambassadors and High Commissioners here. It is a total mystery to me how the President manages to keep a straight face through the tedious ceremony. What an impressive demonstration of self-control! All eight Ambassadors say exactly the same thing; the President receives them in turn and repeats exactly the same thing to each of them. The smiles are flashed at exactly the right time; the photographs are taken and everyone is happy!

A NATION IN A HURRY

In an otherwise bleak and lack-lustre week, it was perhaps predictable that the Senate would provide the flashpoint. On Thursday, the President delivered a serious warning to the Senate which he rightly or wrongly accused of dragging its feet over approval of the Finance Bill. The President had firmly declared: 'We are a nation in a hurry. This filibustering is totally unacceptable. It does not square with the mood of the country.'

The Leader of the Opposition was quickly on his feet: 'Let the President be reminded that the Senate is supreme. It is about time the President was cautioned to stop acting as if he is the greatest thing since the introduction of sliced bread to this country!'

The calm reassuring voice of the 'Chairman' (President) of the Senate was alert to the rapidly escalating tension in the Senate chambers. He pleaded: 'Now, Gentlemen. That remark was uncalled for. I wish to remind you all that the office of President is a distinguished one and certainly deserves your respect. This is not the time to trigger off a contest for supremacy.'

The Leader of Opposition's only response was: 'Amen!'

THE LONG WEEKEND

This was one weekend the President had been looking forward to. Apart from the naming ceremony of his brand new grand-child, there was the promise of a restful Saturday/Sunday at Tarkwa Bay with his family and friends. Instead we have a crisis on our hands!

It all goes back to the President's address on Thursday at the Annual Conference of The Nigerian Chamber of

Commerce and Industries. Usually, this is a predictably civil affair where all the proper protocols are strictly observed. This year, things were different. The Head of State chose the occasion to launch the major thrust of his national policy, the main theme of which revolved around oil; wasteful government expenditure and the urgent need for rapid economic development. With consumate skill, the Head of State produced facts and figures to demonstrate how in the past we had pursued a contradictory Oil Policy – it was now up to us to make a clear choice between a negative policy that would only earn us more enemies and a positive policy that would win us long-lasting friends without compromising our national interest. This was followed by a detailed disertation on wasteful government spending for which he held the civil servants responsible. Then came the knock-out punch – '. . . in terms of true economic growth, we have been standing still for the past twenty years. The only major achievement we can claim is that we have managed to legalise the production and consumption of illicit gin!' This was real dynamite! For the first time in the history of the Chamber of Commerce, the Head of State did not get a standing ovation.

GOOD-BYE TO PROTOCOL

Contrary to all the rules of protocol, the first person to challenge the President was his own 'special adviser' – none other than Alhaji L.P.O. According to the Alhaji, as far as Oil Policy is concerned, apart from a 'positive' and 'negative policy', we have a third option 'the ZERO OIL POLICY'. 'We would probably be better off just stopping oil production. This will take care of all consumer and producer problems, as there won't be any more oil to worry about. We'll just keep it in the ground for the next generation. We're a backward country anyway.' In fact he was quoting the President of another country.

To the consternation of the audience, the next speaker was no less than the Head of the Civil Service who grabbed the microphone in full view of the television cameras and declared: 'I am sick and tired of the civil service being made the whipping boy of each successive government.' It is all very well for the President to wax on about his 'ZERO WASTE POLICY' but I personally feel strongly that it is about time someone stood up for the civil service. To be candid, the Civil Service is a good deal more efficient that it is given credit for. Admittedly, civil servants are advisers but does that qualify them for becoming punch bags? After all we only implement the policies dictated by our political bosses. To put it crudely or to quote one of my predecessors in office, '. . . if the President wants to hang himself, the job of the civil servant is to advise him on the most efficient way of going about it!'

Next to speak was the Director of the 'Think Tank' who launched a savage attack on the President's economic policy. According to the Director of the 'Think Tank', the President has been unduly impressed by the 'Brazilian Experience'. According to legend, Brazil's economic growth is a miracle – within a span of fifteen years, Brazil has been transformed from an undeveloped country' '. . . into what is now the eighth most powerful economy in the world. At the present rate it will rank fourth by the end of this century behind only the United States, Japan and the Soviet Union.' However, this has a price – 'huge foreign investment which flourished in the industrial atmosphere which only generals can create – free from strikes which were illegal, free from political activity which was eliminated, and free from free speech, a right which was exercised only at the risk of arrest, detention, torture and death'.

The Director of the 'Think Tank' who recently visitied Sao Paulo, Brazil revealed how '. . . in Sao Paulo, at least half the population – perhaps seven million, live more than 50 per cent below the minimum subsistence level as defined by the state itself.

They live in rough, home-made houses on the out-skirts of the city or in the slums and shanty towns that cluster like warts around the factories where, in the years of the miracle, more wealth has been created than almost anywhere on earth. Yet most of the people are far poorer now than when the 'Miracle' first struck. Today, a labourer must work twice as many hours to earn the same real wage as 15 years ago. Then it took 40 minutes labour to buy a kilo of beans; now it takes more than four hours. Then, it took three hours work to buy a kilo of meat; now it takes eight hours work.

In Sao Paulo, poverty kills. Each day in the city's largest cemetry, they bury children in rows of specially prepared miniature graves; each year they bury more children than adults. The infant mortality rate – which may be thought to rival economic growth as an indicator of progress – is now 80 per 1000, a rise (since the generals seized power) of no less than 30 per cent. In desperation, thousands of families are forced to abandon their children. In Sao Paulo alone, some 600,000 boys and girls, ranging in age from 6 to 16 live rough on the streets, begging, stealing or prostituting themselves to survive.' The Director was in fact quoting an 'Express' Survey. But Lord have mercy, should we plump for ZERO GROWTH?

THE PRESS

In the ensuing press furor, I think the 'Sunday Punch' got it right when in its editorial it declared:

'The difference between a military regime and a civilian administration is that the generals only need to provide the answers (or what they think are the answers); but a civilian President has a lot of QUESTIONS to answer.'

Quote from Alhaji L.P.O. – any President who can sack his 'Special Adviser'; the Head of the Civil Service; and the Director of the 'Think Tank' within his first week in office certainly deserves our vote.

ONE MAN'S ELECTION . . .
(. . . IS ANOTHER MAN'S POISON)

At the risk of stating the obvious, we have to admit that it is beginning to look as if the controversy over the election of the President is going to be with us for a long time. This is a matter of severe disappointment to those of us who were firmly convinced that the least that could be expected of Africa's most populous (and largest consumer of 'Mateus Rose' – now that champagne is banned) is that the PRESIDENT WOULD BE A UNANIMOUS CHOICE!

The Presidential election has triggered off as many questions as it has generated the sparks that would illuminate the hope that this country has finally come of age. This is not the time for despair – rather it is the time for calm and courage. It is not necessary to insist that all those who dispute the declaration of the winner must be invited to the execution chamber; neither is it necessary to condemn those who support the Federal Electoral Commission as unpatriotic. We must take comfort in the words of George Bernard Shaw who in 'Man and Superman' declared:

'The reasonable man adapts himself to the world. The unreasonable man persists in trying to adapt the world to himself. Therefore, all progress depends on the unreasonable man'.

One indisputable fact that has emerged from the conduct of the election is that for the first time in the history of this country – EVERY CANDIDATE WAS FREE TO CAMPAIGN IN WHATEVER PART OF THE COUNTRY HE CHOSE. This is no mean achievement as those of us who have watched the conduct of elections in this country for the past 20 years can testify!

I have heard fears expressed that we are about to be ruled by a 'minority'. This is a highly debatable point. I think it was Dr Ibrahim Tahir of Ahmadu Bello University who once declared that Nigeria has 'always been ruled by minorities'. At the time, I thought that his statement was nothing more than inspired self-serving nonsense. However, on reflection I have to admit that within the context of macropolitics, he certainly has a point. The 'liberals' have consistenly argued that the Colonial Government as well as its successors could be classified as 'minority' in so far as they represented the interest of a relatively small group. This charge is buttressed with references to the statistics – the divergence between guess-estimates of eligible voters and those who actually voted. Only this week, a Professor of Politics declared that in spite of the publicity given to the last elections, between 15 and 20 per cent of those eligible to vote may not have registered at all or even been aware that elections were going on!

That the elections have been fierce and the artillery deployed by the various contestants have veered from the lofty and principled to the chauvinistic and tribal must provide cause for dismay. But then, we have only caught up with the rest of the world – where power is concerned, 'Winning is Everything'!

Elections by their very nature '. . . speak only of the past – of what has already happened in the minds and divisions of (Nigerians). They tell nothing of the future.' For those who are unduly concerned about the narrowness of the victory, the words of the late President of the United States of America, John F. Kennedy provide the balm. Commenting on his defeat of Richard Nixon in the 1960 election, he declared:

'The margin is thin, but the responsibility is clear. When the votes are counted, however thin the margin, the man who has that margin cannot escape the responsibility of power.' Like the Americans, Nigerians are entitled to expect:

'. . . that the President places himself in the very thick

of the fight, that he cares passionately about the fate of the people he leads . . . reopens the channels of communication between the world of thought and the seat of power.'

That the election of the President has resulted in a less than tidy verdict is of course a sad affair. However, given our past track record, this was predictable. The sociologists are quick to point out that every country has its own intrinsic quirk – for the Americans, it is the spectacular; for the Japanese, it is the electronic; for the British, it is the moralistic; for the Chinese, it is the insular; for the French, it is the exotic; for the Italians, it is the romatic; for the Indians, it is the mystic. Sadly, for the Nigerians – it is the controversial. This country simply thrives on controversy. What is important is to realise that at this stage of our history, it is indeed time for change or else, (to quote Theodore White), this country would be '. . . on its way to the modern torment between its principles and its prejudices, on the way to the yet unmade decision as to whether it is a place, or a nation, an idea or a state.'

THE PRESIDENT AND THE FARMERS

I AM 'reliably informed' (which is another way of saying 'it is only rumour!') that within 24 hours of the swearing in of the President i.e. even before he has got round to picking his cabinet, he would have to issue his policy statement on what he has in store for the rapidly dwindling number of farmers in the country.

It used to be fashionable to think that the problems of the farmers are simple – promise them more money; more land and cheap fertilizers and subsidised seedlings, and they would keep quiet! The reality is a very different story. What seems to have been overlooked is that farmers are a peculiarly proud and canny breed. They are tough too. Years and years of braving a hostile and unrepentant climate day in day out and battling against the vagaries and frustrations of nature somehow make it impossible to think of jumping into bed at the simple whiff of a cold or refuse to go to the farm because of the inhibitions of a mere snake bite.

Neither are farmers fools. For years they may patiently put up with being ripped-off by middlemen and government officials but when they think they have had enough of wrong prices and fraudulent gradings, they simply 'ship' the stuff across the border. They too have got wise to the value of foreign exchange.

One of the problem areas appears to be the Agricultural Credit Scheme to which the Federal Government has pledged ₦100 million with which the government would guarantee 75 per cent of loans made by the commercial banks to farmers. In fairness to the Central Bank and the commercial banks, it must be stated that they have devoted a lot of time and energy to ensure that the scheme produces the right result i.e. increased food production. However, what must not be overlooked is that the Central Bank, (rightly in the view of the experts) insists that such loans must be within the parameters of prudent and usual banking practice.

What this means is that the banks would require evidence that the farmer has a good title; is willing to pledge his assets as collateral; he is willing and able to make the repayments as and when due; and that he is able to keep reasonable financial records etc. THIS IS SOUND COMMERCIAL PRACTICE. Furthermore, from the point of view of the banks, the cost of servicing loans is so high that after taking into account the limits imposed on them as regards what they can charge, it is simply not economical to make thousands of small loans to small-time farmers. For a fraction of the paperwork and headaches they would rather deal in substantial loans to established customers. THIS MAKES SOUND ECONOMIC SENSE.

What the present arrangement simply does not take into account is the mentality of the farmers. The majority of farmers simply do not like to borrow money they cannot hope to repay in full at harvest time. As one of them put it – 'I have no intention of borrowing money which my grand-children will have to repay.' In fact if the farmers had their way, they would only borrow what they can repay next month.

As for pledging their land as security – you can forget it. Most farmers have an in-built suspicion that the government and the banks are in cahoots in order to deprive them of their land – 'the land of their fathers'.

Even the fertilizer programme and agricultural extension scheme are regarded with considerable suspicion. It appears that there is nothing farmers resent more than being told how to run their farms by people who have spent all their lives shuffling between laboratories, classrooms and offices.

It seems clear from the party manifestoes that all the political parties agree that there is an urgent need to come to the aid of the farmers – BUT THE FARMERS INSIST THAT WHAT THEY NEED IS NOT AID BUT BETTER PRICES. I understand that the farmers also insist that better prices do not necessarily mean higher prices.

The farmers certainly have a good case. Unless a lot and I mean an awful lot is done very soon, we may well succeed in producing iron and steel but no food. The towns would be over-crowded but the villages would be desolate.

All is not lost yet – there are some very interesting farms around. The former Governor of Kaduna State, Group-Captain Amin Jibrin runs a very successful farm in Kaduna so also does Mr Justice Nasir. Our former ambassador in the United States, Chief N. A. Martins and Mr Justice G. B. A. Coker also run very successful farms in Iseyin and Lagos respectively.

LAST LINE
PART I

According to Alhaji (Dr) L.P.O. the reason the Ten Commandments are so clear, precise and unambiguous is that unlike our new constitution it was not entrusted to a committee.

PART II

It is beginning to look as if the decision of the Special Tribunal on the Presidential Election headed by Justice B. O. Kasseem on what constitutes 'two-thirds of 19 states' rests as much on legality as on mathematics. I have just been reminded by Alhaji (Dr) L.P.O. that there is a British Judge – Lord Denning (Master of the Rolls) who is eminently qualified for such an assignment. Lord Denning got a First Class degree in MATHEMATICS from Cambridge University before enrolling for the bar.

HOT LINE

WHAT a hectic week it has been for the President. Monday was a really troublesome day because two national Sunday papers had carried bold headlines – 'President condemns The Rich'. This triggered off a lot of panic and many prominent citizens hastened their contigency plans to leave the country. Throughout Sunday and Monday morning, the President's 'direct line' hardly stopped ringing – calls were coming in from all over the country from anxious enquirers, many of whom had overwhelmed the President during the campaign with their generous financial contributions and moral support.

On Monday evening, the President was on television and roundly condemned the Press for not checking their facts before printing sensational headlines. The President was emphatic that he is not against any particular group of Nigerians – rich or poor. According to the President, what he had in fact said was – 'The era of easy or free money is over. Anyone who wants to make money will have TO WORK HARD for it'.

PASSPORTS AND PALAVER

It is quite interesting to observe that even, several weeks after the 'Daily Times' published an editorial in support of Professor Ayodele Awojobi's suggestion that all candidates for the Presidential elections should deposit their passports with the Police, the controversy has still not fizzled out. After all, the elections have since been held.

However, Alhaji L.P.O. is adamant that the suggestion touched on certain basic principles which must be fully debated. Apart from anything else, the 'Daily Times' editorial comments on Professor Awojobi's 'Birthday Lectures' were so ferocious and unwarranted that it was predictable that in order to placate the Professor, the 'Daily Times' was bound to support him next time the Professor went on his intellectual binge. Personally, I do not accept this!

In fairness to the 'Daily Times', it is worth mentioning that the paper's support was based on the belief that 'self interest', if nothing else, would dissuade the Presidential candidates from inciting violence or causing civil disorder as they would find themselves unable to flee the country (without their passport).

Those who oppose the Awojobi/'Daily Times' posi- have pointed out that the really smart politicians certainly know how to acquire more than one passport; and at any rate you do not need to be conducted on a guided tour of our borders to know that thousands cross and recross the borders daily without passports!

Those who oppose the Awojobi – 'Daily Times' position, have pointed out that the suggestion that Presidential Candidates should deposit their passports is a strange one – it is certainly without precedence anywhere in the world. They have also raised the point about whether the idea would not detract from the dignity of being a Presidential candidate.

What I find amusing about the 'palaver' is that if Presidential candidates have to deposit their passports surely the least we can expect is that the head of N.E.P.A. should do the same, otherwise we may not have electricity during the elections! The same goes for the respective heads of the Water Supply Corporation; Nigeria Airways; the 'Think Tank' (we cannot afford to stop thinking during the elections); Nigerian Television Authority etc. Come to think of it, the Managing Director of the 'Daily Times' should be the first to deposit his passport – we cannot afford to be without his newspaper during the election!

LIBERATED WOMEN

A divorce judge in Tel Aviv, Israel tried to reconcile

fifty-one year old Chayim and his 49 year old wife, Esther who wanted to part after 25 years. However, Esther told the judge: (quote from 'News of the World) 'I've got a dog that growls, a fire-place that smokes and a cat that stays out all night. What do I need a husband for?' She got her divorce.

THE PRESIDENT AND HIS PROBLEMS

For several days, the President has been wrestling with the problem of how to handle the new government in Ghana. Having played 'Big Brother' to the previous Ghanaian government as well as its predecessors it was predictable that our reaction to the coup in Ghana would go through a perplexing circle of shock, disbelief, disgust, hostility and now guarded reconciliation. I quote the President:

'The situation in Ghana is a bad mess. One thing is certain – the situation is going to get worse. These boys don't know what they are playing at. Jerry Rawlings is not in control – sooner or later they'll bump him off. Killing people all over the place is not going to solve the problem.'

According to Alhaji L.P.O., there are two remarkable points about the coup in Ghana. First and foremost, it is no longer safe to presume that once a military government has announced the date for civil elections (and it is seen to be pursuing a clear-cut programme towards handing over to civilians), there would be no coup attempt in the intermediate period. Secondly, following the execution of three previous Heads of State, one of whom – General Afrifa was last in government ten years ago, it is equally no longer safe to presume that once a Head of State and his major Lieutenants have been pardoned by his immediate successor, they are safe from punishment by a subsequent regime.

GHANA AND ELECTIONS

I understand that U.N. experts have condemned the elections in Ghana – they could not possibly have been free and fair or how come 'Chairman' Jerry Rawlings did NOT get elected?

HAJJ CONTROL

One of the major problems inherited by the President relates to the ever increasing number of Nigerians who wish to make the piligrimage to Mecca at quite considerable cost and a good deal of discomfort to themselves in addition to the staggering expenditure of scarce foreign exchange. The Government has in the past tried to limit the number of pilgrims to 50,000 per annum and preference was given to those who had never performed the Hajj (or had not travelled to Mecca in the previous three years). Equally, the old and infirm; pregnant women; infants; and those whose adherence to the tenets of Islam was suspect, were eliminated. However, in spite of all these, the number of pilgrims keeps increasing.

I am quite surprised to hear Alhaji L.P.O.'s suggestion that if the President is really serious about limiting the number of people who go to Mecca, preference would have to be given to Christians!

UP NIGERIA

According to the London 'Sunday Telegraph', the Nigerian High Commission is leading the list of embassies and commissions avoiding thousands of pounds worth of fines in London by claiming diplomatic immunity after breaking parking regulations.

In the last six months of last year 3665 parking tickets issued on Nigerian diplomats' cars – nearly £22,000 worth of fines – were cancelled on these grounds according to figures just released by the British Foreign Office.

The main problem area is close to the Nigerian High Commission's Offices in Northumberland Avenue, where only three official parking spaces are provided for the 73 people on the official 'diplomatic immunity list', most of whom have at least one car. The same cars often receive up to four parking tickets a day.

The other aspect of the problem is that since Nigerians

do not obey their own law in their own country – how can they be expected to obey another country's law?

DOWN WITH THE TAXMAN

Here is further proof that the taxman is truly unloved especially by those who wish to dispose of their property. Ted Horley, a former mayor of Altrincham, England, who died four years ago instructed his solicitors to buy a single lemon; divide it into two; and send one each to his home town's Tax Inspector and Tax Collector with the message – Now SQUEEZE THIS.'

QUOTE FROM THE PRESIDENT

Yesterday, the President declared: 'The more I try to educate and inform the country about our gigantic problems, the more I am impressed by the infinite capacity of the human mind to resist the introduction of knowledge. It takes a long while to sink in.'

BUT THIS IS NOT THE 'GRAPEVINE'

IDLE TALK

A few days ago, the 'Daily Times' published an article (headed 'Idleness Is Here To Stay') about the prevalence of idleness in Lagos and the rest of the country. I find that the London 'Daily Telegraph' has plenty to say on the same subject. On 15 October, it reported the experience of a British executive who spent time in Lagos trying to check the credit-worthiness of would-be buyers.

'His day began with proferred bribes of £7500 (about ₦10,000) for his goodwill. Finally, armed with company registration numbers, he got to a dilapidated three-storey building (The Registrar of Companies Office at 31, Oil Mill Street, Lagos). The ledger listing the company files was a well-thumbed hand-written volume with a large proportion of the sheets hanging loose.

He was directed to an office upstairs where there were two typists fast asleep. He got one of them to give him the necessary forms in triplicate to initiate a company search. A more senior official took the forms and got up to make the search – he had been very reluctant to do anything but found one of the two files requested. Unfortunately, the papers in the bundle, all tied up with string, stopped short at 1976! The system of having bundles of papers lying around in no visible order makes it difficult for later returns to get into the files of the earlier returns.

On the way back to his hotel, he adds, he fell into an open sewer!'

MONEY TALKS

As preparations for India's general election build up, leaders of Mrs Gandhi's Congress Party say they expect to raise at least £500,000 (about ₦640,000) towards their election expenses from Indians living in Britain.

Elections in India are an expensive business (same here!) because of the size of the country and because there are 360,000,000 voters. The figures are mind-boggling. The political parties will spend about £200,000,000 (₦250,000,000) on transport, on feeding, and paying 500,000 election agents and on staging meetings.

(i) **POSER ONE**

How much did the last elections cost the Nigerian Government?

1ii) **POSER TWO**

Does anyone seriously believe that FESTAC cost only a paltry ₦241,000,000 as published by the last Government?

WOMEN PALAVER

On 2 November, the 'Daily Times' published a most moving letter by Chief (Mrs) K. A. Pratt decrying the dearth of women among the appointments so far announced by President Shehu Shagari. Her suggestion seems to have been misunderstood – it is not correct that she wants the President to appoint a woman as his 'Adviser on Women's Affairs'. Surely, that is a job for a man! After all, the best choice as 'Adviser on Children's Affairs' is an adult.

THE LAW MAY BE AN ASS BUT . . .

The Nigerian Press is to be congratulated for publishing the full text of the judgement delivered by the 'dissenting Judges' – Justice Andrew Obaseki and Justice Kayode Eso in the Supreme Court verdict on the controversial Presidential Election. It is easy to understand why the Press, irrespective of their party sympathy, found the resonant logic and majesty of language of the two judges irresistable. If I ever have to to the Supreme Court, I would certainly feel a little more comfortable with either of those two judges up there.

THE 'DAILY TIMES' GOT IT WRONG

On 1 November, the 'Daily Times' published an article headed 'Minimum Government' and signed by Stanley Macebuh (does he exist?). The main thrust of the charges levied in the article suggested that the President has been guilty of inertia and ineptitude in his first three weeks in office. A few days earlier, the 'New Nigerian' with uncharacteristic non-partisan candour had echoed more or less the same view in a front page editorial.

While the concept of an all-knowing, all-conquering 'macho' President may be attractive to the Press (incidentally an all-action President helps to sell more newspapers!), it may not necessarily be good for the country. Besides, the Press has failed to grasp one essential factor – the real action is in the States not at the centre. If President Shagari is under-assertive, he is only doing what he (as a candidate) always said he would do – 'play it by ear'.

It is sheer hyprocisy on the part of the 'Daily Times' to now demand action from the President when as a candidate, he was treated with kid gloves at his interviews and conferences with the same paper. In one interview, he fluffed his lines on Foreign Policy (Middle East) and got away with it. Similarly, the candidate quoted a figure of doubtful veracity (₦5000) as the cost of each housing unit to be built by his government but nobody challenged the constituents of the cost or the accuracy of the arithmetic.

It is really amusing that the President is suddenly now expected to deliver the goods on Foreign Policy (Zimbabwe); Education; Energy etc., when throughout the election campaign, the Press through either idleness, reverence or a combination of both never seriously took the candidate to task on the intricate details of his programme.

At any rate, the cynics have long ago concluded that all that the President can do is to 'inspect Guards of Honour and sign documents'. If you are looking for action – go to the States. Besides, during the election campaign, the Press was totally uninhibited in its barely concealed self satisfaction in dubbing the candidate 'an enigma' – well has the enigma already become a riddle?

IDLENESS IS HERE TO STAY

AMONG the many distinguished visitors who came from abroad to witness our 1 October celebrations and the formal handing over by General Olusegun Obasanjo to Alhaji Shehu Shagari in Lagos was Mr John Seeward. His name is not likely to be familiar to many but prior to our Independence in 1960, he had worked for two decades in the old P.W.D. (Public Works Department) of blessed memory. Mr Seeward left just before Independence after collecting his 'Golden Handshake' and has not been back since. In the meantime, he had served in Zambia, the Caribbean, Gambia, and in the last few years – Britain. In none of those places had he felt at home and at ease – the only place that he could truly regard as home was back in Nigeria. All his children were born here and they had considerable difficulties in adjusting to life in Britain. Mr Seeward was determined to come back – 1 October 1979 provided an excellent opportunity. He came in a private capacity full of enthusiasm and affection for a country that had showered him with so much happiness.

I had arranged to meet him at the airport – the brand new Murtala Mohammed Airport. It turned out to be an unforgetable experience! I got to the airport in good time only to hear over the loudspeaker system that the flight would be two hours late. The amazing thing was that only ten minutes after the announcement, the flight arrived bang on time! But my troubles were not over yet.

Even though John Seeward's papers (passport, visas etc.) were meticulously in order, 'immigration' took one hour fifteen minutes of pushing, jostling, pleading and of course sweating, not to talk of the mindless questions.

419

Health control and customs proved to be a repeat performance of the same organised confusion and pandemonium. I began to have fears that I might end up collecting a corpse instead of a friend from the airport.

When he finally emerged from the customs check-point and breathed the first wheeze of fresh air, he fell straight into the arms of ravenous taxi drivers – all yelling 'master, master you want taxi?' They simply would not take no for an answer. We ended up with half a dozen of them following us each with his own special entreaty 'I get air-conditioned car'; 'Me London-trained driver'; 'master, I charge you only small money' etc. Surely, there must be someone at the Nigerian Airports Authority who can get the taxi drivers to queue and pick up their passengers in an orderly fashion like everywhere else in the world.

Mr Seeward was anxious to deliver a letter from his wife to a friend at Agege. We set off for Agege only to find that Agege Motor Road had become a marathon test in obstacle crossing. My guest confessed that he had never seen such huge pot-holes (I beg your pardon, craters) before. Could it be by chance that some of the moon chips fell on Agege Motor Road? How else could one explain the presence on the motorway of a crater so huge that it had almost completely consumed a whole articulated lorry? Traffic had come to a complete standstill and no one seemed to be doing anything about it.

We had to turn back and head for Lagos – which made a trip through Mushin inevitable. Prompted by my guest's remarks, I could not help noticing the incredible number of people milling around on both sides of the road – doing absolutely nothing. Just idling away (at that time of the day when they should be at work) just waiting for some spark of excitement – a temporary diversion from their idleness. Even little kids who should be at school were into the same pastime. Perhaps, they had already reconciled themselves to the belief that the street offered a brand of education far superior to that of any classroom.

It is amazing how one can live in a city and yet be completely blind to all the sores which afflict the sensitivity of visitors. Nobody seems to be doing anything about Ita Faji market. The filth and the flies seemed to have defied the non-exertions of successive governments. Half the population of Lagos must go there for their daily ration of food poisoning in an environment that is infested with 'open' (they are actually blocked) drains; the unpleasant odour of rotten entrails; and partially concealed excreta.

I am reminded of the apocryphal story of how when Chief (Dr) Tai Solarin complained to a past Administrator of Lagos about (dead) corpse lying on the road for several days while the rot set in, the reply he got was: 'Why worry about the (dead) corpse, we are all walking corpses anyway. Lagos itself is the slow poison'.

On our way into Lagos, we passed a number of polling booths. From serving as confessionals during the elections, they had undergone a remarkable metamorphosis. Within a matter of weeks, some enterprising souls had converted them into either urinals or commercials kiosks dealing in petty wares – cigarettes, sweets, soft drinks, soap etc.

Our first call in Lagos was at a Federal Ministry. Amazing, by 1 o'clock virtually all ranking officers were 'not on seat'. The messengers, cleaners and clerks had obtained a temporary relief from their bosses and an impregnable injunction not to attend to any member of the public until the following day.

John Seeward was visibly distraught at the disappearance, from the Marina, of the palm trees that had not only provided a natural shade all the way to the Bar Beach (Victoria Island) but had also conferred a unique majesty on Lagos' 'window of the world' – the quays.

I found myself completely incoherent in explaining to my guest that the only greenery left in the centre of Lagos – the Racecourse that had given so much pleasure to generations of Lagosians was now smothered in concrete, converted into a parade ground – the military's parting gift.

The day after the Presidential ceremony, I accompanied my guest to his old office at the P.W.D. he was truly overwhelmed by the affection of the old carpenters, joiners, drivers etc. who had never forgotten him. As we walked to our car, we could not help noticing the throng of unemployed at the office next door – the Ministry of Labour. John Seeward went up to one young man who was lying in the sun – he had completely given up any hope of employment. My guest could not help admonishing him – 'At this stage of Nigeria's development, how can you afford to spend the day lying in the sun, permanently idle?' Without any hesitation, the young man replied – 'It is not that I am unwilling to work, but I want a good job (level 'yeparipa') in an air-conditioned office, with a Mercedes Benz car; a house on Victoria Island and automatic membership of the Metropolitan Club!'

THE SHAKERS AND THE MOVERS

THE 'Shakers and the Movers' are the very small group of people who are permanently on the Government's Guest List. Irrespective of who or what party is in power, the 'Shakers and the Movers' get invited to all state functions. Needless to add that at the swearing-in ceremony of the President, the shakers and the movers turned out in full force.

For quite a while, I have been puzzled by the number of invitations, that have turned up on my desk, from State House, various embassies, numerous companies etc. to attend banquets, lunches, dinners, banquet cocktails etc. I really do think that there must be a mistake somewhere! After all, I am not a big shot in the Military; or Commissioner; Natural Ruler; Religious Leader; Permanent Secretary; Judge (my arithmetic is hopeless – I know nothing about fractions!); big time contractor or newspaper tycoon. Even among journalists, I have long ago reconciled myself to permanent obscurity.

At any rate, I suppose it was inevitable that three days to the Presidential swearing-in ceremony, a despatch-rider would turn up bearing a large invitation envelope with the Federal Government of Nigeria Crest on it. I am 'cordially invited' not only to the President's swearing-in ceremony but also to the reception at the Officers Mess and of course the evening party at State House.

Reluctantly, I set off for Tafawa Balewa Square where the swearing-in ceremony is scheduled to take place. Rain is pouring with a vengeance and I am suddenly reminded that among pagans – rain is a blessing. By the time I reach Tafawa Balewa Square, my invitation card is too rain-soaked to be legible and I am half hoping that I would be turned back. The place is simply teeming with soldiers, policemen, Air Force chaps and the 'immaculate gentlemen of the Navy'. To my astonishment, not only am I allowed in, I am ushered to my seat! There must be a mistake – I find myself seated right up front, bang in the middle of the 'Shakers and Movers'.

I look around me and I am truly amazed. In 1960, when Dr Nnamdi Azikiwe was being sworn-in as the First President at this same venue (then known simply as 'The Racecourse'), I was an 'usher'. Dressed in my stiff-starched khaki uniform of the King's College Cadet Unit Corps, I ushered these very same people to their seats. Nineteen years afterwards, the same people are occupying exactly the same seats! There are a few notable exceptions of course. Sir Samuel Manuwa, the Chief Medical Adviser is no longer with us. Neither is Alhaji Zana Bukar Dipcharima, whose cap (the 'Kube') became the symbol of the presence of Northerners within the 'Shakers and Movers' in Lagos.

Just behind the First Division of the movers and shakers are the 'new entrants' – dominated by open-faced civil servants who became Permanent Secretaries or the equivalent before age thirty-five and have accepted the 'non-longetivity' of their job. By age 45, they would be 'retired' voluntarily or otherwise and would be quickly replaced and forgotten! Somewhere in the files of the various ministries, their signatures would begin accumulating dust.

One notices with wry amusement the unease of the 'super-technocrats'. They are there as temporary members – 'borrowed' from the universities and various other institutions to carry out special assignments for the Government as heads of the Institute of International Affairs; the 'Think Tank'; Institute of Science and Technology; Enterprises Promotion Board; Universities Commission etc.

Of course, the 'media-executives', the controllers of what we read in newspapers; hear on the radio; and what we see on television are fully represented. But who controls what we neither read, see nor hear? Even among the media chiefs, there is appropriate deference to rank. The heads of the major newspapers are clustered together while the representatives of the minor papers are one row behind.

The Managing Director of the 'Daily Times' occupies the seat dictated by the order of precedence. I can't see him but I know he is there because I can see the largish, longish, brownish cuban cigar.

However, the most subdued group are the diplomats – the heads of various missions accredited to Nigeria. They are like umpires – seated between the First Division and the rest. They seem accustomed to meeting each other virtually every day/night. The seating order as well as the exchange of courtesies are already familiar. One cannot help noticing that the heads of various missions whose home Governments are locked in various international disputes are clearly on non-speaking terms. It emerges that the Ambassadors of the minor countries are on speaking terms with everyone else (they will accept aid from anyone!) it is the Ambassadors of the United States; Britain; Soviet Union; China who can get into serious trouble for speaking to whoever is in conflict with their respective Governments.

There is a sprinkling of politicians – those who insist that politics runs in their blood. As far as they are concerned, the sooner the ceremony is over the better, so they can get on with their own show. In 1960, they came in full force and took their seats by right. This time, the 'old politicians' have sent only a token representation. Their numbers have been decimated by death, old age, disullusionment or the mind-boggling rewards of 'heavy' government contracts. They are supported by the 'new politicians' – the eager new entrants who are anxious to be photographed (for the folks back home).

As for the military, this is truly their day – one last bravura! Lt-General Obasanjo, Lt-General T. Y. Danjuma, Major-General Shehu Yar'Adua are all wearing their uniforms (ironically the uniforms look brand new!)

425

for the last time. The next time you meet them – there is no need to salute! They are a truly interchangeable group. In 1960, they were represented by Aguiyi-Ironsi, Maimalari, Ademulegun, and L. O. Edet (Police). This year, the drill is the same; so are the tattoo; the Presentation of arms; the 21 gun salute etc. Only the faces are different.

On the centre stage is the brand new President – Alhaji Shehu Shagari looking hesitant and rather bemused by the pomp and pageantry. In a matter of weeks, he has gone through the metamorphosis of party nominee, Presidential candidate, President-elect and now the crowning glory. His lean athletic frame cuts a sharply contrasting figure against his flowing white robes (and white shoes). Next to him is the Vice-President, Dr Alex Ekwueme. He is a 'new face' – a graduate of Sociology, Law, and Architecture – now a 'freshman' in the University of life – politics. Suddenly, the swearing-in is on. The Chief Justice, Justice Atanda Fatayi – Williams is resplendent in his ermine robes. Even his polished Cambridge accent falters in the heat of the sun and the solemnity of the occasion.

The gentleman sitting next to me made what struck me as a remarkable observation. His suggestion was that if President Shagari wanted to educate the country that the intervention of the military in politics is an aberration, he should have insisted that the 'handing over' should be done not by Lt-General Obasanjo but by Dr Nnamdi Azikiwe, the last President.

I also overheard someone giving a running account of the various plots by politicians to settle old scores. The result would be predictable chaos and it would not be surprising if the first motion before the National Assembly would turn out to be an invitation – (yes you guessed it) to the military to take over the government once more!

I understand that the reason why the military went to so much trouble and fanfare was because they wanted to make 1 October 1979 a truly historical occasion.

Well, I submit that history cannot be manufactured –

with or without the pageantry and the rattling of sabre, 1 October 1979 would still have been a historical occasion.

THE 1980 BUDGET

IT is really significant that unlike previous budgets which straddled two calendar years, the 1980 budget is an entirely 1980 affair i.e. it would run from 1 April 1980 to 31 December 1980.

It is also significant that it is the first budget to be presented by a civilian administration since the last one was presented by Chief Festus Okotie – Eboh in 1965. The intermediate period was covered by a series of military budgets as regards which both the tone and direction as well as the substance were subjugated to the awe-inspiring directives of the military. In addition, in comparing the present budget with its predecessors, we would also need to bear in mind that whereas previous budgets covered a twelve-month period, the 1980 budget would run for only nine months.

In considering the 1980 budget, we would presume that those responsible for it gave adequate thought to the wider aspects of its economic and political dimensions. To start with, political considerations would prompt a new government, particularly a civilian successor to a military one, to wish to make a complete break with the budgetary policies of its predecessor. There is no clear evidence of this as far as the 1980 budget is concerned. What it has sought to establish is a cautious half-way house between a radical change and a sober appreciation of the realities of the country's economic plight.

Furthermore, we would presume that a meaningful budget would give number one priority to one particular problem e.g. inflation and subserve all others. What we find in the 1980 budget is 'a little something for everyone' without a clear overriding budgetary objective.

Thus we find glaring inconsistencies such as the declaration of 'an all out fight against inflation' while at the same time pursuing increased public spending principally on defence and to a lesser extent on education and housing. Similarly, we are informed of the reversion to 'free collective bargaining' between labour and employers while at the same time imposing a minimum wage of ₦100 for the lowest category of workers. We are not told how the magic figure of ₦100.00 has been arrived at or whether it would not further aggravate the already serious level of unemployment at a time when major employers are laying off staff even at managerial level. Neither are we given any assurances that such imposed increases in wages would be matched by increased productivity. Indeed, considering the havoc caused by the unreliability of water and power supplies in most parts of the country, it would be difficult to measure the relationship between labour and productivity. At any rate, there are many who would argue that compared with the rest of Black Africa, labour in Nigeria is already expensive and any further increases would not only refuel inflation but may also result in our pricing ourselves out of the market where we have to compete with much cheaper (and probably better quality) imports.

The other factor that is forcibly brought to our attention is the 'staggering cost of democracy'! Thus we find that in order to run the new civilian government machinery, the following allocations are revealed in the budget:

	₦
National Assembly	89,108,000
The Presidency	293,473,000
Federal Electoral Commission	7,907,000

Considering that similar votes are embodied in the budgets of the various State governments, we are forcibly reminded that democracy does not come cheap!!

The budget lends further confirmation to the fact that Nigeria is still running a one product economy i.e. OIL.

Out of the projected budgetary expenditure of ₦11,859,824,789, about ₦9 billion is expected to be financed from oil revenue. The lopsidedness this is bound to create in the economy is the equivalent of a man determined to maintain his balance on only one leg. We also find that the sharing out of revenue between Federal and State governments is heavily in favour of the Federal government. Thus while the Federal government is keeping about ₦9 billion for itself, the nineteen states are to share about ₦2.5 billion by way of statutory allocation. The basis of the sharing out of the statutory allocation, we are informed, is 50 per cent 'derivation' and 50 per cent 'population' – a clear departure from the sophisticated formula recommended by the Aboyade Committee. While there is not much dispute about the arithmetic of derivation (even though there are many who insist that derivation should be de-emphasised in the interest of nationhood), the 'population' factor is certainly controversial both in its arithmetic (it relies on the 1963 census figures, which are themselves controversial) as well as its application.

Many would no doubt be relieved to see the demise of the Price Control Board and the advance deposit in respect of Letters of Credit as well as the liberation of imports through the 'Approved User Scheme" and amendment of the ubiquitous 'Form M' – i.e. pre-inspection of imports. For the benefit of those who can afford vacation abroad, the Basic Travel Allowance has reverted to its previous maximum of ₦1000 (one thousand Naira). As regards the granting of car loans to employees, the Government is still fighting shy of accepting full responsibility – probably in deference to the recommendations of the Vincent Committee.

Dividend restraint has been relaxed as companies may now distribute as dividends either a maximum of 60 per cent of profit after tax or 25 per cent of the paid-up capital whichever is higher, provided such distributions are made out of the current year's profit. However, as tax on dividends is to be deducted at source – 'In the case of dividends paid or credited by one company to another, the tax to be accounted for shall be at the rate of 45 per cent . . .' this has created an anomaly whereby a holding company could end up paying tax twice on the same income. For accountants, the change in the accounting year of Government and its consequential effect on assessment years and basis periods is of course of special interest particularly as some of the problems of the transition arrangements have quickly surfaced.

'NA ME CATCH AM FIRST'

FOR the unwary motorist the 'strict' enforcement of the odd/even number regulations in Lagos has become an instructive experience of how the machinery of governmental imposition and private corruption happily co-exist. Both the motorists and the law enforcement agencies have come to terms with the basic economics. If a motorist is caught but insists on his right to be given an official receipt, the fine is ₦100 but if he is willing to do a deal and forget about the receipt – private efficiency swiftly comes into full play. The 'collectors' will happily accept ₦50 or much less on behalf of the 'big man' and let the motorist go.

However, it now appears that the system of private enterprise whereby the 'collectors' share the booty among themselves has broken down. The new arrangement is that whichever 'agent' i.e. road marshall; policeman; off-duty soldier; 'yellow fever', or 'maja-maja' is the first to reach the offending motorist has first claim to work out a deal with the offender and is entitled to keep the proceeds of his deal.

The quintessential experience of this new arrangement (or dispensation?) belongs to Dr Fred Ake-Anyareha who drove into Lagos two days ago but his car bore the wrong number plate for that particular day. He had barely covered fifty metres on Western Avenue before a bevy of 'collectors' converged on his car. Each one of them was yelling 'Na me catch am first' ('I was the first to catch him')!

NEWS FROM MOSCOW

I am informed by 'usually reliable sources' that the Nigerian Government with its characteristic flair for compromise has come up with a suggestion that would avert the disruption of the Moscow Olympics as the United States of America, Canada and several European countries are putting the screws on other countries to join their boycott of the Games in protest at the Soviet invasion/take over of Afghanistan. The Nigerian Olympic Association has been instructed to support the holding of the Games in Moscow but OPPOSE PARTICIPATION BY THE RUSSIANS!!

MOSCOW HERE WE COME

Last night, at the Senate, the Minister of External Affairs put up a very persuasive defence of the decision of the Government to send our athletes to Moscow. Said he: 'If so many countries are boycotting the games – surely this must improve our chances of winning gold.'

HOW TO IMPRESS VISITORS

I wonder whether it is pure coincidence that last week, the Nigerian press chose the visit of several Heads of State to Lagos for the Organisation of African States summit as the occasion for breaking the story of how 'messengers, clerks and typists' at the Central Bank of Nigeria had been arrested by the police for trying to help themselves to a paltry ₦22 million. Surely, that story coming in the wake of the alleged loss of ₦2.8 billion by the Nigerian National Petroleum Corporation must have really impressed our visitors. Incidentally, the aggregate of the national budgets of the countries who were represented at the OAU summit (minus Nigeria) adds up to less than ₦2 billion.

LUCKY AGAIN

In the past, I have had occasion to point out that Nigeria is indeed a lucky country. We proved it again last week – for the first time in the history of the OAU, all the Heads

432

of State returned to their various countries and were pleasantly relieved to observe that their photographs were still being displayed and no coup had taken place in their absence. Had there been any nasty incidents, Nigeria would have been compelled by 'African hospitality' to offer the intrepid Heads of State our Presidential jet and a permanent suite at the Eko Hotel.

WAY AND MEANS

Admiral Akinwale Wey has finally confirmed persistant rumours that the missing '₦2.8 billion oil money' has been quietly lying in his fridge. He has now sent the following message to the Judicial Panel (headed by Justice Irekefe) which is supposed to investigate the missing money: 'MISSING MONEY AVAILABLE FOR INSPECTION IN MY FRIDGE STOP SERIAL NUMBERS AVAILABLE ON REQUEST REGRET KEY TO FRIDGE NOW LOST BUT ARMED ROBBERS WILLING TO RETURN KEY FOR NAIRA TWO POINT EIGHT BILLION RANSOM STOP ROGER OUT WILKO.'

'LOW COST HOUSING' – CAN IT BE DONE

HOUSING in Nigeria has become such a major problem that it should be the subject of commentary from the widest spectrum of society – engineers, architects, sociologists, teachers, doctors, accountants, labour leaders and certainly the workers themselves – the prospective tenants and ultimate beneficiaries of a successful solution to the problem.

It would be only too easy to surrender to the dictates of those who argue that there can never be 'such a thing as low cost housing' – because if it is any good, it won't be cheap and by extension, if it is cheap it won't be any good at all – you simply replace an old slum with a new one! They point out that particularly in Lagos and indeed in virtually all major cities, the cost of land is already so high that it is nonsense to talk of 'low cost' housing – it certainly won't be low-cost by the time you have totalled the cost of acquiring the site; paying compensation; sand-filling; putting in basic infrastructure etc.

The Federal Government is committed to a policy of building 2000 houses in each of the nineteen states in the Federation this year while the Lagos State Government has already commenced building the 50,000 houses it has promised to erect annually. By any definition, these are very high targets which immediately trigger questions about the capacity to deliver. We certainly cannot ignore the constraints of finance, management, materials etc.

There is a clear dichotomy between the approach of the Federal Government and that of the Lagos State Government. Predictably, the Federal Government is having problems acquiring land particularly in states where the political parties in power are not party to the

NPN/NPP accord at the Federal level. Also, according to the budget, only ₦192 million has been voted by the Government for its housing programme. The question that immediately arises is 'how many housing units will not just be started but will be finished with a vote of ₦192 million?'

On the other hand, the Lagos State Government is having trouble justifying its insistence that the prospective beneficiaries of its low-cost housing must be 'evidently low-income workers' but must nevertheless be able to pay a deposit of ₦1000. Also, sooner or later the Lagos State Government would have to deal with the simmering rebellion by its 'middle-class' citizens who claim that they pay disproportionately high taxes which reduce them to 'wealth by qualification only' i.e. they have degrees and professional qualification but very little by way of basic comfort. They claim that they are as much victims of the harsh housing problem as low income workers. Consequently, they see little merit in a scheme that is to be largely financed by their taxes but from which they are automatically disqualified.

Clearly, there is an urgent need to harmonise the Federal Government housing programme with that of the Lagos State Government and all the other state governments. That low-cost housing can be successfully tackled has been demonstrated by a scheme that is currently going on in Bangkok. The Bangkok experiment could become a model for third world countries especially as the emphasis is on self-help. 'The project has its own building materials factory on the site turning out cement blocks, cross beams, foundations, wooden window-frames and doors. All are designed for easy assembly. When the houses are up, community facilities will follow, including fifteen shops, a market, a clinic and a children's playground.'

The centre-piece of the Bangkok low-cost housing scheme is 'building-together' and its organisers believe that by bringing housing costs down to a level poor people can afford, they have found the answer to a perplexing social problem which is at its severest in developing countries. The 'building-together' scheme is a manifestation of a novel approach to housing because it demands labour contributions from the house owners themselves. For example, the subject of our case study is a rickshaw driver who earns less than ₦60 per month and for whom a deposit of ₦1000 would be beyond his wildest dreams. Instead of paying a deposit of ₦1000 'he has been driving foundations and laying building blocks for the first twenty houses, one of which will be his.' His labour contribution is valued at 14 per cent of the cash price of the house and this will be deducted from his repayments.

'Ultimately, there will be two hundred houses on the four-acre site which is only fifteen kilometres from the centre of Bangkok. A West German charity lent the money to buy the land and The Netherlands Government provided water supplies, drainage, sewerage and road. The Thai Government Housing Bank (the equivalent of our Federal Mortgage Bank) provides funds for the building and arranges mortgages.'

When the first twenty houses are completed, prospective owners of the second twenty will move onto the site to begin building with the assistance of those in the first group as well as outside volunteers.

The concept of 'building-together' certainly has a lot to commend it to both the Federal and State Governments who can restructure their role to the provision of basic design, management and technical support.

AMAZING GRACE

Recently in Lagos, those who attended a funeral service for a stalwart of a political party were shocked into utter disbelief. The church was packed full with party members who had decided that the old man should be given a befitting burial as one of the founders of the party, even though he had recently been expelled for 'anti-party activities' – namely for making a grab for the No. 1 office.

To the amazement of the audience, the reverend gentleman who presided at the funeral service devoted three-quarters of his sermon to singing the praises of the successful Governorship candidate of a rival political party whom he declared as 'hardworking' and 'the best Governor Lagos has ever had.'

CAN TAI BE RIGHT?

I know several people who get extremely worried when they find themselves sharing the same point of view with the irrepressible DR TAI SOLARIN. Such agitation of the mind inevitably prompts loss of sleep as they search for some straw that would enable them to declare Tai's latest utterances as nonsense! I have no inhibitions in declaring that in his latest 'jihad' against broken down trailers and lorries which have taken over and ruined Apapa (and indeed the rest of Lagos), Dr Tai Solarin is on the right track.

In urging the Governor of Lagos, Alhaji Lateef Jakande, to tackle the problem urgently, Tai is doing us all a great service. Not only are the broken down trailers and lorries a serious ecological nuisance, they also constitute a severe traffic hazard. Many lives have been lost as a result of motorists crashing into these lorries and trailers especially at night.

I feel certain that in his usual flamboyant manner, Dr Tai Solarin will soon set up a company to offer decent burial nationwide for broken down lorries and trailers! As they say on the Lagos Stock Exchange – 'such a company would offer great prospects'.

DANGER

Last week a young lady narrowly escaped what would almost certainly have been a fatal accident. She was driving her brand new yellow Mazda car along Wharf Road, Apapa when lo and behold her car was almost flattened by the heavy contents of a trailer that had been overloaded with heavy containers. In an almost identical accident on the same date, a young accountant driving a

Peugeot car had a very close shave with death when a lorry fully-laden chose to empty its cargo of huge metal frames, used for constructing bridges and dams, on Ikorodu Road as it ran out of control. Also, it is not so long ago that a young estate surveyor lost his life on Eko bridge. His only 'crime' was that he happened to be driving behind a lorry that was over-laden with iron rods one of which came crashing through the young man's car.

Are we to believe that there is no law enforcing agency to ensure that the mammoth size lorries and trailers are brought under control? Some of them wander all over the place even at peak traffic time with complete disregard for the security of the goods they are carrying and utter contempt for the safety of other road-users.

THE TIMES ARE CHANGING

On learning that His Highness, Oba Adeyinka Oyekan, the 'King' of Lagos had threatened that natural rulers would soon form a 'trade union' of their own in order to preserve '. . . their powers in judicial, political and spiritual matters from Government agencies', the proprietor of one of our largest building contracting companies commented as follows: 'I knew it had to come – after all, many of my workers have been behaving as if they were natural rulers!'

HOW LONG IS A DAY?

Mr Harold Wilson, a former Prime Minister of Britain has often been quoted as saying that: 'In politics, A DAY is a long time.' However, I think that it is stretching the point (or a day!) too far to suggest that this applies to NEPA (the National Electric Power Authority).

A few days ago, it was officially announced that the Minister of Mines and Power held a ONE DAY Conference with representatives of NEPA from all the states in the Federation on the problems of electricity supply and distribution throughout the country. Any one who can deal with the problems of NEPA in one day deserves our unalloyed admiration.

ROBBERY AND UNEMPLOYMENT

Most expatriate visitors to this country usually steer well clear of controversial issues. It is therefore remarkable that Professor Walter Walter-Keen a U.N. expert had no reservations in declaring to students at the Institute of Strategic Studies that 'there is no direct connection between unemployment and the prevalence of armed robberies throughout the country'. According to the learned Professor, armed robbers are generally people who like easy money and who want to live fast. For them, armed robbery has great attraction – the working hours are short and the loot is tax-free.

BLIND BUT NOT FOOLISH

Following the announcement by the Central Bank of Nigeria that the deadline, when the old naira notes would no longer be accepted by the banks, would not be extended in spite of the 'jaw-jaw' at the National Assembly, most people rushed to the banks to get rid of the old notes.

A few days ago a diplomat friend of mine was walking down Broad Street when he was accosted by a blind man who was not actually begging for alms but aggressively demanding it. The diplomat dipped his hand into his pocket only to find that the only money he had was the old naira note. As he had no coins whatever with which to placate the beggar, he handed over the old naira note. To his utter astonishment, the blind man threw the old note back at him after declaring 'Haba! Oga don't you know that the old note is useless?.'

WHERE'S MY SHARE?

ABUJA SPECIAL

ACCORDING to the official Government announcement, the new Federal capital to be located at Abuja is going to cost ONLY ₦10,000,000,000 (ten billion Naira). However, it is amazing how virtually everyone seems to have jumped onto the 'Abuja' hustle – it is like they want to join the gravy train at all costs. The other day, I met an Alhaji whose tender for a job had been turned down by the Federal Capital Development Authority. He complained bitterly and demanded an official reply to his question:

'How am I going to explain to my children that ten billion Naira was floating around but I did not get my share?'

DEAD OR ALIVE

It appears that the Federal Capital Development Authority has been totally baffled by the strange response to its announcement that 2000 plots are available for distribution at Abuja. Apparently, some wise souls have concluded that there is no way any of the plots would be allocated to them. They have therefore decided to apply for burial plots instead! Their thinking suggests that if they are not going to live in the new capital, they can at least be buried there.

CHARLES IGOH SPECIAL

It is quite interesting to observe how within twenty-four hours of being appointed Press Secretary to the President, Charles Igoh has already become a household name.

440

The barman at the Press room at State House has already invented a cocktail drink which he calls the 'Charles Igoh Special'. It is a very potent drink labelled – 'imaginative alcoholic innovation'. It is certainly not a drink to be recommended for the unwary.

PATRICK DELE COLE SPECIAL

A few weeks ago Dr Patrick Dele Cole was hauled before the Senate to answer embarrassing questions about his salary and fringe benefits as Managing Director of the 'Daily Times' Newspaper Group. On the evening news, the TV cameras captured Dr Cole in a poignant flash of 'theatre verite' stoutly defending his position. He very sharply pointed out that he was in charge of a very successful publicly quoted company and that at any rate his remuneration was easily exceeded by that of Ereko market women whose massive earnings from dealing in textiles was virtually tax-free.

However, Professor Milton Friedman, the world-renown and Nobel Peace Prize winning 'monetarist' economist has reacted sharply in defence of the Ereko market women by declaring that:

'They are part of what is now called the 'underground economy' – that section forced by Government interference to make their own rules to cheat in order to survive.'

PRESS FOLLY

I am truly amazed at the cavalier manner in which the Nigerian Press handled the allegations made by the Secretary of a political party that certain political parties were planning secession. Without any inhibitions whatever, several major newspapers splashed the allegation on their front page and relied entirely on quoting the statements of the party executive at a Press conference.

In view of the seriousness of the allegations as well as the recent history of our tragic civil war and the dire consequences of public panic, one would have expected the Press to make a stand there and then that they would not carry the story unless the party spokesman could substantiate his allegations with concrete evidence. Surely, it is in the national interest that the Press should exercise the utmost restraint in such delicate matters especially in these trying times. To quote Andy Akporugo – of the 'Daily Times' – 'Every point on the alleged UPN secession programme revealed last week by the NPN chief scribe was so generalised and vague, that the entire package seemed to strike the note of some queer oracle.'

POLITICIANS AND DEPORTATIONS

As a result of his being deported from Nigeria under very controversial circumstances, Alhaji Shugaba Abdurrahman Darman has become a household name in Nigeria, Chad, Niger and Cameroons!

I am reliably informed that certain politicians whose popularity has been on the decline in recent times have submitted their names to the Minister of Internal Affairs just to let him know that they would not at all mind being deported.

COPS AND ROBBERS

Following the vigorous campaign of the Lagos State Commissioner of Police, Alhaji Mohammed Gambo – the number of armed robberies in Lagos State appeared to have fallen sharply. However, they are now back in business – more ruthless and a good deal more cocky. Apparently what happened during the period of lull was that the armed robbery gangs went into business selling anti-burglar alarms in the streets, in the markets and even tried to sell their wares from door to door. All in the full knowledge that none of these devices could stop them and it made good business sense to make money both ways by selling you junk burglary alarms and then carrying out the raids to prove how inefficient the alarms are!

THE VICE-PRESIDENT GOES BACK TO SCHOOL

Last week the (not His Excellency) Vice-President Dr

Alex Ekwueme – the man who is 'only one heartbeat away from the President' went back to school. He was at the head of the 'Honours List' at the cocktail party hosted by King's College Old Boys Association for the latest crop of 'ever do wells'. I almost didn't go, but I'm glad I did. It was a revealing but chilling experience of the wind of change that cuts across generations, across tribes, across culture and across political party affiliations and religion. I am reminded of Laskin's favourite quotation – 'Every cocktail is a waking upside down'.

There is Mr J. K. Tresize – the 'youngest old boy'. At eighty plus, he is still sprightly and amusing – a very fine gentleman – 'full of wonderful mischief'. Then there is the other 'J. K.' – J. K. McGregor, the architect fresh from the exertions of celebrating his 50th birthday. Suddenly, one is reminded that of all the McGregor brothers, he is the only one who went to King's. All the others went to 'that other place!'

Chief Adeniran Ogunsanya the President of the Old Boys Association is in great form. He never seems to tire of shaking hands, hugging and teasing and somehow seems to know everybody's name and what 'house' they belong to. Had the 'bride' been willing and had the price been right, the Chief would have been the present Governor of Lagos State. What is clear as the Chief leads the joyous singing of the school song – 'Floreat Collegium' is that if it came to choosing between being Governor of Lagos State and being President of the King's College Old Boys Association, the Chief would readily choose the latter! Contrary to the claim by 'Tribune' newspaper, it is not true that the Chief campaigned that Lagosians should vote for him because '. . . he went to (attended) King's College.'

Since the new Government came into power, I have sat through several dinners, lunches, parties etc. in honour of the Vice-President but at none have I seen him (except perhaps the one hosted by his fellow architects) so resplendent with delight. The gaiety is infectious and one is pleasantly relieved to observe that six months of high office have not done too much damage – the easy-going good-natured manner, engaging good humour and quiet elegance are very much in evidence.

Among the 'distinguished old boys' who are being honoured are Mr John Wash Pam, Vice-President of the Senate; Professor Sunday Mathew Essang, Federal Minister of Finance; Mr A. K. Hart, Chairman of the Nigerian National Petroleum Corporation; Mr J. C. Ojukwu, Member of the House of Representatives; and Senator Alhaji Sikiru Shitta-Bey – 'double King's' i.e. King's College, Lagos and King's College, London. Also being honoured are the two Presidential Advisers on Economics – Dr J. C. Odama and Professor E. C. Edozien (a star footballer in his time) but which one, to quote Dr Pius R.A. 'Revenue Allocation' Okigbo, is the President's right-hand 'and which one is his left'? Professor Edozien urbanely declines to be labelled as a 'monetarist' or anything else preferring to regard himself as a 'structuralist'. As for the budget announcement of only a few days ago, he has no comments but would rather wait for public reaction first.

In a corner there is a hilarious argument going on between two 'old fellas' – an argument that has gone on and off for the last twenty-five years as to who snatched the other's girlfriend at the time. It turns out the lady in question married someone else and she is in the audience, having outlasted three husbands – all of whom were King's College old boys!

The wives are very much in evidence – some are attending for the first time while others have been before and certainly there are some who think that 'King's College boys' are terribly boring – all they ever talk about is themselves and cricket. However, the majority of wives are clearly enjoying themselves sharing the gaiety and glory of their husbands and are enchanted by the regaling stories of the pranks their now respectable husbands got into in their formative years.

The true princes of the occasion are of course the all-time great athletes. Traditionally, King's College has always treated its sportsmen like royalty – A. K. O. Amu (athletics, cricket and hockey); M. S. Adewale (cricket and football); Ben Enahoro (cricket, hockey, athletics and football); Dr M. O. Adesanya (football and cricket); Dr O. O. Coker (cricket, football, athletics and hockey); Dr Eben Ikomi (football and athletics); R. A. Oyekan (cricket); Bankole Soetan (football and athletics); S. O. Akpata (cricket, hockey and athletics); Jenkins Coker (athletics and football); Moshood Akanbi (athletics and cricket); R. O. Johnson (athletics and cricket). Strangely, Patrick Ani (cricket, hockey, athletics, squash, tennis and everything else!) is missing.

There is an impressive turn out of former Commissioners and Permanent Secretaries – men who have relinguished high positions to their successors only to be pleasantly surprised to discover that power, influence, peace of mind, happiness and sincere friends are not necessarily corollaries – if you have one, you may not have or even need th others. Chief I. S. Adewale (football and athletics); P. C. Asiodu (cricket and hockey) reputed to be the most brilliant student of his generation; Alhaji Femi Okunnu (athletics and hockey); Dr Tayo Seriki (athletics and hockey); A. A. Ayida (former Secretary to the Federal Government) are all here.

Of course it would be misleading to suggest that all King's College boys end up as doctors, engineers, lawyers, architects, accountants, etc. The truth of the matter is of course that if any have been thrown into jail, or have been involved in nefarious scandal or have deviated from the path of self-fulfilment – they did not show up for the party.

With only a few minutes to the end of the party, a gentleman, obviously overwhelmed by the joyous occasion, declared: 'King's College is a microcosm of Nigeria'. To my utter astonishment, the response from a young man (who had gone on to acquire a degree in Politics, Philosophy and Economics from Oxford University) was: 'Nonsense, sir! The school is colonial and elitist. At a time when every one of its teachers was a graduate, (and predominantly expatriate) there were many schools in Lagos that did not have a single graduate teacher. King's had several laboratories when there were schools in other parts of the country that could not boast of a single laboratory and yet their students were expected to pass science exams.' The young man went on to declare that as far as he is concerned, boarding schools are totally unacceptable – 'Apart from the vast expense of maintaining them for a privileged few, boarding schools represent the total surrender of the responsibility of parents to the state and at any rate the boarding schools have become the centres for serious drug abuse and outright juvenile indiscipline.' At the end of the spirited debate that immediately followed my faith was restored – among old boys you can express any point of view and still have an audience. That is the tradition.

The Vice-President, obviously mindful of the words of Donald Keen – 'The best speeches are the ones that are never made' – did not make a speech. He left quietly on a tide of sincere and affectionate good wishes.

To the two 'barmen' – Remi Odofin and Dapo Odofin (what coincidence, Odofin I and II!) – 'many thanks'.

MOSCOW GAMES

IT is rather ironical that in order to understand the true dimensions of the 22nd Olympic Games held in Moscow, logic demands that we start at the closing ceremony of the Games – on 3 August 1980. For one and a half hours, the capacity crowd that overfilled and overflowed the 100,000 seater Lenin Stadium had been treated to a spectacular display of 'massed calisthenics, Cossack dancers, Latvian milkmaids and Grecian maidens'. Finally, bandsmen from the Red Army, Navy and Air Force took over the arena for a ten-minute display of martial music and military drill. By 9 p.m. the ceremony was over but the pulsating magnificence and the spectacular efficiency which the Russians displayed on the final day had been the anchor that had dominated the Games right from the opening ceremony on 19 July.

As for the Olympic Village in Moscow, it would indeed be rare to find any athlete with complaints about the food or the comfort or the training and recreational facilities. This is no mean achievement! Mind you there were grumblings about the shortage of beer and the 'early' closing of the discotheque at 11 p.m.

For the Press, the facilities provided were truly staggering both in sophistication and efficiency. Even though the sports arena were in various parts of Moscow, they were linked to the automated data management system – ASU – Olympiad; the Main Press Centre; the TV and radio complex and other systems installed to support the Games.

The Main Press Centre is a magnificent tribute to Soviet technology. Located in the Sadovoye Ring it transmitted information about the Olympic competitions

447

to all corners of the world.

The events that had preluded the Olympic Games had more than ensured that whatever success was achieved by the Russians would be overshadowed by fierce controversy over Afghanistan and indeed by haunting questions about the contradiction between the 'free spirit' of the Olympics as opposed to the regimented way of life which is the fundamental anchor of Soviet life. The Russians were of course fully aware of their vulnerability on this score as well as the possibility of direct acts of sabotage perpetrated or contemplated by their ideological rivals for whom the failure of the 22nd Olympiad would have provided gleeful reassurance that the Soviets were bound to fail anyway.

Right from the opening ceremony, the Russians overwhelmed their captive audience with their spectacular fanfare and the uninhibited display of Soviet technology. For three solid hours, there was never a dull moment. By the time the Olympic flame arrived, borne by Sergei Belov, in the Lenin Central Stadium, it had been carried by a relay of 5000 runners through Greece, Bulgaria, and Rumania. As a reminder of Russia's impressive achievement in science and technology, at precisely 18.50 hours, Russian cosmonauts Popov and Bemin who were in outer space beamed their greetings in voices that were not only clear but were evidently full of pride in their country's achievement.

As we trooped out of the stadium, each of us was still stupefied by the magical splendour of the ceremony we had just witnessed yet we were unanimous in our verdict that the Russians deserved a gold medal straightaway.

Within two weeks, the first Olympics to be hosted by a Socialist country had produced the greatest number of records ever – thirty-seven world records were either equalled or bettered while twenty-nine new Olympic records were set.

It was only appropriate that the first gold medal was won by Alexander Melentiev of the USSR in free pistol shooting in which he set a new Olympic and world record. Within a matter of two weeks, we were to be feasted with a sumptuous sporting banquet. In a truly breathtaking finish, Allan Wells of Britain just pipped Silvio Leonard of Cuba by the narrowest margin in the men's 100 metres final in 10.25 seconds. Remarkably enough, three years before Wells was only a second-rate longer jumper! In the 800 metres, the much heralded confrontation between two British athletes Sebastian Coe and Steve Ovett lived fully up to expectation. Ovett won the gold in 1 minute 45.4 seconds while Coe got the silver. The fierce competition between the two was clearly personal and the race lent final confirmation that Britain no longer believed that taking part in sports was all. Coe who ran a badly judged race in the 800 metres was to get sweet revenge in the 1500 metres (3 minutes 38.4 seconds) in which Ovett only managed third place.

The decathlon provided Nigeria with 'half-gold' – as the gold medalist Daley Thompson of Britain is in fact half-Nigerian. His mother is British while his father is Nigerian.

Africa had to wait until the 5000 metres and 10,000 metres for salvation as Mirtus Yifter of Ethiopia, though reputed to be forty years old, won both races easily by sprinting in the last 300 metres of each race as if the race was just starting!

As for boxing, the Cubans virtually made a clean sweep as they captured six out of the eleven gold medals. The high point was of course the victory of Teofilo Stevenson, who with his remarkable resemblance to Muhammed Ali both in looks and style, skilfully jabbed his way to his third Olympic gold medal in the heavyweight division. In the women's hockey, the Zimbabwe team that had been so hastily put together, only three weeks before the Games, that no one noticed they were all white emerged as the champions.

Men's hockey provided one of the moments of hilarity as Tanzanian goalkeeper, Leopold Gracias let in 49 goals in four matches – presumably a new Olympic record!

It was so sad to see Ugandan John Aki-bua the erstwhile 400 metres hurdles world record holder and Olympic champion struggling to qualify. Surely, an actor must know when to quit. Equally sad was the sight of Cuban Alberto Juantorena, the superstar of the Montreal Olympics, finishing an undignified fourth in the 400 metres.

As for the performance of Nigerian athletes, the picture was generally dismal. Apart from Peter Okodogbe who ran a creditable fourth (10.34 seconds) in round 2 of the 100 metres but exited in 7th place in the semi-final; followed by 6th place (21.03 seconds) in the semi-final of the 200 metres, the rest were nowhere! Hammed Adio took seventh place in the second round of the 100 metres while Samson Oyeledun was last in his own heat. In the first round of the 200 metres, Hammed Adio finished fourth in 21.79 seconds. The only respite we got came in heat 3, round 1 of the 400 metres in which Dele Udo came first! The promise of gold was quickly ditched when he came fifth place (45.88 seconds) in the semifinal. Hope Ezeigbo got as far as round 2 only to exit in 6th place (46.88 seconds). In the long jump, Kayode Elegbede did not make any big impression. He seemed to be overawed by the occasion.

The performance of the Nigerian women athletes was equally pathetic. Both Obuzoeme Nsenu and Rufina Uba made their exit from round 2 of the 100 metres by coming sixth in their different heats in 11.55 seconds and 11.60 seconds respectively. In the 200 metres, Uba was eliminated in round 2 (sixth place – 23.55 seconds). This was quickly followed by the round 1 demise of Kehinde Vaughan in the 400 metres (7th place – 53.54 seconds) as well as Mary Akinyemi (4th place 52.64 seconds) and Gloria Ayanlaja (6th place – 53.55 seconds).

The less said about the relays, the better. Nigeria ran seventh in the final of the men 4×100 metres (time: 39.12 seconds); and fifth in the men 4×400 metres round 1 (time: 3 minutes 14.1 seconds). As for the women, they came last in round 1 on the 4×400 metres (time: 3

minutes 36 seconds), and they did not even make it to the final of the 4×100 metres. As regards both the men and women relay teams – someone must have forgotten to teach them how to change the baton!!

It was really galling to watch Nigeria's performance in boxing – a sport in which we had built up a commendable reputation for providing tough intelligent fighters. To my utter horror, apart from one exception, every single Nigerian boxer finished on the canvas in the first round of their first bout!! The only guy who made it to the second leg got there by drawing a bye in the first leg! Rumour has it that some of them were fasting while others deliberately chose to lose their matches because they had not been provided with track suits. As for football, it really does tease the imagination to consider that Nigeria drew 1:1 (but for a disallowed goal it would have been 2:1 in favour of Nigeria) with highly-rated Czechoslovakia – the team that went on to win the gold medal!

Admittedly, the Nigerian team had been seriously 'destabilised' after their gruelling World Cup qualifying round encounter with Tunisia just a few days before the Olympics, and numerous injuries had resulted in the absence of some key players including skipper Segun Odegbami; but nothing could excuse the lack-lustre performance against Kuwait (their first match) in which they were beaten 3:1. Our lone goal was in fact scored by a Kuwaiti defender and even now I still cannot believe that a goal-keeper of Best Ogedegbe's class could let in a shot as feeble as Kuwait's second goal. In their third and final match, Nigeria was beaten by Colombo by a lone goal. In three matches, the Nigerian strikers had managed to score only one goal. In sharp contrast, Zambia (with an attack led by the brilliant Shitalo) gave the USSR plenty of trouble before succumbing 1:3 – but the result certainly belied the dazzling performance of the Zambians.

As for the weightlifters (Cosmas Sampson and Sydney Ikebuaku) and the wrestlers (Mike Bamidele and Augustine Atasie), they made zero impact.

It is only natural that a lot of searching questions are

being asked about the reasons behind the poor performance of the Nigerian team. To my mind, those who think that the answer is money have missed the point. They simply want the Government to pump more money into sports! It is a great pity that Nigerians have conditioned themselves to the money syndrome – if there is a problem, just throw money after it and the problem will disappear! In fact what our various sports organisations need to do is to assert their independence both financially and in forward planning from the vast Governmental bureaucracy that has been woven round them like a web – it is the major reason why nothing gets done: Government keeps blaming the sports organisations which in turn never cease to moan about the meagreness of Government financial support while interference (both subtle and blatant) is continuously increasing.

Also, I do not believe we can expect any vast improvement in sports until there is a concerted effort to widen the spread of sports participation throughout the country. It is not enough for Lagos to solicit the support of the various State capitals – the search must go beyond that, right down to the Local Government Areas. This is no easy task but the truth of the matter is that participation in sports or awareness of its benefits is largely restricted to very few areas of the country. This is a sharp contrast to America, Germany and Russia where surveys have indicated that on average one out of every four persons participates in one sport or the other.

In addition, it is doubtful whether we can make any appreciable progress in sports when virtually none of the equipment are manufactured here. We have to rely on imports with the attendant prohibitive costs. Furthermore, there is clear evidence that our athletes resent the way they are treated by sports officials. They are forever complaining about their paltry allowances as well as welfare which they claim to be a sharp contrast to that of their officials. In fact, they have pointed out that in Moscow, the Nigerian contingent had more officials (both

Federal and State sponsored) than athletes!!

Our sportsmen moan that insufficient thought has been given to their future careers – after several years of continuous training and competitions with the consequent disruption of their studies or job advancement, what follows? After all it was only the footballers who got houses and cars for winning the Africa Cup.

Also, there is an urgent need to remind athletes (and sports officials!) especially when they are outside the country that they are indeed ambassadors and even within the country, they are the best advertisement for sports.

This of course brings us to the 'Moscow Sex Scandal' involving Nigerian athletes and officials. The main gist of the story is already public knowledge – two of the female athletes who were sent home summarily claimed on arrival at the Murtala Muhammed Airport (before TV cameras and radio) that the reason they were disciplined was that they had refused the sexual advances of certain officials. This lent further confirmation to the screaming headlines published by a Lagos newspaper (based on reports fed to it by its Moscow correspondent) that one of the Nigerian officials had been caught making love on the grass lawn of the Olympic Village (an event which was not listed on the official Olympic programme!!)

In addition, it was alleged that one of the female athletes had stabbed a male colleague in a fit of jealous pique even though she later claimed that this was meant to be punishment for his attempt to rape her the night before!

The Minister of Sports has now instituted a panel to probe the matter but what is clear is that there is no way the panel will ever get to the bottom of the matter for two basic reasons: much of the story is based on allegations and would be extremely difficult to prove especially as most of the actors in the drama have displayed great reluctance as regards giving evidence. Secondly, the officials of the Nigerian Sports Commission who were in Moscow unfortunately allowed themselves to be driven into a defensive position by trying to deny the story and then placing an embargo on press reports between Moscow and Lagos. Surely, a much wiser course of action would have been to summon all the Nigerian journalists who were attending the Games and brief them properly about the serious damage which the story could do to Nigeria's image and perhaps invite them to join in investigating the story. That would ensure conviction that the officials had no interest whatever in concealing anything. Even more serious were allegations that selection did not depend entirely on merit and that where female athletes were concerned, there were other considerations (of a sexual nature). Of course, these are only allegations but they are bound to create anxiety among parents who are already wary about allowing their daughters to represent the country abroad.

As for the journalists, there is a raging controversy between those who feel that the reporter who filed the story from Moscow should have checked with the officials before sending the story; and those who feel that it is entirely up to each individual journalist to make his own judgement about the style of his paper and the appetite of its readership for juicy stories!

The interesting question which now arises is whether in the near future, any African country (or indeed any 'Third World' country) should contemplate hosting the Olympics. The Russian experience suggests that only countries with massive financial resources – (the Russians are reported to have spent at least 1.5 billion dollars) as well as superior infrastructure, communications network and excellent technology could successfully handle the modern Olympics. The conclusion to be drawn is that no developing country can afford what is essentially a prestige affair – a jamboree, rather the 'Third World' should concentrate its energies on providing better education, better hospitals, better food etc. for its people. Jamborees can wait!

Towards the end of the Games, (July 31) the London 'Daily Express' with bold front page headlines accused

Russia of cheating. 'Russian judges, it was said, acted unfairly – to put it politely – so that their own athletes could win gold medals.' The paper went on to allege that in the Triple Jump, the only two competitors threatening the Russians, world record holder Joas de Oliveira of Brazil and Ian Campbell of Australia had nine fouls called in twelve jumps though international observers could not see why. In the Discus, Luis Delis of Cuba in his final throw was marked only for the bronze medal although other expert observers 'all thought he had done better than that' – Viktor Rasshchupkin, a Russian stayed ahead for the gold. It was also alleged that in the Javelin, the main gates of the stadium were mysteriously opened as Russian competitors ran up, creating a following breeze for their throws. Even so, Russian Dainis Kula's first two throws were called as fouls. His third throw, said observers, was also clearly a foul, yet it was not only allowed but marked beyond its fall. Kula got the gold. In the Pole Vault, a Soviet official was said to have raised a flag to show wind strength to Russian jumpers.

In addition, the paper reported 'an Olympic storm' because Professor Adrian Paulen, President of the International Amateur Athletics Federation and Professor Beckett, Britain's representative on the International Olympic Committee had declared that drug-taking by athletes 'was still not under control'.

The success of the Soviet Union is not necessarily anchored on the 80 gold medals (which its athletes won) but rather their good fortune in preventing a recurrence of the Munich massacre and their adroitness in blunting the impact of the Olympic boycott orchestrated principally by United States of America, Japan and Western Germany. This of course raises the question: Can sport be isolated from politics? Lord Killian the out-going President of the International Olympic Committee has consistently argued that sports and politics do not mix.

Realism suggests that it would be difficult if not impossible to divorce sports from politics. Even in the case of Russia, it could be argued that: 'There main ambition was political – to bring international credit to the Soviet Union and by implication, its system of government, leadership, ideological line and foreign policy. A successful staging of the Games, it was reckoned, would be an enormous propaganda coup for a government that is exceptionally preoccupied with its image at home and abroad. The Russians were anxious to show themselves as an efficient, organised, contented, stable and hospitable society.'

It is too early yet to determine how much change in the Soviet way of life would be generated by the impact of the Moscow Olympics and the massive influx of and the attendant contact (albeit limited) with foreigners. However, what is certain is that Russia holds all the aces as regards the 1984 Olympics to be held in Los Angeles, U.S. If the Russians decide to go, they would have had the benefit of the rich experience they gained from the Moscow Olympics; but if they choose to pay the United States back in its own coin by boycotting the Games – all the East Europeans, the Cubans and several other countries which are firmly under the thumb of Russia will of course follow suit, there can be only one conclusion – the 1984 Olympics will be in BIG TROUBLE.